DO GOOD FENCES MAKE GOOD NEIGHBORS?

DO GOOD FENCES MAKE GOOD NEIGHBORS?

What History Teaches Us about Strategic Barriers and International Security

BRENT L. STERLING

In Cooperation with
the Center for Peace and Security Studies
Edmund A. Walsh School of Foreign Service
Georgetown University

GEORGETOWN UNIVERSITY PRESS
Washington, D.C.

All statements of fact, opinion, or analysis expressed are those of
the author and do not reflect the official positions or views of the
CIA or any other U.S. government agency. Nothing in the contents
should be construed as asserting or implying U.S. government
authentication of information or agency endorsement of the
author's views. This material has been reviewed by the CIA to
prevent the disclosure of classified information.

Georgetown University Press, Washington, D.C.
www.press.georgetown.edu

© 2009 Georgetown University Press. All rights reserved. No
part of this book may be reproduced or utilized in any form or
by any means, electronic or mechanical, including photocopying
and recording, or by any information storage and retrieval system,
without permission in writing from the publisher.

Library of Congress Cataloging-in-Publication Data

Sterling, Brent L.
    Do good fences make good neighbors? : what history teaches
us about strategic barriers and international security / Brent L.
Sterling.
      p. cm.
    "In cooperation with the Center for Peace and Security
Studies, Edmund A. Walsh School of Foreign Service."
    Includes bibliographical references and index.
    ISBN 978-1-58901-571-5 (hardcover : alk. paper)
    1. Security, International. 2. Fortification—History.
3. National security—History. I. Georgetown University.
Center for Peace and Security Studies. II. Title.
JZ5588.S745 2009
355'.033—dc22
                                      2009008624

♾ This book is printed on acid-free paper meeting the requirements
of the American National Standard for Permanence in Paper for
Printed Library Materials.

15 14 13 12 11 10 09   9 8 7 6 5 4 3 2
First printing

Printed in the United States of America

To my parents,
for making sure no walls ever blocked my way.

Contents

	List of Illustrations	ix
	Acknowledgments	xi
	List of Acronyms	xiii
1	**Introduction**	1
2	**Athens' Long Walls:** *Lifelines to the Sea*	13
3	**Hadrian's Wall:** *Rome's Foremost Frontier Fortification*	64
4	**The Ming Great Wall of China:** *A Dynasty's Unending Pursuit of Security*	106
5	**The Pré Carré:** *Fortifying France's Northeastern Frontier*	157
6	**The Maginot Line:** *France's Great Folly or Reasoned Response to the German Threat*	204
7	**The Bar-Lev Line:** *Citadels in the Sand*	257
8	**Conclusion:** *Lessons Learned about the Use and Abuse of Strategic Defenses*	308
	Selected Bibliography	331
	About the Author	337
	Index	339

Illustrations

Tables

1.1	Selected Cases for Investigation	10
8.1	Summary of Case Studies	310

Maps

2.1	Athens' Long Walls, Fifth Century BCE	16
2.2	Ancient Greece and the Surrounding Area	18
3.1	Hadrian Wall Strategic Defense System, circa 130	67
3.2	Roman Britain and Key Early, Second-Century Northern Tribes	69
4.1	Ming Strategic Defense System	109
5.1	Northwestern Europe in the Late Seventeenth Century	159
5.2	Pré Carré Fortification System, 1680	161
6.1	Metz and Lauter Fortified Regions, 1940	207
6.2	French Frontier Sectors with Key Fortified Areas, 1940	208
7.1	Bar-Lev Line and the Western Sinai, 1969–1970	260

Acknowledgments

THE RESEARCH AND COMPOSITION of this work has been a long journey that would not have been completed without the assistance of family, friends, and colleagues. Above all, I want to express my appreciation to Dan Byman and Dan Chiu for their contributions to the project from its conceptual origins to the final manuscript. They never failed to provide cogent, constructive commentary framed in a positive manner. I am also grateful to Eleanore Douglas for providing valuable feedback on the entire first draft. Avi Beker, Burgess Laird, James Millward, and Joshua Pollack contributed useful observations on individual chapters while Andrew Niebler, Beth Pincus, and Ken Pollack offered helpful suggestions throughout the process.

Beyond these named individuals, I am indebted to legions of specialists who facilitated this comparative, conceptual exploration on strategic defense systems through their primary research. I have taken advantage of their outstanding work, the most significant of which are listed in the selected bibliography. Similarly, I wish to express my appreciation for the many caretakers of history who greatly enriched my travels to China, Egypt, England, France, and Greece to view the relevant terrain and extant fortification elements.

The complexity of the publishing process seemed daunting to this first-time book author, but Don Jacobs has provided yeoman's stewardship as the work's acquisitions editor. I would also to thank the rest of the staff at Georgetown University Press, as well as the anonymous outside reader, for their myriad contributions. No work on strategic defenses and military history would be complete without maps; I have benefited from the skilled cartography of Christopher Robinson. Despite the efforts of all of those involved, errors may exist, for which I take full responsibility.

Finally, I want to thank my family and close friends for their unfailing and unconditional support throughout this lengthy endeavor. They are no doubt giddy at the thought that I will no longer torture them with tales from the walls of history.

Acronyms

CORF *Commission d'Organisation des Régions Fortifiées* (Commission for the Organization of the Fortified Regions)
CSG *Conseil Supérieure de la Guerre* (Superior or Higher War Council)
GNP gross national product
IAF Israeli Air Force
IDF Israeli Defense Forces
RF *région fortifiée* (fortified region)
SAM surface-to-air missile
SD *secteur défensif* (defense sector)
SF *secteur fortifié* (fortified sector)
UN United Nations

1
Introduction

Thou shalt call thy walls Salvation and thy gates Praise.
—Isaiah 60:18

WHILE THE ABOVE BIBLICAL QUOTE reflects a prodefense sentiment often evident since man established boundaries, by the second half of the twentieth century a general disdain emerged for the continuing utility of walls, fortresses, and other barriers. The improved precision and destructiveness of weapons as well as the enhanced mobility of militaries appeared to render physical works obsolete. In the late 1950s, Yigal Allon, one of Israel's early military heroes and strategic thinkers, captured the prevailing view by observing that "no modern country can surround itself with a wall."[1] Fifty years later, however, a range of nations including Afghanistan, Botswana, India, Saudi Arabia, Thailand, and the United States have increasingly been attracted to such barriers, none more than Allon's Israel.[2] Walls stand guard along its frontiers with Lebanon, the Gaza Strip, increasingly the West Bank, and possibly soon Egypt. The relative effectiveness of these ground-based works at controlling cross-border traffic has encouraged adversary attack from the sky. Whether it be the frequent homemade Qassam rockets shot from the Gaza Strip (about three thousand through January 2008), the mixture of rockets and missiles launched by Hezbollah during the 2006 Lebanon War (more than four thousand total), or the longer-range, potentially nuclear-armed ballistic missiles potentially possessed by hostile Middle East states, a high threat perception has arisen.[3] In response, the Israeli Defense Forces (IDF) has pursued multiple missile defense systems, some with colorful names such as Iron Dome and David's Sling, to be part of a multilayer network. Although the West Bank "separation barrier" has controversially deviated from the Green Line (the 1967 Israel–West Bank border) in some areas, defense efforts overall have been met with approval across the political spectrum.

A growing sense of vulnerability has also prompted considerable interest in strategic defenses in the United States, albeit with far less agreement than in Israel. Buffered by the Atlantic and Pacific oceans as well as protected by its overwhelming size and strength, Americans historically displayed a negligible desire to erect artificial barriers along its borders. The military constructed fortifications at times, but these were concentrated on protecting key harbors rather than securing lengthy frontiers. Even this limited effort declined in the twentieth century with the perceived obsolescence of coastal defenses as military and naval technology evolved.

In recent decades a diverse set of political, military, economic, and social challenges (e.g., ballistic missiles, illegal immigration, narcotics, and terrorism) has elevated perceptions of vulnerability. This concern has led to a wide range of efforts from basic fencing to ballistic missile defense. Whether through solid physical structures or virtual walls employing detection sensors, proponents have touted barriers' potential to control population and material flows along the approximately two-thousand-mile border with Mexico. Yet much of the public remains ambivalent, dubious, or even hostile to such an effort. Criticism focuses on the idea of a barrier more than questions of feasibility, although even measures such as the Secure Fence Act of 2006 will continue to leave most of the border without walls.

By contrast, feasibility (cost and technical difficulty) concerns undergird opposition to developing ballistic missile defense. Advocates stress that these hurdles can be overcome with sufficient resources, and they note significant progress to date in obtaining the capability to defeat missiles fired by a rogue state. Even if effective, opponents counter that excessive concentration on this avenue of attack will leave insufficient resources for alternative means by which an enemy could readily turn. With the threats and vulnerabilities to U.S. soil real and likely long-standing, the debate on the value of strategic defenses appears set to continue indefinitely.

While technical examinations and contemporary political analyses represent important tools for assessing barriers' potential, advocates and critics often attempt to bolster their arguments by selectively wielding or distorting history of past strategic defenses. Most problematic is the tendency of journalists, analysts, and politicians to attribute to past strategic defenses blame for broader policy failures and thus reason to oppose contemporary efforts or proposals. An extreme example observes that despite building Hadrian's Wall, the Romans still abandoned Britain.[4] Attributing causality to an event almost three hundred years after the barrier's construction is an absurd standard by which to judge barrier effectiveness. Similarly, proponents of barriers tend to assert extreme claims for their potential contribution to security. The resulting dynamic is for critics and proponents to talk past each other, adding highly subjective versions of the past to bolster their arguments. Even historians, usually more circumspect, have been prone to apply sweeping characterizations on this topic. For example, critic Julia Lovell declares that "perhaps because frontier walls originally cost so much time and money to build, those subsequently left responsible for their upkeep often found it painful to denounce them as a strategically useless waste."[5] By contrast, Martin Van Creveld observes that "history shows that walls, provided people are prepared to do what is necessary to defend them and prevent other people from crossing them, by using lethal force if necessary, work. If not for technical reasons—there never has been, nor can be, such a thing as an impregnable wall—then for psychological ones; and if not forever and perfectly, then for long periods and to a very large extent."[6]

Scholars of international relations and security studies have not significantly advanced understanding of strategic defenses through historic investigation. While academics have engaged in theoretical and technical examinations of the missile defense dimension, most scholarly attention over the last thirty years has been directed at the tangentially related offense–defense theory, which posits that the greater the military advantage for the offense, the more likely war is to occur, all else being equal. By contrast, the greater the edge for defense, the more stable the international system. Offense–defense theory has been a source of considerable debate between ardent proponents and strident critics over substantive, methodological, and definitional issues, including at the most basic level whether "offensive" and "defensive" weapons exist.[7] As unmovable structures, walls represent the most defensive of systems. Yet such an understanding is overly simplistic given an ability to use other weapons in conjunction with barriers to achieve a more potent offensive capability. Moreover, walls placed on disputed or foreign soil may be tactically defensive but strategically offensive. Their application, like all weapons, is context dependent. This reality explains why nations might view a given strategic defense in fundamentally different ways. For example, at the 1932 World Disarmament Conference, the French argued that fortifications were defensive while the Germans contended they were offensive.[8] Such experience highlights the dilemma of trying to classify walls as purely defensive and the need to distinguish between a physical structure and a strategic–military orientation.

Regardless of the merit of offense–defense theory, a need exists for better understanding the general strengths and weaknesses of employing strategic defenses. Most existing studies of strategic defenses are done as individual works, which prevents comparative insights. Moreover, these works tend to focus on the physical elements of the structure (e.g., system design, materials used, and building specifications) or their history in battle. A sound understanding of why such a course of action was adopted is critical to appreciating the barrier's role and accurately assessing its impact, especially the influence on subsequent internal perceptions and policymaking. The few efforts that have sought lessons learned regarding strategic defenses either employed abbreviated barrier sketches or possessed a broader lens related to border dynamics.[9]

All of these works are helpful but fail to exploit the potential of past barrier experiences for generating useful insights to current and future considerations of these structures. If a conference was held for history's greatest wall builders—such as Themistocles, Pericles, Meng Tian, Hadrian, Anthemius, Vauban, Yu Zijun, André Maginot, and Carl Gustav Mannerheim—and their successors who directed security policy under the protection of such strategic defenses, what findings would the group report? The wall builders could be expected to stress the benefits of such structures, but would a clear divide exist between them and their successors? What would have surprised them given previous efforts to construct such a barrier? Could they have done it better, and, if so, how? Alas, no such meeting can take place. Instead, an in-depth exploration of some of their works is both doable and potentially rewarding regarding the pressures and tendencies that result from strategic defenses.

Before addressing the best investigatory approach and case selection, a brief discussion of terminology and basic concepts is needed. As evident from just the few preceding pages, myriad terms exist to characterize man-made security obstacles including barriers, defenses, fences, fortifications, lines, walls, and strategic defenses. In a recent encyclopedic work on fortifications, Guy Le Hallé includes hundreds of defense elements from "abatis" to "zigzag."[10] Historian John Keegan notes that basic fortifications fall into three categories depending on their purpose: refuge—temporary shelter from attack; stronghold—individual positions for sustained, active defense; and strategic defense—continuous or mutually supporting works denying the enemy avenues of attack across a front.[11] This study will focus on the third and most ambitious type—strategic defenses, some of which cover hundreds or even thousands of miles. Barriers, lines, walls, and fences all represent different ways to describe strategic defenses, albeit some with slight variation in meaning. For example, wall is usually applied when a continuous curtain exists (e.g., Hadrian's Wall and the Great Wall of China) while lines tend to represent discontinuous but mutually supporting fortification works (e.g., Maginot Line). When a particular term has been attached historically to an effort, I employ it; otherwise, the terms along with strategic defense should be viewed as synonymous in their basic meaning.

Finally, since the early twentieth century, the invention of aircraft and then missiles transformed the sky into an avenue of attack concerning defenders. The Germans in 1940 erected the first meaningful air barrier, the so-called Kammhuber Line with radars, searchlights, flak guns, and ground-controlled fighters guarding the northwest approach against British night-time bombing sorties.[12] Although different types of systems are employed to guard against ground and air threats, the strategic dynamics are analogous, and thus they can be treated as a common problem.

Regardless of the terminology, using man-made barriers to help seal off or at least safeguard a front may be done for a variety of purposes. States may want to dissuade others from challenging it by demonstrating the polity's greatness through symbolism. Alternatively, leaders may hope to deter attacks by undermining enemy expectations of success, at least at acceptable cost or risk. This type of deterrence, known as deterrence by denial, contrasts with the more common retaliatory-based method known as deterrence by punishment. A lack of confidence in dissuasion and deterrence may prompt a desire for the actual ability to block enemy aggression. Additionally, decision makers have often sought enhanced frontier control to impede low-level attacks, manage human traffic, regulate commerce, or collect taxes. These control goals drive most of the efforts under way or being considered today.[13] Alternatively, strategic defenses along one front may function as a force multiplier to enable concentration of military resources in other areas. Such a system could also serve as a base from which to project power. Leaders usually envision strategic defenses performing more than one of these objectives. An aim of this study is to examine leaders' relative ability to satisfy these varied objectives and under what conditions and constraints.

Strategic defenses are not the only option available to states when facing a threatening adversary. Although the actual courses of action are context specific and infinite in variety, they can essentially be grouped into three basic categories: accommodation, offense, and defense. Accommodation strategies consist of attempts to "demotivate" enemy hostility through political, economic, and informational measures. Offense-based approaches involve projecting military force into territory controlled by the adversary or its allies to eliminate or diminish the danger. Defense-based efforts cover the application of military force along the frontier or within the state. Man-made obstacles can greatly enhance such an approach. Adopting a forward-based defense represents a gray area between offense and defense but is an approach that involves the power projection without fortifications. This typology excludes the always available option of doing nothing and the relatively recently and selectively available approach of emphasizing countervalue threats to coerce the desired behavior. Indecisive leaders often choose to take no action, but such a "choice" represents a temporary delay that environmental pressures will likely make untenable in time. Although nuclear powers can employ countervalue threats without first defeating the adversary's military, this strategy has limited applicability given its lack of credibility against challenges not involving existential danger. This limitation plus the option's lack of existence for most of history has prompted its exclusion from further discussion.

For policymakers, a fundamental distinction separates a defense-based strategy from the other two approaches. Strategies employing offense or accommodation potentially offer ways to eliminate the threat through military and political actions, respectively. By contrast, defense can at best temporarily prevent harm. The enemy's hostile attitude and military capability remain intact with the former possibly exacerbated. "Buying time," however, might provide considerable benefit in the short or medium term, if other options are impractical. Moreover, leaders may attempt to create opportunity with strategic defenses by reducing vulnerability, thus bolstering the potential for either an offensive or accommodation in a combined approach. Complementary efforts are delicate to implement, but the logic for such courses of action appears to exist given the weaknesses often evident with pure approaches.

With these basic policy avenues available, policymakers have been deciding to erect strategic defenses since at least circa 1990 BCE when the Egyptian pharaohs of the Twelfth Dynasty tried to secure the Nubian frontier across the Nile River.[14] Hundreds of such barriers have been built over the subsequent four thousand years. A few defenses retain great fame or infamy, such as the Great Wall of China, Hadrian's Wall, and the Maginot Line, but most are obscure, including the Great Wall of Gorgan (Iran), the Zasechnaya Cherta or Great Abatis Line (Russia), the Great Wall of the Dutch Republic, Offa's Dyke (Britain), the Glomma River Line (Norway), and the Metaxas Line (Greece). Although a quantitative study of all such strategic defenses might reveal some interesting correlations, the enormous variance among the type, composition, context, and purpose of systems creates severe coding problems. More importantly, such a quantitative approach is less apt to provide insights into their effects, especially on perceptions. Rather, the comparative case method with a limited number of in-depth explorations should better enable assessing the value of strategic defenses in three fundamental and interrelated dimensions.

First, how does the barrier affect adversary perceptions of the building state's intent and capability, and how does it shape its subsequent behavior? Second, how does the strategic defense system alter the military balance, both in the immediate and longer term? A very broad conception of "military balance" must be employed for barriers given the objectives pursued range from border control to conventional military defense. Lastly, how does the existence of a strategic defense influence the subsequent outlook, policy debate, and behavior within the originating state? This final dimension is traditionally neglected or underappreciated, but it may be the most critical element for effectively employing barriers. Answering these questions cannot be done exclusively through exploring the postconstruction experience. One must understand the context that shaped the range of options available as well as their relative appeal and the reasoning that ultimately led to employment of a strategic defense system.

The case selection criterion attempts to identify the experiences most germane for answering the key questions raised above. First, I excluded wartime efforts, which constitute most strategic defenses through history. Wartime is defined here as ongoing conventional military hostilities; thus it excludes periodic terrorism or other low-level violence among ardent adversaries. Such conflict barriers tend to be hastily and shabbily built, given the limited time and resources available. More importantly, officials erect these structures with only the simple, albeit demanding goal of blocking or at least slowing down or weakening an advancing enemy through attrition. Typifying such efforts were the dozens of strategic defenses established by the German military during its retreat during World War II. On the Italian peninsula alone, the Germans established more than forty lines, albeit only two (the Gustav and Gothic lines) with relatively robust works.[15] Although usually doomed, some wartime efforts have been notable successes, such as British general Wellington's Lines of Torres Vedras blocking the French assault on Lisbon in 1810–11. These works fail or succeed, but such questions of operational effectiveness are too narrow for our purpose.

Among nonwartime efforts, attention should be on strategic defenses pursued as a matter of choice rather than necessity. Weak states facing a strong adversary have no other viable recourse save capitulation. For example, although Finland's pre–World War II Mannerheim Line obtained great renown as a barrier, Helsinki had no real alternative to building defenses against Stalin and the vastly larger Soviet Union. The primary question for such barriers is their operational effectiveness, especially because the building state lacks the resources to erect robust fortifications. As Keegan observes, the existence of a major strategic defense "is always a mark of the wealth and advanced political development of the people who build them."[16] Such states with significant military, economic, and political resources can pursue the range of policy options discussed here. Moreover, the focus should be on contexts that allowed real options and legitimate debate. These cases are inherently interesting for understanding the relative value of strategic defenses, whether pursued in isolation or combination with another approach. They also belong to a class analogous to the environment faced by Israel and the United States today, the two states most directly engaged in debates about strategic defenses.

Upon narrowing down the candidates to cases of relative powers facing ardent adversaries in a nonwar environment, the remaining criteria reflect their suitability when judged as a group. Variance within the set of cases should allow for more robust lessons learned. First, efforts from distinct historical eras should be included given the combination of consistent political security dynamics and shifting military technology and strategic competition. Second, diverse decision-making structures should exist for the example of wall builders, including both democratic and authoritarian regimes. Finally, the full range of the strategic defense motivations should be operative, including deterrence, frontier defense, and frontier control as well as combination approaches with other strategies. In addition to satisfying these requirements, sufficient information must be available to conduct the examinations, particularly when compared to their contemporary alternatives.

These requirements led to the selection of six cases with considerable historical variance. Study subjects include choices from the ancient (Athens' Long Walls and Hadrian's Wall), early modern (Ming Dynasty's Great Wall and France's Pré Carré), and modern (France's Maginot Line and Israel's Bar-Lev Line) eras. Only the medieval period among key fortification ages is neglected, but individual strongholds rather than strategic defenses were emphasized then. With two of the six cases being French and five of the six being Western, with Israel appropriately being regarded as such, greater geographic diversity would have been desirable. Yet non-European options are less viable candidates given the lack of sufficient information to assess decision making. Thus, I have selected cases without regard to geographic diversity.

The two ancient efforts covered—Athens' Long Walls and Hadrian's Wall—constitute the most noteworthy strategic defense systems of the age. The former, constructed in mid-fifth century BCE, connected the upper city of Athens with its primary ports on the Saronic Gulf to protect against the vaunted Spartan army. This case offers potentially interesting insights into the strategic role of walls for ambitious, rising powers. By contrast, Emperor Hadrian's decision to erect a wall in the early second century CE along the Roman frontier in northern England represents an attempt by an established power to stabilize and control a troublesome front. Limited information makes exploring these cases challenging, but the same constraint affects all ancient barriers, including the most logical alternatives, the Great Walls of the Chinese Qin and Han dynasties.

The early modern era marks perhaps the golden age of strategic defenses, but a compelling rationale exists for including the Ming Dynasty's Great Wall of China and Louis XIV's Pré Carré in northeastern France. The exclusion of the aforementioned Qin and Han walls was in part due to a preference for examining the better-documented Ming decision, beginning in the early 1470s, to build a barrier across its northern frontier. Designed to block penetration by the nomadic Mongols, this case appears to offer valuable insights into questions of frontier defense and control as well as evolving competition dynamics from walling off segments of the frontier gradually. With the introduction of the *trace italienne* fortress and nearly constant war, Europe during the early modern era offers a range of candidates for study. Yet the relatively obscure late seventeenth century effort by French king Louis XIV and his great engineer, Vauban, to establish the Pré Carré, a double line of fortresses facing the Spanish Netherlands, stands out. The regime ultimately expanded fortifications until the *frontière de fer* (iron frontier) guarded an area extending from the Alps to the English Channel. Constructed by the strongest military power in Europe at the time, this system facilitates exploring the dual offense–defense potential for such works as well as the contrasting perceptions provoked between builder and adversary.

Among the modern efforts, any study of strategic defenses must include the Maginot Line, and Israel's usually ignored Bar-Lev Line also warrants examination. As perhaps the strongest fortification system in history, the French pre–World War II Maginot Line barrier needs to be addressed given its powerful legacy with defense critics. Obstructing only part of the frontier threatened by the German army, this case facilitates consideration of combination defense approaches as well as the barrier's effects on French attitudes and political-military decision making. Although existing for only a half decade (1969–73), the Bar-Lev Line helped guard the east bank of the Suez Canal when Israel possessed the Sinai Peninsula. In particular, this case enables consideration of the elements relating to perception, such as deterrence and subjective security, as well as the difficulty of conducting combination military approaches. I excluded the case of the Berlin Wall given the important barrier's unconventional primary purpose of keeping its own citizens from escaping rather than protecting against penetration by external threats.

Although case selection was heavily influenced by a desire to include examples from distinct historical eras, other desirable differences exist among the six subjects. First, the political systems are evenly split between democratic and authoritarian regimes. Similarly, balance exists between examples of essentially continuous walls and discontinuous lines. Finally, while each barrier usually served more than one purpose, the group in toto contains multiple examples of works designed to symbolize greatness and strength; to promote deterrence, frontier defense, and frontier control; to function as force multipliers; and even to facilitate power projection.

Historians themselves are generally loath to compare experiences, with good reason. Every case is sui generis in terms of both the nature of the adversary and the domestic and international factors influencing decision makers, especially if separated by over two millennia. Such recognition should preserve a prudent caution about generalized findings, but it does not preclude gaining crosscutting insights from well-executed explorations. While employing experts on each structure or country would produce better individual case studies, coverage of multiple works by a single analyst enhances the potential for identifying critical commonalities and differences.

To facilitate constructive analysis, this study employs the "structured-focused" comparison technique by applying a common template of questions (structure) to standardize data collection on particular aspects (focus) of each case.[17] The vast disparity of information on the decision making between the

Table 1.1 Selected Cases for Investigation

Barrier	Location	Approximate Dates of Construction	Approximate Operational History
Athens' Long Walls	Fifth century: Connect Athens to key ports on Saronic Gulf	461–457 BCE	457–404 BCE
	Fourth century: Connect Athens to main port of Piraeus	446–442, 394–390 BCE	390–301 BCE
Hadrian's Wall	Across northern England from Tyne River near North Sea to Solway Firth	122–127	127–143; early 160s–410
Ming Great Wall	Initial Segment: Above Shaanxi Province along central northern frontier	1474	1474–1644
	Full System: Along northern frontier from Bohai Sea to Jiayuguan, approaching Central Asia	Mainly 1540s–1580s	1540s–1644
Pré Carré	Initial double line of fortresses along frontier with Spanish Netherlands	1678–1680	1678 through mid-nineteenth century (with major upgrades)
	Expanded fortifications covering French frontier from English Channel to Alps	1680s	
Maginot Line	Along French frontier with Germany and Luxembourg; strongest works on northern border of Lorraine	1930–1936	1936–1940
Bar-Lev Line	Along east bank of the Suez Canal	1968–1969	1969–1973

chapters, particularly when comparing the ancient experiences with twentieth century efforts, has prompted the use of questions relating to the contextual influences affecting leaders. That is, lacking a precise understanding of what motivated officials in some cases, more accessible environmental pressures can suggest likely explanations for known policy choices. This approach is not without some risk given the potential for decision makers to act in spite of contextual pressures. Nevertheless, the potential benefit of this broad exploration warrants proceeding, albeit with caution that a degree of uncertainty exists. Thus the first section of each chapter explores leader perceptions of the key contextual factors: relevant history, threat perception, military capability, strategic culture, resources, and domestic politics as well as the decision-making process through which these influences flow. The ensuing discussion considers how these related factors interact to affect the generation of options and their relative appeal for officials. The remainder of each case study explores the obstacle's effects and evolution, including decisions to expand, alter, or abandon the effort. The conclusion assesses the influences of each strategic defense system on the adversary, the military balance, and the building state as well as briefly discussing the counterfactual of forgoing the barrier. While not attempting to articulate a formal "theory of walls," such an exploration may yield nuanced lessons learned about strategic defenses in each of these key dimensions to enhance assessments of and maximize the potential for future such efforts.

Notes

1. Quoted in Avner Yaniv, *Deterrence without the Bomb: The Politics of Israeli Strategy* (Lexington, MA: Lexington Books, 1987), 17.

2. John W. Donaldson, "Fencing the Line: Analysis of the Recent Rise in Security Measures along Disputed and Undisputed Boundaries," in *Global Surveillance and Policy*, ed. Elia Zureik and Mark B. Salter (Portland: Willan Publishing, 2005), 173–93.

3. Barbara Opall-Rome, "Israeli Defense to Use Artificial Intelligence," *Defense News*, January 21, 2008, 1,10; and Barbara Opall-Rome, "Israeli Missile Defense under Spotlight," *Defense News*, October 29, 2007, 10.

4. Joel Garreau, "The Walls Tumbled by Time," *Washington Post*, October 27, 2006.

5. Julia Lovell, *The Great Wall: China against the World, 1000BC–AD2000* (New York: Grove, 2006), 18.

6. Martin Van Creveld, *Defending Israel: A Strategic Plan for Peace and Security* (New York: Thomas Dunne Books, 2004), 66.

7. For standard works by proponents and critics of offense–defense theory, see Michael Brown, Owen R. Coté Jr., Sean M. Lynn-Jones, and Steven E. Miller, eds., *Offense, Defense, and War* (Cambridge, MA: MIT Press, 2004).

8. George Quester, *Offense and Defense in the International System* (New Brunswick, NJ: Transaction Publishers, 2003), 122.

9. See, e.g., Paul Seguin, *Strategic Performance of Defensive Barriers* (Aberdeen, MD: U.S. Army Environmental Hygiene Agency, 1988); and John Donaldson, "Fencing the Line"; and James Tracy, ed. *City Walls: The Urban Enceinte in Global Perspective* (New York: Cambridge University Press, 2000).

10. Guy Le Hallé, *Précis la Fortification* (Paris: PVC Editions, 2002).

11. John Keegan, *History of Warfare* (New York: Alfred A. Knopf, 1993), 139–42.

12. J. E. Kaufmann and H. W. Kaufmann, *Fortress Third Reich: German Fortifications and Defense Systems in World War II* (Cambridge, MA: Da Capo Press, 2003), 141–42.

13. Donaldson, "Fencing the Line," 173–93.
14. Keegan, *History of Warfare,* 142–43.
15. Neil Short, *German Defenses in Italy in World War II* (Oxford: Osprey, 2006), 5.
16. Keegan, *History of Warfare,* 142.
17. Alexander L. George and Andrew Bennett, *Case Studies and Theory Development in the Social Sciences* (Cambridge, MA: MIT Press, 2005), 67–72.

2

Athens' Long Walls

Lifelines to the Sea

Introduction

During the fifth century BCE, the miles of open, low-lying land between the upper city of Athens and its key ports on the Saronic Gulf represented the city-state's primary vulnerability. Desiring to emphasize naval power despite this intervening gap, the Athenians constructed a set of walls down to the coastline. Athens' adversaries, led by Sparta, quickly learned about the unwelcome Long Walls, but how did they react to its challenge? The barriers eliminated the vulnerability, but what was the general effect of the barriers on the military balance given the contrasting military approaches pursued by Athens and Sparta? Most importantly, how did the mitigation of this rising power's main weakness affect Athenians' security perceptions and policy preferences? Did the fortifications encourage risky behavior or misperceptions about potential dangers? Within a decade of the barrier's destruction after Sparta's victory in the Second Peloponnesian War, Athenians rebuilt the structure and followed up with major reconstruction efforts in the mid-330s and the last decade of the century. These actions provide a useful opportunity to observe what, if any, dynamics result with strategic defenses given the city-state's reduced circumstances. Athens was now a weakened, largely status quo–oriented actor, rather than the rising, expansionist power of the previous century.

The first half of the chapter examines the decision to build the original two long walls in the early 450s, an action that Victor Davis Hanson has characterized as "the most revolutionary development in the history of Greek strategy."[1] Upon the walls' construction, he adds, the traditional strategy of "attacking agriculture to prompt pitched battle or induce starvation" no longer applied to Athens.[2] Instead, these structures would eventually be an integral part of a three-pronged approach involving empire, navy, and long walls that would allow food imports from abroad to sustain the city. Debate exists among scholars over whether the transformative strategy or its fundamental tenets explicitly existed at the time of the initial construction of the Long Walls, a topic that will be addressed later in the chapter.[3] At a minimum, the walls eliminated the city-states' most severe vulnerability and provided emergency protection for both the urban population and rural refugees. Although minimal historical information remains about the decision to erect these structures, the relatively rich contextual history helps us explore all three dimensions of the strategic defense question.

Apparently conceived and employed as a safety net, the Long Walls encouraged Athens' shifting perspective to embrace this more radical strategy relying on barriers, navy, and empire. The discussion considers this transition, which picks up momentum with construction of a third wall in the 440s and culminates in an explicit policy of abandoning the countryside and avoiding the Peloponnesians in a major land battle at the outbreak of the Second Peloponnesian War in the late 430s. The examination considers the war at some length, especially given that the strategy ultimately fails. The rest of the chapter explores Athenian attempts at defenses in the fourth century, especially the three major efforts to reconstruct (390s) and upgrade the Long Walls (330s and 300s) in a time of significantly improved siegecraft. Beyond the fourth century, the Long Walls' value as a strategic defense would decline and, like Athens itself, fade over time.

Around 460 BCE, however, Athens seemed able and interested in dominating the Hellenic world.[4] One can imagine Pericles, Leocrates, Myronides, and other leading Athenian statesmen of the era standing atop the Acropolis with gaze toward the sea, about four miles to the south. Their thoughts would have been filled with visions of future conquest and its associated riches and renown. At the time, Athens appeared to be the most powerful Greek city-state, and it certainly was the wealthiest. Athens' navy—essentially the fleet of the Delian League—could match the other Greek states combined and was viewed as the foundation of the city-state's security success in recent decades.[5] Although not the equal of the Spartans, its relatively large and capable army was better than that of most Greek states. These attributes inspired considerable confidence among the citizenry.

Athenian aspirations and enthusiasm placed great demands on the polis, which would soon be fighting on multiple fronts. Athens dispatched a two-hundred-ship expedition to besiege Persian-controlled Cyprus but redirected it up the Nile River when another Persian vassal, Egypt, rebelled and asked for assistance. Buoyed by the decision of Megara, its southwestern neighbor, to switch allegiances from the Spartan-led Peloponnesian League to the Delian League, the Athenians soon also attacked Halieis in southern Greece (also known as the Peloponnesus). Although the southerners—mainly Corinthians and Epidaurians—repelled the amphibious landing force, the Athenians subsequently defeated them in a naval battle. Athens then moved against another long-time adversary and Spartan ally, the nearby island state of Aegina, which stood as a potential source of opposition in the Saronic Gulf. Visible from the Athenian acropolis, Pericles reportedly labeled Aegina "the stye in Athens' eye."[6] Observing Athens heavily engaged in Aegina and Egypt, Corinth attacked Megara. Corinthian leaders evidently believed that Athens would be either unable to support its new ally or compelled to abandon the siege of Aegina. Instead, the Athenian Myronides assembled a ragtag army of old and young that proceeded to defeat the Corinthians. A few years later the besieged Aegina capitulated.[7]

Fighting with key allies of Sparta highlighted the intensifying struggle between the two great powers of fifth century Greece. Twenty years earlier Athens and Sparta had cooperated to save Greece during the Second Persian War, but by the end of the 460s each state had come to view the other as the primary obstacle to its security and well-being. Recently altered domestic politics in Athens had shifted the polis' relations with Sparta from simmering rivalry to outright hostility. Yet, as Thucydides observed, the reorientation probably was inevitable given Athens' ambition and Sparta's concern about the implications of Athens' expanding power.[8] Despite their tremendous confidence, Athenian statesmen appreciated the danger presented by Sparta with its formidable army. With the city miles from the coastline, Athens' dominant fleet could not ensure its security, let alone the thousand square miles of Attica, the triangular peninsula in the southeastern corner of central Greece over which Athens had dominion.[9]

Eliminating the upper city's vulnerability had emerged as a critical objective given increased tension among the Greek states. Discussion of this critical issue would have taken place at Athenians' primary assembly spot on the Pnyx hillside, just west of the Acropolis. Reportedly capable of accommodating up to fifteen thousand attendees, the Pnyx likely witnessed several well-attended sessions on this important topic although no records exist.[10] Construction of the Long Walls connecting the upper city (*asta*) and its key ports was not the only option available. Other possibilities included expanding and improving the army, creating a border defense system along the Attic frontier, and even relocating the upper city to the more defensible port of Piraeus. Athenians ultimately chose the Long Walls, which allowed them "to protect the city, while still relying on their fleet."[11]

Without precise details on the timing and nature of the construction, it appears that the Athenians initiated this effort in 462 or 461 with the expectation of the coming struggle with Sparta. Building probably intensified after the outbreak of war with completion of two barriers, one to the port of Phaleron and another to Piraeus, achieved by early 457. The exact route of the Phaleron barrier has never been established, but the most likely path was about 3.7 miles in length. The original wall, subsequently known as the northern wall connecting Athens to Piraeus' defenses, was slightly longer at 3.84 miles.[12] Separated by

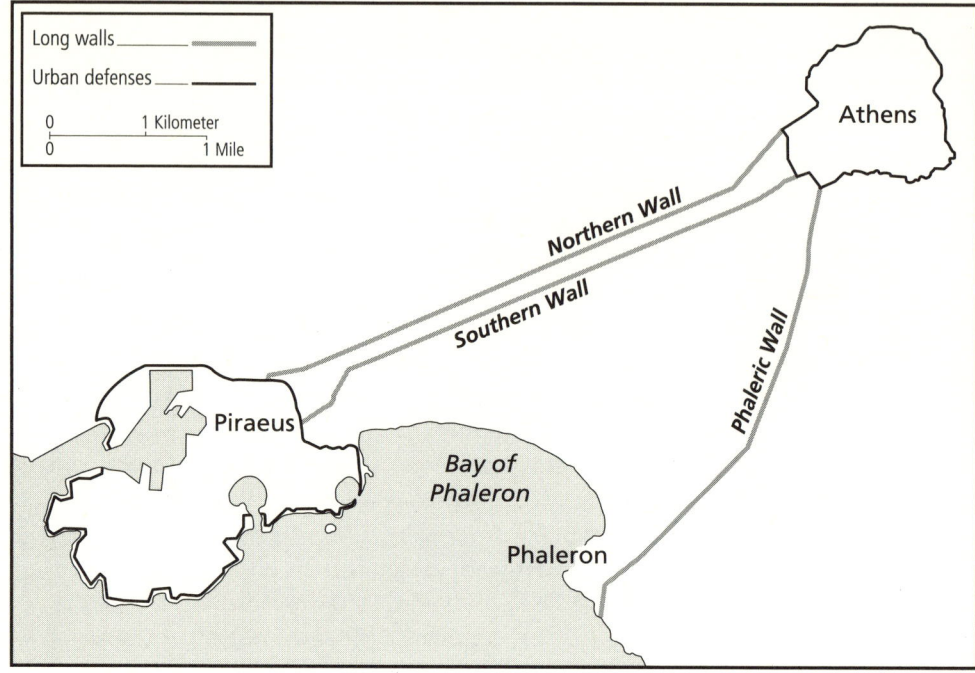

Figure 2.1 Athens' Long Walls, Fifth Century BCE

almost 2 miles along the coastline, these barriers and the dominant navy established a secure, triangular region of almost 5 square miles between Athens and the Bay of Phaleron. With an estimated height of about 25 feet and width of at least 10 feet, construction entailed a major effort. The Athenians built an array of features to enhance functionality and formidability including a parapet-guarded walkway on top of the superstructure; attached towers, especially near the sea where the low-lying plain offered no natural protection; main gates; and smaller posterns/sally ports. Reflecting their limited concern about enemy siegecraft, Athenians built no forward obstacles, such as ditches or palisades.[13]

Rise of a Democratic Power

Any attempt to understand the Athenians in 460 requires an appreciation of their history in the preceding fifty years. This period of extraordinary change resulted in Athens' emergence as a vibrant democracy and imperial power, albeit with brief moments of terror and suffering. The increasing investment of power in the hands of the people—at least adult Athenian males—represents a critical part of the story and important consideration as we later contemplate the effects of long walls on subsequent perceptions and behavior in the building state. Democracy came to Athens with the defeat of the Pisistratidae tyranny in 510 and the introduction of political reforms by Cleisthenes in 508.[14] Subsequent changes over the next five decades continued to reduce elite control over the organs of governance.

Combating the Persians

Almost immediately, the enthusiasm and energy produced by Athenian democracy propelled the city-state to be a central actor in the Greek–Persian struggle for control of the Aegean Sea. Greeks living in Asia Minor revolted with Athenian support. Not surprisingly, an outraged Persian king Darius felt particular enmity toward Athens and after defeating the revolt launched a punitive expedition. Athenian generals debated whether to meet the enemy in the field or seek protection behind the city's modest fortifications.[15] The inadequacy of fortifications probably contributed to the decision to fight the Persian force out in the open, even though the other Greek city-states (excepting the small city-state of Plataea) stayed away or, more accurately in Sparta's case, delayed arriving until two days after the battle. Shockingly to all, the Athenians, led by Miltiades, famously defeated their numerically superior foe at Marathon. Victory saved Athens for the moment, but some statesmen, especially Themistocles, expected the Persians to return with a larger force.[16] Rather than dividing the windfall from the newly discovered silver lodes at Laurium, Athenians accepted Themistocles' argument for building a large naval fleet to protect the city-state and facilitate commerce.[17] By the time the Persians returned ten years later, the Athenian fleet had grown to about 200 triremes—the premier warship of the era with its three rows of oarsmen.[18]

Unfortunately for Athens, the Persian fleet, accompanying an estimated 150,000-man army, exceeded 1,200 ships.[19] In contrast to the punitive mission of 490, the new Persian king, Xerxes, son of Darius, clearly and alarmingly intended to occupy Greece. While many Greek city-states ingratiated themselves with Xerxes, thirty sovereignties joined Athens in an opposing coalition. The Athenians consulted the Delphic Oracle for guidance, which reputedly indicated that Athens would be protected by a "wooden wall."[20] While some citizens interpreted this phrase as the wooden ramparts around the Acropolis, Themistocles among others persuaded a majority that "wooden wall" referred to the navy and that they should evacuate Attica. Such a retreat was inevitable after the Peloponnesian city-states, led by Sparta, decided to erect a defensive barrier on Corinth Isthmus southwest of Athens rather than deploy forces to help defend central Hellas. The Peloponnesian naval forces did join the rest of the Greeks off the Attic coast, where the large Athenian contingent (180 of 368 triremes)

Figure 2.2 Ancient Greece and the Surrounding Area

enabled Themistocles to orchestrate strategy for the entire force despite the titular command of the Spartan Eurybiades.[21] Through clever positioning of ships and superior seamanship, the Greeks achieved a stunning victory in the narrow waters east of Salamis that prompted a distraught Xerxes to return to Persia. The following year, the emboldened Greeks destroyed the remaining Persian army at the Battle of Plataea while a Greek naval force crossed the Aegean to burn the surviving Persian fleet.

Postwar Strategy

These decisive victories, which removed the Persian threat from Hellas for the near future, greatly shaped Athenian thinking about security policy. The primary lesson was the value of naval power, captured in the subsequent writings of Herodotus. He concluded that Athens' "wooden walls" had saved Greece, while Sparta's wall located across the Isthmus was futile since the Persians would have controlled the sea. A pro-Athenian storyteller, Herodotus' views tend to reflect the attitudes of leading fifth century Athenians. Above all, Athenians now regarded the sea as key to their military and economic well-being rather than a traditional orientation toward the land in rural Attica.[22] This shift from a land to sea orientation had profound security and political implications. As Hanson observes, "Athens had now hit upon the formula for radical democratic imperialism that would exempt her from the consequences of hoplite battle and make her triremes and tax-collecting bureaucrats the bother of the Aegean for the next half-century."[23] The challenge would be actualizing this strategy in the postwar environment.

Athens initially met this burden through maintaining a strong navy, erecting fortifications around Athens and Piraeus, and forming an alliance of Greek states to continue the war against Persia. The fleet grew until two hundred to three hundred warships roamed the Aegean and connecting waters, protecting Greeks throughout the region and expanding Athenian economic interests. Soon after victory, Athenians rushed to erect a strong, nearly four-mile circuit around the city to ensure that any siege would be a lengthy undertaking. Subsequently known as Themistocles' Wall for his advocacy, it would last at least in part for sixteen centuries. He also led the effort to fortify the rising port of Piraeus, which lay on a peninsula more than four miles southwest of the city. Given the limitations of siegecraft, which will be addressed later, the new defenses at Athens and Piraeus could not be defeated save treason, but the low-lying, open plain between them left a distinct vulnerability that could be exploited by a major power or coalition. Athens formed the "Confederacy of Delos" in 477 with about 150 Hellenic states to free all Greeks from Persian domination. Notably absent from the Delian League was conservative Sparta and its Peloponnesian allies, who were uninterested in such adventurism.[24]

Their absence enabled the Athenians, led by Aristides and Cimon, to exert considerable influence over the organization. Aristides, a veteran general and capable administrator, set up the league's institutional mechanisms, including determining contribution levels.[25] Cimon, a general and son of Marathon hero Miltiades, aggressively led the alliance into its first combat early in 477. Cimon's political strength grew as he directed the Delian League to repeated successes over the next decade, culminating in a great victory at Eurymedon on the southern coast of modern Turkey.[26] This achievement produced tremendous riches and prestige, yet this distant expedition also symbolized the evolving confederacy. With the Persians pushed out of the Aegean, some league members wanted to end hostilities. Already in 470, the island state of Naxos had attempted to withdraw from the League. Arguing that members could not unilaterally secede, Athens forcibly removed the island's rebellious regime from power to ensure Naxos' continued participation.[27] Calling the Delian League an alliance would become increasingly difficult as it morphed into the Athenian empire over the next few decades.

Escalating Tension between Athens and Sparta

Sparta had watched these developments in Athens with growing concern. The oligarchy's fear of democracy exacerbated traditional balance-of-power concerns. Athens, aware of Sparta's opposition to fortifications, had made its city walls a fait accompli by rapidly constructing the undisclosed defenses. Their existence along with Athens' continued naval expansion concerned the Peloponnesians. By the mid-460s, even conservative Spartans appear to have concluded that prudence dictated weakening their rival. With a heightened threat perception and a probably related shift in internal politics, Sparta learned about Thasos' attempt to revolt from the Delian League in 465. When Thasos urged Sparta to invade Attica to force the Athenian army's recall, the Peloponnesians agreed out of character. However, they soon aborted invasion plans after a destructive earthquake rocked Sparta and prompted the Helots—Spartan serfs from Messenia—to revolt.[28]

Unable to defeat the Helots holed up on Mount Ithome, Sparta sought assistance from other Greek city-states including Athens, regarded as the premier besieger in Hellas. Growing dislike of the Peloponnesians prompted considerable opposition in Athens to the mission on both strategic and political grounds, but Cimon retained enough prestige and power to win approval to take four thousand men to aid Sparta.[29] When this force did not help penetrate the Helot citadel in the summer of 462, Sparta pointedly dismissed the Athenian contingent while requesting all other Greeks remain. This inflammatory step apparently reflected Spartan concern about the infectiousness of Athenian democratic ideals. News of the dismissal, as well as possible discovery of Sparta's aborted invasion plans during the Thasos revolt, infuriated the Athenian polis, undermined the remaining political strength of Cimon, and sparked an explicitly anti-Sparta orientation.[30] Leading figures such as an emerging Pericles seem to have concluded that the city-state "would have to neutralize the power of the Peloponnesian League" if Athens was to continue her progress toward Hellenic superiority.[31] Beyond denouncing the extant if moribund Athens–Sparta alliance against Persia, Athens formed a pact with Argos, Sparta's traditional rival on the Peloponnesus. More significantly, Athens eagerly agreed to protect Megara, its neighbor to the southwest and a long-time Sparta ally.[32] Megaran leaders knew Sparta would not protect them given Corinth's importance as the second strongest member of the Peloponnesian League. The subsequent Peloponnesian attack on the Megaran countryside failed, prompting Corinth's "bitter hatred for Athens" that would last for the rest of the century.[33] Sparta now decided war could no longer be avoided, but both sides were more accurately already in an undeclared struggle to penetrate each other's traditional sphere of influence.

Decision Context

The brief preceding history highlights the military, political, economic, and diplomatic developments that greatly shaped the contextual factors, discussed in this section, that together influenced the Athenian decision to construct the original Long Walls and determined how they would be employed strategically.

Threat Perception

Despite possessing considerable confidence and optimism, Athenians appreciated a significant vulnerability that resulted from the combination of city locale, terrain features, and Spartan adversary. The city proper of Athens was approximately four miles from the Bay of Phaleron, which prevented it from being secured exclusively by naval power. Furthermore, the area between the city and the water was largely a flat, open coastal plain with minimal terrain features and modest population.[34] Thus the region offered accommodating ground for an invading army, which could position itself between the fortified upper city and the sea, and by extension the empire.

Athenians appreciated that Sparta, along with its allies, possessed considerable military strength. Spartan hoplites were recognized as the premier soldiers in the Greek world, something Athenians had witnessed frequently through the years. Sparta fostered a sense of invincibility and fearlessness by refusing to follow every other major Greek city by erecting walls.[35] While Sparta's relatively small population limited the size of its army, most of the other states of southern Greece had joined it in the long-standing Peloponnesian League. They were obligated to "follow Sparta wherever she might lead them."[36] None of these partners could match Spartan combat performance, but some cohorts such as the Eleans and Arcadians were also renowned soldiers.[37] Other allies, especially Corinth, greatly bolstered the size of any Peloponnesian fighting force as well as provided much-needed naval strength. Additionally, most of the towns of Boeotia—the region of central Greece directly west of Attica—were pro-Sparta and possessed abundant infantry and additional naval capability.

Athenians were equally aware of Sparta's glaring military weaknesses. Although the Helot revolt had finally been suppressed in 461, the potential for another revolt was ever present. The Spartans kept close watch on the Helots, but extended army deployments away from southern Greece left them uncomfortable. Such concern undoubtedly contributed to a lack of interest in conducting sieges and thus developing effective siegecraft. Witnessing Sparta's struggle at Mount Ithome almost certainly reinforced Athenian views of the Peloponnesians' ineptness in this area. Sparta had also exhibited a continuing weakness in naval affairs, something its more maritime-oriented allies, especially Corinth, could not offset.[38]

Military Capability

Athenians possessed tremendous confidence in their first-rate military, especially as the premier navy in the Aegean. Beyond their own two-hundred-plus trireme fleet, the Athenians essentially controlled the naval forces of the Delian League. This unmatched force could undertake multiple missions, including sea control of the Aegean. The Athenians also displayed excellent seamanship that gave their vessels and fleets an operational advantage over the Persians and Peloponnesians. Successful naval engagements dating back to the Battle of Salamis had created an almost religious faith in the navy. Although man-for-man inferior to the Spartan hoplite, at this stage the Athenians also had enormous confidence in their fighting capability given repeated successes in combined sea–land operations. In the mid-fifth century, Athens probably could deploy more than ten thousand hoplites, a force larger than any other individual Greek foe, although inferior to the combined strength of the Peloponnesian League.[39]

The Athenians agreed with their reputation as the premier practitioner of siegecraft among the Greeks. Their success primarily resulted from the economic resources that enabled a siege to be maintained until the starving target capitulated rather than any significant ability to penetrate fortifications. Such sieges were usually an effort to ensure that the Delian Confederacy remained intact given the fundamental role of "allies" in Athenian military strength. By the 460s, most allies, lacking enthusiasm for participating in operations, had been allowed to substitute cash for men and ships. In time this subsidy option would evolve into outright tribute. The other Delian League states had the potential to provide significant military assistance, especially of a naval variety, as well as critical resources such as timber and foodstuffs. Beyond the Delian League, more recent alliances—especially with Megara, Thessaly, and Argos—offered the potential to bolster land strength by providing good soldiers. The ties with Megara were of greatest importance given its key location on the northern end of the isthmus and the hilly terrain that severely complicated and imperiled any potential Peloponnesian invasion of Attica.[40]

Strategic Culture

The Athenians' threat perception and military capability emanated in significant part from their evolving view of warfare. At the start of the century, its citizens appear to have possessed the traditional Hellenic belief in agonal (hoplite) warfare—a form of conflict in which heavily armed soldiers formed into phalanxes advancing on open ground. The battles were brief and decisive. Athens, like the other agricultural-based Greek city-states, found this type of warfare desirable because farmers could quickly return to their land and limit the number of combatants to help elites retain political control. Agonal warfare also traditionally discouraged erecting strong walls as well as developing capable siegecraft.[41]

Athenian experience in the Persian Wars generated some revisionist thinking about the nature of warfare that carried over to intra-Greek warfare given its fit with the city-state's strengths. As noted previously, Athenians concluded that naval power, which had largely defeated the greatest invasion in Greek history, was key.[42] The combined sea–land victory over the Persians at Mycale in 479 "set the example for the Greeks in the Aegean for nearly 150 years."[43] As a result, Athens' strategic culture began shifting from pursuing open battles to relying on naval power, raids, and sieges. Hanson labels the emergent Athenian view "anti-hoplite" warfare. By contrast, he characterizes Sparta's strategic culture as "hyper-hoplite" because that city-state essentially replaced farmers with professional soldiers.[44] Scholars of the ancient Greeks such as Victor Davis Hanson, David Conwell, Donald Kagan, Peter Krentz, and Josiah Ober disagree on when this attitude gained dominance among the Athenians. Some scholars, such as Ober and Kagan, regard the transition as being lengthy and not truly occurring until Pericles implemented his strategy at the start of the Second Peloponnesian War in 431.[45] Krentz, among others, contends that by 460, anti-hoplite thinking appears to have been embraced by many leading Athenian statesmen such as Pericles.[46] As Conwell notes, the crux of the issue is the timing in which the Athenians decide, if possible, to avoid land battles and to abandon the threatened countryside without first attempting to protect it.[47] Around 460, aggressive and confident Athenians appear to seek out rather than attempt to evade battle, suggesting a sharp contrast with thirty years later. Similarly, although Athens had evacuated the countryside in 480 and wanted to be able to do so safely in a future crisis, such an option of last resort is fundamentally different from an outright policy of abandonment upon invasion that would be adopted in the 430s. While perhaps logical for some Athenians, such a policy seems unlikely politically without a clearer sense of inferiority at land combat, which did not exist at the time. The key juncture appears to be the setbacks in 446 that prompted an altered strategic environment.

Given the transitional nature of the Athenian strategic culture, it is worth considering Pericles' outlook as indicative of the city's young, rising leaders. Pericles' first mention in the public record occurred in 472 when he bankrolled a series of dramas by Aeschylus. One of them, the *Persians*, relates the story of Athens' narrow escape from domination; Themistocles was portrayed as the savior because of his fleet buildup. Aeschylus would have been unlikely to push this message without the concurrence of his sponsor. Likewise, Thucydides stresses Pericles' defense thinking as a legacy of Themistocles' naval policy. By 460 Pericles probably regarded a strong navy as essential to ensure ally loyalty and prompt Sparta to accept Athens' superiority. This attitude underlay a strategic orientation away from the land empire and the Attic countryside, but no clear indication exists whether Pericles embraced such transformative ideals at this early date. More accurately perhaps, it was not evident that Athens needed to choose between a naval and land empire.[48]

Resources

Athens had obtained great wealth following Themistocles' sea-based policy and could afford high defense expenditures. The evolving Delian League provided the primary source of such funds. Additionally, maritime trade with partners from Carthage to the Crimea enriched the city. The silver mines at Laurium and the recently seized lodes in Thrace provided significant revenue. The state also collected lucrative taxes from owners of slaves employed in mining, and Attic agriculture remained a source of wealth. Affluent Athenians could also be expected to contribute money directly to defense efforts.[49]

Top priority for allocation of these resources would be on maintaining naval superiority, which required huge budget outlays. A two-hundred-ship navy necessitated construction of ten to fifteen triremes annually, replacing casualties of battle and age.[50] A two-hundred-ship armada—vessels and rigging—would cost approximately the same amount of money as a one-hundred-thousand-man hoplite army, a far larger force than employed in any battle during the internal Greek struggles of the fifth century.[51] Moreover, funds would be necessary for operational expenses, although these were the responsibility of the wealthy elite serving as boat commanders.[52] Expensive dockyards and other port facilities also had to be maintained.

Adequate manpower represented another limiting factor for Athens given the city-state's demographics. Athens' fifth-century population is often placed around 250,000–300,000, but this level appears only to have been reached in the 440s–430s, with the influx of metics (resident aliens) drawn by Athens' prosperity and culture.[53] In 460 the total population was probably not more than 200,000. This number included women, children, slaves, and metics, with the latter two categories compromising a significant share. Slaves could not serve in the military, but metics provided an important resource. In exchange for residing in Athens, these foreigners owed public duties including military service, often crewing triremes or serving garrison duty. Each trireme required 170 to 200 men in the galley, meaning that full manning of a two-hundred-ship fleet required 35,000 to 40,000 seamen.[54] Every additional fifty triremes meant finding another 8,500 to 10,000 rowers. Metics and low-class Athenians were not allowed to serve as hoplite infantry, limiting the potential size of the main land force.

While its large population facilitated significant military forces, Athenians likely were sensitive to the taxing demands from fighting on multiple fronts. Corinth's attempt to exploit the deployment of most Athenian soldiers elsewhere by attacking the Megarid had forced the city to turn to the old and young to fill out Myronides' force.[55] The manpower constraints also probably affected thinking about the sustainability of any struggle. For example, although the overall casualty rate is unknown for these years, a surviving marble stelae records that in one year, either 460 or 459, the Erechthesis—one of the ten tribes into which Athens' population was grouped—lost 177 men and 2 generals.[56] If the tribes had equivalent populations, the losses amounted to a conservatively estimated 4 percent to 6 percent of Erechthesian adult males in one year.[57] As Malcolm MacGregor observes, even if the other tribes suffered less, the constant fighting entailed a high cost that money could not replace.[58] This knowledge almost certainly influenced Athenians' thinking about how best to eliminate vulnerability between the upper city and the ports, especially given the priority placed on the navy.

Domestic Politics

Even with its high cost, aggressive pursuit of empire and greatness remained popular in the polis. Given the Athenians' eagerness to support the Ionian revolt four decades earlier, Herodotus wrote that it was easier to convince thirty thousand Athenians to go to war than to convince one Spartan.[59] By 460 the sense that democracy promoted optimism and enthusiasm appears to have grown, especially with the increasingly participatory nature of the political system. At this time the Athenian polis could be divided into three groups: democrats, moderate conservatives, and radical oligarchs. The groups in part reflected different economic classes, but leaders of all three continued to be of noble birth. The democrats favored "rule by many," resulting in support from the poorer classes. With the poor needed to crew the triremes, naval veterans had helped propel the democrats to an increasingly strong position and buttress enthusiasm for a promaritime policy.[60]

By contrast, landholders and farmers tended to support the more conservative groups, which favored "rule by few" and a focus on the countryside. Possessing significant wealth and being the primary source of hoplites, they retained influence. Nevertheless, the shift of the Athenian economy toward maritime trade had weakened the conservatives.[61] In particular, tribute from Delian League members essentially freed the polis from landholders' influence on military decisions by obviating a need for raising taxes to cover defense expenditures.

A split over the relative weight to place on group self-interest versus Athenian national interest further diminished conservatives' clout. The less numerous radical oligarchs focused on undermining democracy.[62] By contrast, moderate conservatives would sometimes support policies that strengthened Athens, such as the Delian League and expansion of naval power, even if they enhanced the relative power of the democrats.[63] Moderate conservatives had generally possessed an advantage in Athenian politics after the Second Persian War, but by 460 the democrats had clearly gained the upper hand. The recent assassination of Ephialtes, the democratic leader, and the ostracism of Cimon, head of the moderate conservatives, meant that both main political groups had something of a leadership vacuum that younger men such as Pericles moved to fill.[64] The widespread hostility toward Sparta neutralized opposition to democrats' views on foreign and defense policy.

Decision-making Process

Ultimately the choice on how best to address Athens' vulnerability would occur in the *Ecclesia* (assembly), to which every adult male Athenian belonged. The demands of the empire now required forty scheduled sessions a year plus emergency meetings, diminishing attendance especially for citizens residing in the rural areas.[65] As a result, urbanites tended to be disproportionally represented among assembly meetings. While the smaller *Boule* (council) explored issues and set the assembly's agenda, the annually elected *strategoi*, a body of ten generals, directed military policy.[66] Wanting to ensure that men of skill and experience held generalships, these positions were the only offices elected by direct vote rather than rotating service or lot. The same men tended to be both political and military leaders, resulting in certain Athenians being elected repeatedly. For example, Cimon had been chosen every year from 479 to 462. Generals and former generals were also the most influential speakers at assembly sessions discussing military issues, although they often disagreed with each other.[67] No commander in chief position appears to have existed, with each general having equivalent power except when designated leader of a particular campaign.

Land Defense Options

When Pericles, Myronides, and other concerned Athenians gathered on the Pnyx hillside for the crucial discussions of how to guard against the Spartan army, the preceding contextual factors probably were on their minds. Because we know nothing about the substance of these meetings except for the outcome, this section must necessarily be somewhat speculative, but it builds on the likely influence of the contextual factors. Some citizens possibly supported taking no action, continuing a two-decade-old policy of relying on the fleet and the already established walls around Athens and Piraeus. Although a status quo policy would leave Athens vulnerable to siege attempts, its advocates could have argued that Sparta would be inclined to avoid the large and lengthy commitment required to besiege successfully a city of Athens' size. Yet, for such a wealthy and strong power, most citizens in the polis likely were open to reducing Athens' primary vulnerability. In his study of the city-state's defense policy in the fourth century BCE, Ober contends that five basic approaches existed to protect it from land attack: deterrence, forward defense, border defense, defense-in-depth, and city-wall defense.[68] The following discussion covers some of these options as potential alternatives in the mid-fifth century.

Enhanced Army

A basic option of expanding and improving the army would have abetted all of Ober's strategies. Athens already possessed an effective and experienced land force that had operated primarily in naval-infantry operations against Persia and rebellious allies. Expanding this force quantitatively and qualitatively was possible. If Athens developed a superior capability to the Spartans, the latter would have significantly enhanced leverage over its rival. This is important to note because the opposite ultimately occurred when Sparta's acquisition of naval power fifty years later finally provided it the key to victory.

Such an initiative, however, held little appeal. The Athenians, although appreciating the strength of Sparta's hoplites, did not regard its own force as clearly deficient. The army had won many battles without any significant defeats. The force of more than ten thousand hoplites when concentrated stood as a major power. More importantly, the polis would avoid any action that might jeopardize naval dominance.[69] A major effort to produce a significantly better and larger land capability would only be possible by constraining the size and effectiveness of the navy given competing resource demands. Athens' strategic culture conditioned by two decades of repeated success discouraged anything that would weaken prioritization on the navy. This option would not appeal to the predominant political group, the democrats, who had less interest in hoplite warfare than naval power.

Frontier Fortifications

A more intriguing notion would have been to prepare strong defenses on the borders of Attica. With the region's eastern and southern fronts protected by water and the navy, the landside western and northern approaches were marked by a series of mountain ranges. These ranges had limited passes, even fewer able to bear significant traffic such as the baggage train of an invading army.[70] Such entry points could be well defended, making penetration extremely difficult. A border defense system would safeguard all of Attica, not simply Athens. This protection would have been extremely appealing to landowners/farmers facing the prospect of Spartan attacks on rural Attica. At the time, a majority of Athenians still resided in the countryside.[71]

Given the underlying logic of this approach, which Athens would employ to an extent in the fourth century, why did the citizens reject it in the mid-fifth century? Ober argues that a border defense system was incompatible with the requirements of Greek strategic culture built around the hoplite.[72] In other words, the need for professional soldiers with specialized skills willing to be permanently garrisoned in remote outposts doomed this option.[73] Although landowners/farmers most benefited from a strong border defense, they tended to be the most conservative citizens with a strong attachment to the traditions of hoplite warfare. If by 460, however, the Athenians had begun shifting to an anti-hoplite strategic culture, should they have been more open to a border defense approach? As discussed earlier, Ober regards Athens as not yet having made this transition, but others have asserted that the fundamentals of the change had taken hold.[74] Herodotus highlights prior examples of Greeks using natural strong points to defend borders, such as at Thermopylae.[75] Some prominent outposts were already in place by the mid-fifth century, apparently designed to limit small incursions and slow down any large-scale attack.[76]

It is clear that Athens did not adopt a border defense of Attica as its primary means of protection against Sparta and other threats. A border defense policy was incongruous with both the anti-hoplite strategic culture based on naval power and the hoplite strategic culture referenced by Ober. Athenians would still have to lay out significant capital to protect against every pass. With the democrats in ascendance at the time, the approach—although seemingly allowing a concentration on the sea—probably deviated too much from the core elements of a naval-based strategy to hold strong appeal. Perhaps most importantly, a border defense system conveyed a status quo symbolism that contrasted with many Athenians' desire at midcentury for a land empire in central Greece. These Athenians would oppose fixed border instillations that might complicate winning political support for additional land conquest.[77]

Upper City Relocation

Relocating the city-state's center from Athens to Piraeus would have fit perfectly with the naval-centered strategic outlook favored by democrats. During the Persian Crisis, Themistocles believed, according to Thucydides, that "Piraeus was a more valuable place than the main city of Athens" given the port's role in facilitating a strong navy.[78] Herodotus relays Themistocles' perspective in his response to Adimantus, a Corinthian admiral attempting to exclude Athenian input on Greek strategy before the Battle of Salamis.[79] Despite the abandonment of the city, Themistocles reputedly declared that "so long as Athens had 200 warships in commission she had both a city and a country much stronger than theirs [Corinth] for there was not a single Greek state capable of repelling them, should they choose to attack."[80] He clearly wanted Athenians to retreat to Piraeus when threatened, possibly even believing in the strategic merit of a permanent relocation of the upper city to the port.[81] No such move occurred, or even was attempted, when Themistocles was at the height of his influence after victory in the Second Persian War.

By 460, with Athens possessing stronger fortifications, vastly greater wealth, and more confident citizens, the political prospects for such a move were nonexistent absent a crisis. Many Athenians, especially conservatives, would have rebelled against it. While Athenian dynamism is often contrasted with Spartan conservatism, most of the former's citizens had a great reverence for tradition, religion, and history. After centuries atop the acropolis, relocating the city was simply too radical an ideal. The less dramatic notion of shifting the city's economic and political locus to Piraeus while retaining religious and historical institutions in Athens probably held little more appeal to the citizens without it being demonstrated that their position was indefensible vis-à-vis Sparta. Such a move may even have worried Athenians as signaling weakness to Sparta and the rest of the Hellenic world. Instead, a palatable precaution would be introduced. Athens built a kind of duplicate city in Piraeus that could function as the capital during times of crisis if the asta—the upper city—had to be abandoned again, as occurred in 480.[82]

Long Walls

Athens' final alternative appeared to offer the strategic benefit of a shift to Piraeus without the perceived negatives of an actual move. The state could build fortified walls to connect the upper city and its ports, eliminating the latent vulnerability posed by an invading army.[83] In an emergency, the Athenian navy would ensure adequate supplies for the upper city, even if control over the rest of Attica was lost. Ober notes that the "Old Oligarch," an unidentified fifth century Athenian, highlighted the resulting advantage as "the strongest of land powers suffer from occasional crop failures, but the state that controls the sea can always import its food from some more prosperous land. In general, the sea power can import whatever it likes or needs from a variety of places."[84] If Sparta invaded, Athens would have the alternative of striking back directly at the Peloponnesians, concentrating manpower on the navy without having to mount a vigorous land defense or even abandon the upper city. Plus, the rural population could obtain safe haven within these fortifications. The Athenians had likely been considering these walls for some time, possibly even dating back to the end of the Second Persian War. Now the need for such a defense had markedly increased. Moreover, the vast wealth generated by the empire had made more affordable such massive structures. Advocates of this approach could trumpet its political as well as practical strengths. Moderate conservatives might have approved it as increasing Athens' naval and imperial power while the democrats certainly would have felt this way.[85] This political appeal would have been enhanced if this was presented as eliminating vulnerability during a wartime emergency rather than part of an explicit policy to abandon the countryside when invaded.

Regardless, some Athenians had strong reason to oppose such a major modification of security policy. Landowners/farmers would have criticized these works as an abdication of defending rural Attica.[86] Even if, as seems likely, the Athenians were not inclined to abandon the countryside without first taking on an invading army, the presence of walls as a safety net would encourage abandoning such efforts prematurely or holding back some strength. Even from a policy perspective, navalists would have some reason for objection. The Long Walls would entail considerable expense, effort, and—most significantly—manpower to guard, potentially handicapping efforts to retain naval dominance.[87] The financial and manning costs of the Long Walls would have been exacerbated by the need to build walls to two ports separated by almost two miles of coastline. As the main naval base with arsenals and dry docks as well as a rising commercial port, Piraeus had to be linked to Athens. Phaleron, although more exposed, remained important commercially and apparently could not be neglected for financial or political reasons. Thus Athenians could not employ a system of closely spaced parallel walls as they would in overseeing, even possibly building, between Megara and its port of Nisaea around the same time.[88] Athens either had to build four walls in two parallel sets or single barriers to each port and rely on the navy to prevent attack on the open coastline between them.

Decision for a Strategic Defense System

Ultimately, despite these concerns, the Long Walls offered the best response from a political, psychological, and security perspective. With the democrats now ascendant, the choice inevitably would have to abet, not detract from, a naval-based strategy. Only the Long Walls and relocation to Piraeus fit this criterion, but the latter approach only had theoretical strategic appeal. Relocation likely did not receive any serious consideration. Some naval purists might have regarded the walls as a distraction, but it would have been easy to convince most citizens that for modest expense they enabled Athens to remain safe miles from the sea while emphasizing the navy. Given that the initial effort likely was presented as a safeguard, not a preordained abandonment of the countryside, it would have been more acceptable. The appeal of the project would have increased after embarking on major war with Sparta for the first time in the fifth century. Advocates for a more transformative strategy of Long Walls, navy, and empire could appreciate these connecting barriers were the last critical ingredient, helping set the stage for Athens to later adopt this revolutionary approach.[89]

Adding to the political appeal of the walls was the psychological comfort (subjective security) they would provide Athenians. Although citizens' confidence from both military victories and political freedom had been a key attribute of the city-state's rise, it rested on a shaky foundation. Athens had been sacked only twenty years earlier. The city's postwar fortifications reduced its vulnerability, but the possibility of isolation and defeat still existed. With the Long Walls in place, Athens could essentially pursue imperial expansion without fear of the city's capture as long as its naval power remained intact.[90] The relationship between objective (actual) and subjective (perceived) security is a central issue in this work and will be addressed throughout, but suffice it to say here that considerations of subjective security play a prominent role in the development and impact of strategic defense systems.

In this case, the objective security matched perceptions given that stout walls could not be compromised by contemporary siegecraft. None of the four general approaches to overcoming barriers offered the Athenians any reason for concern. First, scaling well-constructed curtains was quite difficult, especially for heavily armed hoplites, and attempts would likely result in significant casualties. Second, the Greeks did not yet use tunneling to undermine walls, an approach that would become a popular method of attack in the fourth century. Third, strong walls could not be destroyed by direct assaults. Battering rams for attacking gates would not be introduced into Greece for at least another two decades, and even then they did not present much danger of breeching well-constructed and guarded walls. Finally, encirclement would not work against the Long Walls without the Peloponnesians first gaining naval superiority, an unthinkable condition in Athens. While a border defense approach might have been as effective, Athenians could not be as confident of success given the potential for the outposts being overrun by a determined foe. Given that this option also fit less well with Athens' strategic culture, it not surprisingly lacked appeal.[91]

The Long Walls, however, were vulnerable in one dimension. Traitors inside walls could and at times did compromise their integrity, letting a besieging army charge through opened gates. For Athenian statesmen in 460, concern about traitors was hardly idle with the radical oligarchs implacably hostile to the city's democratic rule, sea-based economic and security policy, and the idea of constructing long walls.[92] Still, the traitor threat could be addressed with vigilance and it did not offset the aforementioned advantages of fortifications. Instead, as F. E. Winter observed, "secure barriers against land attack were an absolute necessity for the Athenians, if they were to be free to concentrate their engines on their fleet."[93]

If the Long Walls offered the best course of action from political, psychological, and security perspectives, did they also have a deterrent appeal? Fifth century Athenians left no record of explicit thinking about deterrence.[94] They may have had notions about the basic concept and its attraction, but in mid-fifth century their behavior suggests little interest or confidence in deterring Sparta from attacking. Clearly, properly constructed, maintained, and manned Long Walls would make the city of Athens invulnerable to Spartan attack, creating the potential for deterrence by denial—convincing an adversary that aggression would not achieve the desired objective—to be operative. For such a situation to deter a Peloponnesian attack, however, Sparta would have to believe that Athens would respond to an invasion of Attica by sitting behind its walls. Such a realization did not even exist thirty years later at the start of the Second Peloponnesian War.[95] Moreover, at the time, the Athenians had no such policy of avoiding land battle and abandoning the countryside. Any ability to deter Sparta would have been constrained by their limited ability to punish Sparta for aggression, but Athens' confidence in being fundamentally superior to its rival probably made the stratagem of little interest anyway. Instead, the Long Walls were most likely perceived as eliminating a dangerous vulnerability in the Themistoclean sea-based strategy.[96] Thus, rather than deterring invasion, at most the hope would be to deter a victorious Peloponnesian army from attempting to cut off the upper city from the key ports.

With minimal evidence and conflicting ancient descriptions, scholars struggle for consensus on the Long Walls' construction dates. The most compelling argument is for a limited, incomplete start in 462 or 461.[97] Plutarch credits Cimon with playing a role in their construction, which if accurate would require work beginning before his ten-year banishment in 461.[98] Cimon's support of the Long Walls may have been part of an unsuccessful effort at political survival after the Spartans dismissed his force from Mount Ithome. Such timing would have meant Athenians acted "in anticipation of hostilities—rather than in reaction to them."[99] Any initial proactive construction efforts appear to have been limited with the bulk progress occurring after the outbreak of hostilities with the Corinthians in 459, at which point Thucydides writes, "Athenians began to build their two long walls down to the sea."[100] The ongoing wars likely hampered efforts, given their funding and manpower needs. Still, by late 458 or early 457 Athens apparently completed its original two Long Walls.[101]

While Sparta would have learned about the new Athenian fortifications under construction, it made no move against them even after a ten-thousand-man Peloponnesian army had been deployed to Boeotia, bordering Attica. This force actually had remained in central Greece, after aiding the allied city of Doris out of concern about safe passage home.[102] The Athenian navy had blocked the sea route across the Corinthian Gulf while the land route required transiting the narrow, vulnerable mountain passes controlled by Megara. At this time radical oligarchs in Athens appealed to the Peloponnesians to move directly against the city-state. Thucydides reports this disgruntled group offered internal assistance "in the hope of putting an end to democratic government and preventing the building of the Long Walls."[103] These aims would have certainly been attractive to the Spartans, but they took no action. Rather, it was the Athenians who acted, viewing the nearby presence of the Peloponnesian army as intolerable.

Although their incomplete status and lack of information about this decision tempers judgment, the advance hints at a tendency for barriers built by rising powers to promote aggressive behavior, not encourage passive conservatism. Athens may have marched out without the long walls rising, but the under-construction strategic defenses reduced the risk of such behavior if they should fail. The Athenians apparently did not consider it necessary to await the barrier's completion, perhaps fearing the Peloponnesians would attempt to prevent it. Combined with its allies, the fourteen-thousand-man Athenian-led force met the enemy at Tanagra in Boeotia.[104] Both sides sustained heavy casualties in resulting combat, but eventually the Athenian side collapsed. The beaten-up Spartan army, however, used the victory as a springboard to travel home safely rather than try to unseat the Athenian democracy and destroy the Long Walls.

The battle of Tanagra would supply a lasting lesson for the Athenians and would have implications for the Long Walls despite the city-state's rapid recovery from defeat. Whereas previously the barriers represented a sound precaution, they now were given heightened importance as workers finished construction.[105] Athenians had gained greater appreciation for Spartan fighting skill and determination. While no explicit indication exists that Athenians sought to avoid fighting the Peloponnesians on land, the Athenians would not engage in another major land battle with them for more than thirty years. Athenian ambition and optimism in general, however, returned after completion of the Long Walls and a series of notable successes.[106] With the Peloponnesian force back in southern Greece, the Athenians soon marched again to Boeotia and defeated the locals at Oenophyta, establishing control over this key neighboring region. Aegina also capitulated, agreeing to remove its fortifications, join the Delian League, and pay the highest tribute level of any member.[107] Tolmides conducted a triumphant raiding mission around the Peloponnesus, burning Sparta's dockyards and capturing the Corinthian city of Chalcis.

While these successes reinforced Athens' image as a strong power, its leaders had already initiated a continuing effort to bolster citizens' confidence in the safety provided by defenses (i.e., subjective security). Krentz highlights this effort by noting how the legendary conflict between Amazon and Athens evolved. The traditional version simply had Theseus and Heracles defeating the Amazonians. In 458, the year in which the Long Walls were likely completed, Aeschylus wrote *Oresteia,* a play in which for the first time Amazon lays siege to Athens. The citizenry fighting atop fortifications repelled the assault. This new version of the legend gained further acceptance in the ensuing years. The imagery of this revised legend encouraged Athenians that they "would overcome any new besiegers just as their ancestors had overcome the Amazons. Their walls would protect them."[108]

Security Developments with the Walls in Place

Within a few years of the Long Walls' completion, the Athenians had suffered setbacks that likely increased perceptions of the barriers' value. These reverses, however, also diminished Athenian naval dominance, which probably highlighted the inseparable link between the strength of the fleet and the utility of the Long Walls.

Setbacks Sour War Enthusiasm

Between 456 and 454 Delian League forces experienced a catastrophic defeat in Egypt, forcing the Greeks to surrender control of the region. While not directly threatening the homeland, sharp losses of men and ships degraded Athenian naval capability. Many Athenians, wearying of conflict, wanted the polis to concentrate on wealth creation and empire building. Cimon had returned from banishment to negotiate in 451 a five-year truce between Athens and Sparta, hoping the agreement would enable an Athenian focus on Persia. His subsequent death while leading an attack on Cyprus, however, soon also ended enthusiasm for that long struggle. With the Persian King also tired of the war, both sides compromised by agreeing to respect each other's sphere of influence.[109]

The end of the Persian war prompted uncomfortable inquiries from Delian League "allies" who expected a cessation of their requirement to supply cash or ships. Athens countered that the break-up of the league would entice the Persians to move against the Greeks residing in modern-day Turkey. Although, as noted earlier, Athenians at the time left no clear written record of formal deterrence thought, at least one scholar argues that the city-state warned its allies that a naval fleet-in-being must continue to exist to deter Persia.[110] Most league members did not find this argument persuasive and a high number defaulted on standing contribution quotas. Thus, Athens—which a few years earlier had relocated the League's treasury from the island of Delos to the "safety" behind its walls—turned to more persuasive economic and military means to ensure continued *"phoros"* (membership dues).¹¹¹ At this point, the evolution of the Delian League to the Athenian empire takes a major step forward as so-called phoros clearly becomes tribute. The transition, however, would be somewhat difficult, temporarily impinging on Athenian naval mastery as well as the potential to rely on the Long Walls if necessary.

No other navy could match the Athenian fleet when a seminal series of setbacks in 447 and early 446 apparently provided a major impetus to embrace the underlying trends toward reliance on the fleet, empire, and Long Walls. First the Boeotians revolted and obtained independence after the decisive Battle of Coronea in 447. The large island of Euboea, just north of Athens, soon launched its own rebellion. As a major food producer and original member of the Delian League, Athens could not allow its defection to stand so Pericles led an expedition to restore order. The Megarans, however, took the Athenian army's movement north as an opportunity to launch its own revolt. Sparta and Corinth, eager to bring Megara back into the Peloponnesian League, moved to help with an invasion of Attica in 446. Pericles reversed course to meet the sudden challenge to the homeland. The Long Walls had been complete for more than a decade, so Pericles' return suggests either the city's leaders wanted to try to defend the countryside or they could not adequately man and defend the Long Walls without the departed troops. Most likely, the Athenians wanted to avoid abandoning rural areas to Peloponnesian carnage if possible, especially with Euboea also in revolt. Ultimately, no battle ensued as the Peloponnesians, having advanced into Attica only as far as Eleusis and Thria, returned home before the Athenians arrived. With the Peloponnesian threat removed, Pericles reversed course again and eliminated Euboean resistance.¹¹²

The Peloponnesian withdrawal had apparently been accomplished by diplomatic overture with Athens agreeing to negotiate what would become the Thirty Years' Peace. Athens surrendered all of its Peloponnesian territory, the Megarian ports of Nisaea and Pegae, as well as most gains in central Greece. Beyond these Athenian concessions, both sides retained their possessions and agreed to refrain from attacking each other. Athens and Sparta also now recognized each other's sphere of influence—Athens in the Aegean and Sparta in the Peloponnesus.¹¹³ Critically, they agreed that allies could not switch sides. Megara's alignment with Athens provided the spark that started the war while its return to Sparta's side facilitated the conclusion. The compromise peace treaty, however, did not resolve the underlying tension of Athens' growing strength and Sparta's concern about the implications of this trend.

Pericles, who had now become the dominant political figure in Athens, took significant lessons from the recently completed conflict with Sparta.¹¹⁴ The experience of the fourteen-year struggle, especially the battles of Tanagra, Coronea, and the recent Spartan advance, prompted him to "see more realistically that

Athens' real forte was by sea."[115] Obtaining and maintaining an empire on land in central Greece did not fit well with Athens' strengths because naval power could not be used to intimidate, isolate, and coerce adversaries. However, the Eubean revolt in 446 and Athens' subsequent struggle to regain absolute control of the Delian League "demonstrated to the Athenians that their sea power was not beyond challenge."[116] They needed to concentrate on ensuring that naval power remained preeminent as well as adopt safeguards appropriate for a state no longer perceiving itself as invincible at sea. Anthony Podlecki sums up Pericles' thinking at the time: "Athens' energies must not be divided between keeping a grip on her maritime empire and acquiring more control over mainland states. The policy of 'no expansion by land' (with concomitant watchfulness for signs of disaffection among the maritime allies) was to become a cornerstone of Pericles' imperial policy, one that he would return to with a tenacious regularity in the years to come."[117] This perspective elevated the importance of the Long Walls; however, Pericles' rush back from Euboea when Sparta advanced toward Athens suggests that the citizenry had not yet embraced an abandonment of the countryside.

Strengthened Strategic Defenses in Athens' Golden Age

Athens commenced what historians have labeled its golden age with both the Persian and the First Peloponnesian wars over, but the calm also facilitated an opportunity to address perceived vulnerability through an additional long wall. Relieved of wartime expenses and collecting a steady flow of allied tribute, the city-state's wealth grew rapidly. Athens continued to expand its empire, establishing new colonies from the Black Sea to Italy. At home, leaders launched a massive building campaign including the Parthenon and the Propylaia. These accomplishments, however, did not distract Athenians from funding a major upgrade to strategic defenses. They might have wanted to strengthen the fortifications for some time, but combat needs received priority while the wars continued. Andocides, a late-fifth-century Athenian historian, attributes the decision to upgrade the defensive walls as a response to the 446 Peloponnesian invasion of Attica.[118] Even if the invasion did not specifically prompt the initiative, improving fortifications made sense given that Athenian statesmen almost certainly expected future hostilities with Sparta. With Megara in the Spartan camp, Attica had become much more vulnerable to land invasion from the south.[119]

Reflecting the growth of Piraeus as the dominant port and the desire to possess a more secure link between it and the upper city, a new long wall ran parallel to the existing Athens–Piraeus structure. Known as "the middle wall" or "southern wall" for its position between the original two barriers, the structure ran five hundred feet east of the Piraeus wall. The resulting corridor to Piraeus, at one-eighth the area between the two original walls, offered a more defensible lifeline. Despite possessing naval dominance and a swampy coastline, the open shore of almost two miles between the two ports left a vulnerability that could be exploited. An alternative remedy would have been to construct a defense barrier along the coastline between the two long walls, but the relative decline of Phaleron apparently encouraged concentration on Piraeus. Athens would continue to maintain the wall to Phaleron to some degree, but periodic challenges to Athenian naval dominance highlighted the value of a fallback position should an adversary land on the Bay of Phaleron. Soldiers also could be rapidly moved between the two Piraeic lines, promoting security with fewer troops.[120]

This Athens–Piraeus corridor, representing the full flowering of Themistocles' defense strategy built around the navy and Piraeus, was probably completed between 446 and 442, although the precise dates are unknown. Athenians built this additional barrier confident that Greek siegecraft had achieved no significant improvement. Thus, as Athens and Sparta drifted toward war in the late 430s, the former had formidable fortifications that altogether exceeded twenty-five miles in length (i.e., the two Long Walls to Piraeus, the Long Wall to Phaleron, and the fortifications of the upper city and Piraeus).[121] Kagan sums up their position: "Once they completed the walls surrounding their city and connecting them by additional Long Walls to the fortified port at Piraeus ... the Athenians were virtually invulnerable."[122] Such a position not surprisingly instilled Athenians with confidence, yet its value depended on maintaining naval dominance.

The Role of the Long Walls during the Second Peloponnesian War

Athens neither wanted nor sought war, but Pericles and other leading citizens regarded the return of the conflict with the Peloponnesians as inevitable and exerted little effort to avoid it by alleviating Spartan concerns. Rather, confident of success in a future fight and feeling protected by the Long Walls and navy, they apparently viewed the risk as low in taking a number of provocative actions that accelerated Sparta's decision to initiate hostilities.[123] Already violating the Thirty Years' Peace by denying Aegina self-determination, Athens in 433 essentially barred trade between Megara and the Athenian Empire in a retaliatory but highly confrontational move. Most destabilizing was Athens' decision that same year to support Corcyra in its worsening dispute with Corinth. Although Athens had attempted to navigate carefully between ensuring Corcyra's safety and alienating Corinth and its Peloponnesian allies, they ultimately supported the former to prevent a combination of the powerful Corcyrean and Corinthian navies that could have threatened Athenian dominance of the seas. As Thucydides relates, this series of events exacerbated Sparta's concern about Athens' growing strength.[124] In the years since the Thirty Years' Peace, the strategic balance had only worsened from Sparta's perspective. Thus it voted for war with the other members of the Peloponnesian League in the summer of 432.

The Archidamian War (431–421)

Pericles' war strategy relied on three components: empire, Long Walls, and navy.[125] Tribute and foodstuffs from "allies" would sustain Athens, eliminating a need to fight directly to protect the Attic countryside. The Long Walls would safeguard the upper city and its primary ports from land attack while providing refuge for the rural population when invaded. Given that "the defenses of Athens were certainly among the most modern and powerful in the whole Greek world" and siegecraft remained limited, it is not surprising that no major upgrades occurred at the outset of the war.[126] Dominance of the seas by the navy's three-hundred-trireme fleet would protect the empire, ensure transport of provisions for the city, and facilitate offensive operations against the Peloponnesians. Without such maritime capability, the other two tenets of the approach lost their value. While the aforementioned debate exists among scholars whether this strategy represented a sharp break from the past, it appears to mark the culmination of a fifty-year trend toward reliance on the navy and urban strategic defense system.[127] Thus, if the original Long Walls had been conceived of more as a safety net, they were now a core part of a security policy designed to abandon the countryside when threatened and avoid major land battle with Sparta. Thucydides has Pericles expressing the essence of this position at the start of the Second Peloponnesian War: "Suppose we were an island, would we not be absolutely secure from attack? As it is we must try to think of ourselves as islanders."[128] The anti-hoplite strategic culture had clearly been embraced. By adhering to its tenets and refraining from expansion of the empire, Pericles believed that Athens' superior staying power in a war of attrition would ultimately convince Sparta to quit. Pericles projected this objective would take three or four years, but the treasury had amassed enough money for at least five or six years of war.[129]

The accuracy of that judgment will be addressed later, but it clearly was not a formula for deterring Peloponnesian aggression. This result is not surprising since the earlier discussion suggested the goal of deterrence had played a negligible role in Athenians' thinking when the walls first rose.[130] With Sparta's continued relative decline and the fear that Athenian dominance would compromise its long-term security and political system, the threshold for achieving deterrence was quite high. Yet Athens' defense strategy did not allow much potential for either deterrence by retaliation or deterrence by denial. Naval raids against the Peloponnesus, exemplified by Tolmides' strike during the First Peloponnesian War, could be launched as a punitive response to any invasion of Attica. Such raids would be popular in Athens but "actually presented the Spartans with little to fear."[131] Athens had not demonstrated an ability to conduct large-scale amphibious invasions of the Peloponnesus, which would ultimately have required defeating the Spartan hoplites on shore.

While Spartans almost certainly realized the virtual impossibility of penetrating the Long Walls, they apparently did not appreciate that Athenians would abandon Attica and sit safely behind these fortifications. On the contrary, memories of Athens agreeing to end the First Peloponnesian War after King Pleistoanax's invasion of Attica in 446 likely dominated Spartan thinking. Thus the Long Walls did not produce a general deterrence by denial. One could argue more narrowly that the Long Walls deterred a direct attack on Athens or an attempt to cut off the city, but the Spartans would not have been inclined to conduct such an attack, if at all, until the Athenians demonstrated an unwillingness to engage in battle. No evidence suggests that Athens tried to convey to Sparta that its hoplite advantage would not yield victory and thus they should refrain from invading. Sparta would likely have attempted a preventive war even if it appreciated Pericles' strategy given the consequences of sustained trends. Ultimately, Athens' belief in the inevitability of war and its ability to win such a conflict probably discouraged attempting to communicate a strong deterrent message.

Thus the Peloponnesians marched off to war in Summer 431 confident of success, but they soon discovered that Athens' strategy made winning problematic. The Athenians did not come out to defend their countryside against the invading army as expected, nor did they attempt to secure the Peloponnesians' departure through offering favorable terms to Sparta. In contrast to 446, peace was unlikely given that Sparta would only agree to terms that produced a fundamental reshaping of the balance of power, something Athenians would not accept without outright defeat. Athens did not fight or capitulate but pursued its unorthodox strategy of attrition warfare without major land combat. At first the rural population displayed some grumbling and hesitance about abandonment of the countryside, but Pericles convinced them to seek protection. Perhaps more accurately, the sixty-thousand-man Peloponnesian invasion force convinced them to relocate. Athens had sixteen thousand soldiers dedicated for defensive purposes as well as another thirteen thousand hoplites, twelve hundred cavalry, and sixteen hundred archers.[132] It has been suggested that, had Sparta sent a smaller expedition, it might have encouraged the Athenians to give battle, but this seems unlikely under Pericles' leadership.[133] Given the strength of the walls, Athens could rely heavily on second-rate troops, including the old, young, and those metics who qualified as hoplites, to guard it. Manpower efficiencies were also obtained by leaving unmanned the least vulnerable areas—the inner long wall to Piraeus, half of the port's defenses, and the inner segment of the upper city's walls. The invasion force's inability to capture the Athenian frontier base at Oenoe or its small ally of Plataea likely boosted Athenian confidence in the city's strategic defense system.[134]

A frustrated Spartan leadership shifted to a new strategy—economic warfare.[135] Soldiers began attacking Attic agriculture, especially the fertile plain of Eleusis to the west of Athens. Initially, the Spartans may have expected the Athenians to sally forth and attempt to prevent such destruction. After this provocation failed, the Peloponnesians broadened the scope of economic warfare as a way to weaken Athens into submission. Thus invasions of Attica occurred in five of the first seven years of the war. Their Boeotian allies also pillaged the countryside from the west and north. Nevertheless, the armies did not inflict lasting destruction during these deployments, which only averaged about thirty days.[136] Heavily armed hoplites could not rapidly roam and pillage while mobile light infantry needed protection from Athenian cavalry. Maintenance of a few border forts and other defenses allowed the Athenians to moderate damage from invasions and repel small raids. Moreover, Hanson has demonstrated the resiliency of Attic agriculture, especially the key olive trees.[137]

Even if the devastation had been far greater, Athens would not have been forced to capitulate. The movement of farmers' livestock to Euboea and continued importation of wheat from the Black Sea region ensured sufficient provisions for the city as long as secure naval transport was available.[138] Recognizing this difficulty, the Spartans in late 429 attempted to circumvent Athens' defenses. The Long Walls presented no vulnerability, but Piraeus offered an opening. Given Athens' naval superiority, the port's defenses were neglected, quite naturally according to Thucydides.[139] With the assistance of their allies, Sparta launched a sneak attack against the port. The Spartans, however, sacrificed the element of surprise through clumsy execution and withdrew after witnessing a vigorous Athenian response. Given the potential danger from a capture of Piraeus, Athens enhanced its security.

Although Pericles' strategy denied Sparta victory, critics at the time and ever since have disparaged it for not providing Athens a way to win. Even with the annual Peloponnesian invasions of Attica entailing significant costs and generating considerable frustration from lack of effect, it remains hard to conceive why Sparta would have quit given the perceived importance of the struggle to their long-term security. Athenian sea-borne raids on Peloponnesian coastal towns, ravaging Megara's countryside, and sporadic cavalry actions in Attica only inflicted limited damage. While the Athenian generals in particular hoped to intimidate Megara to abandon Sparta, these actions were primarily to bolster domestic morale. By the beginning of 430, even Pericles began to doubt his policy would gain Sparta's capitulation, prompting the initiation of larger raids (e.g., against Epidaurus in May 430). These strikes, however, failed to increase pressure directly on Sparta or precipitate an insurrection among its approximately 250,000 Helots.[140]

Growing realization of Sparta's commitment to the struggle coincided with recognition that safeguarding rural Athenians behind the fortifications was not a panacea. These refugees, who tended to relocate in Athens itself, more than doubled the city's population, placing a high burden on government services.[141] The resulting unpleasant and unsanitary living conditions prompted increasing frustration within the polis and in May 430 precipitated an outbreak of the plague that killed up to a quarter of the population. Beyond a devastating decline in resources, the disease inflicted a severe blow to Athenian morale. Thucydides would observe that "nothing did the Athenians so much harm as this [the plague] or so reduced their strength for war."[142] Over a four-year period, Athenian hoplite and cavalry ranks declined by about a third from disease, along with probably a similar percentage of rowers lost.[143] Even though relocation was required for only about one month a year, many refugees did not return to the countryside, especially in the western areas damaged by the Spartans.

After Pericles succumbed to the plague in 429, a second critical weakness with his strategy emerged. It required a charismatic and skilled leader to convince Athenians to stay the course.[144] Instead, by 426 a group of younger generals led by Cleon persuaded the Athenians to pursue a more offensive strategy, with mixed results. A critical victory at Pylos in the southwest corner of the Peloponnesus in 425 punctured the Spartan hoplite's image of invincibility and fueled Athenian hope of victory. Most significantly, the 120 captured, highly valued full Spartiates served as hostages, prompting the Peloponnesians to cease invading Attica. Unfortunately, success motivated the Athenian war hawks to press for expanded aims, especially a land empire in central Greece (e.g., Boeotia, Megara) that would shift the balance of power decisively in Athens' favor. This effort began auspiciously by penetrating Megara's Long Walls through a combination of treachery and commando operations, but momentum soon evaporated with a failed assault on Megara itself and severe defeats at Delium and Amphipolis.[145] These reverses allowed the compromise-minded Nicias to gain the upper hand in Athens and negotiate the fifty-year Peace of Nicias with Sparta in 421.

This agreement reflected both sides' desire for a temporary respite, but clearly hostilities would resume. For Sparta, the increasing power of Athens remained a threat, but it had to find a way to overcome its rival's strategy. For Athens, Sparta would remain an implacable foe that refused to accept its dominance. The refusal of some key Sparta allies, such as Corinth, to accept anything beyond a renewable truce fed this sentiment. While Nicias argued that delaying combat would add to Athens' advantage, other citizens pressed for a more aggressive security policy. Protected by the navy and the Long Walls, they probably regarded such an approach as being low in risk. With Cleon's death at the Battle of Amphipolis in 422, the talented Alcibiades rose to lead the hawks. He soon convinced Athens to enter into an anti-Spartan alliance with three democratic states in southern Greece (Argos, Mantinea, and Elis). This provocative move, vitiating the treaty's spheres of influence principle, threatened the integrity of the Peloponnesian League. In response, Sparta attacked Mantinea in 418 and won a narrow but decisive victory that unraveled the democratic alliance. The following year after regaining power, the democrats in Argos sought Athenian assistance to build long walls to the sea. News of this plan prompted the Spartans to attack Argive territory and destroy the walls under construction. The Peace of Nicias technically remained intact throughout this action, but both sides awaited favorable opportunities to renew the struggle.[146]

The Decelean War (413–404)
The Athenians would supply the spark in early 415 by deploying a large force to Sicily, a highly risky undertaking more than eight hundred miles from the homeland. Alcibiades' hawkish rhetoric and partial recovery from the devastation of the plague contributed to Athenian willingness to launch this effort, but did the existence of the Long Walls protective shield make Alcibiades more seductive? No clear evidence exists, but the majority's willingness to regard such an affair as of limited risk potentially suggests strategic defenses may exacerbate ambitious powers' inclination to skew risk calculations in favor of provocative action. Although ostensibly aimed to empower allies, undercut Sparta's trade, and defeat Syracuse before it attacked Athens, the expedition more accurately appears to have been an attempt to increase the city-state's wealth and power. A rich, populous, and democratic Syracuse, however, presented a challenging target. The Athenians besieged the city at a pedestrian pace, allowing timely assistance from the Peloponnesians to help the Syracusans prevail. Ultimately, the affair ended disastrously for Athens with its entire forty-five-thousand-man force, including a large reinforcement army and the naval armada, essentially lost.[147]

Fear of such a costly debacle had prompted Pericles to caution against attempts at expansion during the war. Even though not technically at war with Sparta in 415, the losses in Sicily now imperiled the Periclean defense strategy in the renewed Athens–Sparta conflict. The loss of 160 triremes and more than 50 allied vessels left the Athenian navy with only about 100 warships, some of which were in poor condition. Moreover, the naval defeat in Syracuse harbor shattered the sense of Athens' invincibility on the water. Disease and losses had reduced the number of available Athenian soldiers and seamen by more than 50 percent since the start of the war. Furthermore, the enormous cost of the Sicilian campaign left the treasury nearly empty. Recognition of Athens' diminished position would lead many of its subject allies (e.g., Euboea, Chios, and Miletus) to rebel in the next few years.[148]

Even before Athens suffered outright defeat in Sicily, the Peloponnesians had seized on its rival's distraction to renew the war by invading Attica early in 413. Recognizing that the annual raiding missions had caused limited damage, Sparta followed the traitor Alcibiades' advice by establishing a permanent base at Decelea (about thirteen miles northeast of Athens along a main trade route).[149] Urban and rural citizens may have been safe behind the barriers, but the Decelean outpost, known as *epiteichismos* ("forward fortification"), entailed serious consequences for Athens.[150] The Peloponnesian army could now sustain control of much of the countryside, restricting Athenian access to fertile lands to the area near the Long Walls. The Decelean base also cut the land route between Athens and Euboea, forcing food imports to travel over the more expensive and time-consuming naval route. The Peloponnesian presence convinced many Athenian slaves to desert, sharply reducing profitable silver production at Laurium. Rural refugees would now be confined behind the fortifications indefinitely. More than a physical or economic handicap, the confinement represented a heavy psychological burden, especially when combined with the devastating defeat in Sicily.

Despite these benefits, the Spartans soon realized their Decelean deployment alone would not force Athens to capitulate. Xenophon reports that King Agis, "who could see from Decelea great numbers of grain-ships sailing in to Piraeus, said that it was useless for his troops to be trying all this long time to shut off the Athenians from access to their land, unless one should occupy also the country from which the grain was coming in by sea."[151] Thus Sparta sought sufficient naval power to embolden other members of the Delian League to revolt and to facilitate directly blocking food imports, especially from the Black Sea region.[152] Sparta's potential to become a naval power materialized when the Persians, seizing upon Athenian vulnerability, agreed to underwrite the effort. Although the Spartans built an impressive fleet, they struggled to develop competent admirals and captains.[153] Thus, outstanding seamanship and able commanders enabled outnumbered Athenian fleets to win a series of stunning victories over the next few years. Nevertheless, the Spartans were better able to replace losses and eventually identified some talented seafarers, in particular Lysander. With its maritime dominance ending, Athens struggled to prevent defections throughout the Aegean, and its empire shrank.

The navy's decline as well as troop losses after Sicily also precipitated an adjustment in Athenian strategic defenses with the apparent abandonment of the Long Wall to Phaleron in or shortly after 413. Lacking consistent sea control of the Saronic Gulf left the exposed port far more vulnerable than the naturally protected harbor of Piraeus. Plus, manpower concerns after the losses in Sicily encouraged concentrating on the more integral Long Walls connecting Athens and Piraeus. Athens' much smaller population as a result of the plague and the war reduced the space needed by refugees. Thus the Phaleron Wall, which always had less strategic utility, probably came to be regarded as an unsustainable luxury at a time of heightened Spartan pressure. While the basic integrity of the Long Walls to Piraeus remained intact, this move served as a harbinger that the strategic defense system was meaningless if Athens lost control of the seas.[154]

In the interim, Sparta attempted three times to intimidate Athenians by advancing a force toward the fortifications, which were apparently now constantly manned. Internal turmoil beset Athens in June 411 when an antiwar group seized power and tried to negotiate a peace in which each side retained its existing possessions. Spartan King Agis, however, deployed a large army in front of the Long Walls to press for a more favorable offer and possibly seize part of the barrier if the internally distracted Athenians were not vigilant. Thucydides relates that a diverse array of Athenian citizens and soldiers led a passionate rush toward the approaching Spartan force, which marched away.[155] In July 410 Agis again returned amid further political turmoil in Athens that eventually restored democracy. Similar to his previous advance, the Spartan king retreated after the Athenians assumed defensive positions and marched out under the protection of missile-throwers on the walls. In 408 or 407, with most Athenian troops deployed abroad, Agis appeared for a third time with a larger Peloponnesian/Boeotian army. Whether attempting to intimidate the Athenians, lure them out to battle, or destroy the rich farmlands near the walls (as perhaps suggested by the heavy presence of light infantry), the Spartan force was unwilling to fight as long as the enemy remained covered by soldiers atop the fortifications.[156]

Three times in five years Sparta had advanced toward the Long Walls or upper city fortifications against a demoralized and weakened Athens without significant effect. No indication exists that Agis seriously contemplated attacking the strong works.[157] Without any significant improvements in siegecraft during the war, the defenses essentially remained impenetrable absent being compromised by internal conspirators as occurred at Megara in 424. Most likely the king hoped his army's presence would intimidate the polis or prompt some traitors to open a gate that could be exploited. Alternatively, he wanted to destroy the fertile land near the Long Walls for material and psychological effects. The Athenian response of deploying its own force in front of the wall, rather than sitting behind it, suggests the Spartans showed no inclination to attack the structures. Apparently Athens could not abide an extended Sparta presence outside its fortifications.

Appreciating the strength of the Long Walls, the Spartans concentrated on nullifying their value by stopping the flow of imports. Lysander's destruction of Athens' last fleet at Aegospotami in September 405 facilitated this objective and ensured Sparta's victory of the war. Having gained control of the Aegean, the Spartan kings Agis and Pausanias again advanced their armies to the Athenian defense works and proposed severe peace terms, including a breach of more than a mile in both of the Long Walls remaining in use.[158] The Athenians, however, rejected any destruction of their valued defenses with the assembly, even making "it a crime for any Athenian citizen to agree to Spartan armistice demands to tear down large sections of the Long Walls."[159] After more than six months of no food imports, the inevitable capitulation occurred in April 404 with Athens apparently agreeing to the destruction of the Long Walls and fortifications at Piraeus as well as a Spartan-installed authoritarian regime and cap on the number of triremes. Conflicting accounts from Xenophon and Plutarch have complicated modern scholars' efforts to understand if the Athenians actually tore down the fortifications or if, in an act of civil disobedience, they refused, forcing the Spartans eventually to do it.[160] Either way, given the labor required, the demolition effort was limited to creating large gaps that rendered the walls ineffective.

The Restored Long Walls of the Fourth Century

Many Athenians apparently retained a strong desire to reestablish the Long Walls as soon as possible. The context in which the decision was made to restore the barriers would be different from the initial mid-fifth century action. The crushing costs and losses of the Second Peloponnesian War combined with the rise of new powers in Hellas ensured that Athens, which had almost immediately reverted to a democracy, would not regain its fifth century position. Even though its economy had partially rebounded after the war, taxable wealth would remain limited.[161] The loss of the empire, in particular, meant far fewer resources available for defense—both finances and needed materials, such as timber. Moreover, the mining industry had suffered badly during the war and would not recover until the mid-fourth century. The number of adult Athenian males was half the total forty years earlier. Moreover, Athens' "previously impregnable self-confidence" had been lost.[162] As a result of these changes, Athens' strategic perspective had been fundamentally altered from an aggressive, confident, offensive-minded state to a humbled, somewhat defense-oriented polis.[163] These perspectives are, of course, generalizations not applicable to all Athenians in either century, but the balance of sentiment had shifted. This contrasting context is important to remember when assessing the decisions to rebuild the Long Walls during the fourth century and their subsequent effects on the city-state's security policy.

After suffering total defeat in the Second Peloponnesian War, the Athenians might have been expected to shift away from the Periclean strategy of empire, navy, and Long Walls. Some citizens did condemn this approach. For example, Plato, often a contrarian, early in the fourth century lambasted "Themistocles, Cimon, and Pericles for having filled Athens with harbors, dockyards, walls, revenues, 'and similar trash.'"[164] In particular, critics reflecting the traditional sentiment behind agonal (hoplite) warfare disparaged walls as corrosive of morale and character.[165] Again, Plato expressed this view often, most cogently in his probable final work, *Laws,* forty years later: "The state should imitate Sparta in relying on her men in armor rather than on walls of stone.... Walls breed a certain softness in the citizens and invite them to seek shelter within, leaving the enemy unopposed. Walls also tempt men to relax their guard and to trust to the false security provided by ramparts and bars."[166] Others, including Xenophon and Isocrates, also condemned the walls for undermining Athenian fortitude. Critics also disliked the Long Walls for exacerbating the tension between rural landowners and urbanites.[167] Nevertheless, for a majority of Athenians the lessons learned from the war appear to have reinforced the value of the navy and long wall elements of the old strategy. Sparta had won by eliminating Athenian naval superiority, thus neutralizing the value of the Long Walls and undermining its empire. Athens aimed to restore its position as a naval power, which Sparta had tried to prevent by limiting it to a dozen warships in the peace agreement.[168]

By the mid-390s, Sparta had alienated most other Greeks, including key former allies, which presented Athens an opportunity. Finding courage in the availability of strong allies, Athens entered into a coalition with Argos, Boeotia, and Corinth to rein in Spartan dominance in what today is known as the Corinthian War. Pharnabazus, a Persian satrap also at odds with Sparta, offered support. Most importantly for the Athenians, the Persians provided triremes. In 394, a combined Greek–Persian fleet led by the Athenian admiral Conon destroyed the Spartan navy in the Battle of Cnidus off the Ionian coast. This victory signaled Athens' reemergence as a naval power, albeit one dependent on Persian support.[169]

Athens' naval restoration had begun a few years earlier, prompting the citizenry to consider reconstructing the Long Walls. Adding impetus to restoration of these barriers was the struggle to rebuild the army from a much smaller manpower base. Relying on soldiers to protect the city in open land battle against the stout enemy remained unwise as the Spartans demonstrated in 394 by winning major battles against the coalition at Nemea River and at Coronea. The Athenians suffered heavy casualties in the former. These setbacks combined with the naval victory the same summer to shift political power in Athens toward the navalists led by Conon. Although the admiral remained deployed until mid-393, political supporters used his rising prestige to push an agenda of restoring naval power and the Long Walls. The virtually absolute advantage of strong defenses in the fifth century had begun eroding, but Athenians evidently did not regard this improving state of siegecraft as problematic. The Spartan army had not demonstrated any progress in this field of arms.[170]

Nevertheless, the improvements in siegecraft and prudence regarding future progress dictated strengthened barriers, especially to limit necessary manning levels. These enhancements included adding more towers and probably increasing the height above the twenty-five-foot level of the original structures.[171] The mid-393 return of Admiral Conon greatly accelerated construction with the resulting influx of money from Persia and labor from the fleet.[172] He had successfully lobbied Pharnabazus to help fund the Long Walls by arguing, according to Xenophon, that "nothing could be a heavier blow to the Lacedaemonians [Spartans]."[173] Within a few years, the Athenians had nearly completed construction on the Long Walls, although Conon's death may have forced any remaining work to occur slowly over a period of years or not take place at all. Nevertheless, enough progress had been achieved to allow the barrier to be functionally finished by the end of the 390s as the Athenians began a push to restore their overseas empire.[174]

The high priority given to rebuilding the Long Walls reflected Athenians' concern about the upper city's security, but the absence of an empire and uncertainty of future naval preeminence precluded resurrecting Pericles' strategy in toto.[175] Without tribute from the empire, the economic importance of Attica had increased significantly, both its agriculture and mineral wealth. Although Hanson has shown that agricultural destruction during the Peloponnesian War fell short of the traditional belief, Sparta had inflicted considerable damage after occupying Decelea in 413. Greek armies, reflecting a lesson learned, now had more lightly armed soldiers and mercenaries, in part to better ravage rural areas.[176] Without imports from the empire, Attica would also have to be a significant source of food for the population during war. Prior experience suggested to the Athenians that Sparta would renew assaults on fertile land as a form of economic coercion during a war if the Long Walls existed.

Thus, prominent Athenian residents such as Isocrates, Lysias (actually a metic), Aristotle, Plato, and Demosthenes persuasively argued for erecting an effective border defense system to protect Attica. The ability of outposts to avoid capture during the Peloponnesian War probably bolstered proponents for such works. With the Long Walls effectively, if not completely, finished, Athens began directing resources toward Attic fortifications.[177] A new generation of leaders may have abetted this focus, which appears to have intensified with the Boeotian War, 378–375. Taking advantage of natural geography and outposts established in the fifth century, Ober notes the city-state's Attic defense system involved three interrelated elements:

- Forts and other defenses guarding the passes from Megara and Boeotia
- Signaling stations linking these defense locations with Athens
- Roads connecting the city and the border outposts.[178]

Precisely dating this effort has been difficult, probably because it evolved over three or four decades from the mid-380s.

Scholars disagree on the relationship between the border defenses and the Long Walls, but they appear to have been complementary in a de facto if not design sense. Some, especially Ober, argue that the border defense system represented a repudiation of the city-based defense strategy that failed in the Peloponnesian War.[179] Even acknowledging the priority placed on rebuilding the Long Walls, he contends that the defeat by Sparta, the loss of the empire, and a defensive mindset prompted Athenians to seek an "Attic-centric" approach.[180] Other scholars view Athenians as pursuing a layered defense strategy to deter and defend by making invading armies have to pass through a series of barriers.[181] Aeneas Tacticus, one of the premier strategic analysts of the fourth century, stressed the application of a combination rural Attica and urban Athens strategy.[182] From this viewpoint, Athens' selective employment of barriers blocking passes within Attica, such as the Dema Wall, would mark an intermediate layer.[183]

Perhaps Athenians regarded the border and urban systems as providing strategic flexibility that allowed leaders to react to particular circumstances. Xenophon suggests such a perspective, noting in 360 that the Athenians had two options against an invading army: advance and engage, or fall back on its walls and navy. He was actually a proponent of engaging forward, but his commentary highlights the continuing consideration of abandoning rural areas.[184] The restoration of the Long Walls was indicative of urbanites' desire to reestablish the navy and empire. Their success would render the Attic countryside less significant, but if they failed or even subsequently lost the navy and empire as occurred during the Second Peloponnesian War, then the border defense system offered valuable security. Moreover, as Ober notes, shrewd figures like Demosthenes and Lycurgus recognized it was "politically more expedient to emphasize the importance of the protection of the countryside."[185] Whether intentional or the result of political compromise within the polis, Athens now employed both a city and rural defense system.[186]

It is unknown whether these defenses deterred enemies from advancing on Athens, but despite frequent conflict throughout Greece in the first half of the fourth century, the city-state suffered only a single brief raid by Sparta in 378.[187] The fortifications probably signaled to would-be allies a strengthened Athens while almost certainly contributing to Athenians' own sense of improved security and recovery. With its Long Walls in place and the navy built up to one hundred triremes by 378, Athens even moved to proximate the old Delian League with "the Second Athenian League."[188] Taking advantage of hostility to Sparta and promising not to levy tribute or implement garrison colonies, the Athenians succeeded and regained their dominant naval position in the Aegean. Kagan goes as far as labeling the new arrangement a "Second Athenian Empire."[189] The league, however, would soon lose strength due to defections.[190]

First, after Thebes' decisive victory over Sparta at the Battle of Leuctra in 371, it and the other Boeotian city-states withdrew. Athens then suffered a severe loss of power when some of the major Greek states in the east (e.g., Chios, Rhodes) successfully revolted in the Social War (357–355). As a result, Athens would possess diminished strength, especially naval power, when facing a new rising threat.[191] Nevertheless, the long period of homeland security and the existence of a defense-in-depth fortification system apparently blinded most Athenians to this approaching Macedonian danger.

Macedonia and the Rise of Effective Siegecraft

While the subjective security provided by walls for Athenians apparently lingered into the second half of the fourth century, their actual ability to protect was declining. Beyond Athens' eroding naval capability, the military balance between defenses and attackers had significantly shifted toward the offense with the emergence of Philip II's Macedonian state. It had the resources and organization to achieve great advances in siegecraft, most critically the torsion catapult, which enhanced the force and accuracy of fired missiles. Although the first clear evidence for "stone-throwing" catapults is Alexander the Great's 334 siege of Halicarnassus, by the 340s a combination of arrow-shooting catapults, siege towers, and battering rams allowed Macedonians to overcome many, but not all, fortifications.[192] This siegecraft capability combined with Macedonia's large, professional army to produce a powerful offensive force that rapidly expanded the empire. Paraphrasing Hanson, only three responses existed when challenged by the Macedonians: capitulation, association, or imitation.[193]

With none of these options appealing to Athens, a divided polis took no action despite the rising Macedonian threat. As early as 351, the great orator Demosthenes had tried to stir a strong forward defense policy to keep Philip away, including disparaging Eubulus' inclination to plaster parapets uselessly rather than take meaningful action. In particular, the Macedonian move into the North Aegean region combined with the decline of the Second Athenian League augured problems given the significant imports of grain and other goods from the area. Aeschines, Eubulus, and other leaders, however, continually weakened or blocked Demosthenes' efforts through effective advocacy for a negotiated solution. Athens and Macedonia finally signed a peace treaty in 346. Philip, however, flagrantly violated the agreement by marching into central Greece and seizing Thermopylae, leaving Attica open to attack.[194]

Nevertheless, the Athenians, despite the last major fortification effort taking place a half century earlier and the notable progress in siegecraft, did not initiate a significant upgrade to defense works. Some citizens had argued for bolstering the structures, but surviving records indicate work on the neglected urban fortifications in the preceding decade was of limited scope.[195] Athens' failure to enhance the Long Walls along with Athens and Piraeic fortifications is puzzling, reflecting either misplaced confidence in the existing structures, a desire to avoid antagonizing Macedonia, or a disregard for the works at a time when naval dominance had been lost. Although one might logically argue that the loss of naval power sapped motivation for an expensive upgrade, Athenians' decision to engage in such a project after the Macedonian threat became undeniable seems to contradict that conclusion.[196] In part, Athenians remained committed to regaining the city-state's position as a naval power, thus ensuring perception of a continued role for the Long Walls. Any decision to avoid antagonizing Macedonia likely served more as a justification for not taking action, especially as Macedonia's hostile intent became clear. Rather, Ober persuasively argues that "considering themselves safe behind their defensive bastions the Athenians were unwilling to acknowledge until it was too late the fact that the efficiency of Philip's siege engineers had rendered the fortresses obsolete."[197]

This failing exemplifies a difficulty often encountered with defenses, as will be identified in the subsequent chapters. Objective (actual) security declines over time while subjective (perceived) security tends to increase save a demonstrated failing. Even if Macedonia demonstrated its siegecraft elsewhere, it had not occurred against Athenian works, thus highlighting another common flaw in military learning. While the fortifications remained unchanged, Demosthenes finally convinced a majority in Athens to take action at the end of the 340s when Macedonia jeopardized Black Sea grain imports by moving against Byzantium.[198] The ability of a strongly walled Byzantium and its nearby blockaded ally of Perinthus to withstand sieges illustrated that limits remained to assaulting well-defended fortifications. A frustrated Philip now declared war on Athens and advanced his army into central Greece. Thebes' decision to fight with Athens gave the Greeks a similar-sized force and some optimism, but the hoplites suffered a crushing defeat to the Macedonian combined arms force at the 338 Battle of Chaeronea.

Seized with a sudden appreciation of their vulnerability, the Athenians initiated a crash effort to strengthen the Long Walls and other defenses.[199] Lycurgus provides a sense of the effort by noting that even the dead gave their gravestones and temples.[200] Emergency work on the improvements stopped when Athens and Macedonia came to an accommodation in which the former essentially became a subject of the latter. Compared to his harsh punishment of land-locked Thebes, Philip offered Athens moderate peace terms.[201] Philip's desire to strike the Peloponnesus and, more importantly, a rich Persia encouraged the Macedonian ruler to forgo attacking Athens if possible. As Raphael Sealey notes, "He might succeed, as he had done at Olynthos [Olynthus], or he might fail, as at

Perinthos and Byzantion [Byzantium] [but] . . . he would at least be delayed for many months."[202]

Athens accepted the terms, but by the summer of 337 it had commenced a major defense upgrade to dissuade Macedonia from attempting to exert more direct control as well as lay the groundwork for restoring complete independence at an opportune future moment. This multiyear effort included increasing the height and thickness of the fortifications to counter advanced Macedonian siegecraft, which was particularly effective on the type of flat, low terrain over which much of the Long Walls traversed. Other measures likely included adding more towers and roofing at least part of the walkway to provide troops cover from catapults. Given the crucial need to keep enemy siege engines away from fortifications, the Athenians constructed outer works including a smaller wall twenty to twenty-seven feet in front of the main curtain and a preceding twenty-two- to thirty-foot-wide ditch. They also may have installed catapults on the towers for counterbattery fire. After the project's completion around 334, the Athenians would be ready when a favorable circumstance emerged.[203]

The chance appeared when the Diadochi (i.e., the Successors—Alexander the Great's generals) began squabbling over the empire's control after the ruler's death in 323. Athens and many other Greek city-states revolted in what became known as the Lamian War. Although Athenians had been undertaking military preparations, including building up the navy for several years, the Macedonians quickly put down the revolt. Most critically, Macedonian-led Phoenician ships destroyed the Athenian fleet off Amorgus in 322. This loss negated the potential value of the enhanced Long Wall strategic defense system, ensured the Greeks' defeat, and permanently ended Athens time as a naval power. In contrast to 338, the victorious Macedonians now garrisoned troops in Piraeus and exerted direct control over Athens' affairs.[204]

Athens would finally regain its independence in 307 as a part of the internecine Macedonian struggle when Demetrius liberated the city from Cassander's control. Expecting Cassander to counterattack, the Athenians initiated work on the badly decayed fortifications while also trying to rebuild the navy. The multiyear upgrade to the Long Walls, as well as Athens and Piraeus fortifications, included roofing the entire parapet, configuring the towers to use torsion-spring catapults, and erecting a new palisade as an outerwork.[205] This effort, despite the advanced stage of Macedonian siegecraft and Athens' lack of naval strength, suggests city leaders expected maritime support from their Macedonian benefactor. With repairs under way, Cassander struck in a conflict known as the Four Years' War (307–304). His initial advance into Attica failed, but in a more determined invasion in 304 he penetrated Attica's border, surrounded Athens, and began assaulting the city's fortifications. The Macedonians damaged the works, possibly even breaching the Long Walls, but the defenses delayed Cassander until the approach of Demetrius' relief force drove him off.[206]

The damage to the walls inflicted by Cassander demonstrated that such barrier defenses were approaching obsolescence. At the time, it was Demetrius, known as Poliocretes ("the besieger"), who employed huge catapults capable of launching massive stones with great destructiveness. Although strong fortifications could delay capitulation, the justification for constructing and maintaining such works was increasingly questionable. For the Athenians in particular, failure to regain naval strength limited the Long Walls' utility. Their vulnerability and the defeat of Demetrius and Antigonus at the Battle of Ipsus in 301 convinced the citizenry to adopt a policy of neutrality. During the third century, Athens would alternate between periods of Macedonian control and independence, but it would never again be a significant power.[207]

Precisely when the Athenians abandoned the Long Walls as an operational strategic defense is uncertain, but it probably occurred early in the third century, leaving the massive, solid structures to slowly decay. The Roman historian Livy reports that by 200 BCE the structures had crumbled to a significant degree.[208] However, they survived somewhat intact until the Roman general Sulla arrived in 87 BCE to punish Athens for shifting support to Pontus king Mithridates. Sulla apparently used a significant part of the remaining Long Walls as material for his siegeworks against the city and port.[209] Construction of an aqueduct two hundred years later added damage to the northern wall. Extant sections remained until the last two centuries when the growth and integration of Athens and Piraeus removed all traces of the Long Walls.

Conclusion

While the impressive remains of the Great Wall of China and Hadrian's Wall in the countryside facilitate envisioning their full glory, the absence of virtually any trace of the Long Walls of Athens, now a heavily urban area, requires considerable imagination. Reflecting back nearly twenty-five hundred years, it is not hard to understand why Athens built and rebuilt these structures. They appealed to the polis from a political, psychological, and military perspective. Both the confident, ambitious citizens of the mid-fifth century and their weaker, less-confident successors of the fourth century shared a common desire to be a maritime power while retaining an urban center miles from the water. By closing the gap, the Long Walls removed the city-state's most pronounced vulnerability and allowed Athenians to pursue their preferred naval emphasis. Even when attaching increased import to the Attic countryside in the fourth century, the barriers provided a final line of defense as a part of a de facto, if not outright, defense-in-depth system.

If the reasoning behind Athens' construction of the Long Walls appears understandable, judging their performance presents more of a dilemma. In a narrow sense, they were extremely effective. For more than a century, until the Macedonian era, the structures could not be penetrated by enemy siegecraft. This negligible prospect of enemy success discouraged adversaries from even testing the fortifications until near the end of the fourth century. As late as the 430s, Macedonian king Philip II compromised to avoid an assault that would be lengthy and costly, even if it produced victory. Their value, however, was inextricably linked to Athenian naval dominance without which the city-state could be isolated and starved into submission. Spartan and Athenian attitudes after the Second Peloponnesian War perhaps best reflect contemporary importance attached to the Long Walls. The Spartans, victorious upon gaining naval supremacy, adamantly demanded their destruction. According to Xenophon, after gaining this concession, they "with great enthusiasm began to tear down the walls to the music of flute-girls."[210] The Athenians had doggedly resisted agreeing to their demolition and restored the defenses as soon as resources and circumstances permitted.

The Long Walls' broader contribution to Athenian security warrants scrutiny. In addition to his antidemocratic bias, Plato's strident mid-fourth century criticism that walls "breed a certain softness" and "tempt men to relax their guard and to trust to the false security provided by ramparts and bars" may reflect frustration that a large part of the Athenian polis ignored the emerging Macedonian threat.[211] The walls almost certainly contributed to this neglect by sustaining subjective (perceived) security long after objective security had begun sharply declining. By this time Athens had become a status quo–oriented, second-tier power leaving it with limited means and interest in competing with this rising force. As Sealey notes, when "confronted with a dynamic power, a sated power is at a disadvantage."[212] Such a reaction seems context dependent, rather than reflecting a constant reaction by wall-building entities. For example, no evidence exists of the defenses producing such an attitude in the glory days of the fifth century.

On the contrary, given that Athens' defeat in that century resulted from overextension, the key question is did the Long Walls encourage rash and misguided offensive action? The Athens–Sparta competition predated the Long Walls' construction, so they may represent an appropriate response to danger, not a precipitant action. They certainly provided a desired freedom of operation for naval actions and imperial growth. It is harder to assess if the Long Walls instilled a sense of invulnerability that prompted risky initiatives including the 415 invasion of Sicily. Aggressive leaders such as Cleon and Alcibiades could more effectively advocate for hawkish behavior. They benefited not only from the safety provided by the defenses but also by the "psychological toll" of a population sequestered behind them while enemies ravaged the countryside.[213] Thus Athenians felt a need to demonstrate the city-state's greatness. Historians have criticized them for ignoring Pericles' caution against overextension, but Pericles' strategy of Long Walls, navy, and empire had already been shown to be lacking enough offensive punch to defeat a determined land power like Sparta in a war of attrition. Perhaps the more aggressive policy was inevitable. Pericles' unwillingness to accommodate Spartan concerns and thus avoid war in the late 430s was also likely spurred by the Long Walls' existence. Again, war with Sparta may have been inevitable, but delaying it almost certainly would have benefited Athens. Thus the existence of the Long Walls appears to have heightened the existing alarm and resistance of adversaries, encouraged balancing tendencies among suspicious third parties, and promoted Athenians' instinct to seek superiority.

Imagining the counterfactual of no walls would seem to augur far greater Athenian caution, especially at the start of the Second Peloponnesian War and the Sicilian expedition. Such restraint seems unlikely to have significantly ameliorated the Athens–Sparta rivalry, which was driven by the rise of Athens' naval-based empire. Rather, it would have left Athens more vulnerable to Spartan and Macedonian pressure. Despite the former's negligible siegecraft, the eventual forward base at Decelea during the Second Peloponnesian War highlights the vulnerability that would have resulted for a walled upper city without connecting to the Long Walls. Their absence in the Macedonian era would have left the city-state with limited leverage to obtain reasonable terms from Philip if it had failed to obtain a more effective response.

Ultimately, we lack sufficient information to assess with high confidence the effects of the Long Walls' presence on Athenian behavior. Once wars came in both the fifth and fourth centuries, the barrier made a valuable contribution to the city-state's security. Athenian policy choices suggest these structures reinforced the offensive (fifth century) and defensive (fourth century) proclivities possessed by the citizenry in the different periods. If so, the walls' broader influence on their security might have been counterproductive because moderating Athenians in the mid-fifth century and rising vigilance among them in the mid-fourth century would have been far more constructive. In other words, the barriers may actually encourage excessive risk over time. For the aggressive, ambitious fifth-century Athenians, the walls promoted risky action, while for the defensive, status quo–minded fourth-century Athenians, they encouraged risky inaction to a changing world. Whether this tendency occurs in other cases will be a subject for consideration in the subsequent chapters. One clear conclusion from examining Athens is that strong, even invulnerable, defenses do not provide a panacea for a state with significant interests and ambitions beyond its protected territory.

Notes

1. Victor Davis Hanson, *A War Like No Other: How the Athenians and Spartans Fought the Peloponnesian War* (New York: Random House, 2005), 26.
2. Ibid.
3. David Conwell, *Connecting a City to the Sea: The History of the Athenian Long Walls* (Boston: Brill, 2008), 61–62, 84–85; Peter Krentz, "The Strategic Culture of Periclean Athens" in *Polis and Polemos,* ed. C. Hamilton and P. Krentz (Claremont, CA: Regina, 1997), 64; Josiah Ober, *Fortress Attica: Defense of the Athenian Land Frontier, 404–322 BC* (Leiden, The Netherlands: Brill, 1985), 35; Victor Davis Hanson, *The Wars of the Ancient Greeks* (London: Cassell, 1999), 117–18; and Donald Kagan, *The Peloponnesian War* (New York: Viking, 2003), 51–53.
4. Anthony Podlecki, *Perikles and His Circle* (New York: Routledge, 1998), 157; and Hanson, *Wars of the Ancient Greeks,* 82.
5. Robert Lenardon, *The Saga of Themistocles* (London: Thames and Hudson, 1978), 95; and Hanson, *Wars of the Ancient Greeks,* 99.
6. J. S. Morrison, J. F. Coates, and N. B. Rankov, *The Athenian Trireme: The History and Reconstruction of an Ancient Greek Warship* (New York: Cambridge University Press, 2000), 62.
7. See Thucydides, *History of the Peloponnesian War,* trans. Rex Warner (London: Penguin Books, 1972), 1.104–6; Malcolm McGregor, *The Athenians and their Empire* (Vancouver: University of British Columbia Press, 1987), 47, 50, 55; and Podlecki, *Perikles and His Circle,* 55–56.
8. Thucydides, *History of the Peloponnesian War,* 1.89–117.
9. David Sacks, *A Dictionary of the Ancient Greek World* (New York: Oxford University Press, 1995), 44.
10. Thomas Cahill, *Sailing the Wine-Dark Sea: Why the Greeks Matter* (New York: Doubleday, 2003), 118–19.
11. Krentz, "Strategic Culture," 62.
12. David Conwell, *The Athenian Long Walls: Chronology, Topography, and Remains* (PhD diss., University of Pennsylvania, 1992), 244, 269.
13. See ibid., 201–3, 398–401, 408–9, 412; Conwell, *Connecting a City,* 4, 59; A. W. Lawrence, *Greek Aims in Fortification* (Oxford: Clarendon, 1979), 156; and F. E. Winter, *Greek Fortifications* (Toronto: Toronto University Press, 1971), 154, 159–60, 238–39.
14. Herodotus, *The Histories,* trans. Aubrey De Selincourt (New York: Penguin Books, 1996), 5.52–78.
15. Ibid., 6.109–10.
16. Hanson, *Wars of the Ancient Greeks,* 94; and Lenardon, *Saga of Themistocles,* 45.
17. Lenardon, *Saga of Themistocles,* 45, 53–54; and Plutarch, *The Rise and Fall of Athens: Nine Greek Lives,* trans. Ian Scott-Kilvert (New York: Penguin Books, 1960), 3.4.
18. Lenardon, *Saga of Themistocles,* 54; for general information see Morrison, Coates, and Rankov, *Athenian Trireme.*

19. Herodotus, *Histories*, 7.138–39; and Barry Strauss, *The Battle of Salamis: The Naval Encounter That Saved Greece—and Western Civilization* (New York: Simon & Schuster, 2004), 41–42.

20. Herodotus, *Histories*, 7.140–44; Plutarch, *Rise and Fall of Athens*, 3.10; and Strauss, *Battle of Salamis*, 63–65.

21. Plutarch, *Rise and Fall of Athens*, 3.9; and Herodotus, *Histories*, 8.40–41, 42–48, 71–72; and Strauss, *Battle of Salamis*, 79–80.

22. Strauss, *Battle of Salamis*, 6, 222; Lenardon, *Saga of Themistocles*, 95; and Hanson, *Wars of the Ancient Greeks*, 99.

23. Hanson, *Wars of the Ancient Greeks*, 99.

24. See Thucydides, *History of the Peloponnesian War*, 1.89, 93; Lenardon, *Saga of Themistocles*, 209–10; Hanson, *Wars of the Ancient Greeks*, 108; Strauss, *Battle of Salamis*, 245; Plutarch, *Rise and Fall of Athens*, 3.19; Conwell, *Athenian Long Walls*, 3; R. E. Wycherly, *The Stones of Athens* (Princeton: Princeton University Press, 1978), 7; and McGregor, *Athenians and Their Empire*, 34–35, 131.

25. McGregor, *Athenians and Their Empire*, 35.

26. Podlecki, *Perikles and His Circle*, 37; and McGregor, *Athenians and Their Empire*, 40.

27. McGregor, *Athenians and Their Empire*, 39; and Thucydides, *History of the Peloponnesian War*, 1.98–99.

28. See Thucydides, *History of the Peloponnesian War*, 1.89–117; Plutarch, *The Rise and Fall of Athens*, 3.19; and McGregor, *Athenians and Their Empire*, 44–45.

29. See Thucydides, *History of the Peloponnesian War*, 1.102; Podlecki, *Perikles and His Circle*, 39–43; Nic Fields, *Ancient Greek Fortifications, 500–300 BC* (Oxford: Osprey, 2006), 51; Plutarch, *Rise and Fall of Athens*, 5.16.

30. Thucydides, *History of the Peloponnesian War*, 1.102; Fields, *Ancient Greek Fortifications, 500–300 BC*, 51; Podlecki, *Perikles and His Circle*, 39–43, 53–55; McGregor, *Athenians and Their Empire*, 48; and Kagan, *Peloponnesian War*, 13–16.

31. Podlecki, *Perikles and His Circle*, 45.

32. Thucydides, *History of the Peloponnesian War*, 1.102, 103; McGregor, *Athenians and Their Empire*, 48; and Podlecki, *Perikles and His Circle*, 55.

33. Thucydides, *History of the Peloponnesian War*, 1.103.

34. Conwell, *Connecting a City*, 4–8, 19, 56–59.

35. Josiah Ober, "Hoplites and Obstacles," in *Hoplites: The Classical Greek Battle Experience*, ed. Victor Davis Hanson (New York: Routledge, 1991), 180.

36. Michael Sage, *Warfare in Ancient Greece: A Sourcebook* (London: Routledge, 1996), 67.

37. Sacks, *Dictionary of the Ancient Greek World*, 36, 88, 168.

38. See Hanson, *Wars of the Ancient Greeks*, 80; Kagan, *Peloponnesian War*, 4; Winter, *Greek Fortifications*, 85–86, 303; Duncan Campbell, *Ancient Siege Warfare: Persians, Greeks, Carthaginians, and Romans, 546–146 BC* (Oxford: Osprey, 2005), 20–23; and Morrison, *Athenian Trireme*, 38–40, 51n1.

39. See Hanson, *War Like No Other*, 39, 260–62; Morrison, *Athenian Trireme*, 62, 107–20; and Conwell, *Connecting a City*, 84–85.

40. See Winter, *Greek Fortifications*, 85–86, 307; Campbell, *Ancient Siege Warfare*, 16–20, 23; McGregor, *Athenians and Their Empire*, 49; and Conwell, *Connecting a City*, 52.

41. See Hanson, *Wars of the Ancient Greeks*, 47–53; Ober, *Fortress Attica*, 32–35, 90–92; Krentz, "Strategic Culture," 56–58; Sage, *Warfare in Ancient Greece*, 31–32; Fields, *Ancient Greek Fortifications*, 16, 47–48; and Duncan Campbell, *Greek and Roman Siege Machinery, 399 BC–AD 363* (Oxford: Osprey, 2003), 3–4.

42. Thucydides, *History of the Peloponnesian War*, 1.93; and Herodotus, *Histories*, 7.144.

43. Victor Davis Hanson, *The Other Greeks* (Berkeley: University of California Press, 1999), 337.

44. Hanson, *Wars of the Ancient Greeks*, 80–81.

45. Ober, *Fortress Attica*, 35; Kagan, *Peloponnesian War*, 51–53.

46. Krentz, "Strategic Culture," 58, 61–62; Conwell, *Connecting a City*, 84–85; and Hanson, *Wars of the Ancient Greeks*, 117–18.

47. Conwell, *Connecting a City*, 84–87.

48. See Podlecki, *Perikles and His Circle*, 11–14, 54; Strauss, *The Battle of Salamis*, 68, 141–42; Thucydides, *History of the Peloponnesian War*, 1.93, 143; and Conwell, *Connecting a City*, 84.

49. See Barry S. Strauss, *Athens after the Peloponnesian War: Class, Faction, and Policy 403–386 BC* (London: Croom Helm, 1986), 46, 48; and Hanson, *War Like No Other*, 251, 262–63.

50. Conwell, *Athenian Long Walls*, 75; and Hanson, *War Like No Other*, 260.

51. Hanson, *Wars of the Ancient Greeks*, 102. This estimation is an extrapolation from Hanson's calculation that a one-hundred-ship fleet would cost nearly a million drachmas while a ten-thousand-man hoplite army would cost two hundred thousand drachmas.

52. Hanson, *War Like No Other*, 116, 251, 262, 264.

53. Cahill, *Sailing the Wine-Dark Sea*, 115–16; McGregor, *Athenians and Their Empire*, 115; Hanson, *War Like No Other*, 6, 27; and Strauss, *Battle of Salamis*, 60.

54. Sacks, *Dictionary of the Ancient Greek World*, 144; and Hanson, *War Like No Other*, 79, 90–91.

55. Thucydides, *Peloponnesian War*, 1.105.

56. McGregor, *Athenians and Their Empire*, 52.

57. Calculating a precise percentage is not possible given uncertainty over the adult male population. This conservative estimate is based on Athens having thirty thousand to forty thousand adult males, the reported size in 432.

58. McGregor, *Athenians and Their Empire*, 52.

59. Herodotus, *Histories*, 5.97

60. See McGregor, *Athenians and Their Empire*, 47; and Hanson, *Wars of the Ancient Greeks*, 78, 102.

61. Hanson, *Wars of the Ancient Greeks*, 74, 77, 102.

62. Thucydides, *History of the Peloponnesian War*, 1.107.

63. McGregor, *Athenians and Their Empire*, 96; and Conwell, *Athenian Long Walls*, 47–48.

64. Podlecki, *Perikles and His Circle*, 47–48, 53–54.

65. Cahill, *Sailing the Wine-Dark Sea*, 118–19; Sacks, *Dictionary of the Ancient Greek World*, 38; and Hanson, *War Like No Other*, 53, 55.

66. McGregor, *Athenians and Their Empire*, 116–17, 120; Debra Hamel, *Athenian Generals: Military Authority in the Classical Period* (Boston: Brill, 1998), 85; and Podlecki, *Perikles and His Circle*, 162–63.

67. Hamel, *Athenian Generals*, 10, 12–13, 84; McGregor, *Athenians and Their Empire*, 120; and Sage, *Warfare in Ancient Greece*, 60.

68. Ober, *Fortress Attica*, 69–86.

69. Thucydides, *History of the Peloponnesian War*, 1.142–43; Krentz, "Strategic Culture," 62–64; and McGregor, *Athenians and Their Empire*, 43.

70. Ober, *Fortress Attica*, 111–12.

71. Thucydides, *History of the Peloponnesian War*, 2.16.

72. Ober, "Hoplites and Obstacles," 173–75.

73. Victor Davis Hanson, *Warfare and Agriculture in Classical Greece* (Berkeley: University of California, 1998), 7, 47; and Ober, *Fortress Attica*, 77, 85.

74. Ober, *Fortress Attica*, 35; Krentz, "Strategic Culture," 58, 61–62; and Hanson, *Other Greeks*, 327–38.

75. For example see Herodotus, *Histories*, 7.172–73, 175, 8.15.

76. Winter, *Greek Fortifications*, 42–43; and Fields, *Ancient Greek Fortifications*, 41–45.

77. Ober, *Fortress Attica*, 206–7; and Hanson, *Wars of the Ancient Greeks*, 47.

78. Thucydides, *History of the Peloponnesian War*, 1.93.

79. Strauss, *Battle of Salamis*, 81, 86.

80. Herodotus, *Histories*, 8.61.

81. Conwell, *Athenian Long Walls*, 100.

82. See Wycherly, *Stones of Athens*, 262; and Conwell, *Connecting a City*, 58, 87.

83. Conwell, *Connecting a City*, 55–62.

84. Xenophon, *Constitution of the Athenians*, 2.6 and 2.11–12, in Ober, *Fortress Attica*, 16.

85. Conwell, *Athenian Long Walls*, 48–49.

86. Thucydides, *History of the Peloponnesian War*, 1.107; McGregor, *Athenians and Their Empire*, 53; and Podlecki, *Perikles and His Circle*, 57.

87. Conwell, *Athenian Long Walls*, 4, 100, 416–7; and Krentz, "Strategic Culture," 63.

88. Conwell, *Athenian Long Walls*, 31–32, 39–41, 100; Lawrence, *Greek Aims in Fortification*, 155–56; and Thucydides, *History of the Peloponnesian War*, 1.103, 107.

89. Conwell, *Connecting a City*, 84, 87–88.

90. McGregor, *Athenians and Their Empire*, 52; Kagan, *Peloponnesian War*, 9; and Conwell, *Connecting a City*, 61–62.

91. See Campbell, *Ancient Siege Warfare*, 15–23; Ober, "Hoplites and Obstacles," 180–87; Winter, *Greek Fortifications*, 303, 306–7; and Fields, *Ancient Greek Fortifications*, 50–51.

92. Ober, "Hoplites and Obstacles," 186–87.

93. Winter, *Greek Fortifications*, 56.

94. Ober, *Fortress Attica*, 72.

95. Hanson, *War Like No Other*, 36.

96. Thucydides, *History of the Peloponnesian War*, 1.93, 142–43.

97. Conwell, *Connecting a City*, 38–54, 64.

98. Plutarch, *Rise and Fall of Athens*, 5.5–7.

99. Conwell, *Athenian Long Walls*, 417.

100. Thucydides, *History of the Peloponnesian War*, 1.107.

101. Conwell, *Connecting a City*, 54, 64.

102. Thucydides, *History of the Peloponnesian War*, 1.107–8; McGregor, *Athenians and Their Empire*, 53; and Podlecki, *Perikles and His Circle*, 57.

103. Thucydides, *History of the Peloponnesian War*, 1.107.

104. Ibid., 1.108.

105. Ibid.

106. Podlecki, *Perikles and His Circle*, 58–59; Kagan, *Peloponnesian War*, 9; and McGregor, *Athenians and Their Empire*, 55.

107. Sacks, *Dictionary of the Ancient Greek World*, 5.

108. See Krentz, "Strategic Culture," 64–65; quote at 65.

109. See Conwell, *Connecting a City*, 62; Thucydides, *History of the Peloponnesian War*, 1.109–110; McGregor, *Athenians and Their Empire*, 57–58, 66–67; and Podlecki, *Perikles and His Circle*, 64, 67–69.

110. McGregor, *Athenians and Their Empire*, 70.

111. See ibid., 55, 75, 79; and Podlecki, *Perikles and His Circle*, 64.

112. See Conwell, *Connecting a City*, 62–64, 86; Podlecki, *Perikles and His Circle*, 60–61, 72; and Thucydides, *History of the Peloponnesian War*, 1.114, 144, 2.21.

113. Kagan, *Peloponnesian War*, 18–19, 59; and Podlecki, *Perikles and His Circle*, 73, 75–76.

114. Podlecki, *Perikles and His Circle*, 72, 76, 86, 158; and Conwell, *Connecting a City*, 70, 72.

115. Podlecki, *Perikles and His Circle*, 158.

116. Conwell, *Connecting a City*, 76.

117. Podlecki, *Perikles and His Circle*, 76.

118. Conwell, *Athenian Long Walls*, 66, 71–72.

119. See Conwell, *Connecting a City*, 63, 65, 70–71, 86; Podlecki, *Perikles and His Circle*, 69–70, 99, 100, 128; McGregor, *Athenians and Their Empire*, 94, 105; Hanson, *Warfare and Agriculture*, 93–94; and Plutarch, *Rise and Fall of Athens*, 6.13, 180.

120. See Conwell, *Connecting a City*, 24, 30–31, 59, 74, 76–78; Conwell, *Athenian Long Walls*, 430; McGregor, *Athenians and Their Empire*, 97; and Thucydides, *History of the Peloponnesian War*, 2.13.

121. See Thucydides, *History of the Peloponnesian War*, 2.13; Conwell, *Connecting a City*, 67–74; Winter, *Greek Fortifications*, 307–9; and Campbell, *Greek and Roman Siege Machinery*, 3–4.

122. Kagan, *Peloponnesian War*, 9.

123. See Thucydides, *History of the Peloponnesian War*, 1.140–41; and Kagan, *Peloponnesian War*, 32–40.

124. Thucydides, *History of the Peloponnesian War*, 1.23, 86–88, 118.

125. Ibid., 1.142–44, 2.13; Kagan, *Peloponnesian War*, 51–52; Ober, *Fortress Attica*, 51–52; Hanson, *War Like No Other*, 29–30; and Conwell, *Connecting a City*, 80–88.

126. Winter, *Greek Fortifications*, 157.

127. Ober, "Hoplites and Obstacles," 118; Hanson, *Wars of the Ancient Greeks*, 117–18; Kagan, *Peloponnesian War*, 51–53; Conwell, *Connecting a City*, 80–81, 84; and Krentz, "Strategic Culture," 64.

128. Thucydides, *History of the Peloponnesian War*, 1.143.

129. Ibid., II.65; Kagan, *Peloponnesian War*, 51–52; Podlecki, *Perikles and His Circle*, 143–44; and Hanson, *War Like No Other*, 27, 30.

130. Kagan, *Peloponnesian War*, 53.

131. Ibid.

132. See Thucydides, *History of the Peloponnesian War*, 2.10, 11, 13, 14, 16; Krentz, "Strategic Culture," 65; Plutarch, *Rise and Fall of Athens*, 6.34; and Hanson, *War Like No Other*, 50–52, 112.

133. Krentz, "Strategic Culture," 69; and Hanson, *Wars of the Ancient Greeks*, 112.

134. See Thucydides, *History of the Peloponnesian War*, 2.13; Hanson, *War Like No Other*, 50; and Fields, *Ancient Greek Fortifications*, 53–54.

135. Thucydides, *History of the Peloponnesian War*, 2.11; Ober, *Fortress Attica*, 35; and Hanson, *Wars of the Ancient Greeks*, 52, 118–19.

136. Thucydides, *History of the Peloponnesian War*, 2.22, 3.1; and Hanson, *War Like No Other*, 50, 56–57.

137. Hanson, *Warfare and Agriculture*, 15, 64, 139, 147.

138. Sacks, *Dictionary of the Ancient Greek World*, 164, 168; and Hanson, *War Like No Other*, 35.

139. See Thucydides, *History of the Peloponnesian War*, 2.93; and Kagan, *Peloponnesian War*, 96.

140. See Kagan, *Peloponnesian War*, 73, 76–77, 162; Hanson, *War Like No Other*, 29–30, 59, 93–94, 111; and Conwell, *Connecting a City*, 82–83.

141. Hanson, *War Like No Other*, 45, 65, 68–71, 77–78, 82; Conwell, *Connecting a City*, 91–92; and McGregor, *Athenians and Their Empire*, 135–36.

142. Thucydides, *History of the Peloponnesian War*, 3.87.

143. Hanson, *War Like No Other*, 79, 81.

144. Thucydides, *History of the Peloponnesian War*, 4.21, 38, 41; and Kagan, *Peloponnesian War*, 146–47, 193, 330–31.

145. Thucydides, *History of the Peloponnesian War*, 4.66–73.

146. See ibid., 4.42–57, 66–79, 5.18–20, 43–47, 63–74, 82; and Kagan, *Peloponnesian War*, 57, 192–93.

147. See Thucydides, *History of the Peloponnesian War*, 6.18, 24, 93, 104, 7.2–4; Hanson, *War Like No Other*, 202, 204–5; and Kagan, *Peloponnesian War*, 284–91.

148. See Kagan, *Peloponnesian War*, 327; and Hanson, *War Like No Other*, 217, 229, 236, 260–61, 273.

149. Hanson, *War Like No Other*, 6, 60, 64; and Conwell, *Connecting a City*, 93–94.

150. Thucydides, *History of the Peloponnesian War*, 7.27–28, 8.69; Hanson, *Warfare and Agriculture*, 153–57, 161–62; and Kagan, *Peloponnesian War*, 299–300.

151. Xenophon, *Hellenica, Books I–IV*, trans. Carleton Brownson (Cambridge, MA: Harvard University Press, 1997), 1.i.35.

152. Kagan, *Peloponnesian War*, 84, 127; Xenophon, *Hellenica*, 1.ii.1; and Hanson, *Warfare and Agriculture*, 90.

153. Hanson, *War Like No Other*, 243, 255; and Kagan, *Peloponnesian War*, 440–41.

154. See Conwell, *Connecting a City*, 95–100; and Thucydides, *History of the Peloponnesian War*, 8.71.

155. Thucydides, *History of the Peloponnesian War*, 8.71.

156. See Kagan, *Peloponnesian War*, 384, 395–96, 420–21, 446; Hanson, *Warfare and Agriculture*, 22, 162; Krentz, "Strategic Culture," 70; Conwell, *Connecting a City*, 101–2; Xenophon, *Hellenica*, 1.i.33–4; and Hanson, *War Like No Other*, 124; Thucydides, *History of the Peloponnesian War*, 8.71.

157. Winter, *Greek Fortifications*, 156–57; Hanson, *War Like No Other*, 124; and Conwell, *Connecting a City*, 101–2.

158. Xenophon, *Hellenica*, 2.ii.10–13; Kagan, *Peloponnesian War*, 478–79; and Conwell, *Connecting a City*, 103.

159. Hanson, *War Like No Other*, 267.

160. Xenophon, *Hellenica*, 2.ii.20; Kagan, *Peloponnesian War*, 481, 483; and Conwell, *Connecting a City*, 104–5, 194–95.

161. Strauss, *Athens after the War*, 47, 50–51, 53–54; and Ober, *Fortress Attica*, 209.

162. Cahill, *Sailing the Wine-Dark Sea*, 220.

163. See Kagan, *Peloponnesian War*, 487; Strauss, *Athens after the War*, 110–111, 113; Ober, *Fortress Attica*, 51–52, 65; Cahill, *Sailing the Wine-Dark Sea*, 220–23; and Raphael Sealey, *Demosthenes and His Time: A Study in Defeat* (New York: Oxford University Press, 1993), 9.

164. Ober, *Fortress Attica*, 54.

165. Ibid., 17, 54–55; Fields, *Ancient Greek Fortifications*, 46–47; and Sage, *Warfare in Ancient Greece*, 109.

166. Ober, *Fortress Attica*, 54–55.

167. Hanson, *War Like No Other*, 198.

168. Kagan, *Peloponnesian War*, 481, 486; Xenophon, *Hellenica*, 2.ii.20, 4.iii.10n1; and Conwell, *Connecting a City*, 105.

169. See Strauss, *Athens after the War*, 105–6, 110–13, 121–22, 160; Sealey, *Demosthenes and His Time*, 9, 13; and Xenophon, *Hellenica*, 4.iii.9–14; and Conwell, *Connecting a City*, 125–26.

170. See Conwell, *Connecting a City*, 110–11, 115–16, 118–19, 125–26; Strauss, *Athens after the War*, 122–25, 126–27; Hanson, *Warfare and Agriculture*, 101; and Xenophon, *Hellenica*, 3.v.16. For the state of early fourth-century siegecraft, see Winter, *Greek Fortifications*, 133, 218, 309, 317–18; Lawrence, *Greek Aims in Fortification*, 39, 56, 240, 423; and Campbell, *Siege Warfare*, 13–15, 24–29.

171. Winter, *Greek Fortifications*, 155–56, 160, 310; and Conwell, *Athenian Long Walls*, 401–3.

172. Xenophon, *Hellenica*, 4.viii.9; Strauss, *Athens after the War*, 126–28; and Conwell, *Connecting a City*, 110–11.

173. Xenophon, *Hellenica*, 4.viii.9.

174. See Conwell, *Connecting a City*, 111–12, 117–18, 125–26; Ober, *Fortress Attica*, 209; and Strauss, *Athens after the War*, 127–28, 152–53.

175. Ober, *Fortress Attica*, 14–15, 28–29, 42, 50; and Conwell, *Connecting a City*, 125–27.

176. Ober, "Hoplites and Obstacles," 189; and Sage, *Warfare in Ancient Greece*, 141–57.

177. See Ober, *Fortress Attica*, 3, 17, 52–55, 63, 77, 207; Conwell, *Connecting a City*, 121–22; Fields, *Ancient Greek Fortifications*, 25–27; and Hanson, *Warfare and Agriculture*, 94–102.

178. Ober, *Fortress Attica*, 3.

179. Ibid., 1–3, 84; and Hanson, *Warfare and Agriculture*, 81–82.

180. Ober, *Fortress Attica*, 65, 195, 207.

181. Conwell, *Connecting a City*, 121–22; and Ober, *Fortress Attica*, 71.

182. Conwell, *Connecting a City*, 121–22.

183. Hanson, *Warfare and Agriculture*, 81–82, 226–27; and Wycherly, *Stones of Athens*, 16.

184. Conwell, *Connecting a City*, 118–19.

185. Ober, *Fortress Attica*, 63.

186. Conwell, *Connecting a City*, 120–21.

187. Sealey, *Demosthenes and His Time*, 55; and Hanson, *Warfare and Agriculture*, 100.

188. Sealey, *Demosthenes and His Time*, 17, 52–58; and Strauss, *Athens after the War*, 136–37, 159–60.

189. Kagan, *Peloponnesian War*, 487.

190. Strauss, *Athens after the War*, 69–71; Sealey, *Demosthenes and His Time*, 81–82, 93, 106–7; and Conwell, *Connecting a City*, 128.

191. Ober, *Fortress Attica*, 222; Winter, *Greek Fortifications*, 111; and Hanson, *Wars of the Ancient Greeks*, 149, 155.

192. Campbell, *Ancient Siege Warfare*, 30–31; Winter, *Greek Fortifications*, 319–20; Hanson, *Wars of the Ancient Greeks*, 149, 155, 158; and Sage, *Warfare in Ancient Greece*, 165–68.

193. Hanson, *Wars of the Ancient Greeks*, 147.

194. See Conwell, *Connecting a City*, 123–24, 129; Hanson, *Warfare and Agriculture*, 97; Ober, *Fortress Attica*, 73–75; and Sealey, *Demosthenes and His Time*, 125, 137–57, 163.

195. Conwell, *Athenian Long Walls*, 125; Conwell, *Connecting a City*, 123–24; and Ober, *Fortress Attica*, 56.

196. Conwell, *Connecting a City*, 123, 129.

197. Ober, *Fortress Attica*, 222.

198. Sealey, *Demosthenes and His Time*, 187–89; Sage, *Warfare in Ancient Greece*, 179; and Conwell, *Connecting a City*, 130.

199. Sealey, *Demosthenes and His Time*, 208; Conwell, *Connecting a City*, 133, 139; and Christian Habicht, *Athens from Alexander to Antony* (Cambridge, MA: Harvard University Press, 1997), 11.

200. Fields, *Ancient Greek Fortifications*, 9, 20.

201. Sealey, *Demosthenes and His Time*, 198–200.

202. Ibid., 199.

203. See Conwell, *Connecting*, 139–43, 145, 147–48; Winter, *Greek Fortifications*, 112, 165–69, 270, 276; Habicht, *Athens from Alexander to Antony*, 11, 23–24; and Fields, *Ancient Greek Fortifications*, 20, 24.

204. See Habicht, *Athens from Alexander to Antony*, 135–38; Sealey, *Demosthenes and His Time*, 215–19; and Conwell, *Connecting a City*, 62, 150–52.

205. Conwell, *Athenian Long Walls*, 145–46, 406; Fields, *Ancient Greek Fortifications*, 20, 24; and Habicht, *Athens from Alexander to Antony*, 70.

206. Habicht, *Athens from Alexander to Antony*, 75; and Conwell, *Connecting a City*, 169–71.

207. See Campbell, *Ancient Siege Wafare*, 45; Conwell, *Athenian Long Walls*, 154, 156–57, 444–45; and Habicht, *Athens from Alexander to Antony*, 81–82.

208. Conwell, *Athenian Long Walls*, 159.

209. Wycherly *Stones of Athens*, 23; and Conwell, *Connecting a City*, 195–96.

210. Xenophon, *Hellenica*, 2.2.23.

211. Ober, *Fortress Attica*, 54–55.

212. Sealey, *Demosthenes and His Time*, 125.

213. Hanson, *War Like No Other*, 136.

3

Hadrian's Wall

Rome's Foremost Frontier Fortification

Introduction

Whereas fifth century BCE Athens offered a rising power looking to eliminate its primary vulnerability, Rome in the early 120s CE presents a somewhat different context and challenge. Although it was among the strongest powers in history, the Hadrianic government strained to manage and secure its domain following the expansionist Trajan era. In one corner of the empire, northern Britain stood as a remote place of instability and violence. The adversary was not a finely honed army like the Sparta hoplites but rather a range of British-Scottish tribes given to raiding and skirmishing. Rome's decision to erect what became known as Hadrian's Wall across northern England constituted an effort to establish better frontier control. Although it was built almost two thousand years ago, this attempt to employ strategic defenses against an irregular challenge correlates well with the modern context. Given the nonexistent knowledge of native decision making, judging their reaction to the barrier must occur through our limited understanding of their subsequent behavior. Did the barrier promote deterrence, a central aim for the overburdened Roman army? With Rome and its adversaries in north Britain possessing sharply divergent approaches to warfare, how did the wall affect the military balance in this asymmetric struggle? The military balance dimension for this case cannot focus simply on effectiveness; it must also address efficiency. With an undersized force for such a large empire, achieving control and stability with fewer soldiers was a highly desired virtue. Hadrian erected this barrier, along with strategic defenses elsewhere in the empire, with an explicit aim to encourage a more status quo–oriented mindset, not the constant expansionism instinctively preferred by Romans. Did he succeed in this regard?

This chapter attempts to answer these questions by focusing on the period from the initiation of construction in 122 CE until the death of Emperor Septimius Severus at York in 211. During this nearly ninety-year period, Roman policy in North Britain goes through considerable flux including an advance to central Scotland and construction of the Antonine Wall. After Severus' death, as Cassius Dio observes, the Romans recognized Hadrian's Wall as the proximate border of their British province and never again tried to advance north except for brief punitive missions.[1] During this later period, higher priority demands, especially in the East, pushed Britain to the margins of the empire. Still, as a strategic defense system, Hadrian's Wall would continue essentially until the end of Roman rule in Britain early in the fifth century. The limited availability of evidence precludes knowing anything with a high degree of certainty, but appreciation of the contextual factors, archeology, and extant writings allows a basic understanding of this wall experience.

In June 122, the Emperor Hadrian sailed across the water toward remote Britain. He would be the first Roman ruler to set foot on the island since Claudius briefly came ashore to oversee the coup de grâce of the initial conquest in 43. Unlike his predecessor's search for glory, Hadrian had real work to undertake. His traveling companions reflected the precarious nature of security on the provincial frontier. In addition to the usual large imperial entourage, Hadrian probably brought with him an experienced governor, Aulus Platorius Nepos, and *legio VI Victrix* (the Sixth Victorious Legion).[2] If not traveling together, they arrived in Britain shortly before the emperor.

Upon leaving the continent, Hadrian likely glanced back toward Germany, the first stop on his swing through key western provinces. His objective was to stabilize and secure Roman frontiers in this region in order to focus attention on the empire's eastern provinces. In the previous months, Hadrian had been attempting to strengthen defenses, most notably ordering the army to build a continuous palisade—a wooden fence—from Mainz on the Rhine River to just west of Regensburg on the Danube River.[3] This front covered a vulnerable area between the headwaters of Rhine and Danube, where over the past forty years the Romans had first established a chain of watchtowers that were later enhanced with forts.[4] Hadrian's addition of a palisade represented a significant evolution in frontier policy. Rather than designed to repel major attacks, it aimed to facilitate a line of control as well as symbolically denote the area that the Romans regarded as their exclusive territory.

Why the Roman Empire stopped expanding is a divisive issue that has generated military, political, and socioeconomic explanations. Addressing this controversial subject is beyond the scope of this chapter, but a brief clarification of the general Roman conception of a frontier or "limes" is needed. Most importantly, the Romans regarded a frontier as a zone rather than a definitive line. The empire, possessing interests beyond its provinces, usually was heavily involved with tribes in these forward areas, which often included "friends" and "barbarians." The Romans did not hesitate to use force in the zone when necessary, but they also engaged in economic trade and social interaction. They even acted beyond the frontier zones when indicated by perceived interests. Initially the term "limes" referred to a road network in the frontier zone, but it later came to be associated with the frontier defenses of Roman provinces, especially in central Europe (e.g., Limes Germanicus, Limes Raetian).[5]

With Germany disappearing behind him, the forty-six-year-old Hadrian's thoughts would have turned toward the approaching island of Britain and the best way to stabilize this troublesome province. Now in his fifth year as emperor, Britain had provided one of his first tests. A rebellion by either the Brigantes or Lowland Scottish tribes, or probably a combination of both, had broken out at the end of Trajan's rule. The redeployment of imperial troops from along this frontier to support the Parthian War in the East likely encouraged native troublemaking. Hadrian deemed the situation serious enough to shift his experienced and able friend, Quintus Pompeius Falco, from his post as governor of the important Moesia Inferior province to Britain. Falco probably defeated the rebellion by 119–20, but only after heavy Roman losses. The situation remained worrisome enough for Hadrian to put Britain on his tour of key western provinces. He probably appreciated the challenge of native resistance given his military service in frontier provinces and Spanish heritage. It took the Romans two hundred years to completely subjugate Spain; they had been in Britain fewer than eighty.[6]

Hadrian's solution to the problem was famously to build a wall. Whether he made this decision during the journey, before departing, or upon inspecting the frontier will likely never be known. Hadrian's biography in the *Augustan History* contains the solitary reference among ancient sources to this action—he "drew a wall along a length of eighty [Roman] miles to separate barbarians and Romans."[7] Over the years, scholars and commentators have offered many explanations for why Hadrian built the wall, what role it played in Roman frontier policy, and how it functioned. "Hadrian's Wall" in this chapter will be used as shorthand phrase for a multifaceted strategic defense system including ditches, roads, watchtowers, and forts as well as the actual wall. All the Hadrianic barriers in Europe, Africa, and Britain had these features, but the particulars varied considerably as a result of terrain and other considerations.

The brief description below captures the initial design in 122 as well as the significant modifications undertaken a few years later, apparently after recognizing the plan's flaws. The wall itself was a continuous barrier that initially ran about 70 statute miles across the Tyne-Solway isthmus and then extended south of the Solway, a body of water that Scottish natives could cross. This path took it along the northern crest of the Tyne, Eden, and Irthing valleys to command the surrounding area. Most advantageously, the central section passed over the Great Whin Sill, an "impressive ridge with craggy, precipitous northern slopes" that reached a maximum height of more than 1,000 feet.[8] The first approximately 40

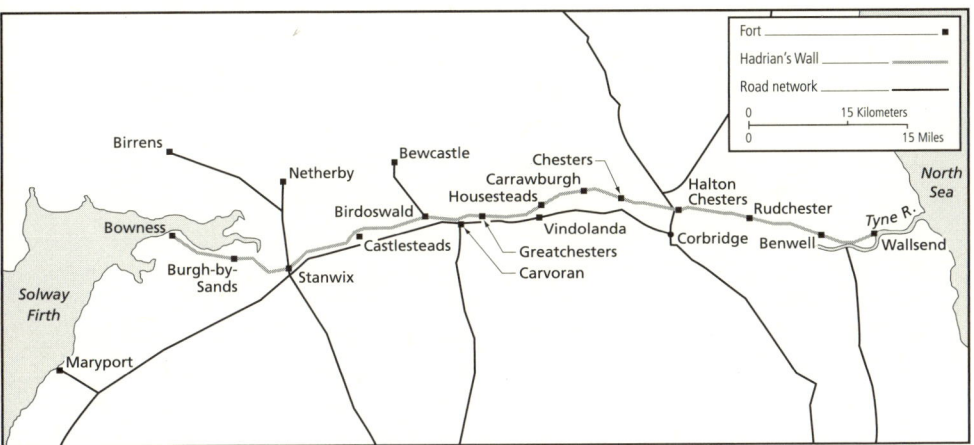

Figure 3.1 Hadrian Wall Strategic Defense System, circa 130

miles from the eastern end consisted of stone, rising to a height of about 15 feet. No evidence exists for a walkway and parapet atop the curtain, but it is likely given the overwhelming logic to facilitate patrolling. As a part of the revision, the Romans extended the eastern end by about 3.7 miles from Pons Aelius (Newcastle) to Segedunum (also known as Wallsend) on the north side of the Tyne River. By contrast, the western approximately 30 miles consisted of turf blocks believed to be at a lower height, especially the section south of the Solway.[9] The region's lack of sandstone for blocks and limestone for mortar is the primary explanation for the change, but the Romans' considerable experience with turf barriers left them comfortable with such structures.[10] It is possible that hostile native reaction necessitated building this section quickly, and turf provided the fastest, albeit less durable, route.[11] With the expanded east end, the total length of Hadrian's Wall increased to approximately 74 miles (80 Roman miles).

Initially, the Romans planned to establish a modest troop presence along the wall in milecastles and turrets. They built a gate with a fortlet every Roman mile (about .92 mile). The emplacement of so many gates is often cited as strong evidence that the wall was not meant as a purely defensive barrier, although some doubts exists whether most of these gates were actually used.[12] In between each milecastle, the Romans built two equally spaced turrets. Housing up to eight soldiers, the turrets essentially functioned as observation posts and troop shelters. With a milecastle or turret every third of a Roman mile, messages could be transferred rapidly along the Wall. The total garrison for these facilities has been estimated at between one thousand and two thousand troops, reflecting Roman intention to base only a small portion of its army on the barrier.[13]

The Romans rapidly strengthened the strategic defense system as part of the redesign, especially by adding forts for cohort-size garrisons every six to nine miles along the wall.[14] At this density, units could march to the next fort in half a day. While employing a few preexisting forts near the curtain, the Romans probably constructed eleven new bases.[15] Some forts were flush with the wall, but the majority extended about one-third beyond the barrier to allow three of the main gates on the north side to facilitate forays into Scotland. The bases often covered key spots such as bridges crossing the North Tyne, Irthing, and Eden rivers. The forts increased the wall garrison to approximately nine thousand to twelve thousand troops.[16] Their addition probably triggered construction of the military way, a parallel road running south of the wall to facilitate rapid army movement in the military zone. The road network provided the critical link between the frontier and the legion bases, none of which were within eighty miles of Hadrian's Wall.

The Romans added obstacles in front of and behind the main barrier. The outermost element was a nearly continuous V-shaped trench, averaging almost 30 feet in width and up to 11 feet deep. Although it is unclear if it was part of the original system, a berm of about 20 feet existed between this ditch and the wall. Recent excavations of this berm toward the eastern end have revealed a previously unknown part of the system—closely spaced pits believed to contain sharpened stakes. The southernmost element of the system was the vallum, a combination mound-ditch-mound obstacle stretching almost 120 feet across and running roughly parallel to the wall. Limiting crossings of the vallum to opposite forts allowed the Romans to funnel traffic and enhance control. They might have always intended such a structure as the last phase of construction but possibly only appreciated the need for it when the initial wall work prompted disturbances among the natives. Altogether, the series of obstacles established a strategic defensive position with a depth in excess of 300 feet.[17]

Roman Experience in Britain

Hadrian, probably landing at Rutupiae (Richborough) in southeast England, arrived in Britain with considerable knowledge of Rome's history on the island. In addition to the normal imperial sources of information, the emperor had ties with individuals experienced operating in Britain. Hadrian began his military service in 95–96 as a tribune with *legio II Adiutrix* (Second Rescuer Legion) at Aquincum (Budapest). Only a decade earlier this unit had been transferred from Britain. It would have been filled with veterans from the legion's fifteen years in the province, a period of constant campaigning against the northern tribes. One can envision many conversations on the subject of a place the Romans always regarded as exotic. Moreover, when Hadrian returned to Rome (probably in 101), he would have crossed paths with Cornelius Tacitus. A leading orator and historian at the time, Tacitus spent many years in Britain with his father-in-law, Julius Agricola, the former governor. He had recently published the *Life of Agricola*, which focused heavily on the Roman's island campaigns.[18]

Figure 3.2 Roman Britain and Key Early Second-Century Northern Tribes

Invasion and Advance

Rome's prior experience in Britain undoubtedly played a role in Hadrian's decision calculus. The Romans had economic and political exchanges with Britons for more than a century before the formal occupation in 43 CE. Although Julius Caesar conducted two brief landings during the Gallic Wars while Augustus and Caligula subsequently considered invasions, the Romans demonstrated reluctance to occupy Britain in part from a belief that the costs would outweigh the benefits of such an undeveloped place.[19] Having been physically unable to serve in the military, a newly installed Claudius needed to bolster his reputation through conquest.[20] The troops initially mutinied when informed of plans to cross the water, but upon restoration of order, the invasion of Britain proceeded without difficulty in 43. Approximately forty thousand troops including four legions (*II Augusta, VIIII Hispana, XIIII Gemina,* and *XX Valeria*) quickly fanned out across southeast England until by the end of the 50s they controlled most of England and Wales.[21]

Disaster struck in 60, while Gov. Suetonius Paullinus and his army were conquering Mona Island (Anglesey) off Wales; the major native revolt prompted a period of consolidation.[22] Harsh Roman management, especially tax collection, and personal humiliations had provoked Queen Boudicca and her Iceni tribe in eastern England to join forces with other disgruntled groups in revolt. The revolt gained momentum with an ineffectual Roman response and destruction of the main Roman towns until Paullinus raced back with ten thousand troops and won a decisive victory. The historian Cassius Dio, writing more than a century later, almost certainly exaggerated Roman and allied Briton losses at eighty thousand lives, but this figure highlights the legendary status that the Boudiccan revolt obtained with Romans.[23] It left a legacy of concern about internal stability that continued to influence Roman officials. Subsequent drawdowns of the island garrison, including a legion for fighting in the East, and the civil war after Nero's death dissuaded expansion for more than a decade.[24] An important factor in Rome's avoidance of serious difficulty in these years was its alliance with the Brigante tribe, the largest group on the island, according to Tacitus.[25] Occupying an area from the Midlands to slightly beyond northern England, Brigantia protected the province's northern front essentially as a client kingdom. The Romans worked to maintain strong ties with the Brigantes, aiding Queen Cartimandua in her struggles to keep the upper hand over anti-Roman tribal factions. The existence of such hostile forces, however, reinforced Roman caution in relying excessively on the Brigantes.

Given their desire to control the entire island, the Romans would have resumed the offensive at some point, but developments at the outset of the 70s provided added impetus. Anti-Roman elements among the Brigantes, led by the Queen's former husband, Venutius, and assisted by allied tribes in Scotland, seized on perceived Roman weakness and overthrew Cartimandua.[26] As a result, the situation in northern Britain radically shifted from the Romans having a protective client kingdom to facing an active, hostile power. This development, as Sheppard Frere notes, "was a turning point of history . . . from this time onward Rome was committed to keeping very large forces in Britain for an indefinite period."[27] Vespasian, a legion commander in the original invasion, won the civil war and dispatched in 71 his son-in-law Petilius Cerialis with reinforcements to defeat Venutius and conquer Brigante territory.[28] Cerialis largely succeeded within a few years, setting the stage for the peak of the empire's expansion in Britain under Julius Agricola. He launched a campaign into Scotland for five consecutive years (79–83), with the last effort pushing beyond the Clyde-Forth isthmus and culminating in a great victory over the Caledonii at Mons Graupius.[29] Nevertheless, the limited size of Agricola's army precluded securing additional territory and the Romans apparently never penetrated the Scottish Highlands in force.

Pullback to the Tyne-Solway Isthmus

Soon after Mons Graupius, the new and jealous Emperor Domitian ended Agricola's unusually long six-year run as governor and precipitated a gradual pullback from Scotland. Domitian worried that Agricola's success and growing fame could be a source of political danger, but he also needed more troops for wars on the continent. After the mid-80s, the Roman garrison in Britain probably never again included four intact legions, the minimal number required to complete the conquest of the island.[30]

With no written record for the period after Agricola, archeologists have provided a general, albeit murky, history of the pullback including the construction of defenses, running north from the Clyde-Forth isthmus to the Tay River.[31] By the end of the decade, however, troop redeployments required abandonment of these positions and a withdrawal to the Scottish Lowlands. Control of this region slowly declined as Trajan continued to recall soldiers for his battles elsewhere, especially the Dacian War in the first decade of the second century. Thus, as Frere notes, Trajan's reign "so glorious in the military sphere elsewhere, in Britain had witnessed retreat."[32]

By 105 the Romans appear to have largely abandoned southern Scotland and concentrated on controlling northern England, beginning at the Stanegate road. Agricola had built this road, just south of the Tyne-Solway isthmus, to connect what is today Corbridge in the east and Carlisle in the west. The Romans had begun expanding fortifications along the Stanegate as the pullback commenced in the late 80s and early 90s. For example, Vindolanda doubled in size. During

Trajan's reign, the Romans added new forts (e.g., Carvoran and Newburgh), increasing base density along the road. Also at this time they constructed smaller fortlets and towers to enhance their presence throughout northern England. Nevertheless, the frontier remained open.[33]

Given its importance for the subsequent discussion of Hadrian's Wall, it is worth considering the location of the Stanegate fortifications. The narrowness of the area across the island at this point, albeit twice as wide as the Clyde-Forth isthmus in central Scotland, obviously appealed to the Romans. It lay in the valleys of three rivers—the Tyne, Irthing, and Eden. Although retaining southern Scotland was desirable, attempting to hold this region with dwindling troop levels likely risked overextension and encouraged rebellions. Any pullback below the Stanegate road would have been even riskier, leaving uncovered a significant part of Brigante territory and probably ensuring the tribe's revolt with strong support from Scottish tribes. In recent years some scholars have contested the traditional view of the area forts as constituting a "Stanegate Frontier."[34] Regardless, establishing forts near or on the Stanegate road offered a way to promote stability in the area and react to periodic attacks from the north.[35] This issue will be addressed when examining the decision to build Hadrian's Wall nearby.

Indications of trouble and ultimately the war mentioned in the introduction suggest the limitations of this approach for stabilizing northern Britain at the end of Trajan's reign. Experience had shown large forces, even entire legions, could be removed from Britain without precipitating an immediate crisis. Yet such actions eventually produced serious consequences. The increasing deployment of unit detachments between forts along the Stanegate road suggests trouble policing the area.[36] The emperor's decision to fight Parthia (114–17) without first expanding the army, in contrast to his Dacian Wars, overstretched the Roman force. It also occupied the most capable commanders, leaving Britain under the control of the inexperienced Marcus Appius Bradua.[37] The rare absence of a veteran and able governor from the island undoubtedly exacerbated Roman difficulties. Thus the demands for the Parthian War appear to have finally undermined stability along the Stanegate as the Augustan history notes that "the Britons could not be kept under Roman control."[38]

Assessing the extent of Roman vulnerability at this time is complicated by the uncertain status of legio VIIII and when it departed from Britain. This is worth considering because the presence or absence of the unit during the trouble of the late Trajanic period would have influenced Hadrian's thinking about how best to stabilize the area. A dedication slab at its York fortress in 108 provides the last dated record of the legion in Britain, although it may have subsequently been deployed along the western end of the Stanegate road. Alternatively, legio VIIII could have deployed to Lower Germany in the 114–17 period as a part of shifting global forces to accommodate needs throughout the empire. Critics of this explanation contend that the Romans would have been unlikely to leave only two legions in Britain. Yet the tremendous need for troops on the continent and the subsequent emergence of trouble in Britain support the logic of this argument. A more cautious Roman policy in Britain might have kept legio VIIII in place. With the Romans having reportedly suffered heavy casualties in defeating the rebellion, legio VIIII might have been unfit for duty, prompting its replacement with a fit new unit (legio VI in 122) for the volatile British frontier. If the Ninth did stay in Britain through Trajan's reign, it makes the eruption of trouble more disturbing as Rome would have appeared and been less vulnerable. A variant of this explanation has legio VIIII transferring to Lower Germany during the Parthian War but being rushed back to Britain after the outbreak of trouble. Legions VIIII and VI could have overlapped deployments given the manpower requirements for the massive construction project. The absence of any recorded work for legio VIIII on Hadrian's Wall—in contrast to the other legions—could be explained by its working on the turf section in the west for which historical inscriptions do not exist. Most likely the need for troops probably resulted in, at least, *vexillations*—detached elements often about one thousand men—of the Ninth deploying to the continent during the Parthian War while the remaining, weakened unit stayed to keep "three legions" in Britain. This reduced force then suffered significant casualties in helping defeat the rebellion and was subsequently reunited with the original vexillations in Germany. Regardless of the Ninth's actual history, the deployment of at least eight thousand Roman soldiers in the early 120s greatly bolstered Rome's position in North Britain.[39]

Decision Context

In addition to Roman history, Hadrian's decision would have been influenced by the nature of the challenge in Britain, military capability, strategic culture (including the emperor's somewhat distinct worldview), resources, domestic politics, and decision-making process.

Threat Perception

While lacking a formidable traditional military like other contemporary challenges (e.g., Parthians, Dacians), the natives of northern Britain presented a dangerous threat to stability and security. Appreciating this difficulty, the regime usually installed as governor a "man of consular rank with proven military and administrative ability."[40] By 100, the position entailed the highest prestige, along with Syria, of any governorship.[41] The failure of inexperienced governors at the end of Trajan's reign certainly would have reinforced the need to install able men. While controlling the troublesome Brigantes was central to achieving provincial security, they also had to deal with a range of Scottish tribes.[42] Three key Scottish tribes resided south of the Clyde-Forth isthmus. The Votadini—occupying fertile ground along the east coast—appear to have been Roman allies or at least not hostile. Next to the Votadini lived the Selgovae in the central lowlands. This extremely hostile tribe always seemed to be involved when conflict with the Romans erupted. Further west resided the Novantae, Rome's other primary opponent in southern Scotland. Bordering Selgovae and Novantae territory was a part of Brigantia that actually extended into the southwest corner of Scotland. The Brigantes maintained a close relationship with these Scottish tribes, especially when dealing with the Romans. As one historian observes it is "rarely that we find trouble with the one without the involvement of the other group."[43]

When facing the Roman menace, the Scottish Lowlanders might also cooperate with the Caledonii, who resided on the Highland massif north of the Clyde-Forth isthmus. Whether characterizing the Caledonii as a single tribe or a loose collection of tribes, the Romans essentially regarded them as a common people with a fundamentally different culture and language than the other natives in the province. Descriptions of "barbarians" on the British frontier seem to fit the Caledonii more than the Selgovae or Novantae. These natives apparently possessed negligible siegecraft capabilities, and after being badly outclassed in the battle of Mons Graupius, they exhibited no interest in fighting a conventional Roman-style battle.[44] Instead they would raid, which, if not stopped, would escalate in scale and frequency. The existence of the Caledonii and their allies as "unconquered (rather than they were unconquerable) might in itself have led to the continuation of a significant army in Britain, especially since the province was relatively isolated as it was an island."[45]

Hadrian could focus on the northern frontier of Roman Britain given the security in the rest of the province. To the east, the fierce waters of the North Sea protected the coastline from native raids until the late Roman period. To the west, excluding the area south of the Solway, the inhospitable shores and mountains along the northwest coast guarded against serious attack from this direction. Within the province, the tribes living south of the Brigantes appear fairly quiescent and a matter of little concern for officials. Even once-troublesome Wales had been relatively stable in recent decades.[46]

Military Capability

While the Roman army continued to be of unmatched fighting quality, the total force size was insufficient to cover all imperial threats. Although Rome had added Britain, Dacia (modern Romania), and some territory in the East in the past 120 years, Hadrian commanded only one more legion than Augustus. The disposition of these core units fluctuated somewhat during Hadrian's reign, but the Romans concentrated legion deployments in Britain (three), along the Rhine (four), along the Danube and in Dacia (ten), and in Syria (five).[47] The total force has been estimated at between 130,000 and 168,000 men, depending on the actual size of a legion (4,500 to 5,800 men)—a disputed subject among experts. Most Italians now avoided service in this all-volunteer force, so that they compromised only 21 percent during the Trajanic period and even less under Hadrian. Overconcentration of these divisions of any particular frontier tended to spark trouble elsewhere and Hadrian sought to avoid such deployments.[48]

The relatively small legion force essentially functioned as a strategic reserve with the Romans employing its auxiliary force along the frontier zones. These complementary units—*cohortes peditatae* (infantry), *alae* (cavalry), and *cohortes equitatae* (mixed infantry and cavalry)—were far smaller and more numerous than the legions.[49] They primarily consisted of 500 men with a limited number doubled for extra punch. Despite possessing less armament and greater mobility than legionnaires, auxiliaries provided considerable strength and should not be confused with light infantry. Moreover, they were veteran, professional soldiers held to high standards. The overall size of this force has been difficult to calculate, but estimates generally range from 150,000 to 225,000 men. Together the legion and auxiliary force consisted of between 250,000 and 400,000 soldiers. Even at the top end of this range, the army is small given the empire's vast size and estimated 70 million population. Moreover, these calculations reflect paper-strength assessments, while units were often under strength.[50]

The Roman garrison in Britain apparently required a disproportionately large share of the army. The arrival of legio VI and other reinforcements probably restored the number of legionnaires to about 15,000, between 9–12 percent of the total force. The size of auxiliary forces is more speculative, but their numbers were clearly substantial. According to one source, about 36,000 auxiliaries were in Britain during Hadrian's reign, down from a high of 48,000 under Agricola.[51] All together, the Roman army in Britain probably had a paper-strength of between 40,000 and 50,000. Documents suggest some units might have been under strength by as much as 25 percent, but unit levels almost certainly grew under Hadrian with the arrival of new troops.[52]

Strategic Culture

Every other chapter introduces the building state's strategic culture as a critical contextual factor, but in this case Roman strategic culture is less relevant given Hadrian's dominant decision-making power and somewhat unorthodox worldview. This variance will be discussed as a part of articulating Hadrian's broader understating of political-military affairs. Only a fragment of his memoirs has survived. Instead, students must turn to the works of classical historians—at least some of whom likely had access to the emperor's writings—and his own actions.[53] As historian Elizabeth Speller observed in a recent book, Hadrian was a complex man who defied conventions.[54] Even Roman writers who preferred to categorize rulers as entirely good (e.g., Augustus, Vespasian, Marcus Aurelius) or bad (e.g., Tiberius, Nero, Domitian) struggled with Hadrian. He is most often associated with possessing a defensive view of empire, especially when compared to Trajan, his expansionist predecessor.[55] For example, Fronto, writing soon after Hadrian's death, typified criticism of the emperor for not emulating Trajan's expansionist behavior.[56] Although such an impression is not inaccurate, it requires some exposition to understand Hadrian's thinking. David Shotter nicely contrasts Hadrian and Trajan by observing that "the new emperor's view of imperial security, whilst no less dynamic than that of his predecessor, was very different in its expression."[57]

A debate exists among scholars over the extent to which the Romans shifted to the defensive after Augustus.[58] His famous testament that Rome should stop expanding is seen as a key turning point by some scholars. Others regard this guidance as tactical, not strategic in nature. They contend that Augustus meant the Romans should employ periods of consolidation. At points between Augustus and Hadrian, especially with the Flavians (Vespasian, Titus, and Domitian), the Romans took steps with forts and other structures to aid control of the frontiers. Still, some significant expansion had occurred, including Britain, Dacia, and territory in the East. Most recent scholarship argues that the Romans did not go into a defensive shell until the third century, especially in the East.[59] Their inclination was to expand if possible, but it just became less possible over time. Moreover, the emperor's need to control the prestige of victory, lest popular generals become political threats, contributed to expansion being far less common in the imperial period.[60]

For Hadrian, his opposition to expansion resulted from a combination of circumstance and personality. Trajan's constant activity had overstretched the army and strained the empire's coffers, necessitating a period of retrenchment, as will be discussed later. Practical considerations aside, Hadrian also appears to have possessed less interest in conquest and glory than a typical Roman.[61] An epigram attributed to Hadrian declares "I have achieved more by peace than others by war."[62] This attitude probably comes from his attraction to Hellenic ideas and values.[63] Greek intellectuals held far less worth in an emperor's military exploits than Romans, regarding conquests as costly and burdensome rather than glorious. Hadrian, who had spent considerable time in Greece before becoming emperor, included notable Greeks in his entourage.

Hadrian seemed to harbor the ambitious goal of establishing an antiexpansionist orientation for Rome that would outlast his reign. He apparently believed that marking the frontiers, at least in the West, would discourage both future Roman adventurism and barbarian aggression. Whether it be the palisades along the *Limes Germanicus*, the *Fossatum Africae* (a series of ditches and walls on the edge of the Sahara), or, as we shall see, the wall in Britain, the emperor enthusiastically shepherded such projects.[64] Historians go to lengths to stress their limited defensive value, but they carried great weight as symbols. Although strikingly different, each was a physical barrier closing off an open frontier. For the barbarians, these impressive structures served to mark Roman territory and signify the empire's strength. For the Romans, Hadrian probably hoped such structures would help prevent a return to Trajan's expansionist policies. Given that most Romans believed that a lack of active campaigning would undermine military capability and discipline, the emperor asserted himself as commander in chief using frequent travels to maintain close relations with units and promote aggressive training and frontier construction to help maintain morale and effectiveness. As a veteran, accomplished soldier, Hadrian ascended to the throne with considerable military expertise and the legions' respect, a status that problematically would not transfer to emperors of a less distinguished background.[65]

Whether expansionist or status quo oriented, impressing the barbarians with Roman power always represented a critical concern for imperial officials.[66] With a relatively small army for its huge empire, the Romans could not maintain security simply "by means of sheer, overwhelming force."[67] Instead they relied heavily on what today is called deterrence, which offered the prospect of acceptable security at feasible cost. Hadrian embraced this approach as he sought "peace through strength, or failing that peace through threat."[68] Arrian, Hadrian's friend and the governor of Cappadocia, seemed to echo the emperor's views on deterrence in his history on battling the Alani.[69] A key question for Hadrian, Arrian, and other Romans was how to make deterrence as robust as possible.

Modern scholars stress that effective deterrence requires capability and commitment, elements that the Romans would characterize as the physical and psychological. It was critical for Rome not only to be strong but also to appear strong and committed.[70] Adversaries apparently discounted overall Roman strength, instead focusing on the army present in their own region. Thus by the second century, the Romans increasingly garrisoned forces close to the frontiers to provide high visibility and enhance rapid response capability. Strategic analyst Edward Luttwak adds that the concentrated power of the legions behind the frontier provided the critical ingredient to "deterrent suasion."[71] Such visibility also created potential vulnerability given that a need to concentrate forces for battle elsewhere would inevitably "upset the local balance of power and neutralize deterrence."[72] Under such circumstances, adversaries had an incentive to revolt or attack. Trajan's Parthian War undoubtedly reinforced this lesson for Hadrian. Moreover, given the army's inadequate size, Rome had increasingly turned to using troop vexillations to create the required presence, but excess splintering risked undermining capability.

The Romans, including Hadrian, appreciated that deterrence could not always be achieved, and when challenged they had to respond to such aggression or risk a precipitous decline in credibility. Themistius notes that the Romans believed, whether responding to external attack or internal rebellion, terror needed to be instilled in adversaries. Any sign of deference or weakness, even against minor breaches, jeopardized Rome's reputation of greatness and courted disaster. Hadrian's extremely harsh reaction to the later Bar-Kochba revolt (132–35) in Judea reflected the emperor's appreciation for this principle.[73] Ultimately, he, like other Romans, believed that a successful frontier strategy depended on a degree of barbarian fear. On occasions when the Romans lacked the ability to respond, they would be sure to launch reprisals even if having to wait years. The zealousness with which the Romans worked "to punish, to avenge, and to terrify" almost makes one consider revenge more than reestablishing deterrent credibility as their true motivation.[74] Still these goals were inextricably linked, allowing Rome to get by with a small army when operative. Unfortunately, adversaries' memories seem to fade over time. Thus, if Rome could influence enemy perceptions not only of consequences for aggression (deterrence by retaliation) but also of their low likelihood of achieving the objective (deterrence by denial), then deterrence would be more robust. Whether Hadrian possessed such an understanding is unknown, but it seems likely he appreciated that strategic defense systems helped facilitate such perceptions by both covering frontier troop movements and complicating adversary attacks.

Resources

Although possessing enormous resources, the empire also required huge expenditures, and the relative balance heavily tilted toward the negative at the end of Trajan's reign. The previous ruler had simply spent vast sums of money and overstretched the army with his long wars. In fighting against the Dacians, and then later the Parthians, Trajan massed armies of up to two hundred thousand men—perhaps the largest of the imperial era. Moreover, Trajan's victories created requirements for large occupation forces. Shortly before his death, insufficient garrisons prompted revolts in the new eastern provinces and probably contributed to a major Jewish rebellion in the established areas of Cyrenaica, Egypt, and Cyprus. Trajan actually had to submit to an armistice in Armenia and shift troops against these insurgencies. He also expensively engaged in the largest public building campaign since Augustus (e.g., *Via nova Triana* road in Arabia, the famous rock-cut road at the Iron Gates near the Danube, and the giant bridge over the Danube into Dacia). While lucrative spoils from the Dacian Wars initially paid for much of this activity, the subsequent Parthian War would not produce the same positive rate of return as the budgetary strain continued to grow.[75]

Upon taking power in August 117, Hadrian faced an even greater demand on limited resources. Trajan's death encouraged opportunistic enemies in several parts of the empire to challenge Rome and its demoralized troops. While Hadrian worked to restore Rome's position vis-à-vis a range of external enemies, he felt compelled to accelerate the retrenchment actually begun under Trajan. Hadrian simply abandoned Mesopotamia and Assyria while relying on allied kings to control Armenia. In southeast Europe, Hadrian also evacuated the plains of Oltenia and Muntenia (the southeastern flank of the Carpathian Mountains) and southern Moldavia as Rome's situation deteriorated along the Lower Danube. Typical of new emperors, Hadrian's need to garner political support required spending generously (e.g., supplying grants to troops and key civilians, putting on games) and reducing taxes. While five years in power had improved the empire's financial position considerably, Hadrian was sensitive about managing resources, especially avoiding hugely expensive, major military campaigns if possible.[76]

Domestic Politics

By 122 Hadrian had solidified his political position as emperor after entering office on somewhat shaky ground. Many Roman elites disliked Hadrian early in his reign, especially after the murder of four senior senators who harbored anti-Hadrian sympathies. The emperor claimed no role in the deaths, but few believed him.[77] He managed to consolidate support through games, financial rewards, and other actions, but he had to avoid taking steps that would outrage the Roman elite and public. The greatest danger involved moves that appeared to undermine Rome's glory. Criticism of his pullbacks from some recently conquered territory prompted the emperor to employ elaborate justifications.[78] Hadrian maintained control over the core of Dacia, Trajan's greatest conquest. As the one province north of the Danube, it would seem logical for a consolidation-minded leader to abandon such an exposed salient. Hadrian's retention of it suggests he lacked the political capital or confidence to adopt such an unpopular move. At least one Roman source indicates that Hadrian's friends dissuaded him from abandoning Dacia, either for strategic or political reasons.[79] Politics thus were not a trivial consideration for the emperor, especially when assessing another fiscally draining province: Britain.

Decision-making Process

Clearly, Hadrian made his own choices. Emperors were far more influential than the governor on policy matters in a province, regardless of the latter's energy and ability.[80] The governor, of course, had to be able to respond in a crisis, but otherwise he needed imperial approval before acting in a significant matter. Strong, confident rulers such as Hadrian exercised power. The challenge for Hadrian was to obtain useful advice, something his intimidating nature did not encourage. For example, Apollodorus, Rome's most prominent architect and military engineer, received banishment after foolishly criticizing Hadrian's architectural designs.[81] More typical was Favorinus, a contemporary chastised for deferring to Hadrian's views. He argued it was only sensible "to believe the man who possesses thirty legions to be more learned than anyone else!"[82]

At times key advisors could play an important role, as they reportedly did in convincing the emperor to retain Dacia.[83] Hadrian would have received counsel from three groups while he pondered options for northern Britain. First, senior officials that Hadrian brought with him to assume key local positions would almost certainly be a part of discussions. Hadrian probably most respected the opinion of Aulus Platorius Nepos, the new governor. Previously governor in Thrace and Lower Germany as well as co-counsel with Hadrian, Nepos had become one of emperor's closest friends and trusted officials by this time. Tullius Varro, commander of the newly arrived legio VI, was apparently close to both Hadrian and Nepos. They shared a Spanish heritage, and Varro's brother had been cocounsel with Hadrian in 119.[84]

Second, key officials who came along as part of the imperial entourage were probably involved in policy discussions. Guard Prefect Septicius Clarus, commanding the Praetorian Guard detachment, and Chief Secretary Suetonius Tranquillus stood out as the most notable such figures. Suetonius' writings suggest he shared Hadrian's opposition to expanding the empire.[85] The influence of both men, however, abruptly ended in Britain with their dismissal, apparently for seditious interaction with the Empress Sabina. By 122 Hadrian hated his wife, whose presence on the trip likely was to keep her from causing trouble in Rome.[86]

In addition, Hadrian likely would have discussed matters with his *comites*— traveling companions from among his friends. Comites on the trip to Britain are not certain, but evidence suggests the entourage included Atilius Bradua. Bradua, a former governor of Britain from the late Trajan period, would have been well acquainted with the province's troubles and a useful advisor for the trip despite his own inability to curtail the rebellion. Another ex-British governor, Neratius Marcellus, may also have been present. Although his term had ended around twenty years earlier, he was reputedly close to Hadrian. Hadrian almost certainly brought along some intellectuals, especially Greeks, because he liked to surround himself with "men of genius."[87] No particular names have ever been linked with the journey to Britain.[88]

Frontier Strategic Options

These contextual factors constrained the options available to Hadrian. Before heading to the frontier, the emperor likely stopped in the provincial capital, Londinium, to meet with Roman officials and discuss the overall state of affairs.[89] Upon the completion of this business and any desired sightseeing, Hadrian and his entourage would have turned north to address the primary concern. The emperor likely sought an approach that accomplished a multitude of aims: demonstrating Roman greatness, enhancing deterrence, solidifying frontier control, and to a degree strengthening frontier defense while reducing the military burden.

Frontier Elimination

The most radical course of action would have been to withdraw from Britain given the province's limited economic and strategic value. Suetonius claims that Nero contemplated such a withdrawal upon becoming emperor in 54, but that occurred after only a decade of occupation. Ultimately he did not want to detract from his father's glory and the Romans remained.[90] By 122 expectations of vast mineral wealth had long been proven erroneous, although lead was heavily mined.[91] With the garrison comprising at least 10 percent of the entire Roman army, one can imagine Hadrian musing about the usefulness of such forces elsewhere in the empire. Appian, a mid-second-century Greek historian and Roman official, observed that the costs of administrating and securing Britain exceeded the benefits from its rule.[92] As Charles Whittaker stresses, if Rome really pursued cost-effective frontiers, then it should not have been in Britain.[93]

It is almost certain that Hadrian never seriously considered withdrawal. Abandoning Britain after nearly eighty years of rule would have been viewed as a disgrace in Rome and a blow to its prestige everywhere.[94] Despite losing money on such provinces, Appian noted that the Romans were "ashamed to set them aside."[95] The second century poet Florus, another friend of Hadrian, captured sentiment of the day by observing, "It was fine and glorious to have acquired them [remote, bare provinces], not for any value, but for the great reputation they brought to the magnificence of the empire."[96] Even if the emperor did not care about prestige and honor himself, their influence on other Romans ensured significant political costs for withdrawal. It would have been far more expedient to pull out of the more recently conquered Dacia—a step, as previously noted, Hadrian decided against.

The emperor would have been even less attracted to the opposite extreme, completing the conquest. Given the existing lack of value of the province, the Roman leaders "do not care for the rest," which offered negligible benefit, especially the Highland massif.[97] Moreover, achieving such a state of affairs would have required significant material and time commitments. History had taught the Romans that at least four intact legions would be needed for capturing the entire island.[98] Furthermore, the reluctance of the Caledonii to fight large-scale battles with the Romans would preclude a rapid victory. Hadrian had no reason to expect stability until after a long period of occupation. While the conquest of Scotland would weaken the ability of natives to resist, rebellions would inevitably ensue. Above all, the conquest of Scotland would conflict with the emperor's overall strategy of halting Roman expansion.[99]

Diplomatic Initiatives

Discounting the possibility of withdrawal from or conquest of Britain, a frontier would have to remain somewhere on the island. Hadrian had employed a range of approaches, including diplomatic initiatives, to enhance security along other frontiers. He had adopted indirect control through client kingdoms in Armenia and probably "a king for the Germans."[100] Rome, however, lacked potential surrogates north of the Tyne-Solway isthmus. The friendly Votadini did not possess the size and strength to assume the burden for protecting Roman interests.[101] The Selgovae and Novantae, the other main tribes in southern Scotland, were implacably hostile. Hadrian would not have deemed the Brigantes a viable option despite their large size and area. Even with nearly fifty years of direct rule over the tribe, at least some Brigantes remained quite rebellious.[102] Rome could have little confidence that the Brigantes would uphold Roman interests rather than use any increased freedom for troublemaking.

Given the absence of potential surrogates, the emperor could have pursued treaties with the adversarial tribes. Less delicately, he could have tried to buy peace. Although once viewed as unthinkable by the Romans, such behavior emerged in the decades leading up to Hadrian's reign. The first major example was Domitian's treaty with the Dacian king Decebalus on the Lower Danube. In the same region, Trajan seems to have paid subsidies to the Roxolani. Hadrian clearly used money in combination with other diplomatic tactics (and threats) to secure peace without fighting in the eastern part of the empire. Such treaties could reduce threats in the short term, freeing up resources for greater priorities.[103]

Hadrian, however, likely would have discounted the value of such treaties in northern Britain. Buying peace undermined the prestige of Rome and diminished its deterrent potential, especially when relied on exclusively. Employing cash subsidies tended to generate heavy criticism, as befell Domitian for his actions. It represented at best a temporary measure, which in the end likely worsened the security situation. Thus, Romans tended to avoid such measures if alternatives existed. The use of such treaties without the other party appreciating Rome's reserve strength encouraged barbarians to defect. Hadrian used such carrots only in combination with sufficient sticks to discourage adversaries from breaking treaty terms. Ultimately, the use of such treaties appears to begin in Britain toward the end of the second century, when Rome faced a more precarious situation than during Hadrian's time.[104]

Alternative Frontiers

After dismissing such courses of action, if considered at all, Hadrian likely weighed three options. First, the Romans could advance the frontier about eighty miles to the Clyde-Forth isthmus in central Scotland. In contrast to the considerable military difficulty of conquering all of Scotland, the Romans could be confident that a limited effort would gain this position. As late as the beginning of the second century, they had maintained some defenses in the area. The terrain advantages of such an advance would have been clear to Hadrian and his advisors given Roman experiences.[105] Tacitus had stressed that the Clyde and Forth line was a "good place for halting the advance ... [the isthmus] carried inland to a great depth on the tide of opposite seas, [which] are separated by only a narrow neck of land."[106] Seizing the region would severely punish the Selgovae and Novantae tribes for their actions of the past decade.[107] In addition, Rome would be better able to protect its ally, the Votadini. The Clyde-Forth isthmus would offer by far the shortest possible frontier in Britain—essentially half as wide as the Stanegate position. A barrier here would also restrict interaction between the lowland Scots and meddlesome Caledonii.

Hadrian almost certainly gave greater weight to the deficiencies of such a course of action. Although a forward shift of about eighty miles might be sold as a tactical readjustment to strengthen Rome's position, it would conflict with Hadrian's antiexpansion agenda. If the option offered indisputable advantages, the emperor might have been inclined to make an exception. However, other negatives existed. Southern Scotland had far less arable and thus less valuable land than below the Tyne-Solway position.[108] While pushing forward to the Clyde-Forth isthmus would be relatively easy, occupation of southern Scotland would require additional resources, perhaps even more troops, for an extended period. Units would be needed not only along the frontier but also throughout southern Scotland to discourage and combat troublemaking. Insufficient troops had prompted the withdrawal from this area two decades earlier.[109] Although positioning the frontier along the Clyde-Forth isthmus would sever the lowland Scots from the Caledonii, it might increase difficulties by extending Roman-controlled territory nearer to these trouble-making Caledonii.[110]

A less taxing alternative was to strengthen defenses along the existing Stanegate road. If the outbreak of troubles had been attributed largely to the reduction of troops, especially the removal of all or a significant detachment of legio

VIIII, then bolstered Stanegate positions might appeal to the emperor. Troop inadequacies had been addressed, at least partially, with the forces Hadrian had brought from the continent. Enhanced fortifications would not entail a major effort, thus limiting required resources. Moreover, maintaining the frontier at its present location would be consistent with Hadrian's desire to avoid expansion. The Romans would undoubtedly be far less vulnerable than the half decade earlier when trouble emerged.

Hadrian probably harbored serious doubts about the wisdom of such a course of action, especially for the longer term. The purpose of this trip early in his reign was to address western security concerns sufficiently so he could focus on the eastern part of the empire.[111] He did not want to have to deal with Britain again. This enhanced status quo option did not fundamentally improve Rome's security position. When problems elsewhere inevitably forced the transfer of troops from the British garrison, the frontier would again be vulnerable to disturbances.[112] Even with Hadrian's reinforcements, the frontier remained open, allowing Brigante-Scottish interaction. As mentioned earlier, this interaction had always been a key source of instability. Moreover, nothing about this option would speak to the greatness of Rome and intimidate the barbarians. Hadrian quite possibly felt such a signal was necessary to bolster deterrence prospects given that for the previous thirty years the natives had witnessed the Romans primarily retreating and reducing their force size. This option would not satisfy his desire to encourage the Romans to regard the existing frontiers as proximate boundaries and not favor further expansion.

Such a signal might have been provided by adding a palisade — a wooden fence — to the north side of the Stanegate road. Hadrian had just ordered such a structure built in central Europe on the first leg of his trip. He almost certainly would have thought about it in the context of the British frontier as well. The different environment, however, likely made a palisade less feasible or advantageous. The lack of timber in the northern part of England may have simply precluded this option. Even with adequate wood, a large fence may have been regarded as insufficient with such a large and hostile population on both sides of it. Another negative of this option would have been leaving the troops without much activity, prompting concern that such idleness would erode morale and effectiveness. Furthermore, the Stanegate road passed through a series of low-lying river valleys, whereas the northern crest of this area offered a far superior observation and control position for a line.[113]

The Idea of a Wall

If the environment suggested the need for something more elaborate than a palisade, Hadrian would have been familiar with the idea of erecting a wall. During his visit to Greece a decade earlier, Hadrian almost certainly observed the remains of Athens' Long Walls. Being well versed in Greek history, he also would have known about the construction of barriers across the Corinthian Isthmus and Gallipoli peninsula. Similarly, Hadrian was aware that Dionysius I erected walls to protect an endangered Syracuse. Among his other accomplishments, Dionysius founded Hadria, the Italian town from which the emperor's family claimed to originate. With a passion for architecture dating back to his childhood, Hadrian would have developed strong ideas about the best form and type of walls.[114]

Hadrian likely appreciated the costs and risks of building some kind of wall in the Stanegate area. The major undertaking would undoubtedly be expensive, not only to construct but also to maintain. Leaving the major threats in place, the erection of a wall probably would not facilitate a reduction in forces along the frontier, at least for some time. While a wall might enhance control to its south, the Romans risked diminishing their influence over events north of it.[115] Hostile tribes might be reluctant to challenge the obstacle but might also regard it as a sign of Rome's reluctance to fight in the Scottish Lowlands. Their ally, the Votadini tribe, would be more vulnerable. Additionally, the Roman army might lose its discipline and fighting fitness if units lay idle along and behind a barrier.[116] Ultimately, as a large expression of the empire's greatness, any wall must be effective at strengthening security on the frontier or risk actually diminishing Roman prestige in Britain.

Decision for a Strategic Defense System

A wall's advantages would have appealed to Hadrian, especially in contrast to the aforementioned alternatives. These positives can be grouped into the personal, the psychological, and the physical. Although Hadrian did not revel in the glory of conquest, he clearly enjoyed receiving adulation and renown for his endeavors. Anthony Birley, Hadrian's biographer, emphasizes the emperor's "burning ambition to excel in every art and science."[117] A grand wall that reflected Rome's greatness and secured a troublesome frontier would undoubtedly have reflected some glory on Hadrian. It would have been associated with him, whatever its actual name.[118]

While personal motivations may have been an attraction, the need to make a powerful statement about the greatness of Rome provided a more compelling rationale for such a structure.[119] As noted above, psychological dominance played a critical role in Rome's ability to rely on deterrence and obtain security. The remote, underdeveloped countryside of the Tyne-Solway isthmus would abet the psychological impression left by the construction of a vast, huge barrier. The Romans would have expected the natives to find it "impressive, even terrifying."[120] A wall would serve as a warning to barbarians that interfering with Roman territory entailed severe consequences. Furthermore, Hadrian would have been attracted to a wall's potential—in conjunction with the palisade under construction in central Europe—to help persuade Romans that the age of expansion had ended.[121]

The physical advantages of a wall would largely accrue from greatly increasing control over native movement. Essentially, a wall and its associated structures would close the frontier. Crossings would require Roman approval, allowing them to channel border traffic and facilitate tax collection.[122] More than generally controlling movement, a wall would allow the Romans largely to "divide unruly Selgovae from equally unruly Brigantes."[123] Separation of Rome's two major problems along the frontier would have been quite appealing as a possible mitigation of their troublemaking potential. In addition to the appeal of physical control, Frere suggests a possible psychological benefit.[124] The Romans might have anticipated that the Brigantes, cut off from the Scots, would become more docile and less rebellious over time.

Modern scholars debate whether the wall was intended to be a stout military barrier, a view that has tended to be in the minority since the 1920s.[125] Nevertheless, as James Crow recently observed, this perspective "underestimates the structure and physical presence of the wall but also assumes that Roman armies were able to control and dominate the military zone beyond and behind the wall, making it . . . in effect redundant."[126] The lack of such dominance appears to have been a central motivation for the construction of a barrier of unprecedented scale. Crow adds that the recently discovered pits with stakes in front of the wall suggest a military motivation if they are to make sense.[127] At a minimum, Hadrian probably regarded the obstacle as bolstering Rome's deterrent capability and the army's effectiveness. As an observation platform, it would provide valuable intelligence on native challenges and impede raiding parties from penetrating Roman territory. It would accelerate the movement of Roman forces along an east–west axis as well as provide a secure base for soldiers advancing into the Scottish Lowlands. The construction of this massive barrier may have promoted defense by simply keeping the army active and engaged. Furthermore, a wall potentially could mask Rome's vulnerability during periods when troops had to be redeployed against threats elsewhere in the empire. Most of Rome's trouble in Britain had occurred during such periods, and given their inevitability, Hadrian might have been drawn to any measure that even partially mitigated the problem. Overall, physically controlling native movement and attempting to influence their psyche seemed to be the primary advantages of a wall over alternative courses of action. Such a barrier appeared to offer the optimal way to stabilize North Britain, especially given manpower constraints, and it fit comfortably with Hadrian's worldview of how Rome could best advance security along its frontiers.[128]

Work on the resulting strategic defense system began on the eastern end of the frontier (Newcastle today). Legio VI had commenced work on Pons Aelius

("Hadrian's Bridge") over the Tyne River. At this spot the Romans also initiated construction of the wall, probably beginning with a sample section for Hadrian's review. The emperor undoubtedly played a major role in the conceptualization and design of the barrier system. A monument commemorated Hadrian's declaration that the future barrier would scatter the barbarians and protect Britania. Such a statement suggests he hoped to separate the Brigantes and Selgovae.[129]

After witnessing the start of construction, the emperor and his entourage apparently headed west for an inspection trip across the frontier.[130] This trek may be what the poet Florus characterized as Hadrian's "walk among the Britons."[131] Vindolanda, a fort halfway across the isthmus, was a likely stopping point, given evidence of preparations for such a visit. The group continued on until at least reaching the Solway, possibly even traveling down the west coast to Alauna (Maryport). Hadrian's friend Marcus Maenius Agrippa, who sailed to Britain with the emperor, had established a new base there with his one-thousand-man, mixed unit, *cohors I Aelia Hispanorum*. The Romans constructed an approximately twenty-five-mile strategic defense system along this Cumbrian coast, apparently to safeguard the western flank and prevent efforts at tax evasion. On his return trip to the east coast, Hadrian would have inspected the construction work, but progress would have been minimal by his departure from Britain before the winter of 122–23.[132]

The emperor would have remained informed of developments through correspondence with Nepos, the man left behind to oversee the work. During 124 the governor's missives must have painted a disturbing picture. Despite only the second year of construction, the Romans in Britain had apparently concluded the initial scheme was fundamentally flawed. As a result, major design revisions were instituted, something Nepos would have been unlikely to order without at least the approval of Hadrian. A range of explanations have been suggested for the modifications.[133] Nepos may have wanted to expedite construction, hoping to complete the project before his departure. However, the nature of some of the changes, especially adding forts to the wall, would seem likely to increase, not reduce, construction time. Another suggestion is that the Romans simply decided to move the forts from the Stanegate road to the wall as a matter of convenience, concentrating forces along one line instead of two. This rationale, however, made sense from the outset.

Most likely the Romans concluded that the original design failed to provide them with sufficient forward-based forces to maximize the barrier's usefulness in the face of a mounting threat perception. Initially Hadrian and Nepos may not have appreciated local conditions and requirements. It has been speculated that the emperor's aesthetic passion for visual appeal over practical considerations could account for the problem.[134] Although such a perspective may explain the flawed design, the rapid recognition of its inadequacy—long before completion of the system—probably was due to native reaction.[135] The Romans would not have expected the Brigantes or Scottish Lowlanders to embrace the wall, but they probably underestimated the extent of angst and hostility provoked by a barrier that would disrupt long-standing economic and social linkages. In particular, cutting off part of Brigante territory may have produced considerable opposition.

These reactions likely heightened Roman concerns about stability, prompting changes to the wall system. Essentially, they merged the forts of the Stanegate with the wall to combine the frontier defense and frontier control missions. The army could now respond more expeditiously to provocations and could possibly employ a more forward-looking policy. The presence of several cavalry and mixed cohort units supports this notion. Still, the need to spread forces among so many forts would limit the size of any rapid response and suggests an attempt to balance presence and policing with defense. Plus, the Romans constructed three strong points (Bewcastle, Netherby, and Birrens) beyond Hadrian's Wall in the southwest corner of Scotland. These forts may have been to protect the small part of the Brigante tribe cut off by the barrier, but they more likely reflected Roman concern about controlling the outlying areas of Brigantia and providing early warning of any trouble. The addition of these outposts bolsters the belief of strident native opposition to the barrier. Surveillance from these outposts would have been particularly valued given their placement in front of the wall's more vulnerable turf segment. The Romans apparently did not believe such formal positions were necessary on the eastern side.[136]

By the departure of Nepos, the Romans had made great progress on Hadrian's Wall. The lack of testimonial citations etched on the curtain referencing his August 127 replacement, Trebius Germanus, suggests the basic structure's completion by that date. Whether driven by security concerns or Nepos' desire to finish the job, the building pace appears to have been rapid. The construction method employed was the type used when the Romans were in a hurry, according to a treatise by Vitruvius, a first century BCE architect.[137] Archeological research has suggested that building all of the components occupied Roman forces for more than a decade, but by the end of the 120s they probably considered the barrier system "operational."[138]

Security Developments with a Fortified Frontier

In 138, while Titus Flavius Secundus, commander of *cohors I Hamiorum sagittariorum* (Hamian archers) at the Carvoran fort, helped secure the British frontier, an ailing and dispirited Hadrian died in Italy.[139] Although the emperor had broken ties with Nepos and most old friends during his ineffectual final years, Hadrian left a tremendous legacy of frontier works, of which the British barrier was the foremost such structure. Along what "was quite clearly the most exclusive frontier line the Romans ever built," northern Britain had apparently been relatively quiet since the addition of the strategic defense system.[140] In the short term, the wall favorably shifted the military balance and introduced some caution among the natives, although trouble existed north of the barrier. With Hadrian's death, the larger question of the barrier discouraging the Romans from contemplating further advancement would now be tested.

Abandonment of the Wall

Hadrian hoped his chosen successor, Antoninus Pius, would continue a defensive orientation rather than initiate a return to Trajanic expansionism. Although the new emperor possessed a restrained nature, he felt politically vulnerable without any army service. Thus, like Claudius nearly a century earlier, Antoninus sought an act of military glory. In searching for an appropriate target, Britain appealed to him and his advisors, again like Claudius. The army leadership on the island may have agitated for an offensive to bolster troop morale, due to limited activity since construction of the barrier. Although only speculative, the symbolism of advancing beyond Hadrian's Wall may actually have increased the political attractiveness of Scotland as the locale for an offensive.[141]

While the political benefits of advancing into Scotland suggest Hadrian had not been able to fundamentally alter the strategic culture in Rome, the barrier's basic contribution to physical security had not been absolute. Local circumstances provided at least a plausible rationale for the desired political act. Hadrian's appointment of Sextus Julius Severus, Rome's top general, as governor in 130 or 131 suggests at least a high threat perception, although an exploding revolt in Judea soon required his transfer east. Julius Severus may have influenced subsequent events in Britain through conversations with Lollius Urbicus, his chief of staff during the Jewish War (132–35). They likely discussed the British situation in the context of how best to achieve security against rebellious natives. In 139 Antoninus appointed Urbicus as governor of Britain, apparently with a mandate to extend Rome's zone of control. Many Roman writers and modern historians have questioned reports of a native attack prompting the offensive, but they accept the general situation in southern Scotland as unstable. One possibility is that the pro-Roman Votadini had been attacked by the Selgovae and perhaps the Novantae. Although Hadrian's Wall provided a strong base from which to project power, the army's limited presence beyond the barrier likely exacerbated trouble in southern Scotland, an area the Romans still wanted to influence.[142]

Seizing control provided the surest path to such influence, which Urbicus and the Roman garrison quickly achieved. Victory coins in 142–43 indicate that the army easily advanced to the Clyde-Forth isthmus.[143] Rather than put up fierce resistance, the more hostile elements of the Selgovae and possibly the Novantae simply retreated north. Agricola had advanced further in the first century, but for Antoninus and Urbicus, apparently enough glory had been achieved. The difficult task of stabilizing southern Scotland remained. Nevertheless, with the narrowest neck in Britain and excellent command of the surrounding area, the Clyde-Forth isthmus facilitated Romanization of southern Scotland by separating it from the more hostile natives to the north.[144]

Although Hadrian's Wall clearly did not completely solve security problems in North Britain, the Romans must have judged it as useful since they immediately began construction of a second wall—this time across the Clyde-Forth isthmus. Named for the emperor, the almost forty-mile Antonine Wall ranged from Bridgeness on the Forth to Old Kirkpatrick on the Clyde.[145] The course of the turf-block structure took advantage of the area's escarpments and crags to gain a dominant position. Initially the Romans planned to space forts every 6 to 8 miles, similar to the intervals along Hadrian's Wall, but before completion of the barrier, the army decided to sharply decrease the gaps between forts from 1.5 to 3 miles to facilitate better surveillance and reinforcement from nearby forces.[146] The threat of Caledonian raiding probably contributed significantly to this change. The Romans also constructed some outpost forts north of the Antonine Wall to abet intelligence gathering and enable protection for friendly locals on the Fife peninsula.[147] As a part of establishing control in southern Scotland, they also rebuilt forts from a half century earlier along Dere Street, the major road running up southern Scotland.[148] The now redundant Hadrian's Wall entered into essentially caretaker status, with the army abandoning most forts, removing milecastle gates, and filling the vallum across from these milecastles.[149]

Return to Hadrian's Wall

British history after the advance to Scotland is poorly understood and disputed, but trouble apparently erupted in the mid-150s south of the frontier. The Brigantes rebelled, inflicting heavy casualties on the Roman army before the situation stabilized by 155. The Romans continued to regard the situation as serious given the arrival of legion reinforcements from Germany and the unusual appointment of Numisius Junior as commander of legio VI. He had previously commanded another legion, and Romans rarely commanded two distinct legions. At some point, an alarmed Governor Verus redeployed forces south to improve policing of the Brigantes area, possibly even withdrawing from the Antonine Wall. A potential benefit of Hadrian's Wall apparently had been separating the Brigantes from the Novantae and Selgovae in southern Scotland, but they were all now south of the Antonine Wall. If the Romans withdrew from the Antonine Wall, it has been suggested that Verus may have acted without the emperor's approval, given his replacement and possible Roman reoccupation of the Clyde-Forth line. Antoninus Pius likely would have opposed abandoning his barrier and surrendering southern Scotland, whose conquest marked one of his main military achievements.[150]

Upon taking over from the deceased Antoninus Pius in 161, Marcus Aurelius considered the proper British frontier without emotional baggage and apparently ordered either Gov. Statius Priscus or his successor, Calpurnius Agricola, to withdraw to Hadrian's Wall. This move happened by 164, at the latest. Beyond the aforementioned improvement in policing Brigante territory, the pullback may have been encouraged by the limited economic value of southern Scotland. A central factor in the shift almost certainly was other growing challenges faced by the empire, especially along the Danube, which required reducing the British garrison. For great powers confronting security threats on multiple fronts, strategic defenses theoretically provide a force multiplier that abets security in such a demanding environment. The lack of secure control south of the Antonine barrier, however, appears to have undermined potential force savings.[151]

After more than twenty years in caretaker status, Hadrian's Wall required heavy expenditures to return it to operational status. The recent instability with the Brigantes highlighted the critical need to ensure a secure military zone along the frontier to limit crossing and potential collaboration. However, either because of reflecting on lessons learned from the earlier period of use or because of an altered tactical situation, the Romans somewhat changed their approach to employing this strategic defense system. The barrier's physical contribution to control and as a base of operations did not seem to obviate the need for a more robust presence throughout the frontier area. Thus the Romans retained forts along Dere Street in southern Scotland to be outposts, thus rectifying the mistake of only placing such structures on the west side in the 120s. By one estimate, 4,300 troops now resided north of the wall, with a heavy emphasis on cavalry to facilitate patrolling. Similarly, the Romans increased policing of the entire Brigante territory, with a majority of the troops in northern Britain—about 18,500 of the 33,000 troops—based south of Hadrian's Wall. The continued rebelliousness of the Brigantes would have been a disappointing, albeit not surprising, state of affairs. The notion that separating the Brigantes from the Scottish tribes would domesticate the former had turned out to be false. Alternatively, the frontier in central Scotland had allowed the Brigantes and Lowland Scot tribes to interact more freely again, reenergizing the former's rebelliousness. Regardless, the unit deployments reflect a desire to maintain tight control over the Brigantes, especially in the northwest region.[152]

A common finding about strategic defenses is that their contribution to security depends on adequate manning and maintenance. When the Romans violated this requirement in the early 180s, native attacks resumed after a couple of decades of apparent calm. As usual, trouble elsewhere prompted imperial officials to redeploy significant forces to the continent.[153] A famous passage from

Cassius Dio at this time comments that the enemy breached the "wall."[154] Historians regard it as unclear if this passage refers to Hadrian's Wall, although damage to the Corbridge fort a few miles to the south favors this interpretation. Some commentators, however, contend that this describes Scottish tribes passing through the Forth isthmus and the abandoned Antonine Wall to challenge Roman influence in the southern Scotland. Either way, the situation had become quite serious, and the governor was killed in 182 or 183 while trying to restore order. The resulting struggle has been labeled the greatest war during the reign of Emperor Commodus.[155]

Although the new governor, Ulpius Marcellus, achieved victory in 184, sustained stability was not possible given internal turmoil, external requirements, and growing adversary strength. Marcellus abandoned Rome's northernmost outpost forts in the Scottish Lowlands—Birrens on the west side and Newstead (and probably Cappuck) to the east—while upgrading those closer to Hadrian's Wall (e.g., Risingham and High Rochester). The martinet Marcellus also apparently alienated the garrison to such an extent that the emperor, fearing a mutiny, recalled him and the legion commanders. Taking advantage of the resulting demoralized Roman force were the Maeatae, a confederacy of Scottish tribes that likely included the Selgovae and Novantae. By the end of the second century, the Scots had essentially coalesced into two main groups, the Maeatae and the aforementioned Caledonii.[156]

A deteriorating military balance prompted the Romans to seek political accommodation with both confederations in the late 190s.[157] These agreements essentially represented efforts to buy peace. While the post-Marcellus era had meant a somewhat diminished Roman force in Britain, the entire empire entered a period of turmoil and civil war after the murders of Emperor Commodus (192) and Emperor Pertinax (193). Clodius Albinus, the British governor, challenged to be the new ruler in 196 by taking a substantial component of the British garrison to fight on the continent.[158] Not surprisingly given Roman vulnerability, the Scots violated treaty terms and attacked. This time they appear to have crossed Hadrian's Wall with a sustained if not deep penetration of Roman territory.[159] The only viable option for new governor Virius Lupus to restore calm was through providing the natives increased financial contributions.[160]

The Severan Reconstruction

Septimius Severus ultimately won control of the empire and began moving in the early third century to bolster Rome's position in Britain. As a part of this effort, he intended a major refurbishment of Hadrian's Wall, which had deteriorated without the necessary maintenance.[161] Any serious upkeep probably ceased when Albinus removed a large part of the garrison as part of his quest to become emperor. Moreover, fighting possibly exacerbated the deterioration through battle damage or preventing repairs. The construction work, likely lasting until 207 or 208, was so extensive that the emperor's biographer in the *Augustan History* actually credited him, not Hadrian, with building the wall "across the island to the Ocean at each end."[162] In recognition of this "greatest glory of his reign," Severus also received the title Britannicus.[163]

Although the Romans had restored control of the frontier and rebuilt Hadrian's Wall, Severus decided to invade Scotland. Several factors encouraged the emperor to travel to Britain in 208 and go on the offensive, beginning with a desire for "Britannicus" to achieve greater glory.[164] He also supposedly wanted to get his sons—Caracalla and Geta—away from the harmful influences of Rome. Concern apparently lingered about the morale and focus of the garrison after the civil war and native struggles, in particular with the building effort over. Severus certainly wanted to punish the Scottish tribes for their previous troublemaking. Reports of their continued aggression, however, probably were Roman propaganda to justify the offensive.[165] Furthermore, because Severus had ordered the largest army expansion of the imperial era with three additional legions and a proportional increase in auxiliary units, he had the troops for such an action. The existence of the wall, even its major refurbishment by Severus, appears to have had no influence in his decision to advance beyond the barrier in force. Again, Hadrian's hope that such barriers would discourage Roman expansion and adventurism does not seem to have been successful.

Whether Severus wanted to conquer the rest of the island is unknown, but his large invasion force suggests considerable ambition. The emperor employed the entire garrison as well as considerable reinforcements from the continent. He used the combined fleets of Germany, Moesia, Pannonia, and Britain as a part of two-pronged advance: by land up Dere Street and by sea up the east coast. Although initial successes prompted some Scottish concessions, problems soon arose as the Caledonii avoided Rome's desired large-scale battle and the Maeatae revolted behind the advancing the army. Coins indicate a peace settlement in 210, but the stubborn Severus was in York planning another offensive when he died the following year. His son Caracalla, the new co-emperor, may have carried out this expedition in a perfunctory fashion, but he held no interest in Britain and soon returned to Rome.[166]

Roman Security in the Third and Fourth Centuries

Before Caracalla departed Britain, he negotiated peace with the Maeatae and Caledonii in exchange for Roman subsidies and withdrawal of all outposts north of Hadrian's Wall. Although the price was high, this agreement produced a long period of relative stability. No wars are recorded for the rest of the third century.

Cognizant of Rome's latent strength, the Scottish tribes apparently had little interest in disturbing the status quo as long as they received their subsidies and the Romans did not interfere in their homeland. Facing increased pressure elsewhere in the empire, the Romans lacked interest in future invasions of Scotland. They maintained Hadrian's Wall, but over the course of the century, its garrison shrank considerably and many forts were abandoned. While some effort was redirected to address the growing naval threat along Britain's southern and eastern shores, decay of the island's legion fortresses further suggests that large detachments had been permanently transferred to the continent. Essentially, Britain became a marginal concern, especially as the Roman Empire suffered through a seemingly endless series of civil wars and ineffectual imperial reigns.[167]

During the fourth century, Roman security in Britain sharply deteriorated. Consolidation of tribes had produced more organized and capable enemies, including the Picts (formerly the Caledonii), the Scots in Ireland, and the Franks and Saxons from the continent.[168] Attacks from the Picts in the north prompted not only a punitive campaign by Constantius in 306 but also apparently the first significant repairs to Hadrian's Wall installations in a century.[169] With all major adversaries now capable of long-range naval actions, especially the Saxons, coastal fortifications continued to receive most resources.[170] In northern Britain, the Romans enhanced the defenses along the Cumbrian coast to protect the vulnerable western flank of Hadrian's Wall from the Picts. They also built new forts farther down the west coast to defend against the Scotti from Ireland. Already, over the course of several decades in the third century, the Romans had constructed a series of forts along the eastern and southern coasts of England in part to deal with the Franks and especially the Saxons.

Despite these defenses, Roman naval and land forces proved inadequate to prevent growing insecurity throughout the fourth century. The garrison's continuing involvement in imperial politics and civil wars contributed to Roman weakness in Britain. In addition to frequent raiding, large-scale uprisings occurred in 342–43 and 367. Ammianus Marcellinus dubiously characterized the 367 attack as a coordinated effort among the Scots, Picts, and Saxons, but he more believably describes the successful Pict operation in northern Britain.[171] Using naval transports, they bypassed Hadrian's Wall and isolated the force along the frontier, humiliating the Roman commander, Fullofaudes. The emperor responded to this attack by dispatching considerable forces to Britain and undertaking the last significant work on the wall system. The outflanking highlighted the barrier's vulnerability once adversaries possessed naval superiority. Moreover, Rome was soon recalling troops again and raiding continued at will along the coasts. By 410 the army had essentially abandoned Britain.[172]

Hadrian's Wall had already ceased to be an operational barrier by this time. Frontier units garrisoned along it had deteriorated until they were of negligible combat value. Instead, Roman commanders, such as Stilicho and Constantine, relied on mobile field armies deployed to defeat adversaries in their late fourth-century operations in Britain.[173] After the end of official Roman Britain, Hadrian's Wall was maintained in a limited fashion by the now independent frontier units that remained in place. Some of the forts on or near the wall (e.g., Birdoswald, Vindolanda) show evidence of construction work and occupation for up to a century after the Roman era.[174] Eventually such efforts ended and the barrier slowly deteriorated. Beyond the erosion of the centuries, its stones provided a near endless supply of building material for local farmers, ranchers, and ultimately the British army in its construction of a road from Newcastle to Carlisle during the eighteenth century.

Conclusion

Standing atop the remains of Housesteads fort (Vercovicium) on the central section of Hadrian's Wall and looking over its magnificent view, one cannot help but be awed by what was the "most elaborate and costly of all Rome's frontierworks."[175] How should we assess its effects and effectiveness? If Hadrian sought personal glory, he succeeded behind his wildest imagination. Today his name is largely known because of association with the famous wall, rather than his myriad other accomplishments as emperor. The more critical questions of effects and effectiveness involve the wall's psychological and physical contribution to Rome's rule of Britain and more broadly the empire.

Maintenance of Hadrian's Wall for nearly three centuries as well as the construction of the imitative Antonine Wall suggests the Romans regarded it as valuable, at least in comparison to alternative policy choices. The scale of the barrier suggests it performed a symbolic role in exhibiting Rome's strength and greatness, although the extent to which the natives found it intimidating is impossible to judge given the absence of their documented views. In modern parlance, the Romans apparently attempted to at least partially substitute deterrence by denial for deterrence by punishment. Long periods of peace occur, but they are punctuated with outbreaks of violence that suggest the barrier's "psychological weight" could not trump concrete contextual factors. Both before and after construction of the wall, difficulties most often emerged when the Romans transferred forces from Britain to address crises elsewhere. Thus the wall could not substitute for a large number of troops nor does it appear to have masked periods of Roman weakness, at least not for any extended period of time. Native attacks during such windows of opportunity suggest limits to Rome's deterrent policy and the wall's contribution to it. This dynamic contributed to the seemingly cyclical nature of rebellions in northern Britain during the second century. Troop relocations would only be safely undertaken in the third century when a distracted Rome abandoned projecting power into Scotland and reached a financial accommodation with the natives.

In assessing the influence of Hadrian's Wall on the military balance, one must define the discussion as being about the entire strategic defense system. The Romans hoped it would facilitate frontier control and, to a lesser degree, frontier defense. In general, through establishing a three-hundred-foot-wide series of obstacles, the barrier allowed the Romans to control frontier crossings. It provided both a physical obstruction as well as an excellent surveillance and communication platform. Individual or small groups might have been able to get through, but not large assemblies. This outcome is not surprising given the lack of alternative passages on this narrow front with water on both sides. The exceptions occurred when the system was not properly manned or maintained. This result reflects a common theme that physical obstacles are not a panacea that eliminates the threat. Rather, they are productive if employed with proper operational status, a core issue in the next chapter on the Ming Great Wall of China.

As a defensive network, the wall was not impenetrable nor, as often pointed out, did the Romans likely expect it to be such a bastion although it did have defensive functions. The wall guarded against external attack, and direct forays against it appear rare. It also provided a base of operations from which to advance to the north or south in response to periodic trouble. The Romans employed outpost and hinterland forts to assist in control of these areas and increased such efforts over time. The need for this expansion highlights the limits of a linear approach across a broad area with an unruly population, especially if one desires to influence events beyond the barrier. The Romans apparently appreciated that conditions in northern Britain did not fit reliance on a pure strategic defense, although they perhaps had excessive expectations for the structure initially.

The most likely counterfactual to a wall would have been building more distributed forts throughout the region. Such an option would have clearly reduced frontier control while possibly facilitating better stability and influence throughout the area given the resources available. It also would not have improved conventional defense performance. Ultimately, a Roman decision to forgo the barrier would have meant either ensuring a larger troop presence in the province or tolerating greater instability and violence. Given that an increased commitment of troops would risk greater instability on other frontiers, this seems unlikely to be provided on a long-term basis because the Romans already allocated a disproportional part of their force structure to this nonstrategic corner of the empire. Thus the province would likely have had less stability, perhaps prompting officials earlier to embrace financial "incentives" to mollify the natives as occurred at the end of the second century. Without the barrier, the price of such arrangements likely would have been higher, if even acceptable to the adversary.

As a delimitation of the Roman frontier, the barrier also appears to have had a modest influence on subsequent regimes, but one inextricably linked to the underlying contextual factors that encouraged the Roman frontier to remain along the Tyne-Solway line. The wall's existence did not prevent Antoninus Pius and Septimius Severus from launching major invasions north within the first eighty years of its existence. Its symbolism possibly even encouraged the advance by the former, Hadrian's successor. In such an authoritarian system, the internal effects of a barrier are sharply constrained by the whims of leaders. The Romans did return the frontier to the wall both times; subsequently, the Tyne-Solway line generally became accepted as the proper border to both natives and Romans. It is unclear whether Hadrian's Wall contributed to this outcome in addition to an underlying recognition that this position marked the appropriate boundary given relative strengths and interests. The Greek historian Appian observed a few years after Hadrian's reign, "The Romans have aimed to preserve their empire by the exercise of prudence rather than to extend their sway indefinitely over poverty-stricken and profitless tribes of barbarians."[176] This view was not embraced by all Romans, and their behavior still ran somewhat counter to it, yet ultimately Hadrian's Wall probably contributed marginally to move the Romans in that direction.

It is the complementary value of Hadrian's Wall that represents the most critical lesson for this barrier. Given its iconic status today, two millennia later, one can easily forget that the Romans employed an array of tools along the frontier. Hadrian's Wall was clearly not a panacea that solved the frontier problem in Britain. The Romans, however, found the wall constructive, especially given that they lacked the resources to conquer the island completely and lacked the political temperament to pull back. For the Romans, the wall provided a range of contributions: (a) bolstering both psychological and physical dimensions of deterrence; (b) abetting control, policing, and protection of the frontier; and (c) facilitating both offensive and defensive combat operations. It worked best when properly manned and maintained and when integrated with other military, diplomatic, and financial resources. The extent to which Roman officials appreciated its value as a complementary tool is not clear. A tension exists between the massive resources from large-scale strategic defenses and the reality of their benefit being maximized not as a stand-alone solution. That is, a question exists whether, even if effective, are they sufficiently efficient to justify the resources required? As the book moves forward through history, this issue deserves close attention because without an appreciation of the conditions under which and the extent to which strategic defenses are likely to contribute to security, it is unlikely they will be used in a constructive manner.

Notes

1. Susan P. Mattern, *Rome and the Enemy: Imperial Strategy in the Principate* (Berkeley and Los Angeles: University of California Press, 1999), 110.

2. Anthony R. Birley, *Hadrian: the Restless Emperor* (London: Routledge, 1997), 124; and Sheppard Frere, *Britannia: A History of Roman Britain* (London: Routledge, 1987), 111.

3. Anthony Birley, *Lives of the Later Caesars: The First Part of the Augustan History, with Newly Compiled Lives of Nerva & Trajan* (London: Penguin Books, 1976), 67–68; and Birley, *Hadrian*, 115.

4. C. R. Whittaker, *Frontiers of the Roman Empire: A Social and Economic Study* (Baltimore: The Johns Hopkins University Press, 1994), 46–47; and Birley, *Hadrian*, 115.

5. See Adrian Goldsworthy, *Roman Warfare* (London: Cassell, 2000), 122, 151–59; Whittaker, *Frontiers of the Roman Empire*, 60–71; Brian Campbell, *War and Society in Imperial Rome, 31 BC–AD 284* (London: Routledge, 2002), 17–18; David Shotter, *Roman Frontier in Britain*, (Lancaster, England: Carnegie Publishing, 1996) 3; and Mattern, *Rome and the Enemy*, 118.

6. See Birley, *Hadrian*, 84, 90, 104, 115, 123; Frere, *Britannia*, 111; Birley, *Lives of the Later Caesars*, 62; Shotter, *Roman Frontier in Britain*, 54; and David Breeze, "The Edge of the World: Imperial Frontier and Beyond," in *The Roman Era*, ed. Peter Salway (Oxford: Oxford University Press, 2002), 184.

7. A Roman mile at 4,856 feet (5,000 Roman feet) is slightly shorter than a statute mile of 5,280 feet. A Roman foot is equal to approximately 11.65 inches. Unless specifically indicated, distances reflect modern standards. Birley, *Lives of the Later Caesars*, 68–69.

8. Frere, *Britannia*, 114.

9. See Guy de la Bédoyère, *Hadrian's Wall: History and Guide* (Stroud, Gloucestershire: Tempus, 2000), 21–23; Nic Fields, *Hadrian's Wall: AD 122–140* (Oxford: Osprey, 2003), 12–13, 36; James Crow, "The Northern Frontier of Britain from Trajan to Antoninus Pius," in *A Companion to Roman Britain*, ed. Malcolm Todd (Malden, MA: Blackwell, 2007), 122–23; and Nic Fields, *Rome's Northern Frontier AD 70–235: Beyond Hadrian's Wall* (Oxford: Osprey, 2005), 12.

10. Fields, *Hadrian's Wall*, 28; Crow, "Northern Frontier," 122; Bédoyère, *Hadrian's Wall*, 20; and Shotter, *Roman Frontier in Britain*, 66.

11. Shotter, *Roman Frontier in Britain*, 63, 66; Fields, *Hadrian's Wall*, 12; and Frere, *Britannia*, 116–17, 122.

12. Crow, "Northern Frontier," 130–31; Whittaker, *Frontiers of the Roman Empire*, 82–83; Breeze, "Edge of the World," 179,188; Fields, *Hadrian's Wall*, 36; and Michael Fulford, "A Second Start: From the Defeat of Boudicca to the Third Century," *The Roman Era*, ed. Peter Salway (Oxford: Oxford University Press, 2002), 58.

13. Bédoyère, *Hadrian's Wall*, 15.

14. Breeze, "Edge of the World," 178; Fields, *Hadrian's Wall*, 16; and Crow, "Northern Frontier," 125.

15. Fields, *Hadrian's Wall*, 16; Bédoyère, *Hadrian's Wall*, 17; Shotter, *Roman Frontier in Britain*, 64; and Crow, "Northern Frontier," 125–26. At least one fort, Carrawburgh, was added in a few years with the construction of Drumburgh and Newcastle much later to close perceived gaps.

16. H. H. Scullard, *Roman Britain: Outpost of the Empire* (London: Thames & Hudson, 1979), 60; and Fields, *Hadrian's Wall*, 40.

17. See Crow, "Northern Frontier," 120, 123–24, 130; Shotter, *Roman Frontier in Britain*, 60, 65; Frere, *Britannia*, 119; Fields, *Hadrian's Wall*, 15; and Bédoyère, *Hadrian's Wall*, 18–19.

18. See Birley, *Hadrian*, 128; Fields, *Northern Frontier*, 6; and Gordon Maxwell, "The Roman Penetration of the North in the Late First Century AD," in *A Companion to Roman Britain*, ed. Malcolm Todd (Malden, MA: Blackwell, 2007), 75–76.

19. Malcolm Todd, "The Claudian Conquest and Its Consequences," in *A Companion to Roman Britain*, ed. Malcolm Todd (Malden, MA: Blackwell, 2007), 42–44; and Mattern, *Rome and the Enemy*, 60, 102, 156, 159.

20. Breeze, "Edge of the World," 173–74; Goldsworthy, *Roman Warfare*, 122; Shotter, *Roman Frontier in Britain*, 17; and Todd, "Claudian Conquest," 44–45.

21. Todd, "Claudian Conquest," 49–50, 53–55; and Richard J. Brewer, ed. *The Second Augustan Legion and the Roman Military Machine* (Cardiff, U.K.: National Museum & Galleries of Wales, 2002), 33, 52, 165.

22. Mattern, *Rome and the Enemy*, 97, 102; Goldsworthy, *Roman Warfare*, 149; and Richard J. Brewer, *Roman Fortresses and Their Legions* (London: Society of Antiquaries and National Museum & Galleries of Wales, 2000), 85.

23. Mattern, *Rome and the Enemy*, 102.

24. Fulford, "Second Start," 43.

25. Frere, *Britannia*, 41.

26. T. W. Potter and Catherine Johns, *Roman Britain* (New York: Barnes & Noble, 1992), 48; and Frere, *Britannia*, 82–83.

27. Ibid., 83.

28. Ibid., 83; and Todd, "Claudian Conquest," 57.

29. Frere, *Britannia*, 90, 100; Fulford, "Second Start," 45; and Breeze, "Edge of the World," 176.

30. See Mattern, *Rome and the Enemy*, 201–2; Antonio Santosuosso, *Storming the Heavens: Soldiers, Emperors, and Civilians in the Roman Empire* (Boulder: Westview, 2001), 152; Fulford, "Second Start," 46; Frere, *Britannia*, 107–8; Shotter, *Roman Frontier in Britain*, 39–40; and Crow, "Northern Frontier," 118.

31. Crow, "Northern Frontier," 116–18; Fields, *Rome's Northern Frontier*, 20–22, 29; and Shotter, *Roman Frontier in Britain*, 39–40.

32. Frere, *Britannia*, 111.

33. See Alan Bowman, *Life and Letters on the Roman Frontier: Vindolanda and Its People* (New York: Routledge, 1994), 13–14, 21, 25, 155; Frere, *Britannia*, 102; Breeze, "Edge of the World," 178; and Fields, *Hadrian's Wall*, 9, 11.

34. Crow, "Northern Frontier," 119.

35. Shotter, *Roman Frontier in Britain*, 53; Fulford "Second Start," 46; and Frere, *Britannia*, 107–9.

36. Breeze, "Edge of the World," 178; Bowman, *Life and Letters*, 24; and Frere, *Britannia*, 109.

37. Anthony R. Birley, *Fasti of Roman Britain* (Oxford: Clarendon, 1981), 93.

38. Birley, *Lives of the Later Caesars*, 62.

39. See Brewer, *Roman Fortresses and Their Legions*, 58, 83–94; Birley, *Fasti of Roman Britain*, 220–22; Frere, *Britannia*, 122–24; Shotter, *Roman Frontier in Britain*, 58; Mattern, *Rome and the Enemy*, 103; and Fulford, "Second Start," 46.

40. Bowman, *Life and Letters*, 51.

41. Peter Salway, ed., *The Roman Era* (Oxford: Oxford University Press, 2002), 211.

42. Frere, *Britannia*, 41–42, 92, 111; Maxwell, "Roman Penetration," 77–78; Shotter, *Roman Frontier in Britain*, 126; and Breeze, "Edge of the World," 187.

43. Frere, *Britannia*, 111.

44. See Mattern, *Rome and the Enemy*, 72; Fields, *Rome's Northern Frontier*, 16–19, 45–46; Maxwell, "Roman Penetration," 77–78; and Duncan Campbell, *Siege Warfare in the Roman World, 146 BC–AD 378* (Oxford: Osprey, 2005), 56–57.

45. Breeze, "Edge of the World," 184.

46. See Frere, *Britannia*, 1–2.

47. Arther Ferrill, *Roman Imperial Grand Strategy* (Lanham, MD: University Press of America, 1991), 22.

48. See ibid., 22, 24; Goldsworthy, *Roman Warfare*, 24, 145; Bowman, *Life and Letters*, 34; and Mattern, *Rome and the Enemy*, 83.

49. Goldsworthy, *Roman Warfare*, 126–27; and Fields, *Hadrian's Wall*, 14, 40.

50. See Mattern, *Rome and the Enemy*, 83; Campbell, *War and Society in Imperial Rome*, 48; and Goldsworthy, *Roman Warfare*, 145. For example, one study from the Antoninus Pius reign (138–161) found that the army included 338 of five-hundred-man units and 48 of the one-thousand-man units (Mattern, *Rome and the Enemy*, 83).

51. Mattern, *Rome and the Enemy*, 103.

52. Breeze, "Edge of the World," 184; and Birley, *Hadrian*, 123–24.

53. Birley, *Hadrian*, 3–4; and Mattern, *Rome and the Enemy*, 33.

54. Elizabeth Speller, *Following Hadrian: A Second-Century Journey through the Roman Empire* (New York: Oxford University Press, 2003), 61–62.

55. Birley, *Hadrian*, 1; Santosuosso, *Storming the Heavens*, 126; and Fields, *Hadrian's Wall*, 35.

56. Mattern, *Rome and the Enemy*, 171.

57. Shotter, *Roman Frontier in Britain*, 54.

58. See Whittaker, *Frontiers of the Roman Empire*, 29, 35–36; Birley, *Hadrian*, 96; and Breeze, "Edge of the World," 178.

59. Whittaker, *Frontiers of the Roman Empire*, 49–53; and Santosuosso, *Storming the Heavens*, 123.

60. Goldsworthy, *Roman Warfare*, 122; and Mattern, *Rome and the Enemy*, 202.

61. Santosuosso, *Storming the Heavens*, 118; Birley, *Hadrian*, 116; and Mattern, *Rome and the Enemy*, 121.

62. Campbell, *War and Society in Imperial Rome*, 135.

63. Birley, *Hadrian*, 62–64, 169, 182; Mattern, *Rome and the Enemy*, 199; and Speller, *Following Hadrian*, 56.

64. Birley, *Hadrian*, 115–16, 209–10; Frere, *Britannia*, 110; Campbell, *War and*

Society in Imperial Rome, 134–35; Fields, *Hadrian's Wall,* 35; Santosuosso, *Storming the Heavens,* 120; and Goldsworthy, *Roman Warfare,* 156.

65. See Birley, *Hadrian,* 1, 32, 49, 52–53, 108, 116–18, 211; Mattern, *Rome and the Enemy,* 112–13, 198–99, 205–6; Crow, "Northern Frontier," 130–31; Fields, *Rome's Northern Frontier,* 46; Birley, *Lives of the Later Caesars,* 60, 81; and Speller, *Following Hadrian,* 69.

66. See Mattern, *Rome and the Enemy,* 108, 111, 119, 122; Birley, *Hadrian,* 212, 287–88; and Edward Luttwak, *The Grand Strategy of the Roman Empire: From the First Century A.D. to the Third* (Baltimore: John Hopkins University Press, 1976), 137.

67. Mattern, *Rome and the Enemy,* 83.

68. Speller, *Following Hadrian,* 69.

69. Birley, *Hadrian,* 287–88.

70. Mattern, *Rome and the Enemy,* 88, 108; and Fields, *Rome's Northern Frontier,* 45–46.

71. Luttwak, *Grand Strategy of the Roman Empire,* 125.

72. Ibid.

73. See Mattern, *Rome and the Enemy,* 115–19, 122, 171, 193–94; Goldsworthy, *Roman Warfare,* 154–55; and Birley, *Hadrian,* 46, 272–73.

74. Mattern, *Rome and the Enemy,* 117.

75. See Birley, *Hadrian,* 56, 73–75, 78; Mattern, *Rome and the Enemy,* 93, 103, 108, 148–49; Shotter, *Roman Frontier in Britain,* 70; and Campbell, *War and Society in Imperial Rome,* 134–35.

76. See Birley, *Lives of the Later Caesars,* 62; Birley, *Hadrian,* 77–78, 84, 95, 97–99; Whittaker, *Frontiers of the Roman Empire,* 57; and Mattern, *Rome and the Enemy,* 103.

77. Birley, *Hadrian,* 87–88, 95.

78. Birley, *Lives of the Later Caesars,* 62; and Whittaker, *Frontiers of the Roman Empire,* 71.

79. Mattern, *Rome and the Enemy,* 7.

80. See ibid., 6, 9–12; Salway, *Roman Era,* 213; and Brewer, *Second Augustan Legion,* 47.

81. Salway, *Roman Era,* 213; Birley, *Hadrian,* 56, 112, 282–83; and Campbell, *Siege Warfare,* 55.

82. Birley, *Lives of the Later Caesars,* 74.

83. Mattern, *Rome and the Enemy,* 7.

84. See Birley, *Fasti of Roman Britain,* 101, 239; and Birley, *Hadrian,* 24, 102.

85. Birley, *Hadrian,* 96; and Mattern, *Rome and the Enemy,* 178.

86. See Birley, *Lives of the Later Caesars,* 69; and Birley, *Hadrian,* 32, 114–15, 138–39.

87. Speller, *Following Hadrian,* 70.

88. See Birley, *Hadrian,* 115, 125, 152, 195; Mattern, *Rome and the Enemy,* 2, 20; and Campbell, *War and Society in Imperial Rome,* 10.

89. Birley, *Hadrian,* 125.

90. Brewer, *Second Augustan Legion*, 64; and Campbell, *War and Society in Imperial Rome*, 15.

91. Frere, *Britannia*, 275–78; Fulford, "Second Start," 64; and Fields, *Rome's Northern Frontier*, 49, 52.

92. Fulford, "Second Start," 65.

93. Whittaker, *Frontiers of the Roman Empire*, 67.

94. Campbell, *War and Society in Imperial Rome*, 15, 21; Mattern, *Rome and the Enemy*, 161, 178; Whittaker, *Frontiers of the Roman Empire*, 67; and Fulford, "Second Start," 46.

95. Mattern, *Rome and the Enemy*, 161.

96. Quoted in Fields, *Rome's Northern Frontier*, 49.

97. Ibid., 51.

98. Fulford, "Second Start," 56; Frere, *Britannia*, 107.

99. See Birley, *Hadrian*, 116; Santosuosso, *Storming the Heavens*, 118, 144; Campbell, *War and Society in Imperial Rome*, 135; Mattern, *Rome and the Enemy*, 105; and Frere, *Britannia*, 107.

100. Birley, *Lives of the Later Caesars*, 62, 70; Birley, *Hadrian*, 150; and Whittaker, *Frontiers of the Roman Empire*, 57, 71.

101. Breeze, "Edge of the World," 181; and Frere, *Britannia*, 92.

102. Frere, *Britannia*, 83.

103. See Birley, *Lives of the Later Caesars*, 64, 76; Mattern, *Rome and the Enemy*, 121, 159–60; and Birley, *Hadrian*, 85–86, 153–54, 226.

104. See Breeze, "Edge of the World," 180, 182; and Mattern, *Rome and the Enemy*, 159–60.

105. Mattern, *Rome and the Enemy*, 115; and Fields, *Rome's Northern Frontier*, 7.

106. Fields, *Rome's Northern Frontier*, 7.

107. Frere, *Britannia*, 108, 141; and Mattern, *Rome and the Enemy*, 116–19.

108. Fields, *Rome's Northern Frontier*, 52; Shotter, *Roman Frontier in Britain*, 84; and Whittaker, *Frontiers of the Roman Empire*, 96–97.

109. Frere, *Britannia*, 107–9; and Fulford, "Second Start," 46.

110. Breeze, "Edge of the World," 198.

111. Birley, *Hadrian*, 113, 150.

112. Fields, *Rome's Northern Frontier*, 45-46; Frere, *Britannia*, 111; and Breeze, "Edge of the World," 187.

113. See Birley, *Hadrian*, 53, 117–18, 128; Frere, *Britannia*, 120; Crow, "Northern Frontier," 129; Fulford, "Second Start," 44; and Mattern, *Rome and the Enemy*, 205–6.

114. See Birley, *Hadrian*, 17, 111, 133; Crow, "Northern Frontier," 129–30; and Salway, *Roman Era*, 213.

115. Frere, *Britannia*, 133–34.

116. Fulford, "Second Start," 44; and Mattern, *Rome and the Enemy*, 205.

117. Birley, *Hadrian*, 112.

118. See ibid; Birley, *Lives of the Later Caesars*, 73–74; and Fulford, "Second Start," 56.

119. Luttwak, *Grand Strategy of the Roman Empire*, 3; Mattern, *Rome and the Enemy*, 114; Goldsworthy, *Roman Warfare*, 159; Birley, *Hadrian*, 128; Bédoyère, *Hadrian's Wall*, 25; and Fulford, "Second Start," 57.

120. Mattern, *Rome and the Enemy*, 114.

121. Birley, *Hadrian*, 133.

122. Crow, "Northern Frontier," 130–31; Fulford, "Second Start," 58; Fields, *Rome's Northern Frontier*, 46; Bédoyère, *Hadrian's Wall*, 25; and Frere, *Britannia*, 119.

123. Frere, *Britannia*, 114.

124. Ibid., 114, 119; and Scullard, *Roman Britain*, 59.

125. Crow, "Northern Frontier," 129–31.

126. Ibid., 130.

127. Ibid., 131.

128. See Goldsworthy, *Roman Warfare*, 156–59; Whittaker, *Frontiers of the Roman Empire*, 82–83; Bédoyère, *Hadrian's Wall*, 25; Frere, *Britannia*, 121; and Fields, *Rome's Northern Frontier*, 45–46.

129. See Birley, *Hadrian*, 130–33; and Shotter, *Roman Frontier*, 60–61.

130. Birley, *Hadrian*, 123, 128, 135, 138.

131. Ibid., 134.

132. See ibid., 138, 198; Fields, *Hadrian's Wall*, 22; Potter and Johns, *Roman Britain*, 58; and Shotter, *Roman Frontier in Britain*, 72, 76–77, 80.

133. See Crow, "Northern Frontier," 126–27; Birley, *Hadrian*, 173; Salway, *Roman Era*, 213; Bédoyère, *Hadrian's Wall*, 16; Shotter, *Roman Frontier in Britain*, 63, 69, 70; Potter and Johns, *Roman Britain*, 59; and Fields, *Hadrian's Wall*, 12, 23, 37.

134. Salway, *Roman Era*, 213.

135. Frere, *Britannia*, 114, 120; Shotter, *Roman Frontier in Britain*, 64, 66, 69; Fields, *Hadrian's Wall*, 37; and Crow, "Northern Frontier," 127, 132.

136. See Breeze, "Edge of the World," 178, 182; Fields, *Hadrian's Wall*, 22–23, 36, 42–43; Frere, *Britannia*, 114, 119, 121; Fulford, "Second Start," 58; Bédoyère, *Hadrian's Wall*, 25–26; and Shotter, *Roman Frontier in Britain*, 61, 69.

137. See Bédoyère, *Hadrian's Wall*, 17, 21; and Fields, *Hadrian's Wall*, 26, 28.

138. Brewer, *Second Augustan Legion*, 189.

139. Altar dedication, Newcastle Museum of Antiquities.

140. Crow, "Northern Frontier," 129.

141. See Potter and Johns, *Roman Britain*, 60; Mattern, *Rome and the Enemy*, 17; Fulford, "Second Start," 65–66; Shotter, *Roman Frontier in Britain*, 85; and Fields, *Rome's Northern Frontier*, 28, 33.

142. See Birley, *Hadrian*, 101, 202, 257, 273–74, 296; Frere, *Britannia*, 123, 133–34; Fulford, "Second Start," 66; Breeze, "Edge of the World," 173–74, 177; Shotter, *Roman Frontier in Britain*, 83–84; Birley, *Fasti of Roman Britain*, 106–7, 114; and Fields, *Northern Frontier*, 33.

143. Fulford, "Second Start," 66; Fields, *Rome's Northern Frontier*, 34; and Frere, *Britannia*, 134.

144. Frere, *Britannia*, 127; and Fields, *Rome's Northern Frontier*, 45, 56.

145. Brewer, *Second Augustan Legion*, 72; Fields, *Rome's Northern Frontier*, 44–45; and Breeze, "Edge of the World," 179.

146. Fields, *Rome's Northern Frontier*, 37–38, 44–47, 49; Breeze, "Edge of the World," 178; Frere, *Britannia*, 127–28; and W. S. Hanson, "Scotland and the Northern Frontier," in *A Companion to Roman Britain*, ed. Malcolm Todd (Malden, MA: Blackwell, 2007), 150.

147. Fields, *Rome's Northern Frontier*, 42.

148. Fulford, "Second Start," 57, 66.

149. Bédoyère, *Hadrian's Wall*, 26; Frere, *Britannia*, 135; and Fulford, "Second Start," 67.

150. See Frere, *Britannia*, 135–36; Shotter, *Roman Frontier in Britain*, 85, 93–95; Fulford, "Second Start," 66–67; Birley, *Fasti of Roman Britain*, 120, 255; Santosuosso, *Storming the Heavens*, 120; and Fields, *Rome's Northern Frontier*, 35.

151. See Frere, *Britannia*, 141; Hanson, "Scotland and the Northern Frontier," 136–37; Santosuosso, *Storming the Heavens*, 125; Mattern, *Rome and the Enemy*, 87; and Fulford, "Second Start," 67.

152. See Bédoyère, *Hadrian's Wall*, 28–29, 148–49; Shotter, *Roman Frontier in Britain*, 94–95, 107; Frere, *Britannia*, 121, 137–38, 141, 145–46; Crow, "Northern Frontier," 120; and Hanson, "Scotland and the Northern Frontier," 138.

153. Fulford, "Second Start," 67; and Fields, *Hadrian's Wall*, 37, 39.

154. Mattern, *Rome and the Enemy*, 110.

155. See Fulford, "Second Start," 67; Mattern, *Rome and the Enemy*, 110; and Fields, *Hadrian's Wall*, 37.

156. See Birley, *Fasti of Roman Britain*, 142; Frere, *Britannia*, 148–49; Shotter, *Roman Frontier in Britain*, 98–99, 102, 107; Fulford, "Second Start," 68; Brewer, *Second Augustan Legion*, 114; and Fields, *Rome's Northern Frontier*, 46.

157. Birley, *Fasti of Roman Britain*, 150; Fulford, "Second Start," 68; and Frere, *Britannia*, 148.

158. Bédoyère, *Hadrian's Wall*, 30; Birley, *Fasti of Roman Britain*, 150; Frere, *Britannia*, 155; Shotter, *Roman Frontier in Britain*, 100–101; Fulford, "Second Start," 68; and Fields, *Rome's Northern Frontier*, 46.

159. Frere, *Britannia*, 155; Shotter, *Roman Frontier in Britain*, 100; and Fields, *Rome's Northern Frontier*, 46.

160. Birley, *Fasti of Roman Britain*, 150; and Fulford, "Second Start," 68.

161. Shotter, *Roman Frontier in Britain*, 101; Frere, *Britannia*, 155–57, 166–67; Fields, *Rome's Northern Frontier*, 46; and Bédoyère, *Hadrian's Wall*, 30.

162. Birley, *Lives of the Later Caesars*, 218.

163. Ibid.

164. Fulford, "Second Start," 68; Frere, *Britannia*, 158–59; Shotter, *Roman Frontier in Britain*, 101–2; and Mattern, *Rome and the Enemy*, 83, 148, 206.

165. Birley, *Fasti of Roman Britain*, 158–60.

166. See Fulford, "Second Start," 69; Frere, *Britannia*, 159, 162; Breeze, "Edge of the World," 199; and Shotter, *Roman Frontier in Britain*, 105–6.

167. See Fulford, "Second Start," 39, 70–71, 184; Frere, *Britannia*, 166; Shotter, *Roman Frontier in Britain*, 106; Mattern, *Rome and the Enemy*, 110; Whittaker, *Frontiers of the Roman Empire*, 218; and Nic Fields, *Roman Saxon Shore: Coastal Defenses of Roman Britain, AD 250–500* (Oxford: Osprey, 2006), 23.

168. Breeze, "Edge of the World," 174; and Fields, *Rome's Northern Frontier*, 19.

169. Pat Southern, "The Army in Late Roman Britain," in *A Companion to Roman Britain*, ed. Malcolm Todd (Malden, MA: Blackwell, 2007), 399–400.

170. Fields, *Roman Saxon Shore*, 4–5, 24, 38–45; Shotter, *Roman Frontier in Britain*, 116–20; P. J. Casey, "The Fourth Century and Beyond," in *The Roman Era*, ed. Peter Salway (Oxford: Oxford University Press, 2002), 87; Fulford, "Second Start," 72–73; and Southern, "Army in Late Roman Britain," 396–99.

171. See Casey, "Fourth Century and Beyond," 84–85, 87; Frere, *Britannia*, 354–55; and Fields, *Roman Saxon Shore*, 11–14; and Southern, "Army in Late Roman Britain," 400.

172. See Southern, "Army in Late Roman Britain," 394, 404–5; Fields, *Roman Saxon Shore*, 13–15; Ian Wood, "The Final Phase," in *A Companion to Roman Britain*, ed. Malcolm Todd (Malden, MA: Blackwell, 2007), 428–29, 432–33; Frere, *Britannia*, 358; and Shotter, *Roman Frontier in Britain*, 124.

173. Goldsworthy, *Roman Warfare*, 170–72; Fields, *Roman Saxon Shore*, 13–15, 47–48; and Frere, *Britannia*, 365.

174. Casey, "Fourth Century and Beyond," 103; and Wood, "Final Phase," 430.

175. Birley, *Hadrian*, 138.

176. Fields, *Rome's Northern Frontier*, 51.

4

The Ming Great Wall of China

A Dynasty's Unending Pursuit of Security

Introduction

Whereas Athens' Long Walls and Hadrian's Wall involved strategic defenses covering limited distances, the Ming Great Wall of China extended across the dynasty's massive northern frontier. Although vastly larger and richer than its Mongol adversaries, the Ming Dynasty possessed an insular, status quo perspective that the wall was intended to support. How did the Mongols, whose well-being depended on some level of interaction with China, react to the emergence of this impediment between the steppe and Ming territory? A central consideration both for influencing the adversary and the wall's impact on the military balance was its gradual expansion over a century. This evolutionary growth facilitates examination of the strategic dynamics involved in cases of partial frontier coverage. Are such efforts doomed to failure or can they be productive given the right context? The enormous scale of the Ming barrier presented immense manning and maintenance challenges, which will be discussed in the last chapter. Given this environment, how does the suboptimal operation of a barrier affect military balance? The Great Wall case presents a good opportunity to observe the effects of the barrier on internal policy debate. Does its allure as a way to "buy time" prompt more fundamental efforts at resolving the acrimonious relationship or does it simply encourage "muddling through"?

This chapter focuses on Emperor Chenghua's decision in the early 1470s to construct the Yansui border wall protecting the Shaanxi Province. The study concentrates on this choice because it led to the construction of the first major section of what would become the Ming Great Wall of China, and because the existing environment allowed a range of possible policy directions. By contrast, during the so-called Second Ordos Debate in the mid-sixteenth century, declining Ming military capabilities made taking the offensive little more than wishful thinking by glory-seeking officials while domestic politics forbade a political accommodation. After examining the Yansui strategic defense system, the discussion considers the expansion of the barrier in fits and starts over the next century. The Ming's long history allows ample opportunity to consider the effectiveness of this obstacle against the Mongols and later the Manchus, as well as its internal effects on policy debate. The Ming, as opposed to earlier Chinese wall-building dynasties, have been selected for examination for both practical and heuristic reasons. As historian Arthur Waldron relates at the beginning of his investigation of the Ming Great Wall, the amount of information available for this era is vastly superior to that for earlier periods.[1]

Among the existing records is a call in 1470 by an alarmed minister of war, Bai Gui, for ideas on how to stop the increasing Mongol incursions from the bordering Ordos region.[2] The Ordos—"territory of the great bend of the Yellow river in the northwest"—functioned as the strategic focus of the Chinese–Mongol struggle during the Ming dynasty.[3] Although mountains or rivers partially protected most of the frontier, no major terrain feature separated this New England–sized area from North China. Throughout history, it has been one of the major invasion routes into China and offered an effective base of operations when nomad-controlled, as was then the case. The Ming government, regarding the desert-dominated area as having no economic appeal, had withdrawn army outposts early in the fifteenth century. Yet the region's modest farming potential from the Mongol perspective exceeded prospects on the even bleaker steppe to the north and had drawn settlements beginning in the late 1450s, to the surprise of the Chinese. Most disturbingly, after a decade the Mongols appeared to be taking up permanent residence in the area.[4]

Faced with increased raiding from these Ordos-based Mongols by the beginning of the 1470s, Emperor Chenghua, Bai Gui, and other senior officials struggled to address the challenge as "an air of crisis pervaded the court."[5] In March 1471 Zhu Yong, a frustrated Ming commander on the frontier, urged the imperial court in Beijing to adopt a clear policy.[6] Rather than responding to Zhu's plea with action, the government avoided choice by dispatching a series of inspection teams to the frontier. In each case, the lead official—Ye Sheng (right vice minister of rites), Yu Zijun (newly reappointed magistrate of Xian in the Shaanxi Province), and Wang Yue (a civilian general)—recommended constructing frontier walls and other defenses, although Wang Yue also supported an offensive.[7] Still Beijing dithered.

The court's caution on how to proceed is understandable given the perceived limitations of each potential course of action. Today historians argue in near unison that there was a clearly preferable choice for the Ming—accommodation.[8] As will be discussed, Chinese officials at the time regarded political and economic engagement with the Mongols as dangerous and demeaning. Instead they mostly debated the merits of launching an offensive versus establishing a defensive barrier between Shaanxi Province and the southern Ordos. Reconquering the region had emotional and strategic appeal, but its feasibility appeared questionable at best. By contrast, construction of a strong defensive barrier was imminently doable, yet many officials doubted it would block the "barbarians." A wall would certainly not remove the nomads from the Ordos or weaken their ability to strike against the dynasty in other directions.

Four years after Bai Gui's call for ideas and an aborted decision to pursue an offensive, the court finally followed the repeated urging of frontier officials and approved a barrier along the Yansui defense sector atop Shaanxi Province. Although the Ming had previously erected defenses to guard key valleys and sections of Liaodong (Manchuria today), this barrier at almost seven hundred miles in length would be the dynasty's first extended wall in North China.[9] It marks the initial step toward constructing a wall across the entire northern frontier. Work on this structure and secondary barriers would continue in fits and starts for the remaining 170 years of the dynasty, especially from the 1540s through the 1580s.

Although the Han Dynasty's Great Wall was longer, the multidimensional Ming fortification effort including ditches, towers, forts, and fortified villages stands as the most ambitious Chinese strategic defense system.[10] The dynasty built it in four phases:

- Phase I: Defenses guarding key northern passes (early years)
- Phase II: Yu Zijun's wall and improvements (1470s and 1480s)
- Phase III: Datong and Xuanfu sectors (mid-sixteenth century, especially 1540s)—also significant upgrade of defenses in the far west
- Phase IV: Northeast and east sectors to the Bohai Sea (1550s through 1580s) unite main defenses into a single east–west barrier.[11]

Following the Mongol threat, the Ming generally extended defenses in an easterly direction until reaching the Bohai Sea. This phased construction, constant modifications, and vastly different terrain along the frontier combined to produce considerable variation along the Great Wall system. Thus, as a prominent scholar observed, "one rarely knows if a particular fact or situation prevailing in one place is applicable to the whole length of the northern border or to the whole duration of the Ming period."[12] With that caveat, the following discussion briefly characterizes the Ming barrier system in its fully developed form.

At the core was the wall, or more accurately a series of walls, covering thousands of miles along the frontier, albeit with a few gaps in areas of extreme terrain. The main line ran from the huge Jiayuguan fortress ("the First Fortified Pass under Heaven") out west to Laolongtou on the Bohai Sea just east of the stout Shanhaiguan fortress ("the First Pass under Heaven"). The terminus at Jiayuguan marked the end of Ming administration and guarded the traditional

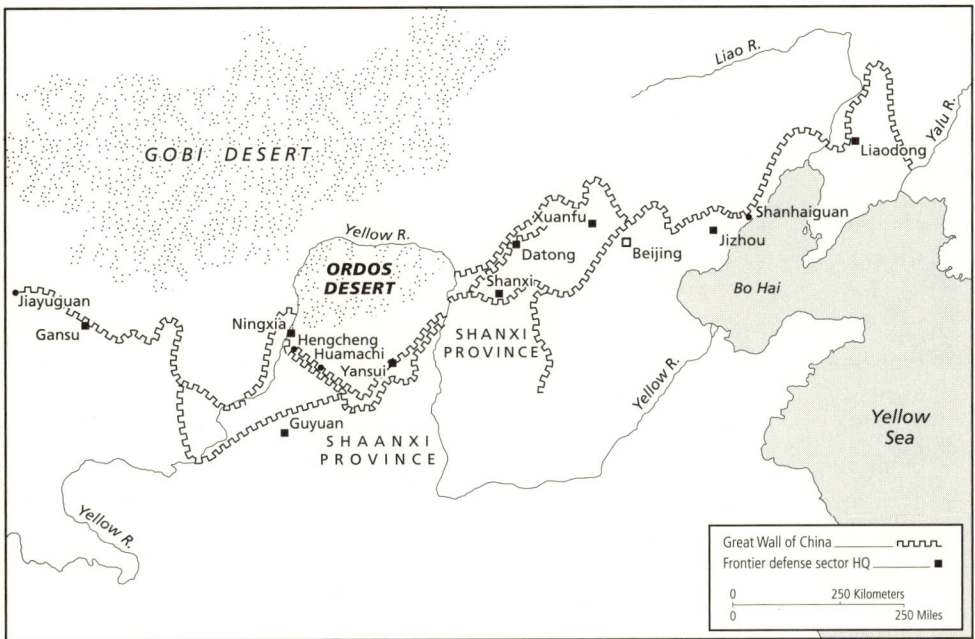

Figure 4.1 Ming Strategic Defense System

route from Central Asia. In the west, the wall generally did not exceed fifteen feet, although upgrades late in the dynasty raised this level in places. A physically more imposing barrier guarded the final section built in northeast China with defenses about thirty to thirty-five feet high and twenty feet wide. This width allowed four horses or ten soldiers to march side by side on top of the curtain, except for narrowed passages over steep terrain. Commentators vary on counting as a part of the main wall an additional 650-mile barrier that extended from Shanhaiguan north around Ming-controlled territory in Liaodong until reaching the Yalu River.[13]

The Chinese augmented the main line with secondary walls in many places, especially to enhance protection of Beijing. Most notably, north of the capital, the main wall splits into the inner and outer great walls as it heads in a westerly direction until reconnecting near the junction of Shanxi Province, Shaanxi Province, and the Ordos. The most visited section of the Great Wall today at Badaling, near Beijing, is actually part of the Inner Great Wall. In the critical Datong and Xuanfu sectors, up to four layers provided defense-in-depth against attacking raiders breaking free into the North China plain.[14] Similarly, out west, a major secondary line ran through the Guyuan sector (southern Ningxia region) to enhance defense of the valuable Central Plain.

A variety of factors account for construction differences, including the period when the work took place, but the most significant factor appears to be location, as the long frontier covers places of sharply different terrain and available building materials. The early efforts of the Ming consisted of rammed or tamped earth, following a two-millennium Chinese tradition. Erosion required such earthen walls be rebuilt approximately every two decades. Officials frequently discussed the need for maintenance, but "one gets the impression that once constructed, they were soon neglected and allowed to disintegrate under the erosion of wind and rain."[15] In the second half of the sixteenth century, officials increasingly shifted to using large brick walls and stone foundations for the structures near Beijing and along the northeast frontier. These materials allowed sturdier fortifications, but they also greatly increased the requirement for skilled labor and high expenditures. Regardless of the means and material employed, wall building was an arduous physical task that tended to lower morale in northern garrisons.[16]

Supporting structures played important roles in the strategic defense system, albeit in varying degrees as terrain shifted. In mountainous regions, a moat was neither feasible nor necessary. But in relatively flat sections, the Ming sometimes added a water barrier, usually known as an "outer trench."[17] The need for people, animals, and water to travel through the barriers required the inclusion of frequent gates that the Ming attempted to protect with added defense works. Each sector of the front had a primary fortress that housed the region's commander and main garrison, as well as numerous smaller bases of varying concentration depending on perceived need.[18] The Ming constructed hundreds of fortified villages along the frontier to house most of the forward-based soldiers and provide a safe haven for the local population during attacks.[19] Finally, thousands of square or rectangular platforms dotted the frontier zone to the north, south, and along the walls. Their total number is unknown, but the Yansui sector alone had well over one thousand with another nine hundred in the Datong sector. On the main barrier, towers were usually located every third of a mile, but the gaps varied from two and a half miles to eighty feet with concentrations increasing in key sectors. The Ming intended these "fighting towers" to provide shelter and storage for troops repelling attacks while "signaling towers" north of the wall enhanced early warning, and those behind the wall abetted communication with the government. In practice, the functions of fighting and signaling towers tended to merge. Effective signaling was vital to counter Mongol mobility with the Ming army spread out along a vast frontier and the capital only a day's ride from certain parts of the Great Wall. Although not definitively known, signal rates probably at least matched the earlier Tang dynasty's coverage of more than 650 miles in a single day and night.[20] Ultimately, by the end of the 1580s an essentially complete Ming Great Wall of China guarded the entire frontier, although repairs and modest enhancements would continue until the end of the dynasty in 1644.[21]

China's Struggle for Security in the North

The Ming decision to build a strategic defense system and the subsequent form of that system were inevitably influenced by a long tradition of states in northern China erecting barriers. The most common and important rationale for such structures was guarding against nomad attacks. Walls could also facilitate power projection into the steppe, a clear attraction for the early dynasties. Moreover, the Chinese, like the Romans, employed barriers to demonstrate military might and regulate commerce. Domestic incentives included preventing regime subjects from escaping north to evade taxes or enforced labor as well as keeping the masses occupied. Leaders usually possessed some combination of these motives.[22]

Contrasting Frontier Approaches

The prevalent image of a continuous barrier existing for more than two millennia is inaccurate; the Ming had to erect their own Great Wall system. Instead, Waldron and others have persuasively shown that some dynasties engaged in wall building (e.g., the Qin, 221–206 BCE; Han, 202 BCE–220 CE; Northern Qi, 550–577 CE; and Sui, 581–618 CE) while others eschewed such works as unnecessary or ineffective and pursued alternative frontier policies (e.g., Tang, 618–907; Song, 960–1279; and Yuan, 1279–1368).[23] These divergent approaches to frontier security as well as China's shifting border ensured that the passage of time would erode extant defenses. Ming officials' familiarity with prior Chinese defense efforts likely influenced their perspective. Significant barriers have been traced as early as the Chu Dynasty in the seventh century BCE with considerable construction during the Warring States Period (475–221 BCE).[24] After emerging victorious over the other states in 221 BCE, Qin Shi Huangdi soon directed his dynasty's attention toward the troublesome nomads from the north by dispatching general Meng Tian and a large army to drive the enemy into the steppe. Upon accomplishing this goal, Qin ordered Meng to cobble together many existing barriers with new construction into what famously became known as *Wan Li Chang Cheng* ("ten thousand li long wall"—a *li* being approximately one-third of a mile).[25] The tortuous exploitation of an estimated five hundred thousand laborers building the structure, along with other projects, contributed to the collapse of the dynasty soon after its founder's demise.

The successor, Han, would erect the longest wall of all time, although other dynasties would construct less expansive barriers. Initially, the weak and internally focused regime's only recourse to increased raiding was to bribe the northerners through the euphemistically labeled Peace and Friendship policy. In late second century BCE, however, the Han embarked on a wall-focused frontier policy similar to the Qin after pushing the Xiongnu out of the Ordos. The Han barrier ran from North Korea to Yumenguan (near today's Lop Nur in Xinjiang Province), making it the westernmost of all the Chinese great walls by about 250 miles. The dynasty eventually integrated a trading relationship (in effect subsidizing the Xiongnu) with a wall-based security policy, a combination that brought relative peace for almost a century. Although Julia Lovell attributes this calm entirely to the relatively inexpensive trade relationship, the continued employment of walls suggests a Han view that they helped limit the price for Xiongnu restraint and discouraged outright nomad transgressions. The brief Northern Qi reign (550–577) erected about 2,000 miles of barriers, notably including parallel lines to promote defense-in-depth. The sixth century Sui Dynasty (581–618), despite lasting only thirty-seven years, also aggressively embraced wall building. Comparisons of Sui to the Qin inevitably arise, due not only to a similar political history (a strong authoritarian founder followed by swift collapse under an incompetent successor) but also to their robust fortification efforts. Subsequently dynastic officials apparently observed a correlation for the Qin and Sui between short reigns and wall building, making such efforts unpopular and "associated with defeat and political collapse."[26]

In particular, the Tang regime (618–907) would rule for almost three hundred years with a radically different frontier policy. While they engaged in diplomatic and economic relations with the northern "barbarians," the dynasty also maintained a strong military presence on the steppe.[27] Taizong, the second Tang emperor, argued to the troops, "Emperor Yang [Sui dynasty] exhausted the country in building long walls to defend against attack. Now I use you to protect the north and the Turks dare not come south—you are much better than a long wall!"[28] This Tang approach worked for a century and a half, but ultimately the growing influence of southern Chinese in the government reduced the regime's contact with nomads and eventually prompted the dynasty to pull back forces from the steppe.[29] As a result, the government increasingly relied on untrustworthy northern allies, a move that contributed, along with domestic rebellions, to its collapse.

After completing the conquest of China in 1279, Khubilai Khan, the Mongol grandson of Genghis Khan, established the Yuan dynasty and pursued a border policy that stressed diplomacy and trade.[30] Controlling the entire region, this dynasty had no use for erecting defenses. By the late thirteenth century, earlier frontier barriers would have largely withered from time and weather. The great chronicler Marco Polo makes no mention of such defenses during his visit at this time; he almost certainly would have noted any such work if he had observed it.[31] This dynasty's main threat would not arise on the steppe but rather among the impoverished Han Chinese who periodically rose up. In 1368 one of these rebellions drove out the Yuan and founded the Ming Dynasty. Except for defenses at a few key passes, it inherited an essentially open northern frontier beyond which the Mongols had retreated.

Although some of the dynasties discussed here are easily labeled as wall-builders (Qin) or accommodationists (Tang), most regimes displayed a similar pattern with their frontier policy. Dynasties initially attempted to engage steppe leaders but subsequently undermined such efforts with their own politically and culturally motivated restrictions. Such constraints almost inevitably provoked retaliatory nomad raids. In response, dynasties either launched offensives or constructed defenses, depending on officials' assessment of relative military strength. The high resource requirements and palpable danger of advancing into the steppe usually encouraged a defensive strategy. Whether facing offensive or defensive approaches, Chinese success tended to push the nomad tribes toward greater cooperation and increased military strength. Thus, Chinese regimes continually struggled "to find a permanent solution to the tendency of the nomads to invade."[32]

Active Early Ming Frontier Policy

The Ming policy toward the Mongols emerged as a central preoccupation from the dynasty's beginning. Officials initially attempted to combine economic engagement and military force to achieve frontier security. The court approved limited trade, but it would not subsidize the nomads as the preceding Yuan regime had done. A somewhat open attitude of the Ming toward "barbarians" continued, as exemplified by many Mongols remaining in China and even in the army. Their cavalry and archery expertise abetted the hard edge of Ming frontier policy as early emperors Hongwu (1368–98) and Yongle (1403–25) projected military power into the steppe. Difficulty supplying these campaigns across the Great Desert prevented absolute victory and left the frontier somewhat fluid with considerable Chinese–Mongol interaction.[33]

The Ming in this initial era applied with shifting emphasizes the three basic approaches to the nomads: accommodation, offense, and defense. They harbored no serious territorial aims on the steppe given its lack of agricultural productivity, but the Ming wanted to exert influence in the area and support future invasions. As a result, the army established numerous early warning towers and eight outer garrisons (strongpoints) on the steppe up to about 150 miles north of Beijing. Along the frontier, the Ming erected strong defenses at key points, such as at the three main passes (i.e., Juyang, Gubeikou, and Shanhai) into North China. Although many officials regarded such border defenses as of secondary importance, these safeguards allowed campaigning with less risk of Mongol counterstrikes. Still, disputes over resource allocation between proponents of the forward and frontier positions reflect the initial exchanges in what would be a long-running battle between advocates for offensive- and defensive-oriented approaches to the Mongol problem.[34]

During the reign of Yongle, two key changes would significantly alter long-term Ming–Mongol dynamics. First, the emperor decided in 1403 to relocate China's capital from the centrally located Nanjing to the far more northern Beijing. Although scholars have suggested several military and political reasons why Yongle would make the change, Beijing was a "questionable choice for a native Chinese dynasty" given its proximity (a day's ride) to the northern frontier.[35] The capital would require strong protection in the form of massive walls, but officials would still feel vulnerable even with such protection, especially as time passed. Yongle's other lasting strategic legacy was a gradual withdrawal from the outer garrisons on the steppe so that only one strongpoint (Kaiping) remained when he died in 1424, and it would soon be abandoned.[36] The resulting vacuum over the semiproductive buffer zone between the steppe and the Middle Kingdom allowed initiative to shift to the Mongols and opened up the Ordos region to them. Waldron goes as far to argue that the "withdrawal marked the first major turning point away from an effective steppe policy."[37] The dynasty's fiscal difficulty probably best explains the policy change.[38] Yet any short-term savings from the abandonment of these outposts came at a steep, long-term cost, trying to counter a highly mobile, militarily proficient enemy.

Ming Military in Decline

Fortunately for the Ming, the steppe tribes' preoccupation with internecine conflict, something Chinese diplomacy attempted to exacerbate, left the frontier relatively calm until midcentury. By this time Chinese officials appreciated that the deteriorating military balance augured danger.[39] Inadequate spending and incompetent administration had resulted in the army's qualitative and quantitative decline, especially with the archery and cavalry forces needed to counter the mobile Mongols. In contrast, an extremely charismatic and capable Mongol leader known as Esen had unified much of the steppe by the late 1440s with a corresponding increase in military strength. Requiring wealth to maintain this unity, he pushed the Ming for larger tribute embassies (essentially elaborate rituals in which the nomads received goods, particularly grain and iron, in exchange for acknowledging subservience to the Middle Kingdom). Viewing the nomads as greedy, Chinese officials responded by reducing the gifts provided, which provoked the Mongols to menace Chinese territory.[40]

These intensifying Mongol raids sparked a debate among Ming officials over the proper response. While most government bureaucrats urged caution given China's anemic military, the eunuch Wang Zhen, a self-interested and powerful court figure, argued for a punitive invasion of the steppe. It was his own path to glory and riches, but such an offensive also appealed to the twenty-one-year-old emperor Zhengtong, who longed to be a great soldier like his predecessors. With the emperor in command, the poorly planned and organized invasion force arrived at the Datong frontier base to find its garrison routed. Possessing a demoralized army, Zhengtong decided to declare "victory" and return to Beijing. His force waited in an exposed position at Tumu for news of its already-destroyed baggage train when Esen sprung a trap crushing the Ming army, killing Wang Zhen, and capturing Zhengtong on September 1, 1449. A reigning emperor had not previously been seized by nomads during battle to the humiliation of the Ming. Esen demanded a huge ransom for Zhengtong's return, but his empowered brother, Jingtai, refused to pay given that it would end his reign. A frustrated Esen launched further raids, but court officials would not capitulate. The Mongol leader's failure to capitalize on his hostage portended domestic problems that culminated in his own 1455 assassination. Steppe historian Thomas Barfield cites Esen's downfall as exemplifying that "a nomadic leader who failed to establish a lucrative extortion relationship with China was building a political structure on sand."[41]

The material and psychological ramifications from the crushing defeat at Tumu were profound for the Chinese. They had to accept that "the possibility that the Ming might eventually succeed to the Yuan's position as hegemon of the steppe, which still had been plausible even a few years before, now seemed out of the question."[42] Given the woeful state of the army, the Chinese ability to protect the frontier for at least the near future now appeared questionable to many Ming.[43] When intra-Mongol fighting after Esen's assassination pushed some tribes south into the Ordos, the Ming army lacked the ability to prevent such migration. Some worried officials even urged relocating the capital to the more secure south, but the court had no interest in such a symbolically significant step. Rather, Ming weakness only appeared to discourage political and economic relations with the Mongols.[44] Thus Tumu's legacy was "driving the Chinese towards stubborn isolationism and the Mongols towards further aggression."[45] The Ming commenced significant defense work, especially improving fortifications covering key passes, but otherwise ineffective governance and political turmoil prevented stabilizing the frontier.[46] The situation continued to deteriorate, and Mongol settlement of the Ordos accelerated after Chenghua became emperor in 1465. He would be under considerable pressure to bring stability to the frontier.

Decision Context

The influence of Chinese and Ming history occurred in part through shaping perceptions about the contextual factors that most weighed on decision makers such as Emperor Chenghua, especially threat perception, military capability, and strategic culture.

Threat Perception

Ming officials viewed the Mongols as their most dangerous external enemy. This strongly held threat perception resulted from a view of the Mongols as "barbarians" who were uninterested in coexistence and an appreciation for the Mongols' military prowess. Continuing to see the nomads as descendants of the Yuan dynasty promoted a false fear that the Mongols sought to regain dominion over China.[47] Their constant raiding reinforced this perspective, rather than signaling a need for Chinese goods. In contrast to earlier Chinese dynasties, "the Ming was no longer willing to see the nomads as simple extortioners."[48] Racist attitudes about the so-called barbarians among Ming elites not only exacerbated threat perceptions but also constrained potential responses.[49] The Han Chinese, especially southerners, possessed contrasting economic and cultural ways that hampered relating to their steppe neighbors. By contrast, the similarities between the Ming and the majority non-Chinese population in their southern provinces encouraged policies of assimilation and self-government.[50] Even during a time of a more nuanced security policy, the first Ming emperor, Hongwu, set the tone by labeling the Mongols as "barbarians of the northwest."[51] By the mid-fifteenth century, officials' references to the Mongols as "fierce and wild" (Yu Qian) who "could not really change their nature" (Qiu Jun) were common.[52] In essence, the court in the decades following the Tumu disaster regarded this as a zero-sum conflict, turning "security against the north into an obsession."[53]

Historians disagree on the extent of Ming knowledge about steppe politics, but officials had at least a limited awareness of the different Mongol groupings that lived across two thousand miles from Manchuria to the Pamir Mountains in Central Asia. Of these groups, the Eastern Mongols constituted the primary "enemy" for Ming officials. Esen's rule marked the high-water mark for the extremely aggressive and ambitious Oirat, or Western Mongols, who after Esen's death retreated toward their northwest base of the steppe. Although the legacy of the Tumu disaster prompted the Ming to regard the Oirats as a latent threat, the Eastern Mongols occupied the territory closest to the key Central and North China plains and accounted for most attacks by the early 1470s. Ming sources often divide the Eastern Mongols into two basic factions as the "5 tribes of Khalkh" and the "6 tribes of Chahars."[54] The Khalkhas, who resided more to the north, possessed the largest Mongol population and outstanding cavalry. The more southerly Chahars had greater interaction with the Chinese, leaving them wealthier but less formidable warriors. Nevertheless, Ming officials worried about the Chahars given that their leader, at least in terms of a figurehead, was descended from Genghis Khan and heir to the Yuan dynasty. Given that the Ming had never been able to coerce the Yuan line to abdicate, its successors had "a certain moral force" that fueled Chinese suspicions.[55]

Beyond their perceptions of the Mongols as hostile barbarians, Ming officials' appreciation of Mongol military prowess intensified concern. The mobility and skill of nomad cavalry made them a formidable power that could quickly concentrate force at a chosen time and point of attack. Today the word "raid" evokes images of a handful of mounted warriors, which was typical, but during the Ming era, raids could consist of thousands or even tens of thousands of nomads. By the late fifteenth century, the declining availability of cavalry had left the Ming army more vulnerable to Mongol units that could range up to sixty miles a day. Exacerbating Ming concern was the recognition that "never before in imperial history had the capital been located so close to the northern frontier."[56] In the Chenghua regime, senior official Ma Wensheng typified attitudes by characterizing the Mongols as "China's constant calamity"[57] while Grand Secretary Liu Dingzhi fretted "that since ancient times the calamity brought by the Yi and Di [barbarians] has never been greater than today."[58]

A series of recent events explain the elevated Ming concern. First, the previously calm northeast frontier had become turbulent after Tumu when some formerly allied Jurchen chiefs rebelled.[59] Even after a joint Sino-Korean army finally ended the violence in 1467, tension continued into the 1470s, albeit largely due to acts of aggression by the Ming governor. Second, at the opposite end of the frontier in the northwest, Tu-ta Mongols (Tatars) living in China revolted in May 1468.[60] A Ming army defeated the rebellion within a year, but the uprising dashed hopes that the increased wealth resulting from farming within the dynasty would engender loyalty and spurred suspicion that Mongols north of the border had been provocateurs. As Frederick Mote observes, "militarily it was a relatively simple affair, but its political impact was profound."[61] Finally and most seriously, in the frontier's central sector, Mongol raiding had reached its largest scale since the days of Esen. The emergence of Bolai, an aggressive and capable leader who was able to unite some tribes, had precipitated the increasing attacks.[62] By 1469, strikes ranging from Manchuria to south of the Ordos had grown into a serious problem. Even when the Chinese scored some successes, the nomads always returned to raid another day. The Mongols' strengthening base of operations in the Ordos suggested the situation would continue to deteriorate without fundamental action.

Ming officials were free to focus on their northern problem, given the absence of perceived threats on the dynasty's other frontiers. Beginning from Hongwu's characterization of the other Asians (e.g., Japanese, Koreans, and Annamese) as "no more than mosquitoes and scorpions," court officials over the decades had directed decreasing attention to its other neighbors.[63] The Ming maintained "distant and cool" relations with Tibet, the primary power to the west. Although officials always worried about a Mongol–Tibetan alliance, relative national interests made such a partnership unlikely.[64] The Ming had stopped pursuing southern expansion into Annam (Vietnam) decades earlier. Despite possessing a four-thousand-mile plus coastline, the Ming displayed little interest or attention to the sea at this point in the dynasty.[65] Their blasé attitude about coastal piracy and hyperventilation over Mongol attacks represents a noteworthy contrast, probably resulting from a combination of the Yuan legacy, the Mongols' proximity to the northern frontier, and a strategic culture that focused internally on the Middle Kingdom.

The Ming did worry about maintaining internal stability given that the late 1460s and early 1470s represented one of the periodic spasms of rebellion that plagued the dynasty. In 1465 the largest native revolt of the fifteenth century erupted in western China. Suppression attempts failed until a frustrated Ming court in 1471 dispatched a huge 250,000-man army to crush it. A Yao tribal rebellion in the mid-1460s had also proved difficult to eliminate. The Ming particularly stressed preventing uprisings in the four provinces with predominantly non-Chinese populations (Guangxi, Guizhou, Yunnan, and Sichuan). Officials, however, regarded this task as more of a political than military challenge that could be solved by policies of assimilation and self-government. At least during the 1470s, the Ming's concentration of its military strength on the northern frontier could occur without jeopardizing broader Chinese security policy.[66]

Military Capability

Ming officials recognized that the army suffered from chronic organizational, financial, and operational weaknesses that not only exacerbated threat perceptions but greatly complicated their response to the Mongols.[67] On paper, the Chinese army had an impressive strength of 2.5 million to 3 million men, but units often failed to reach even 50 percent of their assigned size.[68] The Ming military establishment was based on the flawed *weisuo* system—"the concept of a self-perpetuating, hereditary soldiery" in which designated families provided farmer-soldiers.[69] Poor soil along the border and less land under cultivation prevented the hoped for self-sufficiency, and after the mid-fifteenth century, the decline and migration of military families reduced the quality and quantity of soldiers.[70] Harsh government efforts to force local able-bodied men to fill needs only exacerbated desertion rates. One source notes that manpower shortages limited Beijing to deploying approximately three hundred thousand troops along the northern frontier despite its top priority.[71] Logically, the Ming kept frontier units at a higher level of preparedness, but this relative standard was a low threshold with troops lacking adequate training and supply. As censor Chen Xuen reported after a 1464 inspection, the poor state of Chinese forces and defenses invited Mongol aggression.[72] One historian sums the army up as a "corrupt, under-disciplined, under-trained, and under-supplied" force.[73] Ultimately, by the 1470s, the Ming had to pay recruited volunteers to fight, especially "in all situations requiring more than passive defense."[74]

The first Ming emperor had eliminated a unified chain of command to protect against coups, but the decentralized command structure exacerbated military weakness. With the rest of the empire divided into five independent military commands, the Ming segmented the northern frontier into the *jiu bian zhen* (the nine defense garrisons or areas).[75] From east to west, the frontier commands were

- Liaodong—Yalu River to Shanhaiguan
- Jizhou—Shanhaiguan to north of Beijing
- Xuanfu—Northwest of Beijing
- Datong—Northwest border of Shanxi Province
- Shanxi (aka Taiyuan)—Western stretch of Shanxi Province
- Yansui (aka Yulin)—Northern border of Shaanxi Province
- Ningxia—Yellow River through Ningxia region to northeast Gansu Province
- Guyuan—South of Ningxia front (supporting sector)
- Gansu—Gansu region to end of the Ming realm at Jiayuguan.

Commanders controlled forces in their area with periodic transfers of authority over one or even two neighboring sectors during times of heightened alarm.[76] This decentralized system had the potential of facilitating rapid reactions, but it hampered efficiency of effort and strategic planning for a chronically underresourced force. Moreover, Beijing tended to inhibit local commanders' freedom of action in the key sectors near the capital, undermining the primary benefit of a decentralized structure.[77]

Ming officials had been aware of the military's shortcomings since at least the Tumu disaster, but internal politics inhibited the fundamental policy changes necessary for meaningful progress. A special council had been established at the outset of the Chenghua's reign to debate potential military improvements and advise the new emperor on security matters. It generated some ideas, such as establishing twelve "integrated divisions" with infantry, cavalry, and artillery, yet political infighting severely hampered this effort. Chenghua and his officials lacked the will to institute fundamental reforms, taking only modest steps that resulted in limited improvement. Beyond the military system's institutional problems, a lack of competent generals mostly accounted for its failings. The inability to find skilled commanders contributed to an ever-increasing role for civilian officials in military operations. The talented civilian Wang Yue, dispatched to Yansui area in 1469, demonstrated the value of a capable commander to bolster local operations by temporarily driving off Bolai the following year and winning other victories. Yet civilians were hardly a panacea, and many hindered effectiveness, especially supervising eunuchs. Despite Wang Yue producing limited Ming victories in the early 1470s, overall military capability had not improved significantly.[78]

Strategic Culture

Ming decison makers were influenced not only by a venerated strategic culture regarding the efficiency and manner of force but also more basically a culture with strongly held beliefs about China's place in the world. Some significant differences of opinion exist, however, on the nature of the "Chinese" perspective.[79] Waldron argues that "Chinese" culture is actually "a complex alloy of elements drawn from two sources: the steppe civilization of the nomads and the settled civilization of the people who are today called 'Han.'"[80] The relative influence of each tradition shifted over time. The preceding Mongol-led Yuan Dynasty naturally reflected more of the steppe perspective. The early Ming regimes retained some of this steppe mentality while also embracing the Han culture as the first native dynasty to rule over all of China in many centuries. This combination accounts for the relative success of the Hongwu and Yongle regimes along the northern frontier. The steppe influence began diminishing with the death of Yongle in 1424, and the catastrophic defeat at Tumu more than twenty years later sent it into permanent eclipse. By the early 1470s, the traditional Han view had become culturally dominant in the government.[81]

A core element of this worldview, dating to the long ago Han Dynasty, was China's place as center of the world (i.e., "the Middle Kingdom"). This conception encouraged the Chinese to possess a strong sense of superiority. They wanted foreigners to acknowledge China's greatness and their own subordinate position. Thus the Ming required all trade relationships to occur under the auspices of tribute in which other states or nations acknowledged themselves as "vassals" to the Middle Kingdom. During times of trouble, the Chinese sense of superiority would exacerbate their insularity, essentially closing themselves to outsiders as much as possible. As Edward Farmer observes, "Ming cultural conservatism was manifested both in a defensive stance toward the outside world and in a preoccupation—obsession would not be too strong a word—with ritual production of social order."[82]

This cultural perspective combined with lessons learned from preceding dynasties shaped the strategic culture in the Ming era. Military officials were required to examine historic works while many high-ranking civilians who generally dominated security policymaking also became devoted students.[83] Attention centered on the teachings found in the "Seven Military Classics"—a single volume that compiled the writings of the foremost ancient Chinese strategists, including Sunzi (more commonly known as Sun Tzu). These renowned works provided guidance on a range of security issues from battlefield tactics to grand strategy, most notably discouraging active combat. Officials would benefit most from employing defenses, diplomatic intrigue, and alliances. Nevertheless, despite the value of and knowledge about these teachings, their role in the development of policy during the Ming era has been somewhat disputed. In particular, scholar Alastair Johnston thoroughly examined the subject for the Ming Dynasty and found the presence of two distinct strategic cultures.[84] Johnston characterizes the traditional approach as assuming that "war is aberrant and preventable; that conflict is variable sum and that the enemy has a price; and that highly coercive strategies are generally the least efficacious and are last resorts (or at least not first resorts)."[85] While such views appear often in Chinese writings, he finds tenets of this strategic culture are "disconnected from the programmatic decision rules governing strategy, and appears mostly in an habitual discourse designed, in part, to justify behavior in culturally acceptable terms."[86] In other words, Ming decision makers employed these concepts to rationalize a policy direction chosen for other reasons.

Instead, Johnston finds that an alternative strategic culture, which he labels the parabellum paradigm, exerted far greater weight on Ming security deliberations. This mindset "assumes war is inevitable or extremely frequent; that war is rooted in an enemy predisposed to challenge one's own interests; and that this threat can best be handled through the application of superior force."[87] Such a perspective promotes offensive strategies above static defense and especially accommodation.[88] His argument may not be applicable to other Chinese dynasties, but it appears, as even critic Huiyun Feng observes, to have validity for the Ming—a dynasty that replaced and then engaged in an essentially continuous struggle with the Mongols.[89] Waldron adds "for purposes of ruling the territories that were culturally Chinese, the classics sufficed. But for dealing with the horse nomads, something quite different was necessary."[90]

Johnson's argument is most persuasive with regard to the "highly contingent" nature of Chinese security thinking. He observes that strategic preferences were "mediated by a powerful notion of absolute flexibility."[91] Leaders must "determine or weigh (*quan*) the constantly changing nature of the conflict (*bian*) with the enemy."[92] The key to policy choice for the Ming was to consider the practicality of actions when evaluating options. Johnston sees Bai Gui, minister of war in the early 1470s, exemplifying this practice by noting that he argued "in the face of larger or superior Mongol forces the Ming should 'consolidate defenses' and ride out the attack until the Mongols retreated. But when weaker or inferior Mongol forces appear the Ming should concentrate its military power and 'exterminate' them. The key rule was 'to attack or defend depending on opportunity.'"[93] Such thinking suggests a less distinctive Chinese strategic culture than characterized by adherents of the traditional view. Moreover, as Waldron observes, it is a corrective that "closing the frontier was not, as is sometimes thought, a fundamental Chinese cultural preference."[94] Nevertheless, Johnston contends that the flexibility of choice extended only to military options, excluding nonviolent strategic approaches. Truly embracing "absolute flexibility" would have meant being fully open to accommodation, but this approach apparently contradicted the Chinese overarching moral sense of superiority.[95]

Resources

Given the dynasty's size, wealth, and prioritization of the Mongol problem, decision makers should have been able to consider policy options without resource concerns, but they actually operated under considerable limitations. Population figures vary widely, but even a middle-of-the-road estimate places the number of Chinese at more than 150 million in the 1470s. Ming officials appreciated that their numbers hugely outweighed the Mongol population, which during the Ming era has been estimated at 2–3 million.[96] Beyond its massive edge in population, China's wealth and prosperity contrasted sharply with the nomads' impoverished existence on the steppe. Moreover, the plentiful rivers facilitated the movement of people and goods throughout the dynasty. Unfortunately for Ming decison makers, political, economic, and demographic factors inhibited their ability to harness resources and direct them toward frontier security despite its high priority. Displaying considerable political sensitivity, Ming rulers were extremely cautious about extracting revenue from society. Government funds largely came from agricultural and land taxes, but local landowners had progressively gained the upper hand over government officials. As a result, the level of taxation in China was relatively low compared to that of contemporary governments in Europe at the time.[97] Moreover, in contrast to some earlier dynasties (e.g., Tang and Song), Ming fiscal administration was seriously deficient.[98] The government's necessity to both fund the ineffectual weisuo system and underwrite an improvised force to provide an actual army inefficiently consumed resources.

The most severe constraint on the Ming's access to resources was a political schism between northerners and southerners. The south possessed most of China's wealth and population. The preceding Yuan Dynasty had critically mobilized the region's resources for campaigns and subsidies in the north, abetting an effective policy.[99] By contrast, politics prompted Ming fiscal policy to leave "most of the wealth generated by its productive people in the regions where that wealth was produced."[100] During Chenghua's reign, this northern–southern division was quite sharp, and the emperor was unable or unwilling to breech the difference.[101] Frontier security had to be underwritten by the adjacent provinces along with some limited government annuities given that none of the nine defense areas was self-sufficient.[102] Shaanxi and Shanxi, the provinces closest to the Ordos, were among the most impoverished areas in China.[103] The twin scourges of drought and nomad raiders had only exacerbated their poor circumstances in the early 1470s. Southerners also largely avoided serving on this remote frontier, leaving the approximately 12 percent of the population residing in North China (15–18 million) to fill out army ranks.[104] Even most of these northerners resided some distance from the frontier and avoided service. For Ming officials, the bottom line was that although able-bodied Chinese along the frontier wall outnumbered the Mongols, they knew this population was neither large enough nor wealthy enough to produce an adequate covering force against such a mobile enemy.

Domestic Politics and the Decision-making Process

In this case, the overlap of domestic politics and the imperial decision-making process warrants combining these two contextual factors because the weak government structure ensured that factionalization and politics would greatly influence policy choices. At the outset of the dynasty, Hongwu eliminated the positions of prime minister and commander in chief to guard against domestic challenges. He even issued an ancestral injunction that anyone who tried to bring back the prime minister would be "immediately executed."[105] Instead the first Ming emperor established six function-specific ministries and the aforementioned independent military commands under his executive authority. This system required an extremely hard-working and able emperor to serve as his own prime minister and commander in chief. Although the system worked reasonably well under Hongwu and Yongle, their weak or incompetent descendents struggled and factionalization intensified, inhibiting governance.[106]

Chenghua, who rose to the throne in 1465 at age sixteen, has been labeled a mediocre ruler—a term that seems appropriate. The eighth Ming emperor has been characterized as being of limited intelligence, slow to act, and easily misled. He would eventually become "paranoid and tyrannical," but in the early 1470s he at least appears dedicated to governing well.[107] On defense issues, the emperor "identified with his military-minded grandfather and father ... [and] aspired to their vigorous, even aggressive military postures, and rewarded successful military leaders generously."[108] Still, unlike most Ming predecessors, he had never actually campaigned or obtained practical military experience. This shortcoming probably added to his inability to act in a timely fashion.[109]

Although the emperor ruled authoritatively in the Ming governing system, his inner court exercised enormous influence over policy, especially with a leader of Chenghua's nature. The court consisted of two key components: the eunuch bureaucracy and the grand secretariat, whose proximity to the emperor fueled their growth in stature and power. In particular, the eunuchs, entirely dependent on their relationship with the ruler, worked to ingratiate themselves.[110] Their pandering tended to reinforce imperial views, a dangerous phenomenon under militarily incompetent rulers. As a part of the eunuch bureaucracy's enormous growth in size (approaching ten thousand officials) and scope by the 1470s, it had begun exerting increased influence on security issues.[111] Some "good" eunuchs labored for better governance, but most of them sought wealth and career advancement in part through winning military battles. Thus they tended to urge emperors to attack the Mongols and, at times, manipulated the decision environment to promote combat. By contrast, the grand secretariat, consisting of a small number of top scholar-officials, exercised influence through counseling the emperor. Hongwu had not viewed this group as becoming a major policy-making force, but "because of its long-term continuity, the influence of the office steadily expanded during the middle period of the dynasty."[112] Senior grand secretary Li Hsian initially had great sway with Chenghua, but after Li's death in 1467, no other grand secretary established such a relationship.[113]

Despite many talented individuals, divisions within the regular bureaucracy exacerbated the struggle to govern effectively. More than any other previous Chinese government, the Ming bureaucracy was "dominated by civil servants recruited and promoted on the basis of merit."[114] Its performance, however, suffered from an inability to coordinate policy among the six ministries (i.e., personnel, revenues, rites, war, punishments, and works) without a prime minister or similar executive. Instead each department dealt directly with the emperor and court officials. This decentralized structure greatly handicapped designing and implementing policy toward the steppe. The ministry of war dealt with military affairs against the Mongols while the ministry of rites handled tribute issues, essentially trade and diplomacy.[115] Moreover, both departments in addition to the ministry of revenue had taxation authority to help fund frontier policy.

Beyond these governing entities, select civilian officials exerted influence on Ming security policy in the early 1470s. These civilians had been able to usurp the power of military officers given the latter's generally incompetent performance and resulting low prestige.[116] Some of these civilian bureaucrats were also talented contributors on the battlefield, such as Wang Yue, who would become one of the Ming Dynasty's greatest generals. Among the key civilians debating and influencing military issues were Wang Yue, Han Yang, Xiang Zhong, Ma Wensheng, and Yu Zijun. Possessing considerable experience and expertise on frontier affairs, these officials tended to be sensitive to resource constraints and more open-minded on how best to deal with the nomads.[117] Yet, as Waldron laments, both the prevailing culture and institutional framework limited their impact on court decisions.[118]

Not surprisingly, this decision-making process fostered intragovernment conflict, especially between the eunuchs and grand secretaries. Emperors often fueled this competition by playing them off against each other, although Chenghua's tendency to do this has been characterized as "by default more than by design."[119] Regular government bureaucrats shared a more natural affinity with members of the grand secretariat, but at times they established useful alliances with eunuchs. In particular, the preference of many southerners, predisposed to viewing the Mongols as "barbarians," for a hard line in policy dovetailed with eunuchs' desire for conducting offensives. The battle over policy on the Ordos region played out in a struggle to build alliances and influence imperial preference. Such political maneuvering was essential for officials outside the inner court, but given the distance Chenghua maintained from everyone at this point of his reign, it behooved all parties to bolster their position. As will become evident in the next section, every policy option possessed weaknesses that opponents could exploit.[120]

Frontier Strategic Options

These contextual factors weighed heavily on decision makers as they contemplated how best to address the Ordos problem—"Ming China's most basic security issue."[121] A wide range of options had been employed historically against the Mongols, but three basic approaches were viable in the early 1470s: accommodationist, defensive, and offensive. Before examining them, a brief caveat needs to be introduced on the meaning of "policy choice" for the Ming. Students of the dynasty's decision making, such as Johnston and Waldron, have stressed that the three approaches were not necessarily discreet strategies considered against each other.[122] Johnston writes, "to the extent that grand strategic options were debated in Ming policy circles, these were generally not disaggregated into fine-grained policy categories.... [The options] were not viewed as mutually exclusive approaches to handling the barbarian problem."[123] In particular, accommodation and defense were not viewed as mutually exclusive.[124] For example, although he was the most enthusiastic proponent of wall building, Yu Zijun believed that trade with the nomads would help stabilize the frontier. Such openness to accommodation reflects a clear appreciation by at least some Ming wall proponents that barriers alone were unlikely to provide security against an adversary unwilling to accept the status quo. Similarly, some wall advocates also supported limited attacks to weaken the Mongols.[125] The appeal of such combination policies becomes a common theme throughout the cases. The Ordos debate of the 1470s, however, marks an instance where the Ming court appears to have considered these options as mutually exclusive in practice, at least in a temporal sense.[126] The rest of this section explores the strengths and weaknesses of the options available.

Offensive

The most ambitious and demanding strategy was to launch an offensive to reconquer the Ordos. Successful execution required completion of three tasks: organizing an invasion force, defeating and driving out the nomads, and setting up measures for lasting Chinese control of the area. Most advocates of an offensive focused on the intrinsically appealing matter of the second element, driving the Mongols out.[127] A victorious offensive fit with Emperor Chenghua's desire to follow the military successes of his predecessors. Many eunuchs favored offensive action, which offered the lure of great individual rewards. In general, conquest of the Ordos had popular appeal among the educated elites as the best way to deal with the "barbarians."[128] Fueling this sentiment was the parabellum strategic culture that, according to Johnston, prioritized offensives as the optimal response to the Mongols when possible.[129]

Beyond its psychological and personal attractiveness, regaining control of the Ordos potentially offered strategic benefits. Officials now better appreciated that this area between the steppe and North China provided the enemy a strong base from which to attack the dynasty.[130] The danger would only grow if the Ming let the region's occupation progress. Reconquest would provide China with a "natural frontier" by pushing the Mongols north of the Yellow River. For this reason, in early 1472 the minister of war contended that control of the Ordos offered the only long-term solution.[131] The extent of this sentiment prompted some officials, such as Wang Yue, to even associate themselves with "eunuchs and discredited courtiers" to bolster the cause.[132]

Although these considerable benefits prompted some decision makers to overlook feasibility concerns, other officials vigorously stressed both the high cost and risk of an Ordos campaign. Beyond the initial expense, the Ming would have to allocate funds to maintain control of the area, including forward garrisons in the Ordos and perhaps defensive works along its northern loop on the Yellow River. The Ming had been unwilling to expend the resources for such garrisons earlier in the fifteenth century. Although subsequent events may have convinced leaders that the previous decision was penny-wise and pound-foolish, the occupation and defense of the Ordos would have been expensive in an era of reduced means. Given that the poor neighboring provinces would have been heavily taxed to pay for the offensive and subsequent measures, the ongoing drought diminished their potential contribution as well as the willingness to provide it without generating strong antidynasty sentiment. Even if financially affordable, many Ming doubted the prospects of an offensive given the strong Mongol presence and the decline of the Chinese army. In particular, critics questioned whether the army possessed sufficient mobility and commanders to avoid a repeat of the disastrous ambush at Tumu. Ye Sheng and others stressed the impracticality of organizing the 150,000-man force, which Minister of War Bai Gui had indicated the campaign would require.[133] Moreover, they added even if the Ming managed to regain the Ordos, nearly a century of experience showed that the Mongols would simply withdraw to the steppe and counterstrike when they desired rather than capitulate. Thus critics concluded that a major attack entailed both considerable short-term and long-term risk.[134]

Accommodation

In stark contrast to pursuing an offensive, the Ming could have sought an accommodation with the Mongols. This nonmilitary approach offered a way to coexist or even cooperate with the nomads. For the Chinese, accommodation included "diplomacy, political trading, economic incentives, bandwagoning, and balancing alliance behavior."[135] The crux of any engagement policy would be trade, under the auspices of tribute, given the Mongol's economically motivated aggression. By the 1460s, inadequate tribute relations had prompted the nomads to intensify raiding. Rather than signaling the need for more trade, the failure of such half-measures soured many officials in Chenghua's court on the basic merit of engagement. Thus Beijing had completely severed the tribute relationship by the decade's end.[136]

Some officials, however, would advocate its reestablishment during the ongoing debate over policy toward the Ordos region. An accommodationist-based strategy made sense in light of the relative decline of Ming military power. Earlier dynasties, such as the Han and Tang, had become more accommodationist as their strength dissipated.[137] Not surprisingly, it was officials along the frontier, such as Yu Zijun, who, facing reality, tended to urge "more accommodations in meeting the nomads' demands for markets and subsidies."[138] Beyond quieting the border, such advocates saw this policy enhancing the Ming's long-term strength by bolstering the local economies and gaining time and resources for military improvement. In particular, they would be able to obtain through trade much needed, high-quality horses for the inadequate cavalry. Thus, even if suspicious of Mongol intentions, some Ming officials stressed the merit of accommodation.[139]

Proponents of accommodation, however, faced formidable political and strategic barriers. While regarded as tactically necessary at times, for the Middle Kingdom to appease the malevolent "barbarians" was generally viewed as "humiliating and expensive" by the Chinese.[140] Not surprisingly, it was deeply unpopular. Given that tribute was a matter of private concern for emperors, it would inevitably be a strongly politicized issue in which eunuchs played a key role. The financial gains received by eunuchs and courtiers from restricted commerce encouraged their opposition. The court's involvement also led the ministry of rites, which handled tribute relations, to emphasize politics over economics.[141]

Overcoming this unfavorable political environment might have been possible if Ming decision makers perceived accommodation as effective. But, in an era where the Mongols were regarded as malevolent "barbarians," such a policy appeared to be appeasement, no matter how well it fit the underlying context. Historians lament the shortsightedness of court officials for not adopting an accommodationist policy, but modern scholars have the benefit of knowing that the nomads simply needed and wanted access to Chinese goods.[142] Ming officials at the time held a pervasive fear that the Mongols actually sought to regain control of at least northern China. They believed any accommodation policy would abet that nomad goal by disproportionately benefiting the Mongols.[143] Prior experiences reflected the Mongol tendency to expand the size and frequency of trade missions until the Ming balked. Officials at that point feared the Mongols would have "the means, the horsemanship, and the hunting skills to seize it [desired goods] with force."[144] In this regard the Ming appeared to focus on the Song Dynasty's experience. Struggling to defend its northern border, the Song provided significant subsidies to the Khitans, Jurchens, and eventually the Mongols, but these neighbors still seized North China and later South China. Thus, despite "economic problems and military difficulties far worse than those encountered by the Han and Tang," the court did not see value in pursuing an accommodation.[145]

Wall

The Ming considered erecting a long defensive barrier south of the Ordos, essentially connecting "principal garrison points."[146] Given the abundant prior dynastic experience with walls, officials knew the advantages of such a strategic defense system. For example, Gao Lu, an oft-cited fifth century official, contended that a wall contributed to frontier security because "first, it eliminates the problems of mobile defense. Second, it permits the northern tribes to nomadize [beyond the wall] and thus eliminates the disasters of raiding. Third, because it enables us to look for the enemy from the top of the wall, it means we no longer wait [to be attacked, not knowing where the enemy is]. Fourth, it removes anxiety about border defense, and the need to mount defense, when it is not necessary. And fifth, it permits the easy transport of supplies, and therefore prevents insufficiency."[147] For these combined reasons, the Ming had been erecting limited defenses since the beginning of the dynasty. Most notably, in 1442 and 1447, the dynasty constructed its first walls in Liaodong to safeguard settlers in the empire's northeast corner.[148]

Proponents for building a long wall south of the Ordos, led by the experienced civilian officials Yu Zijun and Ye Sheng, argued that it would significantly curtail Mongol raiding into Shaanxi Province.[149] As noted earlier, inspectors touring the frontier had regarded the poor condition of Ming forces as actually inviting large-scale Mongol attacks. Embracing Gao Lu, those arguing for a barrier noted it would facilitate secure communications and frustrate and channel attacks.[150] Moreover, a barrier would function as a force multiplier, allowing the Ming to accomplish these objectives with fewer troops. The most ardent defense proponents, such as Yu Zijun and, in the 1450s, Gao Deng, even suggested walls could fundamentally change Mongol behavior.[151] If Mongol raids produced high causalities and no booty, then the nomads would be reluctant to launch attacks. Thus the walls would achieve what Gao Deng termed "not fighting and subduing the enemy," which is known in modern parlance as deterrence by denial.[152] This argument depended on Mongol aggression being motivated by opportunity rather than need, a diversion from reality that would prevent this fundamental benefit.

Regardless of its deterrent potential, proponents argued that a wall represented the superior approach given the infeasibility of a major offensive. Even if the offensive had appeal as a "more fundamental answer to the security problem," the influential notion of *quan bin* (flexibility) meant that building defenses would be consonant with China's parabellum strategic culture.[153] Wall advocate Ye Sheng actually favored seizing the offensive when favorable circumstances existed, but the current environment did not provide such a context. Yu and others stressed that a wall would actually facilitate the necessary transition for an offensive by allowing the population and economy of the Shaanxi Province to recover. They bolstered this argument by noting that a solid thirty-foot-high earthen barrier could be rapidly built. Finally, they nuanced their approach by supporting occasional forays into enemy territory to weaken the adversary.[154]

Critics, many of whom possessed a political and strategic predisposition to favor conquest, countered that defenses were costly and ineffective. Not allowing themselves to be exclusively tarred with the high costs label, offense proponents asserted that a long wall also involved great expense because earthen walls required continuous and costly maintenance to combat erosion. Unless the appearance of a wall would modify Mongol behavior, the barriers would not solve the problem and would have to be sustained indefinitely. These expenses would be largely paid by the Shaanxi border province and strain its already burdened economy. Wang Yue typified opponents by asserting that it was actually the wall-building approach rather than the offensive that exceeded Ming resources.[155]

Beyond costs, critics questioned the strategic effectiveness of such a barrier. They noted that past efforts with walls had contributed to the fall of the short-lived Qin and Sui dynasties. Yu's use of the term "*bianqiang*" (border wall) instead of "*changcheng*" (long wall) possibly represented a preemptive effort to distance the project from the Qin barrier.[156] Nevertheless, pro-offensive officials particularly stressed the unsuccessful frontier policy of the Sui, "the last dynasty to have built one [a wall] in this area."¹⁵⁷ This defense-based approach inevitably left the initiative to the Mongols, forcing the Ming to not only maintain the walls in top condition but also support border garrisons in perpetual readiness.¹⁵⁸ Any knowledgeable student of Chinese history would not expect such an effort to be sustained. Even if the proposed wall south of the Ordos protected the population along its five-hundred-mile expanse, the mobile Mongols would undoubtedly strike elsewhere.¹⁵⁹ Thus, whatever its tactical effectiveness, the barrier would not benefit Chinese security more broadly. Efforts to erect strategic defenses across part of a frontier against a mobile adversary are always vulnerable to this criticism.

Decision for a Strategic Defense System

Prodded by frontier officials and a high threat perception, the Ming court met on May 24, 1472, to address the Ordos problem. Given officials' understanding of the Mongol challenge and political sentiment, an accommodation strategy had little appeal and received at most a cursory discussion. Even a protrade advocate such as Yu Zijun reflected the almost universal attitude of officials that "only because of military preparations can one suppress conflict."¹⁶⁰ The question before Emperor Chenghua was whether to adopt an offensive or defensive approach, with proponents on both sides claiming their approach entailed greater fiscal and strategic merit. Lacking indisputable evidence, the emperor and his court appear to have embraced the instinctively more appealing course of action. While technically shelving Yu's wall proposal for further study, the court had rejected it as an expensive and likely ineffective response to the Mongol problem. In particular, Chenghua fretted that the wall would undermine rather than promote regional prosperity given his expectation that the necessary local taxes would drive the Shaanxi population away. Instead the court approved an operation to capture the Ordos as the only available solution to the problem.¹⁶¹

The nature of the decision process helped undermine the already difficult and risky offensive strategy. Either the war faction had manipulated its presentation of facts to Chenghua or they were actually delusional about the true requirements for a conquest of the Ordos. Regardless, troubled by continuing raids and anxious to realize the advertised gains, Chenghua and his courtiers wanted a rapid victory. As a result of this pressure, the army would not be able to conduct the careful, nearly year-long preparations that Minister of War Bai Gui had stressed as necessary when recommending an offensive. Instead, the court concluded that the "existing" eighty thousand frontier forces under inspired, new generalship could advance at once. The appointed campaign commander (Zhao Fu, "the General who pacifies the barbarians") and his deputy (Wang Yue) were quick to point out that "existing" forces were at most forty thousand troops, and they vigorously resisted Beijing's call for action until better resourced. Tension remained high as Yu Zijun reported that eighty thousand Mongol warriors with seventy-five thousand horses were hovering ominously close to the border. With the onset of winter, the issue remained in limbo as Zhao and Wang would not attack without a larger, better-supplied force, which the imperial court would not provide. Despite having initially outlined the need for careful preparation, the pressured Bai Gui now chastised Zhao and Wang for their tentative, insubordinate behavior.[162]

Amid this stalemate, proponents of a barrier began gaining traction. By late 1472 a frontier official warned that the taxes extracted to underwrite the offensive were excessively burdening the area's small and drought-suffering population. Prodefense forces, whose policy had been effectively attacked for the same fiscal reason, now argued that the stressed peasants needed relief or they would abandon the region or, even worse, become bandits. In December 1472 Yu sent another letter arguing that the precarious situation required the construction of a wall before the next raiding season (fall 1473). He stressed that the past six months demonstrated that the conquest of the Ordos was impractical, whereas a thirty-foot barrier could be erected in months with only a fifth of the personnel required for a campaign. Then in January 1473, Zhao, after consulting with key border officials such Yu, Wang, and Ma Wensheng, sent a particularly pessimistic report to Beijing. With half of the original force of 40,000 having deserted, Zhao now required 130,000 more troops for success. As the drought continued to plague the Shaanxi and Shanxi provinces, they could supply limited resources and not enough soldiers. Zhao boldly suggested that reinforcement would have to come from elsewhere, and, if not available, the Ming should withdraw the local Chinese population to a more defensible region. A frustrated court removed him from command for excess caution and ineffectiveness, but memorials by Yu and Zhao from the frontier for a joint active–passive defense had begun shifting sentiment in Beijing. Chenghua, worried about overtaxing the locals, increasingly regarded the campaign as a grave risk, if it was at all possible. Yu tried to seize the momentum by reiterating that a wall would allow the raid-plagued Shaanxi Province to recover and better supply a future campaign. The court called off the offensive, but instead of approving a wall, it decided to reconsider all options. Apparently even the inherently disliked approach of "restoring peaceful tribute relations" now received some attention.[163]

Fortuitously, as the court dithered, circumstances actually improved along the northwest frontier in October 1473. Although unwilling to launch the invasion, Wang Yue adroitly carried out a small-scale raiding campaign to push the Mongols away from the Ming border. He won a major victory over Mongol leader Bag Arslan, by using 4,400 handpicked cavalry to attack defenseless Mongol camps of women and children and then ambush nomadic warriors rushing back to the bases. These defeated Mongol tribes withdrew from the southern border of the Ordos, which theoretically improved the prospects of all three strategic approaches but most benefited the wall-building proponents by providing a temporary respite in which to construct a strong barrier. The war faction could stress that Wang's successes showed the time was right for a big push, but the military balance had not been fundamentally improved vis-à-vis conquest of the entire Ordos. Even though the Ming could pursue accommodation with less trepidation of exploitation, it remained politically and strategically unappealing.[164]

Thus in early 1474 the court finally opted to pursue a strategic defense, albeit without much passion. War Minister Bai Gui was "unenthusiastic, but lacking any better ideas," he did nothing to stop it.[165] The minister's perspective appears to be emblematic of an official demonstrating "absolute flexibility" against the nomads. Similarly, Chenghua approved construction of a wall despite concern about its potential cost.[166] In general, Waldron argues, if Ming officials believed a nonmilitary approach was impossible, then "exclusion and wall-building makes a certain amount of sense."[167] Lovell offers a harsher judgment, declaring that after a quarter century of "racist arrogance, military incompetence and murderous factionalism, only one course of action was beginning to look both defensively viable and psychologically satisfying: wall-building."[168] In essence, the insular regime now hoped to physically and mentally block out the problem.

The Ming proceeded to build their first long wall in North China. Actually, the government built two barriers of tamped earth, totaling almost 700 miles (2000 li) in length. Following along the path of the old Qin dynasty barrier, Yu's main wall ran about 560 miles west from the Yellow River, across the top of Shaanxi Province to Huamachi, near the convergence of Shaanxi Province, Ningxia Province, and Mongolian territory. A second barrier, built by Wang Yue, continued for 129 miles from near Huamachi through part of Ningxia to Hengcheng in Lingwu County. Forty thousand laborers toiled away for at least a few (and probably several) months, constructing an impressive wall that averaged thirty feet in height. At some key spots, the Chinese built two or even three lines to enhance protection while further bolstering defense along the barriers with 10 strongholds, 810 fortresses (strong points), 15 defense towers, and 78 small observation towers. Although the system was rapidly completed as advertised, Yu would continue strengthening it during his remaining three years as the local governor.[169]

The Yansui defense sector (atop Shaanxi Province) remained secure in the years following construction of the "border wall," but did the calm result from Wang's victory over Bag Arslan, the strategic defense system, or a combination of both developments? As mentioned earlier, once the impracticality of conquering the Ordos had become evident, some offense advocates, such as Wang Yue, emphasized employing an active defense through counterattacking the

Mongols. Wang observed that "although this [policy] cannot cause [the Mongols] not to invade, it is sufficient to cause [the Mongols] not to dare to penetrate deeply."[170] His ruthless campaigning deserves some credit for the increased security. Futhermore, Yu's long barrier also almost certainly contributed to Mongol unwillingness to attack the area. Ultimately, despite opposing perspectives, Yu and Wang "brilliantly performed tasks of complementary character."[171] Then, in 1482, the Mongols finally decided to test the wall. Their major raid against it ended in a decisive defeat, with the strategic defense system working particularly well in trapping the nomads who penetrated the initial layer. While the Mongols mourned their considerable casualties, the Chinese along the border regarded the outcome as vindication of Yu's wall-building policy.[172] Many government officials also felt that "frontier walls, for the time being, had shaken off their bad historical reputation."[173]

Tactical effectiveness, however, only gave way to the larger question of strategic merit. Finding this section of the border well defended, the Mongols logically shifted raiding in other directions, particularly eastward toward the Shanxi, Datong, and Xuanfu sectors that guarded approaches to the capital. Moreover, maintaining the long-term effectiveness of defenses in sectors with barriers was a practical challenge. In 1484 Wang Shu, minister of war in the Nanjing capital, pointed out that if a strategic defense produced calm, the Ming would inevitably divert resources elsewhere, precipitating a dangerous atrophy of the barrier and associated troop readiness. Wang stressed that this weakened condition would invite future attacks, so the Chinese had no reason to expect lasting serenity. This cycle reflected a dilemma that bedeviled the Ming in trying to secure their mammoth frontier through a defensive approach that could not produce victory. More generally, it highlighted the limitations of an exclusively defense-based strategy against a highly motivated and mobile adversary.[174]

Security Developments along a Partially Fortified Frontier

Continuing uncertainty about the value of walls at the imperial court helps account for its vacillation on building additional barriers despite increased raiding in neighboring provinces and the urging of such efforts by frontier defense advocates. Nevertheless, the increased pressure from Mongols attacking eastward out of the Ordos prompted the court to dispatch Yu to investigate in 1484.[175]

Stalemate Blocks Wall Expansion as Mongol Challenge Grows

After visiting the critical Datong and Xuanfu sectors northeast of his wall, Yu reported the absence of adequate protection and the population's suffering from repeated assaults. Benefiting from high prestige after his barrier's 1482 success, Yu won Chenghua's approval for a new wall modeled on the previous structure and appointment as governor-general of the Datong and Xuanfu frontier defense sectors. The emperor apparently felt he had little choice given the army's inability to stop the increasing raids. Yu planned to initiate major defense construction in early 1485, building a 433-mile barrier from near the capital west to the Yellow River as well as more than tripling the number of signal towers in these sectors. A requirement for eighty-six thousand laborers, more than double the number who built the far longer Yansui wall, reflects the construction challenge of these mountainous areas. Approval of this second barrier suggested to defense advocates that they were moving toward a general wall-building policy along the frontier.[176]

Sharing this conclusion were offensive-minded civilian officials, such as Wang Yue and the eunuchs, who were motivated to go all out to scuttle the project. Tension between Yu and the eunuchs had been longstanding, but the official's unwise call for the eunuchs' role to be limited to their original domain of household affairs exacerbated court hostility. He abetted opponents' cause by not personally overseeing construction of the new barrier, which suffered from a lack of timely progress in marked contrast to the closely supervised first wall. An inspector in late 1485 reported significant cost overruns and a discontented local population, a development that always upset the emperor. Opponents used this information, even alleging corruption by Yu, to sour Chenghua on the project. By November 1485 he had suspended the wall's construction, leaving Yu to retire with a tarnished reputation. Some officials would continue to advocate for barriers, but stronger resistance now blocked their approval. The Datong-Xuanfu walls would not be resumed for many years, and there would be no frontier-wide security policy.[177]

Batu Mongke, a talented Mongol leader, emerged to exploit the Ming's lack of overall strategy and put increasing pressure on the dynasty to address the frontier. Descended from the Yuan, Batu proved better at unifying Mongol tribes than any leader since Esen in the mid-fifteenth century. Moreover, he introduced during a thirty-eight year reign a number of key innovations, such as the organization of an elite striking force, that enhanced the Mongols' raiding ability. With Chenghua's death in 1488, a new emperor, Hongzhi, was left to address the Batu challenge. He initially attempted to mollify the Mongols by reestablishing a trade relationship, which somewhat improved stability for more than a decade. Then, as usually occurred, Ming suspicion and hostility toward their neighbors prompted a suspension of trading rights in 1500, with an entirely predictable response.[178]

An outraged Batu initiated aggressive raiding and built up camps in the Ordos into enduring bases that would facilitate more continuous and larger strikes against Ming territory. The Mongols struck east against Shanxi Province, west against Gansu, and even southwest against the wall that protected the Shaanxi region. After a quarter century, Yu's structure had apparently suffered considerable decay, proving correct Wang Shu's prediction that any successful barrier would not be maintained. This situation highlights a dilemma for policymakers—the effectiveness of a strategic defense declines over time, but it is difficult to appreciate the rising vulnerability and gain the resources to mitigate the problem without attacks. Irritated and concerned by the frequent raiding, Hongzhi wanted to launch a major offensive into the Ordos to clear out Batu's camps. Convinced by officials that such a campaign exceeded the army's capability, he abandoned the idea but would not approve construction of new border walls. Instead the emperor dispatched an experienced general, Qin Hong, to reform the army and refurbish the extant defenses in the Yansui, Ningxia, and Guyuan sectors. Qin added considerable embankments and ditches to bolster security, but the emergence of Turfan, a powerful new Central Asian state, forced him to further divide an already overstretched force. Then, in 1506, thousands of Mongol raiders penetrated the old barrier in the Guyuan sector southwest of the Ordos.[179]

This latest calamity prompted a now predictable series of events. New emperor Zhengde, who took office the same year, reacted cautiously by sending respected scholar Yang Yiqing to the frontier on a fact-finding mission. Yang's report mirrors the views from thirty years earlier that highlighted the Ming strategic dilemma. He concluded that regaining control of the Ordos and establishing a defensive perimeter on its northern border along the Yellow River loop represented the optimal security approach. Yang added that such a strategy currently exceeded Ming military capability. He urged building border defenses to protect China as much as possible until it accumulated the strength to conquer the Ordos. Barrier critics led by eunuch Liu Jin convinced the emperor to replace Yang and other prodefense frontier officials after the completion of only thirteen miles of the new wall. The solitary and limited success of Yu's barrier south of the Ordos was insufficient to convince emperors that additional walls would enhance security, especially given the presence of strident defense critics at the court. The stark realities, however, prevented even this instinctively aggressive ruler from launching a major campaign. Instead the Ming essentially continued to operate without a frontier policy while Batu strengthened control over the Ordos and security further declined.[180]

The dynasty's shaky financial position during the early decades of the sixteenth century contributed greatly to its inability to adopt either an offensive or defensive frontier policy as well as ensuring the further deterioration of the army. The government's lack of funds left many units without pay for long periods, which inevitably prompted mass desertions. They often exacerbated instability by forming bandit armies, exemplified when such a force brought chaos to the region south of Beijing in 1509. The government ultimately recalled some of its most capable units from the frontier to restore control, accepting increased vulnerability to Mongol raids. The cycle would repeat itself during the 1520s and 1530s, raising suspicion that the Mongols actively instigated or worked with these bandit armies. With their mobility and the initiative, the northerners could easily outmatch beleaguered Ming defenders with "raids" of up to sixty thousand warriors.[181]

Beyond financial constraints, the growing influence of southerners politicized Ming frontier policy. Having accumulated great wealth, southerners had obtained more positions in the inner court and government from which to advocate their beliefs that the Mongols, regarded as barbarians, should be isolated.[182] Internal politics, while always a factor, increasingly colored frontier policy discussions, especially discouraging consideration of any accommodation. This perspective became magnified with the succession of Zhengde by Jiajing in 1522. The new emperor, a southerner, "loathed the Mongols and felt they were an insufferable affront to his dignity and majesty."[183] Jiajing thought the Ming should avoid any diplomatic or economic interaction with the Mongols. Moreover, his disputed rise to power left the ruler obsessed with protocol and personal prestige while producing an intensely factionalized court.[184] The competing groups found frontier policy to be a favorite arena in which to battle, and discussions usually ended in deadlock. Experienced government officials managed to scuttle attempts to launch major attacks, but they could not win support for policies that might bolster security. Instead, government policies only provoked more raids, which prompted more Ming hatred—"a vicious diplomatic circle" that now reached its apex.[185] The only mitigating factor for the Ming was the aging and ultimately the passing of Batu Mongke in 1524, which prompted the Mongols to be distracted by internecine conflict on the steppe.

Second Ordos Debate

The power struggle on the steppe ended with the victory of Altan Khan in the early 1540s, which heralded a much greater threat. Rather than take advantage of the respite, the Ming had taken no meaningful measures to address frontier security. An underfunded government and overwhelmed military struggled to respond to the increasing scale and cohesion of Mongol attacks. Growing problems of internal unrest, demanding Portuguese traders, and, most significantly, the explosion of piracy along the coast now competed for Ming resources and attention, pulling the army in different directions. Despite the deteriorating situation, Jiajing would not consider a trading relationship with Altan Khan, who harbored no territorial ambitions in China. The Mongol leader simply sought goods, especially grain, as an ongoing drought had hit his power base particularly hard. The Ming court's brusque rejection of his overtures prompted the aggravated and needy Mongol leader to retaliate with attacks, seeking booty for supporters and pressure on the Ming to allow trade.[186]

As the ferocity and depth of these raids grew, the Ming finally initiated construction of extensive long walls in the Datong and Xuanfu sectors sixty years after Yu's aborted effort. While questions about their military effectiveness still existed for many officials, strategic defenses were the only option that could garner a green light from the heavily factionalized court. By the late 1540s, China had covered the eastern border of the Ordos with approximately 525 miles of barriers and considerably more signal towers and garrisons.[187] This strategic defense system usually had two defense lines, but in key areas, a third or even fourth wall had been added for depth. Local commander Weng Wanda, while ably directing the defense program, also urged the court to pursue trade and diplomacy given that the military was "incapable of resisting" the Mongols.[188] Other frontier officials echoed Weng's sentiment as improved defenses "made raiding more difficult and costly for the Mongols; but they did not remove the cause of the raiding."[189] Attacks continued and the Ming generally fared poorly against the Mongols in battle. Most disturbingly to the Chinese, "the nomads were settling down along the border in a strategically ominous way" with the founding of a Chinese-style city at Hohhot, fewer than 250 miles from Beijing.[190] Nevertheless, the emperor, while respecting Weng's judgment and funding his request for robust defenses, "refused to consider petitions for trade."[191]

Instead the continued attacks prompted the Ming government in the 1540s to consider seriously a large-scale offensive for the first time in decades. Given the state of the Ming army, this exploration seems surprising, but any potential escape from the nightmarish status quo made an offensive appealing to some officials. Moreover, the reliably pro-offensive eunuchs now exerted greater influence over military policy.[192] Thus, in 1547, the war faction seized on a two-step proposal from Zeng Xian, joint commander of the Yansui, Ningxia, and Guyuan sectors, to drive the Mongols out of the Ordos. His plan called for an army of at least three hundred thousand soldiers to sweep the enemy from the region, after which defenses would be constructed along the Yellow River loop that provided the northern border of the Ordos. The bold, if unrealistic, proposal gained critical momentum when Grand Secretary Xia Yan indicated his support, albeit largely for internal political reasons.[193]

The emperor found the plan appealing, but not surprisingly, many officials, led by Minister of War Chen Jing, opposed it as excessively costly and risky. Given the relative military strength of the Mongols and Ming, the common criticisms used to counter pro-offensive advocates in every debate since the 1470s had never been stronger. Even if the initial campaign succeeded, the Ming's ability to hold and defend the Ordos appeared highly questionable. Projected costs for the invasion and subsequent defense, although far below likely actual costs, were still substantial. Whether Jiajing would have been persuaded to ignore these negatives is unknowable because the plan also faced a daunting political obstacle. Grand Secretary Yan Sung, Xia Yan's rival for power in the court, regarded the Ordos campaign as a political threat to him. Appreciating that Xia supported the campaign as a way to increase his clout, the politically superior Yan made sure to block it. On February 15, 1548, Jiajing indicated his concern about the campaign for the first time, prompting its support to unravel. A combination of political and military pressure ultimately doomed the plan to reconquer the Ordos, which the Ming would never again seriously consider.[194]

The Ming almost certainly avoided a military disaster by rejecting the offensive, but border security continued to deteriorate. The construction of significant barriers in the Datong and Xuanfu sectors had only prompted the Mongols to shift most attacks elsewhere on the frontier, especially the open area northeast of Beijing. By this route, the Mongols conducted a succession of large raids in June 1548, October 1548, November 1548, and March 1549. Altan Khan left word during this last raid in March 1549 that unless the Ming allowed a trade relationship, he would launch a major attack on Beijing in the fall. Even such a grave threat could not mobilize the deeply divided Ming to action. Perhaps the capital's multilayered impregnable walls and the Mongols' disinterest in remaining in Ming territory caused court officials to be unmoved. In September 1550, Mongol detachments circumvented the well-fortified Gubeikou Pass northeast of Beijing and opened the way for a large nomad force to reach the outskirts of the Chinese capital. Although the Mongols could not enter Beijing, they spent three days looting the surrounding area before returning to the steppe.[195]

Altan Khan had made his point as greatly alarmed court officials scrambled to respond to an intolerable situation, even initiating a surcharge on land taxes for the only time in the sixteenth century. The funds obtained, however, could not offset Ming weakness in the near term, prompting the court to finally follow the advice of Weng Wanda and reluctantly agree to limited trade in April 1551. The Mongols discontinued raids in return for semiannual fairs at which they would exchange horses for Chinese textiles. The Ming, however, balked when the Mongols subsequently sought to add trading cattle and sheep for beans and grain. Accommodation had quickly lost favor among Ming officials after the pressure of major Mongol raids ceased. Many decision makers worried, as one official noted, that "if China displayed weakness by acceding to formal trade relations, it would lose its awesomeness and would appear fearful of the Mongols."[196] The Ming knew this rejection would prompt a renewal of Mongol raiding by the winter 1551–52, but they now felt less vulnerable. Instead, the new raids prompted Jiajing to end all trade and reputedly forbid any official from even raising the topic.[197]

Having rejected offensives for good and backed away from accommodation, the Ming began "wall-building on an unprecedented scale" to seal off the frontier and, in essence, mimic the safety of Beijing on a much grander scale.[198] The potential for this approach depended on officials' understanding of the previous breeches of the frontier. Rather than viewing periodic penetrations of walls as an indictment of such structures per se, at least some Ming officials focused on a pair of practical flaws—one more correctable than the other. With the Mongols probing for weakness and directing attacks—"like water"—against identified areas to the west and especially the east of the capital, incomplete defenses left North China vulnerable.[199] Of course, such a deficiency prompted wall-building advocates to argue successfully for more barriers, especially northeast of Beijing to close off an approximately eight-hundred-mile gap.[200] The scope of the strategic defenses by this time covered thousands of miles, making maintenance an expensive, unmanageable task.

Even more problematic for the Ming government, barriers required an effective army. Genghis Khan had zeroed in on this point by allegedly uttering "the strength of walls depends on the courage of those who guard them."[201] Whether apocryphal or not, recent mass raids had shown "the Wall was not a defense in itself, but a defense installation that required manning with well-armed, well-trained, and most of all, well-commanded and motivated troops."[202] Quantitatively and especially qualitatively, Ming forces did not measure up to the challenge. Frequent fraternization between imperial soldiers in frontier towers and Mongol warriors provided the adversary valuable intelligence.[203] Unfortunately, the government found building physical structures easier than fixing the army's endemic problems. Only with the 1567 assignment to the frontier of Gen. Qi Jiguang, a hero from fighting Japanese pirates, would a serious effort at training be undertaken.[204] Qi appreciated that security could never be achieved without a capable force, but too many Ming officials failed to realize this requirement or lacked the will and ability to satisfy it. Thus the government concentrated on completing the barrier defense system across northern China while the Mongols continued to conduct successful major raids.

By the end of the 1560s, the Ming government's deteriorating financial and strategic position forced it to reexamine the practice of relying exclusively on a defense-based security policy. With a barrier now essentially extending across the front, the location of future Mongol attacks became less predictable. Sometimes the nomads coordinated raiding parties across the frontier, further complicating Ming efforts to concentrate forces. Efforts to bolster frontier garrisons as much as possible, combined with the increased need for coastal protection from pirates, prompted military expenditures to soar until the army accounted for between 60 to 70 percent of the government budget. It was still not enough because the troops manning the northern nine defense areas remained inadequate both quantitatively and qualitatively. Essentially a vicious circle or, more accurately, a downward spiral, plagued the Ming as increased Mongol attacks prompted walls for improved defenses and thus greater expenditures, which further strained government effectiveness without resolving the underlying problem.²⁰⁵

Faced with an untenable position, the Ming finally escaped when political changes permitted a reconsideration of reaching an accommodation with the Mongols. First and most critically, after forty-five years on the throne, Emperor Jiajing died in 1567. His successor, Longqing, displayed more openness than did his predecessors on integrating trade and diplomacy into security policy.²⁰⁶ Second, Grand Secretary Zhang Juzheng, through a close relationship with the new ruler, succeeded in centralizing authority to a degree unseen in decades.²⁰⁷ Given his considerable influence and sensitivity to the precarious Ming finances, Zhang worked to establish a viable frontier policy. Rejecting the always-present calls for preemptive strikes, Zhang and his allies concluded that the best response to the Mongol challenge combined strengthened defenses with economic and political interaction.²⁰⁸ This combination had long been urged by the most astute frontier officials, such as Yu Zijun and Weng Wanda. The court apparently feared that a purely accommodationist approach would engender Mongol perceptions of Ming weakness and precipitate attempts to extort more goods or launch greater assaults. Thus the Ming continued to upgrade defenses while finally moving to engage the Mongols.²⁰⁹

The Chinese achieved the needed diplomatic breakthrough in 1571 when Gen. Wang Chonggu convinced Altan Khan to accept a mutually beneficial peace.²¹⁰ For the Mongols, swearing allegiance to the Ming was a worthwhile price for reestablishing trade. Profiting more from exchanges than from raids, attacks immediately lost their appeal and largely stopped. For the Ming, the frontier population enjoyed much greater security while cuts in manning observation towers and conducting patrols along the frontier quickly reduced military expenditures. The defenses remained in place to encourage Mongol cooperation, in part by ensuring that trading would be more profitable than raiding. Wall sections even received upgrades after occasional raids from tribes beyond Altan Khan's control or local leaders dissatisfied with current trade terms. Most notably, a 1576 attack through a gap in a remote, mountainous area by one of Altan Khan's sons sparked a significant improvement to the Jizhou sector, northeast of Beijing.²¹¹ Despite the overall success of this combination policy, infighting between hardliners and engagement advocates returned after Zhang fell in 1582.²¹² Fortunately, Altan Khan's death the same year left the Ming to face a less unified and thus less dangerous Mongol foe.

Rising up to thirty to thirty-five feet in height with a crenellated brick top, the recently built Jizhou sector's approximately 666-mile course from north of Beijing along the Yanshan and Taihang mountains until reaching the Shanhaiguan fortress created a striking impression.²¹³ It is this monumental section, labeled "ostentatious exhibitionism" by a critical historian, that provides today's image of the Great Wall.[214] Another historian asks why the Ming erected such structures over mountains that clearly would not be crossed by Mongolian cavalry.[215] The desire for a symbol of China's awesomeness may have been a compelling motivation for such construction. Nevertheless, given that the front had repeatedly been exposed by small numbers of Mongols, such as the aforementioned raid by Altan Khan's son, frontier officials had pushed for defense improvements, especially towers. Resource constraints limited the rate and extent of work, but the Ming managed to strengthen the wall and erect twelve hundred additional towers by the end of the 1580s.[216] Repairs and modest enhancements would continue until the end of the dynasty in 1644, but the essentially complete Ming Great Wall of China now guarded the entire northern frontier.

End of the Ming and Their Defenses: The Manchu Challenge

While relative stability persisted on the Chinese–Mongol front in the early seventeenth century, a new and ultimately more dangerous threat emerged to the northeast on the Liaodong Peninsula—the Jurchens (Manchus, after 1635). This region had the earliest Ming strategic defenses in the 1440s, but its works, although connected to the main line, were less robust than the adjoining areas. The fortifications played a role in securing this corner of the empire, but more importance had been standing alliances with Jurchen tribes. This policy began faltering in the late sixteenth century when an independent-minded and military-gifted Jurchen leader named Nurhaci emerged and began unifying disparate tribes. Chinese officials at first ignored him, distracted by a Japanese invasion of Korea and native revolts in the southern provinces. Whereas the Ming overestimated the Mongol threat to their rule by correlating its leaders with the Yuan period, they underestimated the Jurchens, who—like their ancestors—were much more likely to threaten dynastic rule. The Jurchens shrewdly pursued both Chinese sedentary knowledge and Mongol martial prowess. Any foreign entity aiming to supplant the Ming needed such a skill set; otherwise, they would be limited to raiding as the Mongols had done for the past two hundred years. Struggling to obtain the considerable resources needed for his fledgling state, Nurhaci began attacking Ming territory in search of goods as the Mongols had, but he already indicated greater ambition by proclaiming the restoration of the Jin dynasty (1115–1234).[217]

Rather than bolster defenses or generally prepare to meet the challenge, the overconfident Ming responded by cutting off trade to punish the Jurchens. This step naturally provoked an escalation of attacks that ultimately led to outright war in 1618. For the Ming, the northerners quickly demonstrated their martial strength by capturing the border city of Fushen. Beyond material gains, Nurhaci hoped to highlight Chinese weakness and convince holdout Jurchen tribes to switch sides. Wanting to reassure its frontier allies and undercut Nurhaci, the Ming rushed a one-hundred-thousand-man army north in 1619. This poorly led and unprepared force, however, was defeated on consecutive days at Sar Hu. With the resulting damage to Chinese prestige in Liaodong, the remaining pro-Ming Jurchen tribes closed ranks with Nurhaci, and many border cities capitulated after their undersupplied and underpaid garrisons defected. By 1621 the Jurchens controlled all former Ming territory on the peninsula east of the Liao River.[218]

The Chinese now appreciated the threat, but officials disagreed on how to respond. Again, accommodation appears not to have been an option, and the debate focused on either aggressively pursuing Nurhaci or accepting some retrenchment and husbanding resources. Rising military expenditures had already severely strained Ming finances, prompting some bureaucrats such as censor Zhang Quan to warn that increased government taxation risked provoking major internal rebellions. The discrepancy between societal wealth and Ming government resources had grown sharply over the course of the dynasty. Some officials doubted that even a well-resourced Chinese military could retake the lost territory, given its lackluster army. While this antiwar faction favored conserving resources, the predominant view contended that the Jurchen military challenge had to be met directly. This effort resulted in a string of defeats until the Ming in November 1625 repulsed the Jurchens and fatally wounded Nurhaci at Ningyuan, fewer than fifty miles north of Great Wall.[219]

Although suggesting limits to the Jurchen threat, the battle actually proved counterproductive by clearing a path for the rise of Nurhaci's even more capable son, Abahai. Whereas the military-focused Nurhaci lacked political organization skills, Abahai excelled in this regard. Realizing that defeat of the Middle Kingdom required a stronger political foundation, he first attempted to make peace with the Ming. The court dismissed the proposal, appreciating that a stoppage of war would likely be temporary. By this point, accommodation was not an option. Moreover, Ming officials now possessed greater military confidence, especially with the recently imported European cannons having proved so valuable at Ningyuan. They knew that between the Jurchens and North China stood the strongest section of the Great Wall system, including Shanhaiguan fortress blocking the only major pass in the area. In essence, they adopted a combination offense–defense policy against the Jurchens, but Ming resource limitations and bureaucratic incompetence hampered the approach.[220]

Abahai's restrained reaction to the Ming rebuff showed his savvy. First he invaded Korea to coerce its government into providing needed financial support. Then, after a failed attempt to penetrate Ming defenses demonstrated that the Jurchens lacked the strength to achieve a breakthrough, he achieved a diplomatic and military coup by gaining the support of key Mongol tribes. Growing similarities between the two steppe peoples, especially with the Mongols' declining nomadic ways, had set the stage for such an alliance. Beyond his Mongol partners' valued military assistance, Abahai could shift raids westerly through their territory. Striking this more vulnerable sector of Chinese defenses allowed the Jurchens to penetrate the Great Wall in 1629. After breeching the barrier, the raiders stayed in China for a few months, even probing near Beijing, to the dismay of Ming officials.[221] Their lengthy "visit" ominously stood in contrast to the quick-hitting Mongols. In subsequent years the Jurchens would repeatedly penetrate this sector of the barrier while the area facing Manchuria remained stout. This episode reiterates that strategic defenses with variable strength have significantly reduced effects on the military balance. It is important to observe that by blocking the most critical avenue, the Ming had raised the difficulty and cost of Jurchen attacks while limiting their danger.

The symbolism of the barrier's penetration exacerabated the Ming court's ineffectual response. After the initial penetration, it recalled Yuan Zhenghuan, China's ablest commander, from Manchuria and ultimately executed him. His fate shows that "political rather than military concerns drove the defense system" even at this vulnerable stage.[222] Without his leadership, the Chinese position in Manchuria rapidly deteriorated. The northerners' ability to cross the Great Wall from this time until the end of the dynasty was likely abetted by the Ming army's budget constraints.[223] Again, this experience highlights that physical fortifications' effectiveness sharply deteriorates without proper maintenance and manning.

Unable to reach an accommodation with Abahai and lacking sufficient military strength to defeat him or even secure the frontier, the Ming largely ignored the potential benefit of establishing alliances with key Mongol tribes. Such a diplomatic coup would have enabled the Chinese to outflank the Jurchens. Even neutralizing the Mongols would have been valuable, denying the Jurchens needed horses and territorial access. Yet the Chinese government undermined its one attempt at such alliance manipulation by eliminating the subsidy to Lighdan Khan, the Chahar Mongol leader. The Ming court was simply too conservative by this time to engage in steppe politics effectively. The existence of its strategic defenses, despite limited penetrations, probably encouraged the natural conservatism of the Ming. Their fortifications had allowed the dynasty to "muddle through" against the Mongols. However, the Mongols had no interest in overthrowing the Ming and muddling through worked to reduce the danger especially given the tendency for internecine warfare to break out on the steppe and weaken the nomads. By contrast, Abahai managed an increasingly cohesive political entity, which he established as the Qing Dynasty in 1636 to signal his intention to replace the Ming. As long as the Great Wall defense system remained impenetrable to an army in the northeast, the Manchus (Abahai changed their name in 1635) lacked the ability to win militarily. Instead Abahai followed a de facto strategy of pressuring the Ming with raids while strengthening his control over Manchuria.[224]

Manchu pressure would exacerbate the internal weakness of the Chinese state to undermine the Ming dynasty. The "crippling effects of fiscal mismanagement" not only hampered defense, they also imposed great hardship on soldiers, especially those serving in the neglected units of northwestern China.[225] Inadequately paid and provisioned, soldiers deserted in increasing numbers, and many formed bandit gangs. In the late 1630s, Li Zicheng and Zhang Xianzhang united these disparate forces into large armies. The emergence of this threat, in addition to the Manchus, created a strategic dilemma for the Ming. Manchu pressure prevented the Ming from concentrating against the rebels, and combating these restive Chinese hampered responding to the Manchus. The court focused on whichever problem seemed more acute, but it switched direction whenever that situation improved, preventing a lasting result against either threat. For example, at the end of the 1630s, China's most able commander, Hong Zhengzhou, gained significant ground against the rebels, prompting the government to transfer him to the neglected Manchurian front and allowing rebel forces to recover.[226]

By the early 1640s, Abahai's de facto strategy of "pressure and wait" had crystallized into an actual policy with his awareness of the Ming Dynasty's precarious position. In 1642 Chinese defenses north of the Great Wall almost completely collapsed. This Ming setback probably suggested to Abahai a more fundamental weakness given his information that Li Zicheng's rebel army had grown to four hundred thousand men. The army rapidly approached the capital, which was protected by twenty-one miles of strong walls that had always been impregnable. As the ultimate example of a barrier being only as strong as the men defending it, the walls would not save the Ming this time. The government's only effective fighting force was more than two hundred miles away facing the Manchus. In the spring of 1644, a majority of the capital's soldiers had already abandoned the bankrupt regime, leaving a small force of second-rate troops and die-hard eunuchs to defend the emperor. When Li attacked, most of these remaining guards scurried away, leaving an isolated Emperor Chongzhen to hang himself on April 25, 1644.[227]

While the dynasty was over, Wu Sangui, commanding the last effective Ming army, had the ability to serve as kingmaker. Both the rebels and the Manchus sought his support. Finding the prospect of a Manchu dynasty more appealing than peasant rule of China, Wu allowed the Manchu army access through the Great Wall and joined forces with it to end Li Zicheng's so-called Shun dynasty.[228] Possessing strong organizational skills at first, the Manchus' Qing Dynasty would survive into the twentieth century. After debating the utility of the Ming long walls, the new regime generally abandoned them.[229] The barriers made little sense given the Manchus' desire to expand the Chinese empire to encompass the steppe and their priority on directing resources against the growing European threat along the coast. Moreover, defeat had soured the scholar-official class within China on defenses as "a symbol of Ming Chinese military weakness, collapse, and conquest by, yet again, foreign 'barbarians.'"[230] Nevertheless, the immense barrier remained in a state of benign neglect into the twentieth century, when it suffered considerable damage during the fighting of World War II, the Chinese Civil War, and finally the carnage of the Cultural Revolution.

Conclusion

Most of Yu's original barrier has vanished, and the remainder only provides modest cover from the area's worsening sandstorms. By contrast, visiting the Great Wall at Simatai, northeast of Beijing, with its 70-degree slope up 2,500-foot peaks, leaves one awestruck. A stop at this place or another section near the capital has become obligatory for any first-time visitor. It has been estimated that one-third of the Ming Great Wall is still in fairly good condition with another third remaining in poor shape. Construction of the barrier has actually begun again in recent decades, reaching about twenty miles according to one recent study.[231] Now, however, this work is done to lure tourists rather than repel raiders. Many of the sightseers are Chinese, who in the past century have come to view the Great Wall as a source of pride and accomplishment. For Chinese and foreigners alike, the barrier stands as the most famous symbol of the Middle Kingdom.

Does this fond memory accurately reflect the Ming Great Wall of China's contribution to Chinese security? Given that "the Ming experienced more attacks over a longer period than any other Chinese dynasty," such fortifications had been regarded as essential by government officials.[232] At the same time, the existence of such attacks undermines claims of its value as a strategic deterrent. Most historians characterize the structure as unsuccessful.[233] Mote typifies this view by concluding that "China's Great Wall wasted vast amounts of treasure and it defined a foreign policy that was shortsighted and doomed to failure."[234] The high military expenditures not only failed to tame external challenges but also contributed significantly to the emergence of an internal climate that finally brought down the dynasty. Instead scholars generally regard the ignored approach of accommodation as offering the best chance for stability and prosperity along the northern frontier.[235]

Before addressing this strategic assessment, the tactical performance of the barrier needs to be considered. Adversaries, both the Mongols and Manchus, appear to have struggled against well-constructed and guarded defenses, suggesting tactical effectiveness.[236] However, a defense system that cannot be maintained in robust operating condition lacks operational effectiveness regardless of its optimal performance. Places with worn-down defenses or inadequate and demoralized (or even disloyal) soldiers created severe vulnerabilities. Unfortunately, one or both of these shortcomings frequently appear to have been operative. Possessing the initiative and probing for weaknesses, the highly mobile adversaries could generally avoid the Great Wall's most robust sections, albeit at some cost. Given the vastness of the frontier and the government's limited resources, the Ming simply found it impossible to maintain the defenses in satisfactory condition.

The discussion of strategic effectiveness must be based on a permeable barrier, albeit one presenting raiders with far greater difficulty than open terrain. During the Ming Great Wall's episodic construction lasting over a century in the middle of the dynasty, its circumvention reflected a clear indictment of a partial defense strategy. After the frontier was almost continually blocked by walls in the 1580s, the Chinese had made raiding much more difficult, despite the aforementioned weaknesses. The strategic problem with relying on long walls, however, lay in the nature of the opponent. The Mongols were a thoroughly revisionist actor that needed Chinese goods, if not for their existence, then at least for any quality of life. Some Ming officials prophesied that the Mongols would cease attacking if the defenses proved impenetrable. The defenses, however, never achieved enough success to test the potential for such deterrence by denial. Nevertheless, one doubts that the Mongols—given their motivation (need, not opportunity) and lack of alternatives—would ever have stopped attacking until given trade rights. Thus, at a minimum, the Chinese would have had to maintain this expensive security policy indefinitely.

With an offensive-based solution impractical from the second half of the fifteenth century, the primary counterfactual to relying on defenses would have been accommodation. Although many historians argue that such an approach offered the path to stability, one can question if this approach alone would have been sufficient. After agreeing to trade in 1571, most Mongol attacks ceased as the nomads found peaceful exchanges more lucrative than raiding. But that calculation occurred with the Ming continuing to upgrade their defenses. Given the Mongol tendency to constantly seek a better trade deal and attack when rebuffed, they would have had far greater leverage over the economic relationship if the Ming adopted a purely accommodationist approach. Whether that leverage would have produced enough gains to offset the cost of defenses earlier in the dynasty cannot be empirically assessed. Regardless, the political consequences of accommodating increasing Mongol trade demands should raise doubt about such a policy's sustainability without a metamorphosis in the antibarbarian Ming political environment. No rationale exists for such a metamorphosis occurring. A severe danger would seem to lurk in growing Chinese frustration over the likely escalation of Mongol trade demands. It quite likely would have prompted a rash decision or series of decisions for offensives into the steppe. Almost certainly, these flights of fancy would have repeated the disastrous Tumu experience and perhaps badly destabilized the dynasty. Maybe accommodation would have achieved the required metamorphosis in Chinese thinking, but it stands as a questionable proposition.

The Ming decision to pursue a combination defense–accommodation approach in the 1570s appears the most strategically sound course of action. Wiser Ming officials, such as Yu Zijun and Weng Wanda, had long advocated for such a frontier policy. The Ming experience highlights the general point that defenses work most effectively in combination with another approach that more directly affects the adversary. Not only did trading reduce Mongol incentives to strike, it also greatly reduced the need for maintaining strategic defenses and thus allowed for a reduced budget. The extant barriers still contributed by readiness and shaping enemy calculations of cost and feasibility for abandoning agreements or attempting to lever better terms. Despite its success, such a combination approach proved fragile given the preponderant political disinclination to accommodate the barbarians. The period of improved relations does not seem to have had a salutary effect on the Han perspective toward northerners.

The Ming primarily relied on the Great Wall strategic defense system to "muddle through." Lovell reflects a standard condemnation of the barrier as providing only a "temporary advantage" demonstrating its bankruptcy as a policy approach.[237] However, "buying time" should not be condemned outright; at times, it is the best possible outcome. Unfortunately, the Ming case illustrates the common phenomenon that in such cases regimes do not productively use the time "bought." Rather, the short-term gain often discourages decision makers from adopting a companion part of the strategy to produce a long-term solution, especially if such a course is politically costly or risky. In the Ming case, the grandiose, symbolically powerful wall structure probably abetted a Chinese mentality of dissimilarity with the "barbarians" that exacerbated the political and psychological obstacles to engagement. Ultimately, the availability of fortifications prompted the Ming to forgo painful reforms until "muddling through" was no longer possible.

Notes

1. Arthur Waldron, *The Great Wall of China: From History to Myth* (New York: Oxford University Press, 1990), 7–8.

2. Waldron, *Great Wall of China,* 97; and Frederick Mote, "The Chenghua and Hongzhi Reigns," in *The Cambridge History of China,* Vol. 7, *The Ming Dynasty, 1368–1644, Part I,* eds. Frederick Mote and Denis Twitchett (New York: Cambridge University Press, 1988), 401.

3. Waldron, *Great Wall of China*, 55.

4. See ibid., 55–56, 61–62; Mote, "Chenghua and Hongzhi Reigns," 400–401; and Alastair Ian Johnston, *Cultural Realism: Strategic Culture and Grand Strategy in Chinese History* (Princeton: Princeton University Press, 1995), 185.

5. Mote, "Chenghua and Hongzhi Reigns," 401.

6. Waldron, *Great Wall of China*, 97, 100.

7. Ibid., 100; and Mote, "Chenghua and Hongzhi Reigns," 401.

8. See, for example, Frederick Mote, *Imperial China, 900–1800* (Cambridge, MA: Harvard University Press, 2003), 693, 697; Waldron, *Great Wall of China*, 171–72, 187; Julia Lovell, *The Great Wall: China against the World, 1000 BC–AD 2000* (New York: Grove, 2006), 17–19; and Thomas J. Barfield, *The Perilous Frontier: Nomadic Empires and China, 221 BC to AD 1757* (Cambridge, MA: Blackwell, 1989), 231, 248.

9. Waldron, *Great Wall of China*, 98, 100.

10. See ibid., 147–51; William Lindesay, *The Great Wall* (New York: Oxford University Press, 2003), 57–62; Henry Serruys, "Towers in the Northern Frontier Defenses of the Ming," *Ming Studies* 14 (Spring 1982): 10; and Luo Zhewen, *The Great Wall: History and Pictures* (Beijing: Foreign Language Press, 1995), 17–23.

11. Mote, *Imperial China*, 693; Lindesay, *Great Wall*, 43; and Waldron, *Great Wall of China*, 141.

12. Serruys, "Towers," 9.

13. See Qiao Yun, *Defense Structures: Ancient Chinese Architecture* (New York: Springer-Verlag, 2001), 128, 133, 135, 139–40; Waldron, *Great Wall of China*, 141; Luo, *Great Wall*, 17, 22, 80, 146; Lovell, *Great Wall*, 219–22, 226–27; and Lu Shun, *The Eternal Great Wall* (Beijing: China Nationality Art Photograph Publishing House, 2005), 80. The Ming Great Wall lacks an agreed upon length given differences of opinion on which of the myriad lines/spurs should be counted.

14. Waldron, *Great Wall of China*, 143, 151, 157; Luo, *Great Wall*, 17, 31, 96; and Stephen Turnbull, *The Great Wall of China, BC 221–AD 1644* (Oxford: Osprey, 2007), 44–45.

15. Serruys, "Towers," 24.

16. See Qiao, *Defense Structures*, 127–28; Waldron, *Great Wall of China*, 9, 72–73, 141; Turnbull, *Great Wall of China*, 17–23; Lovell, *Great Wall*, 219, 223–25; and Lindesay, *Great Wall*, 45–46.

17. Qiao, *Defense Structures*, 127, 130.

18. Ibid., 132, 137–38; and Waldron, *Great Wall of China*, 140, 150.

19. Turnbull, *Great Wall of China*, 29; and Serruys, "Towers," 60.

20. Waldron, *Great Wall of China*, 151.

21. See Serruys, "Towers," 11, 16, 21, 23–26, 37, 53; Qiao, *Defense Structures*, 126–27, 134, 140; and Turnbull, *Great Wall of China*, 25–28, 37.

22. Lovell, *Great Wall*, 21, 43–44, 58–59, 83–84.

23. Waldron, *Great Wall of China*, 3, 7, 22–29, 37, 47; Lovell, *Great Wall*, 15–16, 138; and Lindesay, *Great Wall*, 16, 20, 25–26.

24. Waldron, *Great Wall of China*, 2, 13, 15.
25. Ibid., 2, 13, 15–18; and Lovell, *Great Wall*, 53–55, 57, 61–63.
26. Lovell *Great Wall*, 17. See also ibid., 17–18, 64, 67, 69–70, 74–75, 88–90, 118, 125–26, 133–34.
27. Waldron, *Great Wall of China*, 47–48; and Lovell, *Great Wall*, 138–45.
28. Lovell, *Great Wall*, 143.
29. Waldron, *Great Wall of China*, 47–48; and Lovell, *Great Wall*, 95, 145–46, 150.
30. Waldron, *Great Wall of China*, 70; and Lovell, *Great Wall*, 177–78.
31. Waldron, *Great Wall of China*, 21.
32. Lindesay, *Great Wall*, 7; see also Waldron, *Great Wall of China*, 33, 37, 171; and Lovell, *Great Wall*, 44, 69–71, 87–90, 138.
33. See Waldron, *Great Wall of China*, 70, 73–75; and Lovell, *Great Wall*, 183, 188.
34. See Waldron, *Great Wall of China*, 9, 72–73, 76–79, 86; Serruys, "Towers," 14; and Turnbull, *Great Wall of China*, 14.
35. Barfield, *Perilous Frontier*, 234; see also Mote, *Imperial China*, 567, 618–19; and Lovell, *Great Wall*, 182–83, 193–94.
36. Mote, *Imperial China*, 611, 695; and Waldron, *Great Wall of China*, 80, 86.
37. Waldron, *Great Wall of China*, 81.
38. Ibid., 80–81.
39. Barfield, *Perilous Frontier*, 230, 238, 240; Waldron, *Great Wall of China*, 86, 88; and Lovell, *Great Wall*, 191–93, 196.
40. See Barfield, *Perilous Frontier*, 238; Lovell, *Great Wall*, 191–93; and Mote, *Imperial China*, 692–93.
41. Barfield, *Perilous Frontier*, 238; see also Waldron, *Great Wall of China*, 89–92; Mote, *Imperial China*, 627–28; Lovell, *Great Wall*, 193, 195–98; and Barfield, *Perilous Frontier*, 241–42, 249.
42. Waldron, *Great Wall of China*, 91.
43. Johnston, *Cultural Realism*, 185; Waldron, *Great Wall of China*, 91; and Barfield, *Perilous Frontier*, 238, 242, 246.
44. Waldron, *Great Wall of China*, 88, 91–92.
45. Lovell, *Great Wall*, 190.
46. Waldron, *Great Wall of China*, 92, 94–95.
47. Barfield, *Perilous Frontier*, 238, 249; and Lovell, *Great Wall*, 33, 186.
48. Barfield, *Perilous Frontier*, 249.
49. Johnston, *Cultural Realism*, 188–89; and Waldron, *Great Wall of China*, 58.
50. Mote, *Imperial China*, 702, 706.
51. Ibid., 685.
52. Johnston, *Cultural Realism*, 188.
53. Lovell, *Great Wall*, 186.
54. Mote, *Imperial China*, 689.
55. Barfield, *Perilous Frontier*, 232; see also ibid., 233, 238, 242; Mote, *Imperial China*, 610, 688–89, 691; Arthur Waldron, "Chinese Strategy from the Fourteenth to

the Seventeenth Centuries," in *The Making of Strategy: Rulers, States, and War*, eds. Williamson Murray, MacGregor Knox, and Alvin Burnstein (New York: Cambridge University Press, 1994), 91; and Morris Rossabi, "The Ming and Inner Asia," in *Cambridge History of China*, Vol. 8, *The Ming Dynasty, 1368–1644, Part II*, eds. Denis Twichett and Frederick Mote (New York: Cambridge University Press, 1998), 224.

56. Lindesay, *Great Wall*, 37.
57. Johnston, *Cultural Realism*, 187.
58. Ibid., 224.
59. Rossabi, "Ming and Inner Asia," 269.
60. Mote, "Chenghua and Hongzhi Reigns," 399.
61. Ibid., 399–400.
62. Ibid., 399–401; Barfield, *Perilous Frontier*, 243; and Waldron, *Great Wall of China*, 97–98, 103.
63. Lovell, *Great Wall*, 186.
64. Mote, *Imperial China*, 701.
65. Ibid., 685, 719–20.
66. See Mote, "Chenghua and Hongzhi Reigns," 377–80, 384, 387.
67. Ibid., 372–73, 376; Lovell, *Great Wall*, 196, 200; and Waldron, "Chinese Strategy," 98, 105.
68. Mote, "Chenghua and Hongzhi Reigns," 373; and Charles O. Hucker, "Ming Government," in *Cambridge History of China*, Vol. 8, *The Ming Dynasty, 1368–1644, Part II*, eds. Denis Twichett and Frederick Mote (New York: Cambridge University Press, 1998), 55, 100.
69. Hucker, "Ming Government," 62.
70. Ibid., 65, 70–71; Ray Huang, "The Ming Fiscal Administration," in *Cambridge History of China*, Vol. 8, *The Ming Dynasty, 1368–1644, Part II*, eds. Denis Twichett and Frederick Mote (New York: Cambridge University Press, 1998), 150; and Waldron, *Great Wall of China*, 82–83.
71. Mote, "Chenghua and Hongzhi Reigns," 373.
72. Barfield, *Perilous Frontier*, 242; and Lovell, *Great Wall*, 201–2.
73. Lovell, *Great Wall*, 196.
74. Hucker, "Ming Government," 67.
75. Mote, "Chenghua and Hongzhi Reigns," 373; Hucker, "Ming Government," 13, 75; and Luo, *Great Wall*, 17–21. The Ming later added two commands around Beijing to bolster its protection.
76. Hucker, "Ming Government," 103.
77. Lu, *Eternal Great Wall*, 63.
78. See Mote, "Chenghua and Hongzhi Reigns," 367, 373–76, 400–401; Waldron, *Great Wall of China*, 97–98; Shih-shan Henry Tsai, *The Eunuchs in the Ming Dynasty* (New York: State University of New York Press, 1996), 64; and Marvin Whiting, *Imperial Chinese Military History, 8000 BC–1912 AD* (Lincoln, NE: Writers Club, 2002), 439.

79. For example, see Johnston, *Cultural Realism*; Huiyun Feng, *Chinese Strategic Culture and Foreign Policy Decision-Making: Confucianism, Leadership, and War* (New York: Routledge, 2007); Andrew Scobell, *China and Strategic Culture* (Carlisle, PA: Strategic Studies Institute of the U.S. Army College, 2002); Shu Guang Zhang, *Deterrence and Strategic Culture: Chinese-American Confrontations, 1949–1958* (Ithaca, NY: Cornell University Press, 1992); and Waldron, "Chinese Strategy."

80. Waldron, "Chinese Strategy," 88.

81. See ibid., 85, 88–89, 95, 100–101; and Lovell, *Great Wall*, 200, 260.

82. Edward Farmer, "The Hierarchy of Ming City Walls," in *City Walls: The Urban Enceinte in Global Perspective*, ed. James Tracy (New York: Cambridge University Press, 2000), 486; see also Rossabi, "Ming and Inner Asia," 223; Mote, *Imperial China*, 686, 692–93; Waldron, *Great Wall of China*, 32–33, 58, 84; and Lovell *Great Wall*, 5, 26, 36.

83. Johnston, *Cultural Realism*, 25–26, 40, 44, 66; and Feng, *Chinese Strategic Culture*, 17–35.

84. Johnston, *Cultural Realism*, x, 153, 155.

85. Ibid., 106.

86. Ibid., x.

87. Ibid., 106.

88. Ibid., 151, 172.

89. Feng, *Chinese Strategic Culture*, 4.

90. Waldron, "Chinese Strategy," 91.

91. Johnston, *Cultural Realism*, 59.

92. Ibid., 151.

93. Ibid., 221.

94. Waldron, "Chinese Strategy," 93.

95. See Johnston, *Cultural Realism*, 149–51, 172, 216, 221; Waldron, *Great Wall of China*, 58; and Waldron, "Chinese Strategy," 91–92, 101–2, 113–14.

96. Mote, *Imperial China*, 688–89, 745.

97. Mote, "Chenghua and Hongzhi Reigns," 7.

98. Waldron, "Chinese Strategy," 98-99; and Huang, "Ming Fiscal Administration," 111, 113, 118, 126; and Waldron, *Great Wall of China*, 82–83.

99. Waldron, "Chinese Strategy," 97.

100. Mote, "Chenghua and Hongzhi Reigns," 7.

101. Ibid., 360.

102. Huang, "Ming Fiscal Administration," 125, 149; Barfield, *Perilous Frontier*, 234–35; and Mote, *Imperial China*, 621.

103. Lovell, *Great Wall*, 202, 204.

104. Calculation is based on a 1491 survey that counted 18.4 million Chinese in the four northern most political provinces (Hucker, "Ming Government," 14).

105. Mote, *Imperial China*, 575.

106. See ibid., 574–75, 636; and Waldron, "Chinese Strategy," 93–94, 100, 102–3.

107. Tsai, *Eunuchs in the Ming Dynasty*, 229.

108. Mote, "Chenghua and Hongzhi Reigns," 371.

109. See Mote, *Imperial China*, 630–31, 633; and Mote, "Chenghua and Hongzhi Reigns," 345, 362, 371.

110. Mote, *Imperial China*, 575; and Lovell, *Great Wall*, 194–95.

111. Hucker, "Ming Government," 21; and Mote, "Chenghua and Hongzhi Reigns," 362, 365, 371, 400.

112. Ray Huang, *1587, A Year of No Significance: The Ming Dynasty in Decline* (New Haven: Yale University Press, 1981), 18.

113. Waldron, *Great Wall of China*, 95; and Mote, "Chenghua and Hongzhi Reigns," 360–62.

114. Hucker, "Ming Government," 29.

115. Waldron, "Chinese Strategy," 94.

116. Mote, "Chenghua and Hongzhi Reigns," 372; and Hucker, "Ming Government," 55, 80.

117. Waldron, *Great Wall of China*, 104, 117; and Mote, "Chenghua and Hongzhi Reigns," 401.

118. Waldron, "Chinese Strategy," 93, 102–3.

119. Mote, "Chenghua and Hongzhi Reigns," 363.

120. See ibid., 362–63; Tsai, *Eunuchs in the Ming Dynasty*, 225–26; and Hucker, "Ming Government," 78–79.

121. Waldron, *Great Wall of China*, 62.

122. Johnston, *Cultural Realism*, 113, 116–17; and Waldron, *Great Wall of China*, 42–46, 62.

123. Johnston, *Cultural Realism*, 117.

124. Ibid., 230; and Peter Hessler, "Walking the Wall," *The New Yorker*, May 21, 2007, 63.

125. Johnston, *Cultural Realism*, 216, 219–220.

126. Waldron, *Great Wall of China*, 92.

127. Mote, "Chenghua and Hongzhi Reigns," 400; and Waldron, *Great Wall of China*, 97–98, 102.

128. Lovell, *Great Wall*, 203.

129. Johnston, *Cultural Realism*, 219, 221.

130. Waldron, "Chinese Strategy," 105–6; and Mote, "Chenghua and Hongzhi Reigns," 401.

131. Waldron, *Great Wall of China*, 97–98.

132. Mote, "Chenghua and Hongzhi Reigns," 400.

133. Waldron, *Great Wall of China*, 97–98, 100–2; and Johnston, *Cultural Realism*, 226.

134. See Waldron, *Great Wall of China*, 33, 56, 97–103; Mote, "Chenghua and Hongzhi Reigns," 400; and Johnston, *Cultural Realism*, 226.

135. Johnston, *Cultural Realism*, 112.

136. See Waldron, *Great Wall of China*, 95–96; Mote, *Imperial China*, 692–93; and Mote, "Chenghua and Hongzhi Reigns," 396.

137. Barfield, *Perilous Frontier*, 231, 248; and Mote, *Imperial China*, 692.

138. Barfield, *Perilous Frontier*, 249.

139. Waldron, *Great Wall of China*, 103; Lovell, *Great Wall*, 202–3; and Mote, *Imperial China*, 693.

140. Waldron, *Great Wall of China*, 33.

141. See ibid., 37, 172; and Mote, "Chenghua and Hongzhi Reigns," 396.

142. See, for example, Mote, "Chenghua and Hongzhi Reigns," 390, 396, 472, 477; Waldron, *Great Wall of China*, 171–72, 187; and Lovell, *Great Wall*, 183–84, 230–31.

143. Johnston, *Cultural Realism*, 187–89; Barfield, *Perilous Frontier*, 238, 249; Mote, "Chenghua and Hongzhi Reigns," 390.

144. Lindesay, *Great Wall*, 12.

145. Ibid., 248–49.

146. Mote, *Imperial China*, 696.

147. Quoted in Waldron, *Great Wall of China*, 45.

148. Ibid., 98.

149. Johnston, *Cultural Realism*, 192, 225; Waldron, *Great Wall of China*, 100; and Mote, "Chenghua and Hongzhi Reigns," 401–2.

150. Barfield, *Perilous Frontier*, 242; Lovell, *Great Wall*, 201–2; and Waldron, "Chinese Strategy," 93.

151. Johnston, *Cultural Realism*, 224.

152. Ibid.

153. Ibid., 185.

154. See ibid., 192, 219, 221; Waldron, *Great Wall of China*, 100, 103, 105; Mote, "Chenghua and Hongzhi Reigns," 401–2; and Lovell, *Great Wall*, 204–5.

155. See Waldron, *Great Wall of China*, 33, 97–98, 100–101; and Johnston, *Cultural Realism*, 220.

156. Lovell, *Great Wall*, 203, 206.

157. Waldron, *Great Wall of China*, 101.

158. Ibid., 35; Johnston, *Cultural Realism*, 220.

159. Waldron, *Great Wall of China*, 100–101.

160. Johnston, *Cultural Realism*, 192.

161. Waldron, *Great Wall*, 98–103; Johnston, *Cultural Realism*, 230.

162. See Waldron, *Great Wall of China*, 98–99, 103; and Lovell, *Great Wall*, 204.

163. Waldron, *Great Wall of China*, 103; see also ibid., 99, 102; Lovell, *Great Wall*, 204–5; and Mote, "Chenghua and Hongzhi Reigns," 401.

164. See Waldron, *Great Wall*, 104, 105; Mote, "Chenghua and Hongzhi Reigns," 389, 401; and Lovell, *Great Wall*, 205.

165. Lovell, *Great Wall*, 203.

166. Mote, "Chenghua and Hongzhi Reigns," 401.

167. Waldron, *Great Wall of China*, 35.

168. Lovell, *Great Wall*, 201.

169. See Waldron, *Great Wall of China*, 105; Lovell, *Great Wall*, 206–7; Mote, "Chenghua and Hongzhi Reigns," 401; and Serruys, "Towers," 34.

170. Quoted in Johnston, *Cultural Realism*, 220.

171. Mote, "Chenghua and Hongzhi Reigns," 401.

172. Waldron, *Great Wall of China*, 107; Mote, "Chenghua and Hongzhi Reigns," 401–2; and Lovell, *Great Wall*, 207–8.

173. Lovell, *Great Wall*, 208.

174. See Waldron, *Great Wall of China*, 114; Mote, "Chenghua and Hongzhi Reigns," 402; and Johnston, *Cultural Realism*, 187, 198.

175. Waldron, *Great Wall of China*, 108, 116; Mote, "Chenghua and Hongzhi Reigns," 401–2.

176. See Waldron, *Great Wall of China*, 108, 116; Mote, "Chenghua and Hongzhi Reigns," 401–2; and Lovell, *Great Wall*, 208.

177. See Lovell, *Great Wall*, 208–9; and Waldron, *Great Wall of China*, 112–13, 118.

178. See Mote, "Chenghua and Hongzhi Reigns," 398; Waldron, *Great Wall of China*, 108, 111; and Lovell *Great Wall*, 212.

179. See Whiting, *Imperial Chinese Military History*, 441; Waldron, *Great Wall of China*, 105, 108, 112, 118–19, 243; Rossabi, "Ming and Inner Asia," 236.

180. See Rossabi, "Ming and Inner Asia," 236; Waldron, *Great Wall of China*, 105, 118–20; and Johnston, *Cultural Realism*, 201–3.

181. See Huang, "Ming Fiscal Administration," 151; James Geiss, "The Zhengde Reign," in *The Cambridge History of China*, Vol. 7, *The Ming Dynasty, 1368–1644, Part I*, eds. Frederick Mote and Denis Twitchett (New York: Cambridge University Press, 1988), 412–13; and James Geiss, "The Jiajing Reign," in *The Cambridge History of China*, Vol. 7, *The Ming Dynasty, 1368–1644, Part I*, eds. Frederick Mote and Denis Twitchett (New York: Cambridge University Press, 1988), 450–52, 468, 472.

182. Waldron, *Great Wall of China*, 58, 109.

183. Geiss, "Jiajing Reign," 471.

184. Ibid.; and Waldron, *Great Wall of China*, 120–21, 174.

185. Lovell, *Great Wall*, 212.

186. See Barfield, *Perilous Frontier*, 244–45; Waldron, *Great Wall of China*, 122; Lovell, *Great Wall*, 212–13; Johnston, *Cultural Realism*, 185; Mote, *Imperial China*, 672; and Geiss, "Jiajing Reign," 471, 491, 495–96.

187. See Geiss, "Jiajing Reign," 472; Waldron, *Great Wall of China*, 105, 110; and Lovell, *Great Wall*, 214–15.

188. Johnston, *Cultural Realism*, 229.

189. Geiss, "Jiajing Reign," 472.

190. Waldron, *Great Wall of China*, 122.

191. Geiss, "Jiajing Reign," 471.

192. Tsai, *Eunuchs in the Ming Dynasty*, 63–64; and Huang, *1587, A Year of No Significance*, 118.

193. See Johnston, *Cultural Realism*, 206; Waldron, *Great Wall of China*, 125–28, 130; and Geiss, "Jiajing Reign," 474–75, 482–83.

194. See Geiss, "Jiajing Reign," 474–75, 482–84; Waldron, *Great Wall of China*, 122, 125, 130, 134–38; and Mote, *Imperial China*, 671.

195. See Geiss, "Jiajing Reign," 474–75; Waldron, *Great Wall of China*, 139, 159–60; Barfield, *Perilous Frontier*, 245; Mote, *Imperial China*, 619; and Lovell, *Great Wall*, 182, 216.

196. Johnston, *Cultural Realism*, 215.

197. See Geiss, "Jiajing Reign," 471–72, 476; Waldron, *Great Wall of China*, 123, 160; Huang, "Ming Fiscal Administration," 153; Johnston, *Cultural Realism*, 209; and Mote, *Imperial China*, 697.

198. Waldron, *Great Wall of China*, 160.

199. Ibid., 158.

200. Ibid., 158, 161, 182; and Hessler, "Walking the Wall," 63.

201. Lovell, *Great Wall*, 17.

202. Lindesay, *Great Wall*, 76.

203. Serruys, "Towers," 45; and Lovell, *Great Wall*, 245–46.

204. Lu, *Eternal Great Wall*, 63; and Luo, *Great Wall*, 40.

205. See Geiss, "Jiajing Reign," 477; Johnston, *Cultural Realism*, 235; and Waldron, *Great Wall of China*, 121.

206. Mote, *Imperial China*, 697.

207. Waldron, *Great Wall of China*, 183–84, 187.

208. Ibid., 183–84; Ray Huang, "The Longqing and Wanli Reigns," in *The Cambridge History of China*, Vol. 7, *The Ming Dynasty, 1368–1644, Part I*, eds. Frederick Mote and Denis Twitchett (New York: Cambridge University Press, 1988), 524; and Johnston, *Cultural Realism*, 236.

209. Johnston, *Cultural Realism*, 215; and Waldron, *Great Wall of China*, 162–64.

210. Barfield, *Perilous Frontier*, 246–47; Waldron, *Great Wall of China*, 186; Mote, *Imperial China*, 697; and Huang, "Longqing and Wanli Reigns," 520, 525.

211. Huang, "Longqing and Wanli Reigns," 557; Hessler, "Walking the Wall," 63; Waldron, *Great Wall of China*, 164; and Johnston, *Cultural Realism*, 181.

212. Waldron, *Great Wall of China*, 187–88; and Lovell, *Great Wall*, 231.

213. Waldron, *Great Wall of China*, 162–64; Lindesay, *Great Wall*, 45; and Hessler, "Walking the Wall," 63.

214. Lovell, *Great Wall*, 222.

215. Turnbull, *Great Wall of China*, 32.

216. Hessler, "Walking the Wall," 63; Waldron, *Great Wall of China*, 163; Turnbull, *Great Wall of China*, 26; and Huang, *1587, A Year of No Significance*, 182.

217. See Barfield, *Perilous Frontier*, 250–54; and Mote, *Imperial China*, 697, 733–35, 785.

218. See Barfield, *Perilous Frontier*, 252, 255; Mote, *Imperial China*, 789; and Lovell, *Great Wall*, 241–43.

219. See William Atwell, "The Taiching, Tianqi, and Chongzhen Reigns," in *The Cambridge History of China*, Vol. 7, *The Ming Dynasty, 1368–1644, Part I*, eds. Frederick Mote and Denis Twitchett (New York: Cambridge University Press, 1988), 590, 602; Lovell, *Great Wall*, 229; and Mote, *Imperial China*, 769.

220. See Barfield, *Perilous Frontier*, 258, 261; Mote, *Imperial China*, 790; and Turnbull, *Great Wall of China*, 40.

221. See Barfield, *Perilous Frontier*, 261; Atwell, "Taiching, Tianqi, and Chongzhen Reigns," 616–17; Mote, *Imperial China*, 786–87, 793–94; and Lovell, *Great Wall*, 234.

222. Mote, *Imperial China*, 794.

223. Lovell, *Great Wall*, 229.

224. See Barfield, *Perilous Frontier*, 254, 258, 260–63; and Atwell, "Taiching, Tianqi, and Chongzhen Reigns," 600, 629.

225. Mote, *Imperial China*, 776.

226. See ibid., 776, 796–97, 804–5; and Atwell, "Taiching, Tianqi, and Chongzhen Reigns," 621, 629–30.

227. See Barfield, *Perilous Frontier*, 263; Mote, *Imperial China*, 799, 804–6; Atwell, "Taiching, Tianqi, and Chongzhen Reigns," 631, 636; and Lovell, *Great Wall*, 235–37, 241.

228. Barfield, *Perilous Frontier*, 266–67; and Lovell, *Great Wall*, 252–54.

229. Lindesay, *Great Wall*, 78–79; Lovell, *Great Wall*, 258–59; Turnbull, *Great Wall of China*, 18.

230. Lovell, *Great Wall*, 259.

231. Lindesay, *Great Wall*, 81.

232. Barfield, *Perilous Frontier*, 248.

233. Mote, *Imperial China*, 693, 696; Waldron, *Great Wall of China*, 164, 171–72; Barfield, *Perilous Frontier*, 231; and Lovell, *Great Wall*, 17–19.

234. Mote, *Imperial China*, 696.

235. See Waldron, *Great Wall of China*, 171–72, 187; Lovell, *Great Wall*, 183–84, 230–31; Mote, *Imperial China*, 693, 696–97; Barfield, *Perilous Frontier*, 231, 248; and Geiss, "Jiajing Reign," 472, 477.

236. Waldron, *Great Wall of China*, 164; Serruys, "Towers," 24; Turnbull, *Great Wall of China*, 35–36; and Hessler, "Walking the Wall," 63.

237. Lovell, *Great Wall*, 17.

5

The Pré Carré

Fortifying France's Northeastern Frontier

Introduction

While the Ming Great Wall of China stands as the preeminent example of a strategic defense system, the other early modern case involves a rising power with great ambition yet suffering from a chronic sense of insecurity. The seventeenth-century French Pré Carré also marks a technologically driven transition from the first three cases, essentially continuous walls, to the last three efforts of discontinuous lines of fortified strongpoints. Whereas in all the examples the strategic defense systems affect the adversary by reducing their leverage, the potential of the frontier fortifications in this case to enhance the formidable French army's offensive potential is particularly worth investigating. It caused a vast divergence between French intentions and adversary perceptions of French intentions, raising a basic question: Could the French have signaled a lesser threat while still producing enhanced security, and if so how? In an era when positional warfare was dominant, a strategic defense of strong fortresses would inevitably affect the military balance. But what was the extent of their impact, especially given the emergence of extremely powerful siegecraft? Finally, for a leader and government hypersensitive to its security despite possessing the best army in the world, how do such frontier fortifications affect perceptions as well as future behavior? Although involving a different political system and military-technology context, in some important ways this situation seems surprisingly analogous to the United States today, which suggests the potential for some interesting lessons learned.

This chapter explores these questions by examining French king Louis XIV's decision to establish a *pré carré* to protect his kingdom and its resulting effects. The first half lays out the decision context over the winter of 1675–76 upon which the king determined French strategy. With this background, the discussion analyzes Louis' assessment of choices and his rationale for pursuing a forward pré carré. The chapter then outlines the 1680s expansion of strategic defenses from opposing the Spanish Netherlands to safeguarding France's eastern frontier from the Germanic principalities and the Austrian Empire. The examination concludes by considering the impact of the strategic defense systems during the two great wars that dominated the last twenty-five years of Louis' reign (the Nine Years' War and the War of the Spanish Succession). Near the end of the latter conflict, the enemy had penetrated deeply into this barrier on the northeast frontier, but the time and cost required for advancement allowed diplomatic and military changes that ultimately saved France from defeat.

More than thirty years earlier, in late 1675, a chagrined King Louis XIV had faced his first crisis after nearly a decade and a half directing French affairs. The Dutch War, promisingly begun three years before to promote the king's *gloire* and punish the Dutch Netherlands, had exploded. Abandoned by most of its allies, France now essentially stood alone against the other powers of western Europe. The army would face this challenge without its two most distinguished marshals, given Henri Turenne's recent battlefield death and the Prince of Condé's health-related retirement. Earlier in the year, a necessary sharp increase in taxes precipitated revolts in western France. Although limited in scale, such uprisings had not occurred during the king's adult reign. He feared returning to the persistent rebellions experienced earlier in the seventeenth century.[1] Even Louis' personal life had entered a particularly turbulent time with the "three queens"—his wife, Marie Thérèse, and two favorite mistresses, Louise de La Vallière and Madame de Montespan—stressing the ruler.[2]

Confronted with these military, political, economic, and personal problems, Louis and his advisors contemplated how to proceed for the coming year and more generally how best to protect France. They essentially had three strategic options. First, despite the challenges, the monarch could press on aggressively attempting to defeat France's enemies and establish dominance in western Europe. Second, Louis could abandon the war and surrender conquests to date in an attempt to restore the diplomatic harmony and robust security that he inherited in 1661. A final option involved establishing a pré carré, translated as either a dueling field or square meadow.[3] A more conceptually useful, if less literal, translation of "ring fenced estate" has been suggested.[4] That is, France could pursue a straightened frontier with strong fortifications that resulted in a more defensible position along the border with the Spanish Netherlands, the front closest to Paris. Two variants of such an approach could be pursued: abandon exposed locations or advance to capture the necessary territory to establish a forward pré carré.

Ultimately, the king opted to pursue a forward pré carré. The talented and respected French military engineer Sébastien le Prestre de Vauban had first suggested this concept to Louis and the Marquis de Louvois, secretary of state for war, two years earlier. Facing a deteriorating strategic environment, Vauban had reiterated his advice in a September 1675 letter by urging capture of Condé,

Figure 5.1 Northwestern Europe in the Late Seventeenth Century

Bouchain, Valenciennes, and Cambrai because "their seizure would assure your conquests, and create the pré carré so much desired."[5] The plan for the 1676 campaign season would set the foundation for French strategy over the next fifteen years on its northeastern and then eastern frontiers. In comparison to pre-1675, French strategic policy "was far more defensive in its goals, though often aggressive in its means."[6]

After the Dutch War was victoriously concluded, Louis and Louvois approved Vauban's plan for defending the approximately 150-mile frontier facing the Spanish Netherlands. In a November 1678 memorandum, the brigadier had urged "two lines of fortresses . . . like an army drawn up for battle."[7] Although disagreement exists on the inclusion of some smaller forts as a part of the Pré Carré, Vauban proposed a first line of fifteen works (thirteen fortresses, which encompassed towns, and two forts) from the English Channel to the Ardennes Forest (in order):

- Dunkirk — Bergues — Furnes — Knocke — Ypres — Menin — Lille — Tournai — Mortagne — Condé — Valenciennes — Le Quesnoy — Maubeuge — Philippeville — Dinant[8]

A second, reserve line of thirteen fortresses ran roughly parallel to the first at a distance ranging from approximately fifteen to thirty-five miles (in order):

- Gravelines — Saint-Omer — Aire — Béthune — Arras — Douai — Bouchain — Cambrai — Landrecies — Avesnes — Marienbourg — Rocroi — Charleville[9]

Almost all these locations already had fortifications, but the French undertook major upgrades, including new walls, citadels, and free-standing forward structures, as well as erecting a few entirely new locations.[10] Vauban placed great import on personally inspecting sites, adapting to the terrain, and using good sense rather than formal rules and systems, so individual fortresses differed markedly.[11]

The Pré Carré did not include a continuous physical barrier, despite awareness among French officials of the growing importance of entrenched lines, especially to block raiding parties. Protection against such attacks initially existed in the form of outposts along the frontier. Copying the Dutch, the French army built a modest, thirty-mile entrenched line from the English Channel to the Lys River.[12] After seizing Ypres in March 1678, Vauban proposed building another line from Ypres to Commines. He declared that "it is impossible that the enemy parties could carry out their designs beyond these entrenchments."[13] Because they required constant upkeep and continuous manning, the appeal of such lines

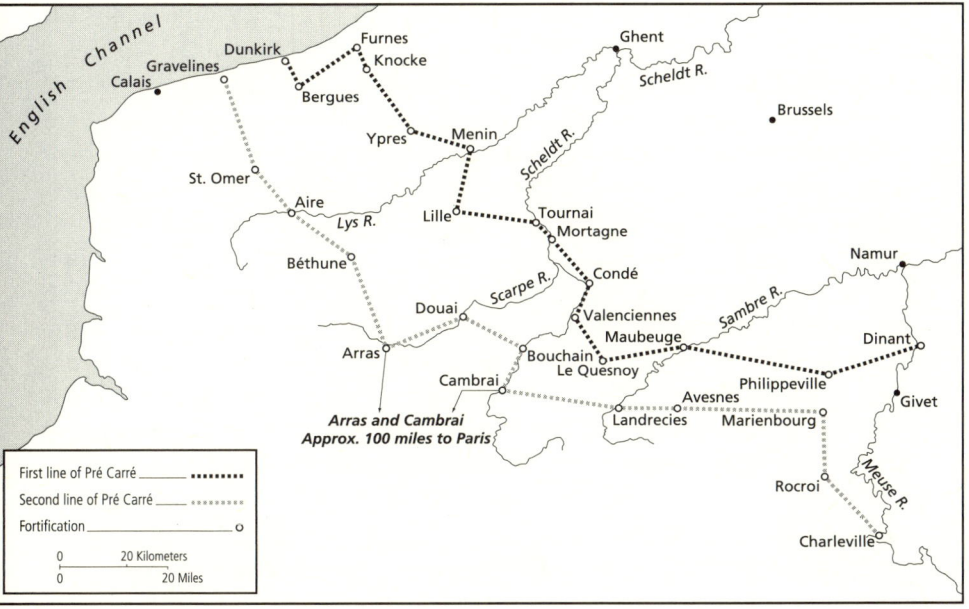

Figure 5.2 Pré Carré Fortification System, 1680

declined with the war's end. However, they could be established when needed; therefore, the French government concentrated on its frontier fortresses, which were rapidly constructed or upgraded.

Vulnerable but Expanding Frontiers

French history greatly influenced the decision making of Louis XIV and his advisors, most notably their concern about the Habsburg threat. In the sixteenth century, a smaller and weaker France had constantly been on the defensive with enemies frequently penetrating its soil. Although the Spanish and German Habsburg lines split in 1556, "their policies were often in accord, and the French saw them, and often fought them, as a single foe."[14] Still, the French regarded Madrid as its primary antagonist, with the so-called Spanish road linking the home country with its Netherlands territory through land controlled directly or indirectly by Spain and potentially cutting off France from the rest of the continent. The French government had periodically erected barriers to enhance security, but such efforts tended to be insufficient and short run. King Henry IV constructed numerous works along the eastern frontier, but this large-scale fortification program along with overall government effectiveness declined with the monarch's assassination in 1610.[15]

Cardinal Richelieu, who began directing government policy in 1624, pursued a two-pronged strategy to break France's potential encirclement by the Habsburgs.[16] First, he encouraged foreign heretics, essentially Protestants, to distract the Austrian Habsburgs. Second, France launched a series of limited attacks in the hopes of weakening its enemies, helping to fuel the Thirty Years' War. However, the cardinal ultimately could not avoid full-fledged French participation in the draining struggle after war with Spain commenced in 1635. Richelieu neglected frontier defenses and divided his army, quickly precipitating disaster. After the initial French offensive failed, the Habsburgs counterattacked in 1636 with great success against "the appallingly neglected Picardy frontier."[17] Enemy troops quickly captured the fortress at Corbie allowing a rapid advance across the Somme until they reached Compiègne, about thirty-five miles from Paris. News of the Corbie disaster and subsequent enemy advance not surprisingly caused panic in the French capital, whose own fortifications were no longer intact. Although the Habsburgs did not move on Paris in large part because of the onset of winter, the infamous Year of Corbie "served as a long-remembered object lesson to that generation and the next on the dangers of weak and unprepared frontier defenses."[18]

France would remain on the defensive for several years until a signal victory over the Habsburgs at Rocroi in 1643 marked the beginning of an increasingly favorable military balance. Spain would fight on for another sixteen years, including supporting an internal uprising in France, known as the Fronde, which involved many of the kingdom's noble families and premier soldiers.[19] Ultimately, the monarchy defeated the rebels and the supporting Spanish forces in turn after a long struggle, greatly strengthening the central government's power. Gains in the resulting Peace of the Pyrenees in 1659 "eliminated the dangerous Artesian 'bulge,' and placed France firmly on the 'forward slope' of the Netherlands border."[20] The kingdom now "stood as Christian Europe's preeminent land power."[21] Jeremy Black, however, usefully reminds that the decline of Spain so evident from today's perspective probably was not clear to French policymakers at the time. Instead Madrid's weakness likely seemed a temporary phase that France needed to exploit in the long-run competition between the two main powers in western Europe.[22]

Although Louis XIV had become king as a four-year-old child in 1643, the Italian cardinal Mazarin capably ran the government for the next eighteen years. He effectively promoted ties with key actors in Europe, such as the Dutch Republic and the German principalities, to guard against the Habsburgs. Historians tend to exalt the cardinal's work, exemplified by the observation "that never did France enjoy such near perfect security on its frontiers as in the last year of Mazarin's life."[23] Sustaining this advantageous situation for a long time only required France "to renounce further conquests ... indeed, moderation was the secret of his success in bringing the gift of security to his adopted country."[24] Yet despite "for the first time since advent of the Capetian kings [987], the country did not have a single declared enemy," some Frenchmen worried that "the yawning gaps through which foreign armies had invaded so many times remained open."[25] Even though they were ultimately beneficiaries in the Treaty of Westphalia and Peace of the Pyrenees, French leaders "shuddered at what they had sometime only barely survived."[26] Given that diplomatic allegiances could always shift, counting on alliances to help preserve security entailed a certain degree of risk.

King Louis Takes Charge

Would such risk be acceptable to the young Bourbon king who took over French policy after Mazarin's death in March 1661? French officials had some reason to expect a continuation in security policy. Extremely close to Louis, the cardinal stressed the value of allies and moderation in overseeing the king's education. Despite their connection, the young, aggressive ruler wanted to establish a reputation and push the nation "into a predominant position by French wealth and arms alone."[27] He also sought to ensure his dominance over policymaking by abolishing Mazarin's position as de facto prime minister. Louis spent the initial years of his reign mastering a monarch's duties while maneuvering to gain the Spanish Netherlands. Opportunity and danger arose in 1665 when the ailing and childless Charles II became King of Spain. Louis asserted his succession rights to the Spanish crown after Charles based on the unpaid dowry for his marriage to the Habsburg Marie Thérèse; ominously, he recognized control would be more likely to transfer to the Austrian Habsburg line. While diplomatically attempting to prevent such an outcome, the French king wanted to exploit Spain's temporary weaknesses to seize valuable land, especially in the Netherlands.[28]

The French king confidently advanced an improved army to seize "his" territory [Spanish-held Flanders] in May 1667, compelling Madrid to declare war on July 14. The dominant French army rapidly captured a series of frontier towns, including Lille, capital of the Spanish Netherlands; another force seized the much-desired Spanish region of Franche-Comté (west of Switzerland). Recognizing that the entire Spanish Netherlands could be grabbed, the alarmed Dutch organized an alliance with London and Stockholm in January 1668—all current or recent allies of Paris—to block the French king. Unwilling to face such a coalition, Louis in May 1668 agreed to the Treaty of Aix-la-Chapelle, which returned Franche-Comté to Spain but allowed France to retain twelve fortified towns in the northeast, including Lille, Tournai, and Charleroi. The resulting ragged frontier left a French salient with "enemy fortresses poised dangerously on the flank and rear," a situation that clearly would not be stable.[29]

Disentangling the situation required Louis to eliminate the impediments to expansion—above all, Dutch opposition. Therefore, while Vauban labored to improve or build fortresses in the newly acquired French territory, the king sought to isolate the United Provinces. Louis' aggressiveness complicated the task, especially with regard to the leaders of German states, whose alliance had been a linchpin in Mazarin's security strategy. In contrast to the French king, Austrian emperor Leopold's restraint prompted numerous German princes to "perceive that the threat to their liberties no longer emanated from Vienna."[30] Louis further alarmed the Germans by seizing the independent Duchy of Lorraine in 1670. French opponents highlighted such behavior in a skillful propaganda campaign whose influence cannot be definitively ascertained, but it is "worth noting that for many years such a level-headed man as William III was to labor under the delusion that Louis XIV, whose objectives were always strictly limited, really did aim at 'universal monarchy.'"[31] Nevertheless, by the beginning of 1672, the French had essentially isolated the Dutch through financial support, especially to the cash-poor British king Charles II. The Austrian emperor successfully convinced the elector of Brandenburg to side with the Dutch, but Leopold himself signed a neutrality pact with Louis in November 1671. Imperial forces would not intervene unless France attacked Spanish territory. Of course, attacking Spanish territory is precisely what Louis wanted to do, but the way was now clear to first deal with the troublemaking Dutch.[32]

The Dutch War

In February 1672, the king led 120,000 men forward to secure glory, obtain revenge, and end Dutch interference. Louis had reason to be confident given the United Provinces' isolation, French possession of a vastly superior army, and a combined Anglo-French navy that on paper matched the enemy's great maritime fleet. After witnessing rapid French capture of several Dutch fortresses, an increasingly desperate Hague offered generous peace terms. While Secretary of State for Foreign Affairs Simon Arnauld de Pomponne urged acceptance, the director of the war effort, the Marquis de Louvois, pushed for greater concessions.[33] Intoxicated with success, Louis sided with Louvois, seeking "exaggerated demands that would have reduced the United Provinces to a marginal state."[34] The Dutch responded with their one trump card—flooding the countryside—while shifting diplomatic sentiment complicated French strategy. The advance of Marshal Turenne's army into Germany to defeat the Dutch ally Brandenburg prompted a concerned Austrian emperor to end his neutrality. Louis continued to have a third force covering the Spaniards in Flanders, hoping forlornly to provoke Madrid into declaring war.[35]

France remained in a strong position, but a daring December 1672 siege by the Dutch prince of Orange against the Charleroi fortress brought home the potential danger of war. A quick reaction prompted the Dutch to abandon the attack and any plans for a deeper penetration. Nevertheless, it left the French king "surprised and shaken" given that he "was accustomed to visiting the ravages of war beyond his own frontier provinces. He had not expected to relive the fears that had swept the court of his father in 1636, the terrible year of Corbie when the Spanish threatened Paris itself."[36] This observation may exaggerate the extent of the king's concern, but the raid certainly served as a wake-up call for Louis and his advisors. It also crystallized a growing appreciation of the existence of superfluous fortifications, which tempted the enemy and required significant men and material.[37]

In particular, Vauban, who by this time had become the de facto fortification expert, wanted to rationalize the frontier security approach. He first expressed the need for a pré carré in a January 20, 1673, letter to Louvois: "Seriously, Sir, the King must think some about creating a pré carré. I do not like this pell-mell confusion of fortresses, ours and the enemy's. You are obliged to maintain three for one; your men are plagued by it; your expenses are increased and your forces are much diminished.... That is why, be it by treaties, be it by a good war, if you believe what I say, Monseigneur, always preach squaring things off, not the circle, but the *pré*."[38] Louvois responded that "everything in your letter looks good to me, but things cannot be done as quickly as one would wish. You must be patient and hope that after some time; your advice will be useful."[39] The king's general attitude about the pré carré concept at this time is fuzzy, but he remained focused on more grandiose aims that seemed increasingly possible.[40] Most notably, under the brilliant direction of Vauban, French forces captured the fortress town of Maastricht, the one prestigious Dutch target not protected by floodwaters. The rapidity of this June 1673 victory stunned Europe, covered the king with glory, and freed the main French army for further action early in the campaign season. Simultaneously, Turenne's army knocked Brandenburg out of the war and pushed imperial forces back to Austria.

These successes, however, set the stage for a series of decisions that would quickly undermine the French position. Unable to provoke Spanish entry into the war, Louis sent his main force to bolster French positions in Alsace and Lorraine, and then into the German state of Trier. Harboring no territorial ambitions in Germany, the French king apparently saw the advance as defensive, especially controlling Koblenz at the convergence of the Rhine and Moselle rivers. This move, however, proved a critical mistake, marking "the first time French troops occupied the land of an important prince of the Empire without invitation or declaration of war."[41] With Louis exerting pressure on the local rulers for support, European leaders perceived him as pursuing "universal monarchy." This view fueled the emergence of a powerful anti-French coalition including both Habsburg branches (Spain and Austria). France had not faced such a large coalition during its seventeenth century rise, but Louis did not back down. Rather, he unsuccessfully attempted to reach a settlement with the Dutch to concentrate on the Habsburgs.[42]

By fall 1673 the overstretched French military struggled with its multiplying tasks, including the long-awaited opportunity to seize Spanish territory. Louis' failure to reinforce Marshal Turenne in central Germany led to his retreat under pressure from imperial forces. The king's October 22 withdrawal of troops from most conquered Dutch territory has been characterized as "the beginning of the end to Louis' youthful lust for armed conquest as a route to gloire."[43] The French court now concentrated forces on the Spanish Netherlands and the Rhineland, but their redeployments were too late to block the enemy from capturing Bonn. The loss of a key German ally's capital dampened Louis' confidence while demonstrating to German princes that the French army was not invincible. Thus the 1673 campaign season ended disturbingly with France on the defensive.[44]

Angst would grow in Paris over the next six months as Louis paid a price for not better supporting allied war aims.[45] The British parliament and public—never enthusiastic about the conflict—had lost patience, abandoning the French with a separate peace in February 1674. Several German allies switched sides, including Cologne and Münster. Most German princes balanced against rather than bandwagoned with Louis. The German shift culminated on May 28, 1674, with the Imperial Diet declaring a *Reichskrieg* (war of the Holy Roman Empire), a "virtually unprecedented step" highlighting the extent of anti-French sentiment.[46] Although many individual principalities were small, the great French marshal Condé had forewarned Louis that "the strength of the [Holy Roman] Empire is awesome when it is united."[47]

Europe's best army continued to reward the faith of the French court, but the growing isolation prevented accomplishing desired war aims and increasingly worried officials. With the Spanish concentrating forces in their Netherlands territory, French troops seized Franche-Comté. Meanwhile, Condé's army, guarding the Dutch frontier, won a rare battle of field armies at Seneffe in July 1674, albeit producing little tangible benefit at the cost of heavy casualties. Finally, in Germany, Turenne fought a brilliant maneuver campaign to frustrate allied intentions. Nevertheless, memory of these military successes quickly faded as Louis and his advisors came to appreciate underlying enemy strength. Although Turenne started 1675 with another great victory at Türkheim, allied pressure persisted as "Louis XIV continued to fear for this frontier."[48] Coalition troops' rout of Swedish forces in Pomerania that June revealed the reduced strength of his major remaining ally. Then, in July, France suffered a severe blow with the death of Turenne at the battle of Salzbach. Condé, France's other leading commander, would soon retire due to poor health. France ultimately averted disaster by year's end largely through the quality of her army and the "inability of Louis's enemies to mount a concerted action against him."[49] Still, the next campaign season augured ill.[50]

Beyond the military setbacks, the war's growing strain on the homeland concerned the French court. The army's voracious need for bodies was increasingly difficult to satisfy. Capital requirements forced an unpopular hike in taxation, especially the detested *gabelle* (salt tax). This unhappiness evolved into a rebellion in early 1675 that began in Bordeaux, spread to Guyenne, and ultimately became most severe in Brittany. The arrival of French troops ended resistance, but Louis quartered ten thousand soldiers in Brittany over the winter to ensure calm and set an example.[51] Although stability had not seriously been threatened, the first major disturbance of Louis' adult reign served as a reminder of recent history when domestic revolt was common. More pointedly for the king, it probably refreshed a painful and influential childhood memory "of fleeing at night from a Paris threatened by revolt and the Fronde."[52] Vauban gloomily summed up the overall situation at year's end by observing that "things are still going from bad to worse, and are making me tremble."[53]

Decision Context

The preceding history, especially the Dutch War, has been relayed at some length because of its influence on policymakers directly and indirectly through the other contextual factors. With Louis XIV dominating the French government, it is his perspective of the subsequent elements that matters above all.

Threat Perceptions

Despite France's inherent strength, Louis continuously worried about the nation's insecurity. One historian observes that "no one reading his letters can miss the fact that all his life he had an almost pathological fear of an invasion of 'my kingdom.'"[54] His knowledge of French history, including his father and grandfather facing invasions, fueled that concern. France's central location in western Europe intensified threat perceptions. Vauban encapsulated the problem by highlighting that France was "almost in the middle of the most considerable powers of Christendom, ... equally in range of blows from Spain, Italy, Germany, the Low Countries, and England."[55] The formation of a large anti-French coalition in the current war exacerbated concern, especially given the perceived reason. As Vauban noted, France had "attained a high degree of elevation that renders her formidable to her neighbors, in a manner that they all interest themselves in her ruin, or at least in the diminution of her power."[56]

Although the adversary coalition imperiled multiple regions, French threat perception varied sharply between the kingdom's five frontiers—the northeast (Low Countries), the east (Germany), the southeast (Italy), the south (Spain), and the coastline (England). Above all, Louis and his advisors worried about the northeastern frontier with the Spanish Netherlands from which the Habsburgs had invaded the kingdom several times in the sixteenth and seventeenth centuries. This frontier alone lacked natural barriers, such as mountains or rivers, to aid in defense. Despite Madrid's recent setbacks, the king "had grown up in the shadow of the Spanish colossus" and continued to regard Madrid as his primary adversary.[57] Exacerbating this frontier's importance was the fact that, "by an accident of history, the political center of the French monarchy was not near the middle of the realm—somewhere in Touraine—but far to the north."[58] The enormous growth of Paris had prompted the French court to decide it would be impractical to replace the old fortifications razed in 1670. Although a reasonable conclusion, it reinforced concern about the northeastern frontier where a major defeat potentially jeopardized the capital.[59]

The neighboring eastern region represented the other troublesome frontier for French officials. Growing French strength and influence in the lands to its east—Lorraine, Alsace, and even Germany—had essentially transferred this frontier into the Moselle and Rhine river valleys. While this expansion reduced worry about Spanish encirclement, French concern shifted toward the Austrian emperor, especially after his vigorous opposition in the Dutch War. The huge, and at times wild, Rhine River stood as a potential barrier, but only if the French controlled its bridge crossings, which they did not at this point. Within a decade this area would obtain the highest threat perceptions for Louis and his advisors, but in the winter of 1675–76 it was a secondary, albeit growing, concern.[60]

French officials did not ignore the other three frontiers, but they perceived far less vulnerability.[61] The rugged Alps and the Pyrenees guarded against large-scale invasion on the southeastern (Italian) and southern (Spanish) frontiers, respectively. Even if an enemy could penetrate the mountain passes, it would have to cover a great distance to reach the heart of France. Less obvious or logical is the limited French concern about the extensive coastline, which provided the British and Dutch maritime powers ample places to strike. Louis would undertake significant improvements to the navy and coastal fortifications; nevertheless, he continued a royal tradition of treating the water frontier with secondary import.[62] The primary sources of danger, means of power, and prestige for most officials and officers were the northeastern and eastern frontiers.

Military Capability

This threat perception fueled and was reinforced by the French government's focus on the army, the finest such institution in Europe at the time. Under the steady direction of Michel Le Tellier and his son Louvois, the army had improved considerably in recent decades. In contrast to the private French and foreign forces employed during pre-1635 conflicts, the government had essentially become responsible for all aspects of unit recruitment, provisioning, training, and organization with a corresponding increase in both performance and loyalty to the crown.[63] This approach facilitated the growing need for technical expertise, large wartime armies, and sizeable peacetime forces. The service's performance during the first years of the Dutch War illustrated its continuing progress, not only in combat but also in crucial combat support areas.

Beyond general improvement, the French army excelled at siegecraft and fortification. Vauban's innovations, including parallel trenches, doomed even the strongest fortress if provided adequate resources. The rapid capture of Maastricht in 1673 with negligible casualties provided the clearest example of this new reality. Such sieges consumed enormous resources, but Louvois' talented administration ensured adequate supplies. Although Vauban's fortification concepts do not match his siege innovations, the engineer oversaw construction of improved defenses with an emphasis on antisiege artillery.[64] The combination of French successes and adversary failures at siegecraft during the Dutch War had bolstered confidence about their superiority in this key area. In particular, observing enemy attacks, such as at Oudenaarde and Grave in 1674, had revealed to French senior officers that "the allies were gratifyingly incompetent at the business of fortress warfare."[65]

While the French army's qualitative advantage seemed clear, the emergence of a large enemy coalition created pressures for a significant force expansion. Whereas the maximum French army size during the Thirty Years' War had been 125,000, by the winter of 1675–76 the army was approaching its estimated Dutch War high of 253,000 soldiers. A sharp increase in French wealth and population allowed such expansion, but its continuation was becoming increasingly difficult, and only modest growth seemed likely in the near term. For example, Louis had recently demobilized several naval units to generate more ground troops while Vauban urged abandoning unneeded fortifications to save manpower. Garrison requirements functioned as a significant driver of army expansion, with the increased number and size of fortresses approximately quadrupling demand over the past decade.[66]

Despite its second-class status in the French military, the navy had undergone phenomenal growth in recent years. From a relatively small force in 1661, the fleet had become the world's largest by 1675 under the aggressive naval minister Jean-Baptiste Colbert. It consisted of 134 warships with many first and second-rated vessels, including the world's largest combatant, the 120-gun *Soleil Royal*. Colbert had visions of challenging Dutch and British naval dominance, but prodigious shipbuilding was far easier to achieve than finding able seaman. Performance of the French navy in the war to date had been lackluster at best. Moreover, despite Colbert's herculean efforts, Louis saw the navy "as an extension of his army," created to support land campaigns rather than command the high seas.[67] During crises such as that now being faced, the king could be expected to redirect resources toward the army.[68]

Strategic Culture

With Louis XIV's dominant personality driving policy, any discussion of French strategic culture must be suffused with his worldview. Historians stress that pursuit of gloire—perhaps best translated as reputation or prestige—strongly influenced the king's deliberations and choices.[69] The French ruler, reflecting the prevailing aristocratic mentality, regarded military success as the best way to obtain prestige. Thus, from 1661–75, which John Lynn characterizes as Phase I, "Louis aggressively sought to advance his gloire by conquering new territory for France."[70] Nevertheless, while military success was glorious and even taking on most of Europe had an ennobling aspect for a ruler who selected the sun as his symbol, defeat would be catastrophic. By 1675, having obtained considerable glory through his military successes and facing a deteriorating balance of power, Louis could appreciate the logic of pursuing prestige in a more nuanced fashion through protecting the enlarged kingdom.[71] As has been suggested by a prominent scholar, "for all his obsession with gloire, Louis harbored in his heart more fear of invasion than lust for conquest."[72]

Nevertheless, one is struck by the continuous risks taken by the king, especially since he has been characterized as "very cautious by nature," only embarking, if given a choice, on undertakings likely to be safe.[73] Rather than being risk acceptant, perhaps Louis lacked the ability to calculate risk accurately. The king was reputedly "a confirmed optimist" who expected every campaign to be successful and "always seemed a little astonished when it did not."[74] Lynn has suggested that the psychological phenomenon known as prospect theory might provide an explanation.[75] Individuals accept far greater risk to prevent loss than to obtain gain based on their frame of the issue. Louis, witnessing the extent of anti-French hostility throughout western Europe, probably framed issues in terms of preventing loss. The king had to ensure his realm's security against invasion, and if achieving that goal involved some risk, so be it. The driving, if problematic, mentality was that "any threat to his possessions, no matter how remote, was very real to Louis."[76]

The king was a product of his times and country, reflecting common perspectives on employing military power and securing frontiers. Overlapping frontier zones often existed during the first half of the seventeenth century, deemphasizing attention to juridical borders and complicating defense considerations. French decision makers tended to focus on *portes* (gates) through the frontiers, which were critical for blocking enemy entry into the kingdom as well as projecting force forward. As the century progressed, however, the French conception of state frontiers evolved toward more clearly defined and defensible boundaries. During this evolution, some figures, particularly Jesuit geographers and historians, highlighted the value of rivers and especially mountains as natural frontiers.

Despite not defining French security policy as once believed, this concept of natural frontiers "gave shape to an imagined national space" that Louis could employ in service of his strategies.[77] The French king sought "more defensible and better delineated frontiers, where natural barriers provided important demarcations."[78] In particular, Vauban "appears to have had a very clear idea of an 'engineered' boundary that is often conflated with a natural geographic boundary."[79] But in the northeast no such "natural frontier" existed; it would have to be created artificially with fortifications.

This evolving frontier conception had been enhanced as civilian and military decison makers came to appreciate the growing dominance of positional warfare. Marshals Turenne and Condé had been advocates for fighting in open fields, but once "these two warrior gods disappeared" no influential advocates of field battle remained.[80] Condé's horrifically costly victory in 1674 at Seneffe helped undermine support for a battle culture, especially in the eyes of the king. This pyrrhic success had earned France minimal advantage in contrast to the Maastricht's capture with minimal casualties. In 1677 German J. H. Behr would write that "field battles are in comparison [to sieges] scarcely a topic of conversation."[81] Although tempting, a fortress could not be bypassed without significant risks because "its garrison could cause mischief entirely out of proportion to its numbers."[82] The enormous proliferation of fortifications made this a reinforcing phenomenon. Given that siege logistical requirements generally precluded engaging in more than a few in northern Europe's six-month campaign season, the era's wars usually turned into long attrition struggles. While progress was slow, positional warfare offered the potential for lasting gain. As Vauban wrote, "one can say that today it alone offers the means of conquest and concentration."[83]

Resources

French leaders appreciated the kingdom's vast resources.[84] With a population of approximately 20 million, France far exceeded any other state in Christian Europe (e.g., 8.5 million Spanish, 12 million Germans, and 8 million English/Scottish/Irish).[85] Excepting the limited uprisings earlier in 1675, the nation had been essentially unified and at peace in recent decades, which allowed the French economy to prosper into Europe's richest. This stability also enabled the crown to destroy or neglect hundreds of city walls and fortifications in the French interior, saving considerable funds. A sufficient resource base existed to underwrite expensive defense measures, including a large and well-armed military as well as frontier fortifications.

The crown, however, labored to extract the necessary funds for its expansive military operations. Although Louis certainly exceeded his predecessors' relative strength vis-à-vis society, today's image of an all-powerful monarch is not accurate. The aristocracy, which controlled most of the nation's wealth, was partially tax exempt. The church, the other major source of wealth, maintained its tax-exempt status by making limited payments to the crown. The combination of direct taxes on wealth, indirect taxes on purchased goods (e.g., the hated salt tax), and fees raised from other levies (e.g., the sale of offices) was insufficient to support the monarchy's activities, especially during wartime. The recent tax revolts in western France highlighted the dangers of efforts at increased revenue collection. Instead the government turned to alternative financing vehicles with deleterious consequences. First Louis and his advisors increasingly used short-term credit to finance the war, an expensive method of raising capital that abetted corruption and caused long-term economic harm.[86]

The French government also increasingly sought "contributions" from occupied or neighboring areas to support the military. Armies seeking sustenance from local populations had long been a feature of martial activity, but beginning with the Thirty Years' War, this behavior evolved into "a more regular form of extortion" known as contributions.[87] In particular, the wealthy Low Countries attracted French attention. Such extortion had become more efficient and appealing in part because funds now went directly to the state's coffers rather than individual units. Louis regarded contributions as vastly preferable to the traditional "tax of violence" in which the army similarly extorted the French population. Essentially, the government wanted war to feed itself; of course neighbors and adversaries detested such a system that required deploying military forces on or nearby foreign territory.[88]

Even with credit and contributions, the enormous increase in expenses unavoidably strained the French economy as the scope and length of the conflict expanded. Government outlays had skyrocketed from an annual average of 63 million *livres* in the mid-1660s to more than 100 million livres by the middle of the Dutch War. The need for money undermined Colbert's financial reforms that had contributed to improving the nation and government's fiscal position in the preceding decade. From 1672, the monarchy would run a larger deficit each passing year. The war also had damaged or ruined many French business ventures, especially those involving foreign trade and commerce.[89]

Domestic Politics and Decision-making Process

Essentially, one decision maker existed in 1675 France—Louis XIV. Whether with the army in the field, staying at Paris, visiting the under-construction Versailles or other parts of the nation, the king ruled as a true monarch. Louis did not employ a prime minister.[90] It has been observed that he "was the first king of France who could live up to the ideal royal image depicted by Catherine de Medici."[91] Effectively assuming such a dominating role over the government required great energy and effort, which Louis supplied enthusiastically. The king concentrated on military and foreign affairs, knowing these areas would shape judgments of his reign.[92] Louis considered himself a soldier and was fascinated by military matters in contrast to economic affairs. In 1673 he stayed at the front with the army for more than 150 days. He particularly enjoyed discussing fortifications and "directing" sieges, more than twenty of which he attended in person.[93]

Nevertheless, Louis only set military policy and strategy after receiving considerable input from trusted counselors.[94] For an absolute monarch, he was surprisingly open to advice, recognizing "that others knew more than he did about many aspects of government and war, and he sought the most expert opinion that could be found."[95] Louis found it valuable to hear issues debated, even if he was irritated by excessive fighting among subordinate rivals. His own prodigious efforts to be well informed made such discussions productive, rather than the pro forma exercises occurring before the Ming emperor described in the last chapter. The primary forum for meeting on national security issues was the Conseil d'en-Haut (High Council), whose participation Louis had sharply restricted after taking power to consolidate his dominance.[96]

The dynamics of council sessions depended heavily on the key personalities. The 1671 death of Hugues de Lionne, Louis' wise and respected foreign minister, removed a force of restraint with his replacement, Pomponne, exerting less influence. By contrast, the energetic Colbert had continued to amass greater power with his direction of the French economy and government finance. Generally the only impediment to the influence of Colbert and his family was the Le Tellier clan, with whom they often battled. In particular, on military and strategic matters, Louvois surpassed Colbert as Louis' most trusted servant. His aggressive support of the army and hawkish advice dovetailed with the king's inclinations. Not pleasant or popular, Louvois possessed tremendous ability and dedication. The military setbacks in 1674 had briefly jeopardized his position, but by the end of 1675, the politically adroit official had recovered.[97]

Since the start of the Dutch War, Louis and Louvois had used the High Council to assume more control over military affairs, and the departure of Turenne and Condé cemented this "guerre de cabinet" approach. No other soldier possessed their prestige or willingness to act independently. Louis and Louvois, however, did eagerly seek military advice from capable officers, such as Marshal Luxembourg and the recently promoted Brigadier Vauban. Jules-Louis Bolé, the Marquis de Chamlay, was another important figure who had recently begun traveling with the king during campaigns and who often advised him on military matters, although his role would not become central until the death of Louvois in 1691.[98]

Among military officers, Vauban stood out as a strategic advisor. His successful conduct of sieges and design of fortifications had earned him great credibility.

Vauban would not technically become Commissaire Général des Fortifications until the 1677 death of his mentor, Chevalier de Clerville, but he had been regarded as the true expert for almost a decade. In a sign of respect for his abilities, Vauban had been promoted to the rank of brigadier (1674) whereas no previous engineer had risen above captain. Traveling an average of more than 2,500 miles annually in this period to inspect frontier fortifications and terrain, he relayed his observations and broader strategic thoughts to Louvois in an extensive correspondence that reveals a mutual respect. Moreover, they frequently met to discuss these issues. As one Vauban biographer observes, he was "far ahead of his contemporaries. He thought of defense as a whole, not as a matter of scattered and isolated details, and there was always in the back of his mind this idea of a ring fence, the strong barrier that would preserve the Pré Carré inviolate, and embrace the whole circuit of France."[99] Although it had been two-and-a-half years since his first mention of the pré carré defense approach, Vauban now argued that the deteriorating situation made its serious consideration paramount.[100]

Frontier Strategic Options

With the upcoming campaign season approaching, Louis and Louvois needed to choose a course of action, and they had to point French security strategy in a general direction. Although the two requirements did not have to be precisely correlated, prudence dictated that the latter should influence the former. France had essentially three strategic options, although the first two seemed infeasible. The first approach entailed a quest for French dominance in western Europe. In opposition, the monarchy could fall back and attempt to resurrect Mazarin's network of alliances and France's benign reputation. Finally, an intermediary option entailed pursuit of a defensible frontier. In essence, the government could seek Vauban's pré carré. Because French officials did not regard the existing frontier as suitable for such a barrier, this approach would require either abandoning exposed terrain or pursuing limited advances to gain the ground necessary for a secure forward frontier.

All-Out Expansion

Many European leaders believed Louis had been pursuing the first option in the Dutch War, but he more accurately had been focused on accumulating gloire through limited conquest. The difference would have been lost on the king's adversaries. Plus, early French successes had enhanced the court's appetite, most notably when the capture of Maastricht temporarily fueled a notion of eliminating the Dutch as a major power. Even with the diplomatic situation worsening in September 1673, Louvois held to ambitious aims by noting that a long war was a "necessary evil that is impossible to avoid unless we make a peace like that of

1668. The king is a long way from doing anything like that."[101] Yet, even in the heady days of 1673, Louis did not indicate a desire to pursue control of western Europe. Most notably, despite considerable French military activity on German soil, he harbored no territorial aims in this region.[102] Already by the end of 1673 French withdrawal from most Dutch territory rendered any grandiose notions seemingly unobtainable.

Two years later an even more isolated and weary France did not seem capable of expanding the struggle. Seeking major territorial gains was problematic given that "the need to defend multiple fronts kept Louis from marshalling the full military might of his kingdom on any single one of them."[103] A significant additional increase in French army strength appeared undoable with the current effort provoking tax revolts and a manpower shortage. French diplomats certainly endeavored to undermine the adversary coalition, but recent experience revealed the proclivity of German leaders to balance rather than bandwagon. Any effort at dominance would be expected to intensify resistance. A more promising, if delicate, diplomatic gambit involved distracting Vienna by supporting subversive forces in eastern Europe (e.g., Hungarian rebels, the Ottoman Empire). Even if the coalition could be temporarily weakened, French officials appreciated that the ascendancy of positional warfare would limit the speed and scale of any advance. Gaining dominance in western Europe would be a lengthy, costly, and probably unachievable endeavor. Whatever the gloire attached to such a success, failure would tarnish Louis' reputation and jeopardize the security of his kingdom. Lynn concludes that "if he ever strove to dominate Europe, it was neither his first nor final goal, simply an arrogant, and passing, fancy."[104]

Accommodation

If pursuing dominance was futile and thus unappealing, could and should France return to Mazarin's strategy of relying heavily on alliances and a benign reputation? Historians have come to regard Mazarin's network of alliances as creating an extremely safe kingdom.[105] In particular, allied protection of the eastern front had allowed the French to concentrate forces in the northeast, where nothing stood between the kingdom and the Spanish Netherlands. Denying Spain, its implacable foe, allies represented a critical benefit of such an approach. The policy could potentially provide enhanced security at significant fiscal savings.

For Louis, however, returning to Mazarin's strategy was both undesirable and probably infeasible. First and most importantly, the king would essentially be repudiating his prior position. Such an explicit acknowledgment of erroneous judgment would tarnish Louis' reputation and have potentially damaging political repercussions. Although offering money could perhaps generate some interest, France would not have been able to resurrect alliances without surrendering considerable territory, possibly all gains since the 1659 Peace of Pyrenees.

Such a pullback would have been unpopular among French elites, especially the military, given that the nation had not been defeated on the battlefield. Moreover, given his chronic fear about invasion, the French king would have been uncomfortable with even a partial reliance on an alliance system for security.[106] The repeated shifts in ties over the past five years only highlighted the fragility of such commitments. As a result, the king would have felt compelled to erect significant fortifications in conjunction with this accommodationist approach, especially fearing its interpretation as evidence of French weakness. Such a precaution would certainly limit the fiscal benefits of an accommodation-based approach and possibly compromise its success by sustaining perceptions of French war potential. In reality, a decade of aggression had convinced many European leaders of Louis' hegemonic tendencies; thus "France's system of security—Mazarin's brilliant achievement—was destroyed beyond any hope of resurrection."[107] The point is moot, however, because Louis would not have adopted a course of action that he believed so damaging personally, politically, and strategically.

Pré Carré

The shortcomings of both dominance and reassurance strategies left the king and his advisors to ponder the merit of a defensible frontiers' approach. Such a policy entailed some negatives that had contributed to Louis' reluctance to embrace it previously. Most notably, this approach ensured that the struggle between France and her adversaries would continue indefinitely with high military expenditures. Beyond the major investment in frontier fortifications, the government would have to fund a large peacetime army to garrison them adequately.[108] French military experts, such as Vauban, stressed the peacetime force could not be less than the minimum needed for protection in wartime— "any less, and fortresses would become prey to enemy action at the outset of the next conflict."[109] Increased fortifications had already quadrupled garrison forces from the twenty-five thousand troops needed in the mid-1660s. The demand for both large garrison and field forces facing an enemy coalition troubled military analysts.[110] Additionally, the currently intertwined territorial alignment on the northeast frontier was ill suited for a strong strategic defense, and this option would require targeted advances or selective withdrawal. In general, significant advances entailed international political consequences while major withdrawals had domestic political effects.

Decision for a Strategic Defense System

Despite these negatives, the king found the establishment of a defensible frontier to be the most appealing option for psychological, political, and military reasons. The fearful and combative Louis probably never envisioned that a time of blissful peace would be possible in an age of nearly continuous warfare. Although expenses for the current conflict had fueled some instability, the wealth of the kingdom could support strong strategic defenses, especially if it reduced costly future wars. Moreover, Louis and Louvois probably did not fully appreciate that relying on frontier fortresses would result in such a permanent expansion of the army. Given the poor siegecraft demonstrated by the enemy to date, a strategic defense system appeared likely to be effective. Even if component fortresses were captured, they would slow down an advancing enemy and gain time to react, especially given France's geography-facilitated internal lines. Holding a strong, defensive position would not only preempt adversaries from challenging France but it would also enhance the gloire of its king by safeguarding the realm.[111]

If adopting this course of action was clearly preferable, the court still had to decide either to "sacrifice advanced positions, falling back to a defensible line, or add new pieces of territory to form a defensible line forward."[112] Given the struggles of the last two years, pulling back from exposed areas represented the easiest variant. It would not require any military gains and could likely be parlayed into a peace settlement to end the war. Although any pullback would diminish the prestige of Louis and possibly generate some domestic discontent, the king had demonstrated a willingness to withdraw when necessary, as occurred in his abandonment of most Dutch territory in late 1673. Moreover, he had established a significant reservoir of gloire with his military successes to date. Nevertheless, French leaders exhibited no interest in this variant. In contrast to the tactical abandonment of Dutch territory, Louis had declared his intention to keep captured parts of the Spanish Netherlands. For a French monarch "who insisted that not a foot of his territory should be violated," such a declaration had created a strong disinclination to any withdrawal from "new" parts of the realm.[113] Moreover, military advisors, in particular Vauban, argued that an advance pré carré was preferable, especially "eliminating the Spanish fortresses to the right (east) of the Lille salient" (i.e., Condé, Bouchain, Cambrai, and Valenciennes).[114] Whether Vauban actually believed that only moving forward would create a satisfactory pré carré, or whether he recognized that Louis would frown on a pullback is unclear. Regardless, the engineer's advice reinforced the king's inclination to press forward.

Louis' military policy for the remainder of the Dutch War reflected this pursuit of a defensible frontier through limited gains in the Spanish Netherlands.[115] Given the prowess of the French army, such minimal gains appeared achievable, especially against a coalition that had difficulty coordinating its activities. The French willingness to increase their vulnerability on the eastern frontier by concentrating force in the Spanish Netherlands enhanced their prospects.

Upon obtaining a pré carré, the French would erect fortifications—*frontière de fer* (iron frontier)—to provide the desired defense-in-depth. From this point in his reign, Louis sought limited territorial additions to enhance French security, albeit often through military threats and action.[116] The strategy fit the king's personality and thinking, but it entailed the high price of projecting a defensive-oriented ruler as threatening to the other leaders of Europe.

Implementation of the New Strategy

In early 1676 the army began pursuing the Pré Carré–required territory by laying siege to the Spanish fortifications at Condé and Bouchain on the Scheldt River.[117] After their rapid capitulation, the court showed commitment to its new strategy. Instead of simply advancing forward, Louis returned to Versailles and the French troops took up defensive positions. Then on 7 July, when the Prince of Orange besieged French-held Maastricht, the king did not order a major relief force be sent to the old Dutch fortress whose capture had brought so much glory. Instead Louis directed an advance on Aire, one of the two remaining Spanish-held fortresses in the Artois region, much closer to Paris. Either the king had already decided to advance on Aire as a necessary part of the Pré Carré, or he now concluded its possession would "better serve the French defensive system than the distant and exposed Maastricht."[118] While the French army quickly captured Aire, its force at Maastricht valiantly resisted the ineffective Dutch siege until a relief force arrived at the end of August. Although it is possible Louis believed all along that Maastricht could hold out until the army seized Aire, clearly the latter now had more value to the French than the former. The unsuccessful Dutch effort only reinforced notions of allied incompetence at siegecraft. Despite nearly fifteen years of continuous warfare, adversaries had captured only a single meaningful French-held fortress (Bonn, in 1673).[119]

A lack of progress at the Nijmegen peace talks allowed the French to continue pursuing pré carré territory. In the next campaign season, the army would target key positions on the northern and southern flanks of the Lille salient.[120] To the north, the army concentrated on Spain's last fortress in the Artois region, Saint-Omer, "such a useful prize that the French could afford to suspend all work on their rearward fortresses in Picardy."[121] To the south, the French built on gains in the previous campaign by advancing along the Scheldt River to capture the now isolated Valenciennes and Cambrai. The limited targets of Louis' campaigns in 1676 and 1677 showed "he now identified his personal gloire with defending his lands rather than with seizing more territory."[122] In contrast to these French victories, another Dutch siege failed, this time at Charleroi.

Louis had now seized the desired terrain for a robust pré carré, but he needed to legitimate these acquisitions through a peace treaty. The French ruler could not achieve peace simply by saying he only wanted defensible frontiers, especially with the allies demanding that the king relinquish the captured terrain necessary for the Pré Carré. Louis' opponents hoped an increasingly anti-French England would join them prompting the crown's ambassador in London to urge an end to the war. The court recognized that the Dutch were the key to breaking the coalition and rapidly ending the war. While declaring no interest in Dutch territory, Paris moved to frighten The Hague into submission. They achieved this goal early in the 1678 campaign season by overwhelming the historic old Spanish fortifications at Ghent near the Dutch border and then capturing the Ypres fortress.[123]

The completion of a French–Dutch accord in August 1678 undermined the prospects for British participation and collapsed the opposing coalition. Without Dutch support, Spanish continuation of the struggle would be counterproductive. Thus, in mid-September Paris and Madrid agreed to terms. The departure of the Dutch and the Spanish would quiet the northeast, shifting the French focus to the eastern frontier. Paris had previously neglected this region, enabling imperial forces to seize the bridges over the Upper Rhine at Philippsburg and Strasbourg as well as much of the Alsace region. Given this success, the Austrian emperor demonstrated greater reluctance to end the war, but prudence dictated that the relatively isolated Vienna agree to peace in February 1679.[124]

A combination of military success and diplomatic triumph had established France as the war's biggest winner and Spain the primary loser.[125] The former finally retained the Franche-Comté region while keeping eleven towns previously part of the Spanish Netherlands, including Aire, Cambrai, and Saint-Omer. Individually none of these towns matched the import of Luxembourg or Namur, but Louis collectively "had gained almost everything he wanted on his northern frontiers."[126] The squared or rationalized border could now be effectively defended with robust fortifications. The king returned to Spain the more exposed fortresses such as Charleroi and Ghent. By contrast, a confused outcome resulted in the Rhineland, not surprisingly since "neither side could claim a clear military victory."[127] The emperor retained control of Philippsburg, which, along with the independent but affiliated city of Strasbourg, left him essentially possessing two of the three bridges across the Upper Rhine. Louis obtained garrison rights to Freiburg east of the Rhine, which ensured access to Breisach and the other bridge.

Lessons Learned from the Dutch War

Before turning to Louis' postwar policy, it is worthwhile to review his lessons learned from the Dutch War. Although covered in glory as the "Sun King" and receiving accolades from victory, Louis realized he needed to be more cautious.[128]

The arduous struggle to achieve modest goals had a sobering effect even with the army's strong performance. For Louis "the impetuosity of youth was gone, and he and his advisors made few grand gestures again like the invasion of the Dutch Netherlands."[129] Second, although the French had ultimately unraveled the opposing coalition, the king now appreciated the danger of a large anti-French alliance.[130] Given that most European leaders continued to fear Louis, such a coalition could easily be resurrected. Moreover, the French ruler had to face that "Louis's two implacable enemies—the Austrians and the Dutch—had formed a working alliance."[131]

These two lessons combined to inform a third conclusion for Louis and his advisors—France needed to continue to improve the defensibility of its frontiers. Louis' military success after 1675, "when neither Condé nor Turenne were at his side," promoted the soundness of a defensible frontier in his mind.[132] The king believed intensifying his unilateral, defense-oriented policy would better protect the realm than attempting a diplomatic offensive to alleviate the inhospitable climate. Evidence of this attitude quickly emerged in November 1679 when Louis used trumped-up charges to dismiss Pomponne.[133] A popular view in Paris that France should have received better terms given its military success prompted the criticism of diplomats. Replacing the moderate Pomponne with the aggressive Marquis de Croissy, the naval minister's brother, signaled that the French government would press for every advantage to strengthen its frontiers. Although such behavior might seem incautious, for the French at the time, safety was defined in the reality of stout strategic defenses, not the possibility of improved foreign relations.

Security Developments along a Fortified Frontier

With the war over, Louis and his advisors directed their attention and resources to creating the "iron frontier" with fortified cities and strong points. Although not a static line or single wall, the works functioned in toto as a strategic defense system to bolster security, especially in areas devoid of naturally protective terrain.[134] This approach has been characterized as "an innovative way of thinking at a time when any given fortification had quite recently been seen as only a very localized matter, which might fit into a scheme of provincial defense at best, not a truly national one."[135] Another historian notes it was "like a giant *trace italienne* [fortification] between the North Sea and the Meuse."[136] Although scholars differ somewhat in characterizing the two-line system as a defense-in-depth or a tight seal of the border, they agree that the French sought to protect the kingdom from three types of threats: external invasion, enemy "contribution" raids, and to a lesser extent, internal uprisings in recently conquered territory.[137] While the frontier fortifications clearly enhanced protection, they also abetted

France's ability to strike outward. This dual offense–defense effect perhaps best defines the nature of the Pré Carré and its significant influence on the strategic dynamics of western Europe for the next few decades. While Louis identified the Pré Carré as "forming an impenetrable wall that protected and defined a border," foreign rulers focused on its offensive potential.[138] Fortresses served as large supply magazines, advantageously facilitating attacks earlier in the season and enabling more profitable exploitation of neighboring populations through "contributions."[139]

Expanding the Frontière de Fer to the Eastern Frontier

Securing the frontier with the Spanish Netherlands highlighted to the French court the relative vulnerability of areas to the southeast. Imperial forces had used their control of bridgeheads over the Rhine in the late stages of the Dutch War to move into the Alsace region and cause great difficulty. Despite somewhat strengthened defenses in the Lorraine region, Louis and Louvois regarded them as insufficient to protect this critical area below the Pré Carré. Instead, "more and more the idea of lineal frontiers defended by great works at key points came to dominate the thinking of the war ministry."[140] The king, regarding such an approach as the key to risk mitigation, was eager to pursue its broader implementation. Whereas the Ming tended to be reactive after the Mongols circumvented extant barriers, the French moved proactively to secure the fronts perceived as vulnerable. Erecting major strategic defenses on French soil alone would have been disturbing to adversaries, but the king's belief in the Pré Carré meant obtaining the territory best suited for such fortification, fanning alarm throughout Europe.[141] Although Vauban was sensitive about the political consequences of French expansion, his arguing for Dixmude, Courtrai, Luxembourg, and Strasbourg "began to reveal ever more clearly his thoughts for a line of strategic bases, or *frontière de fer*" along all of France's exposed borders.[142]

The French government aggressively pursued the desired territory.[143] Despite wanting to avoid major war, "military action was the hallmark of Louis's policy" as the French lacked diplomatic aplomb and political sensitivity.[144] The French historian André Corvisier labels this approach as "la défense aggressive," using bullish means for limited gains.[145] The effort began dramatically on September 30, 1681, when French forces seized both Strasbourg and Casale; "the double coup ... stunned European statesmen."[146] With the formerly independent city of Strasbourg, the French controlled the two most southerly bridges on the Rhine. By contrast, the seizure of the Casale fortress east of the Alps near Turin appears counter to a defensive orientation. Rather than focus on the natural mountainous frontier, France now possessed two strong outposts facing Italy to the understandable concern of European leaders. Louis' motives for Casale remain unclear; possibilities include another bridgehead across the Alps, a valuable chit to exchange for desired territory elsewhere, or leverage to exert pressure on adversaries. The crown ultimately retained Casale and its other forward positions, prompting Vauban to later lament, "if instead of flying like a butterfly across the Alps we had stuck to arranging the frontier decently, the king would have had his mind at rest."[147] In an attempt to gain further territory without appearing so threatening, the French government employed reunions—"a strategic mixture of legality and force."[148] French troops seized desired areas, but Louis asserted his rights by characterizing them as "dependencies of territories ceded to the French crown."[149] Validation of his claims came from bodies set up by the French government in the various territories. These groups not surprisingly found the land seizures legitimate while the rest of Europe viewed them as outright thievery.[150] The arrogance of Louis and the abrasiveness of his secretary of state for foreign affairs aggravated and alarmed others, only intensifying the French belief in the need for strategic defenses.

Despite their concern about France, a renewed Ottoman assault on the Austrian Habsburg Empire in 1683 took priority for European leaders and created a window of opportunity for Paris.[151] Louis, as a Christian ruler himself, needed to act delicately to avoid appearances of abandoning coreligionists, but the other western European powers could not provide Spain tangible assistance. After advancing an army onto Spanish soil for sustenance, the French attacked the great Luxembourg fortress on September 1, 1683. Given its isolation, Madrid refrained from declaring war until learning in October that Christian forces had routed the Ottoman army besieging Vienna. This victory would eventually prove fundamental to the course of Europe because "for the first time the Habsburg Empire was free to bring all its power to bear in the west"; for now, the Austrians and Germans remained preoccupied with the Turks.[152] As a result, the French overwhelmed the Spanish in the so-called War of the Reunions, seizing numerous fortresses, including Beaumont, Dixmude, Courtrai, and finally the main prize, Luxembourg, in early June 1684.[153]

At this point, all the parties wanted a respite, leading to the 1684 Truce of Ratisbon, which "marked the high water mark of Louis's territorial acquisitions."[154] Some advisors pressed for seizing the entire Spanish Netherlands, but the king realized further ambition risked war against a strong coalition. The opportunity might seem grand, but "1673–4 served as a warning about how a situation could suddenly deteriorate."[155] During the agreed upon twenty-year truce, France would retain its reunion acquisitions as well as Luxembourg and Strasbourg while returning Dixmude and Courtrai to Spain after destroying their fortifications. France now "came closest to realizing Vauban's goal" of strong, fortified strategic defenses along the nation's exposed frontiers while marking "the peak of Louis XIV's international power and prestige."[156] From the perspective of

Louis and key advisors, they regarded their recent aggression as defensive since they "were convinced that once Leopold had achieved peace with the Turks on his terms, he would turn against France."[157] The French paid a steep price for these limited gains as European leaders' view of Louis XIV as an intolerable menace continued to grow.[158]

Louis and Louvois, possessing a high threat perception, intensified efforts to fortify the kingdom's frontiers. In the east, captured towns such as Strasbourg and Luxembourg received substantial defense upgrades while the French built new fortresses at Fort Louis, Landau, Mont Royal, and Belfort. Priority may have been placed in the east, but the government improved fortifications on every frontier, including the coasts. The 1680s marked the apex of defense construction, with annual expenses quadrupling the rate of the mid-1660s and peaking at more than 12 million livres in 1689. By then Vauban began to worry that the huge costs of fortresses—both in terms of money and manpower—might actually be creating vulnerability by weakening the army. Because of his concern, several superfluous fortifications were abandoned, but the overall effort remained robust. It seems that each new or upgraded work only raised internal concern about other spots being vulnerable, as the king appeared to be pursuing an unobtainable absolute security.[159]

The contrast between France and other European leaders regarding these structures is striking, exemplifying a critical need for wall-builders to appreciate and address adversary perceptions of such efforts. European leaders did not see these strong defense positions as an attempt to deter or defend attacks against French soil.[160] Instead the works, particularly those east of the Rhine, "confirmed the feeling that Louis was unwilling to confine himself, notwithstanding specific assurances."[161] Beyond its symbolic import, the strong French position east of the Rhine combined with the east–west direction of the great river's German tributaries abetted French offensive potential. The dual offense–defense capability of French fortresses fueled a classic security dilemma. Lynn captures this dynamic well by stressing that "in seeking to deter his enemies by constructing 'impregnable' borders during the 1680s, he so alarmed his foes that he made virtually inevitable the very war he sought to avoid. Paradoxically, in demanding ever more guarantees of his security he appeared the insatiable aggressor. Louis never appreciated how his quest for absolute security threatened his neighbors."[162] Dutch leader Prince William III, also outraged by Louis' treatment of French Huguenots (Protestants), maneuvered to establish a strong counter. The French king's plundering of weak Catholic Spain and aiding the Muslim enemy also increased hostility from Catholic leaders, especially after Pope Innocent XI excommunicated him in 1687. By contrast, Emperor Leopold appeared deserving of allegiance given his heroic stand against the "barbaric" Turks. As a result, a militarily and politically stronger Austria joined with the United Provinces,

Sweden, Spain, and many German states in forming the League of Augsburg to prevent further French expansion.[163]

Nine Years' War

Whether the League of Augsburg would attempt to reverse French gains was unclear, but Louis and his advisors feared such an effort with the approaching defeat of the Turks.[164] Rather than try to ameliorate the tension diplomatically, Louis attempted to cement his prior gains by demanding in early 1687 a permanent peace treaty to replace the Truce of Ratisbon. Leopold and other European leaders had no incentive to submit to such a brazen ultimatum. Rather, their position improved throughout the year, especially after a decisive victory over the Turks at Mohács. A frustrated and worried Louis responded to the diplomatic rebuff by initiating a preventive military strike to strengthen his defense position. The French king's decision to advance rather than sit behind his vast fortifications system says more about the ruler than how the defenses affected the military balance. As mentioned earlier, Louis had an unquenchable desire for the unobtainable absolute security, but his attitude reflects a basic dilemma for all wall-builders—reliance on strategic defenses alone leaves the adversary with the initiative both operationally and politically. Louis now wanted to seize Philippsburg, just east of the one bridge over the Upper Rhine that remained out of his control.[165] Its occupation would eliminate "the weakest link in the French defenses" and effectively seal the Rhine.[166] The army quickly captured this objective in September 1688 despite some stout resistance, but its gain had to be weighed against the outrage that erupted throughout Europe. Louis had no desire to start a large-scale war, but there would be no peace now as a large and determined coalition moved to punish the king and weaken France.[167]

His continuous need to eliminate weak spots had helped the French ruler stumble into a great war, but the existence of an overall strong frontier fortification system may have filled him with the confidence to undertake such rash actions. The king displayed an almost schizophrenic alarm and confidence that prompted highly risky behavior, although in his own mind he was apparently attempting to minimize risk. At the outset of the conflict he wrote, "whatever happens in this war, it is certain that the good state of my frontiers and of my troops, will prevent my enemies from troubling the peace of my kingdom and will give me the means to extend my possessions."[168] He had certainly invested an immense amount on these manmade obstacles, which were manned by 166,000 troops.[169] Beyond their strength, Louis was buoyed that effectiveness did not depend on capable field marshals. Rather, the court could direct the war strategy. Louis' personal military adviser, the marquis de Chamlay, captured this perspective in October 1688 by writing,

> The difference that exists between the present situation of the King's affairs and that of [the Dutch War] is that in those previous times, the fortune of His Majesty and of his kingdom was in the hands of men who, by being killed or by making a bad decision, could lose it in a moment, or at least compromise it in some way by the loss of a battle [from] which it had been difficult to reestablish. Whereas, presently, because of the great conquests that have been made, and because of the advantageous situation of the places that have been fortified, the King finds himself able to grant command of his armies to whomever it pleases him, without having anything to fear from the mediocre capacity of those to whom he confides it.[170]

Chamlay has been quoted at length because this attitude reflects the general tendency of wall-builders to erroneously expect the physical structures to minimize the role of the human element in defense and security policy. Typically, Louis' view on the unimportance of talented commanders would prove erroneous.

Somewhat ironically, Vauban, the fortification advocate, had become worried that the heavy reliance on fortified frontiers, especially with the growing strength of France's adversaries, reflected an excessive faith in defense works. If the allies actually cooperated, the French army's superiority and stout defenses might not be enough to block coalition attacks. Adding to his angst was knowledge of "the state of the frontier fortresses, some of them in poor shape ... from neglect and false economies."[171] As with the human element, the need for adequate maintenance of defenses has been a lesson many wall-building states have tended to neglect. The engineer was particularly concerned about a breakthrough on the northeast frontier given the older works on the original Pré Carré and their proximity to Paris. Thus, Vauban proposed in 1689 reestablishing the capital's defenses on the surrounding hills with walls able to withstand modern artillery salvos. Louis acknowledged the value of such structures, but he regarded fortification of Europe's largest city as prohibitively expensive. There would be no safety net.[172]

France's challenge grew immensely more difficult after November 1688 when the Dutch leader William III conquered England. Fear that England's weak, catholic king James II might accept alliance overtures from Louis XIV (or that a de facto partnership already existed) had motivated William while the French attack on Philippsburg increased Dutch enthusiasm for the venture.[173] Concentrating on central Europe, the French failed to protect the Stuart regime. William's stunning success unified the two great maritime powers under Louis' most ardent foe. Every major power in western Europe had now joined the struggle against the French kingdom.

Although the French faced this isolation confidently, the primary strategic question for Louis was how to win the wider conflict.[174] He could not defeat all of the powers arrayed against him, so that left either intimidating some members to drop out or simply grinding out victory slowly. The purely defensive option of relying on his fortifications left the initiative to his enemies and a likely expensive attrition war. Uninterested in this costly approach, the king hoped to reprise the successful maneuvers that cracked the coalition in the Dutch War a decade earlier. In particular, Louis thought that the German princes might be "persuaded" to abandon the Dutch and the Habsburgs.[175] The French also hoped action in Germany would keep Turkey fighting the Austrians. Once it became evident Louis could not convince the German princes to capitulate, he decided to protect the frontier by "clearing a firebreak to the north and east of the French fortress line that ran from Breisach to Strasbourg to Philippsburg to Landau."[176] As a result, the French army turned this region into a wasteland, leaving more than twenty towns and the surrounding countryside destroyed.[177] The firebreak had been achieved, but so had a "hatred of France [that] lasted for generations in Germany" and intensified hostility throughout Europe.[178]

Given adversarial determination and positional warfare dominance, an attrition struggle commenced. Facing so many enemies and garrisoning so many fortresses, the army had grown to 273,000 troops by 1691 and two years later reached a maximum of approximately 340,000 men under arms.[179] In these early years of the conflict, the army actually gained territory, including the line of Spanish fortresses along the Sambre River (e.g., Namur, Charleroi). Vauban declared in late 1693 that the frontier was "the best France had had for a 1,000 years."[180] Nevertheless, decisive victory eluded the French, ensuring continuation of the war. Supporting such a massive army—a size that would not be reached again until after the French Revolution—increasingly burdened the kingdom. Louis sacrificed the grand battle fleet as an unaffordable luxury, but he hesitated to abandon nonessential outposts and refused to withdraw from Casale beyond the Alps, despite the urging of Vauban.[181] A disastrous harvest in 1693–94 exacerbated pressure on the French economy and led to the death of as many as 2 million nationals.[182] Compounding concern was the evident decline of France's qualitative military advantage. Most disturbingly, the Dutch, under the direction of Menno van Coehoorn, had finally gained significant siege warfare capability as evidenced by their rapid success against the strong fortress at Namur in 1695. Vauban disparaged Coehoorn's cavalier waste of men and material as a form of unsustainable attack, but Namur's seizure shocked most French and raised questions about artificial barriers' ability to provide security.[183] Heavily fortified strategic defenses can contribute significantly to perceptions of safety, but such benefits are susceptible to rapid deflation if such works prove to be vulnerable as occurred at Namur.

As a part of the effort to enhance strategic defenses during the conflict, the French had increasingly constructed continuous barrier lines. As previously mentioned, such entrenchments had been used in a limited fashion in the Dutch War to block the enemy from obtaining "contributions." At the outset of the Nine Years' War, Louis ordered these lines on "a much grander scale," especially facing the Spanish Netherlands.[184] They proved effective against raiding parties, even blocking an attack by fifteen hundred cavalry and fifteen hundred horse-transported infantry in August 1690 near Ypres. Armies, however, could easily overcome the barriers as evidenced by the Duke of Württemberg penetrating the same area with approximately fifteen thousand men. Vauban had begun arguing for constructing stronger lines integral to the overall strategic defense system vice exclusively protecting against contribution raids. He feared that the enemy's growing siege capabilities meant "that static permanent fortresses alone were incapable of staying the Allied counter-offensive."[185] The king ordered in April 1695 a ten-mile line between Courtrai and Avelgem that would "be eight feet deep and eight feet wide with earthen parapets rising beyond them a full nine feet tall and six feet wide in front of a firing step."[186] While presenting a clear obstacle, the French lacked the resources to build and man such entrenchments across the entire frontier.

Ultimately, mounting military and especially economic exhaustion prompted Louis to accept the less than favorable Peace of Ryswick in September 1697.[187] France had to relinquish most of the Spanish territory garnered under the reunions as well as Charleroi, Ath, Courtrai, and, to the particular disappointment of Vauban, Luxembourg. Louis also had to surrender all his strong fortresses east of the Rhine: Breisach, Freiburg, Kehl, and Philippsburg. This component of the treaty helped establish France's eastern border at the Rhine River. Beyond the territorial losses, the long, costly conflict had sapped relative French strength. A chagrined Louis now "pursued a policy of peace at nearly any price," even accepting deployment of Dutch garrisons into ten fortresses in the Spanish Netherlands.[188] Despite such efforts, French leaders realized peace was tenuous and security policy needed to be reinvigorated. The collapse of Namur prompted some French officials to question the value of fortifications; however, Louis and his advisors perceived no real alternative. In the northeast, the Pré Carré remained largely intact with refurbished fortifications, although Charlemont-Givet replaced the dismantled fortress at Dinant on the first line's southern flank.[189] The loss of Luxembourg required that the French restore the strategic defense system employed on that front prior to 1684. Most importantly, Vauban concentrated on "building the formidable *barrière de l'est*," a line of fortresses, including the massive Neuf-Brisach, on the western side of the Rhine to maximize the river's defense potential.[190] Within a few years, defenses—almost three hundred fortified positions—guarded the full length of the kingdom's northeastern and eastern frontiers.[191]

War of Spanish Succession

Louis' effort to avoid further conflict floundered with the long anticipated death of Spain's Charles II.[192] Lacking a direct heir, his empire would fall to either a French Bourbon or Austrian Habsburg. Versailles and Vienna had attempted to defuse the predictable crisis by agreeing to split the Spanish realm, but Charles undermined this effort by designating Louis XIV's grandson Philip as heir. If the Bourbon did not take over the entire empire, however, it would be transferred to Archduke Charles, one of Leopold's sons. These terms essentially forced Louis to accept the will or enable the unification of the Spanish and Austrian empires under one Habsburg family for the first time in nearly 150 years.

Despite their misgivings, other European leaders might have accepted Philip V's accession in 1700 if Louis had not reinvigorated fears of French hegemony. He had asserted that the two kingdoms would not be ruled uniformly from Versailles, but Louis quickly fostered that impression.[193] In particular, he antagonized William III by surrounding the Dutch-occupied fortresses in the Spanish Netherlands with French troops. These forces remained even after the Dutch soldiers left, with Louis declaring they would defend the Spanish Netherlands until Madrid could assume the task. This move, along with similar deployments into the bishoprics of Liège and Cologne, threatened to eliminate any buffer between France and the Dutch Netherlands.[194] Louis further exacerbated tension with his recognition of James II's son as successor to the British throne. Even after the accidental death of William, the French king's aggressive actions prompted an opposing coalition led by the United Provinces and the Austrian Empire to declare war on May 17, 1702.

To the dismay of its senior officers, France's defensive position was actually weakened by Louis' decision to advance forces into the Spanish Netherlands, which had so alarmed William. In April 1701, after completing an inspection tour, Marshal Boufflers observed that "you will scarcely credit the state of decay of all these fortresses. It defies description."[195] The works, including structures or refurbishments overseen by Vauban, had been completed more than twenty years earlier, and the Spanish had neglected proper maintenance in this now remote part of the empire. Per Louis' guidance, the French army would have to defend this Spanish territory beyond the Pré Carré. Holding the position against coalition forces would require a large French presence that inhibited the army's ability to concentrate forces in other sectors or engage in offensives.[196] Louis' decision to safeguard the Spanish Netherlands with French forces was a political and military blunder, but it highlights a drawback of relying on strategic defenses in a fluid environment: strategic defenses do not facilitate flexible policy without increasing vulnerability.

While time did not permit significant refurbishment of the Spanish Netherlands fortresses, the French did move to bolster their defenses at the outbreak of hostilities by erecting the robust Brabant entrenchment lines.[197] These barriers ran for almost 130 miles from the port of Antwerp across the frontier until reaching the Meuse River between Namur and Huy. The lines, growing in scale and range for thirty years, reached their fully developed form with "a curtain, furnished with bastions and redans, and preceded by a ditch twenty-four feet wide and twelve feet deep."[198] The performance of such entrenchments, however, depended on adequate manning. Therefore, the allies probed for weaknesses knowing their length stretched the French army's capacity. Again, the mobility of an opponent's forces and the number of avenues of attack critically shaped the potential effectiveness of strategic defenses.

In contrast to the previous war, France actually began this conflict with noteworthy allies (Spain, Savoy, Cologne, and Bavaria), but their assistance would soon be compromised by military setbacks. The possession of allies does not fit with a purely defensive strategy of relying on one's own fortifications because it leaves partners vulnerable. Facing a wealthier and more powerful coalition, Louis was not inclined to surrender the initiative and engage in another attrition struggle. Thus the French and their partners pushed deep into Germany with the aim of knocking the Austrian emperor out of the fight.[199] This strategy foundered on the Blenheim battlefield in 1704, where a crushing defeat gravely weakened Louis' army and deprived him of German allies. The war would continue for another decade, but now France had to adopt a strategy of essentially frontier defense, "a course of action that made it difficult to gain allies, that posed a serious logistical strain and which made victory impossible."[200] The situation further deteriorated after severe loses at Turin and Ramillies in 1706, which pushed the French back to the Alps on the southeastern frontier and eliminated a strong presence in the Spanish Netherlands. The Spanish region's relatively weak fortifications had become easy prey, and several towns including Brussels, Ghent, and Antwerp capitulated without resistance.[201] Still, reflecting the nature of positional warfare, seizure of even the mostly weak and dilapidated fortifications in the Spanish Netherlands "did force the Allies to conduct eleven sieges and delayed an advance into France proper until 1708—six years into the war."[202]

As the enemy gained control over most of the Spanish Netherlands, the French adjusted their defenses to the border regions. Marshal Louis-Joseph Vendôme began construction on new lines to replace the abandoned Brabant entrenchments.[203] Known simply as the 1706–7 line, this barrier ran for more than one hundred miles from Ypres through Lille, Tournai, and Mons before traveling along the Sambre River to Namur. The section from Ypres through

Tournai connected key fortresses on the first line of the Pré Carré. With peace talks producing no diplomatic solution, the army stood guard as a determined foe approached France in force for the first time since Louis adopted the defensible frontiers strategy thirty years earlier. At a minimum, the strategic defense system prompted caution from the allies, whose unwillingness to advance aggressively resulted in a few years of stalemate.[204]

Rather than be encouraged by the allies' hesitance, French officials worried that preparedness levels would be unsustainable should the status quo continue, and growing allied firepower would overwhelm fortifications should the allies attack.[205] Typifying this latter concern, the Marquis de Chamlay, still Louis' primary military advisor, had noted that "even a very considerable garrison would likely be unable to save Lille [Vauban's great fortress] if the enemies were to attack it with an artillery train as large as what they usually employ in their sieges."[206] In 1708 the French launched an offensive into the Spanish Netherlands to break the stalemate, lest they have to capitulate due to exhaustion. The allies routed this force at Oudenaarde, creating an opportunity for the Duke of Marlborough and Prince Eugene to resume their own advance. Marlborough advocated attacking along the coastline with resupply from the Royal Navy to bypass the main Pré Carré fortifications, but his allies regarded such an approach as excessively risky. Instead, the Dutch and Prince Eugene successfully pressed to launch an attack directly against Lille, the heart of the first line.[207] Although it offered some stout resistance, the great fortress, as Chamlay feared, could not withstand the overwhelming firepower directed by the allies and fell by the end of the year. This seminal defeat brought "the Allies literally to the front door of France," and combined with a poor harvest to prompt a reinvigorated French effort for peace.[208] The allies' severe terms, especially "no peace without Spain," prevented a diplomatic solution.[209]

Louis did not have to capitulate because even the successful allied capture of frontier fortresses would be a time-consuming and costly process despite a shift in the offense–defense balance toward the former. With a large garrison and strong works, Lille demonstrated that progress would be slow by holding out from September until early December. Moreover, as with the previous assaults on fortresses at Kaiserwerth and Menin, the allies suffered significant casualties (more than twelve thousand men including the loss of sixty-five badly needed engineers).[210] Even with the capture of Lille, the allies would have to overcome several additional Pré Carré fortresses before opening a path to Paris. The allies "found that it was far easier to launch subsequent attacks sideways into Vauban's first line of fortresses than it was to venture forward into the second line, let alone capture the main prize of Paris."[211] While the viability of Marlborough's proposed strategy of maneuvering around the main fortresses will never be known, the results of a direct assault were clear. The allies spent the next two years slowly expanding the Lille salient, exemplified by a lengthy and costly, albeit ultimately successful siege against Tournai.

French resistance had been invigorated not only by fighting on their homeland but also by the placement of Marshal Villars in command. Louis' belief that the quality of commander did not matter given France's iron frontier had proven erroneous with the army suffering greatly under a series of incompetent or mediocre leaders. Villars, however, was of the caliber of past stalwarts of the Louis XIV era (e.g., Turenne, Condé, and Luxembourg). Possessing a traditional general's mindset, Villars thought "hiding behind entrenchments (or fortress walls) was enfeebling and demoralizing" and sought to go on the offensive whenever possible.[212] Thus, when the allies moved to attack Mons in 1709, Villars led a skilled effort to block them at nearby Malplaquet. Although the allies achieved victory, it was a pyrrhic one—costing them 25 percent of the force—in sharp contrast to their overwhelming successes at Ramillies and Oudenaarde.[213] Nevertheless, the enemy continued to advance in a seemingly relentless, albeit slow, manner that included the capture of second line Pré Carré fortresses at Aire, Béthune, Saint Venant, and Douai by the end of 1710.

With the enemy inexorably approaching the Oise Valley, historically the avenue toward Paris, the French took defense preparations as best as possible but regarded the upcoming 1711 campaign season with dread.[214] French-held fortresses at Arras, Cambrai, Le Quesnoy, and Landrecies still obstructed a direct move against the capital. While reinforcing these Pré Carré positions, Villars bolstered strategic defenses by building new entrenchment lines, which he famously labeled *Ne Plus Ultra* (No Further). With France facing a direct threat, the role of such lines had evolved "from being a mere shield against 'contributions' . . . into prepared fields of battle for entire armies."[215] The French now occupied approximately two hundred miles of entrenchments in northeast France and the Spanish Netherlands, although they continued to lack the troops to cover properly their entire length.[216]

The alarmed court operated unaware that "the weary old process of shuffling along the frontier" had taken its toll on enemy forces and produced political problems especially in England.[217] The four sieges in 1710 produced twenty thousand additional allied casualties and generally diminished morale among the troops and within the participating nations despite the victories.[218] In August 1711, Queen Anne replaced the prowar Whig cabinet with members from the opposition Tory party.[219] Wanting to focus on colonialism and trade, the Tories undertook direct talks with the French to extricate England from the war. Then, in January 1712, the government replaced Marlborough as commander of British forces, removing the allies' most aggressive and talented commander. Britain remained in the war with negotiations ongoing, but it would begin the next campaign season without any enthusiasm for further combat.

The failure to end Britain's participation exacerbated French fear that 1712 would be the year of allied breakthrough, but it would not occur. Pessimism was so rampant at the French court that some advisors suggested Louis relocate south to the Loire Valley. The king, bolstered by the determination of Villars and other French military officers, refused to retreat.[220] Facing an enemy twice its size, the beleaguered French forces concentrated between Arras and Cambrai to protect the Oise Valley. Prince Eugene's superior army continued to push forward, capturing Le Quesnoy in early July and then heading for Landrecies, the last Pré Carré fortress before the Oise Valley. After four years of slogging, Eugene would never reach this long sought objective. Now deprived of British troops, the allied force had become overextended allowing Villars to launch an effective counteroffensive against enemy rear lines that captured several key depots. Appearing on the verge of victory, this sudden setback combined with the loss of English support and worn down troop morale evaporated allied determination.[221] In the end, the iron frontier "was never completely broken through even in the blackest days of the War of Spanish Succession."[222]

The changed military and diplomatic environment allowed Louis to negotiate a far better settlement than he would have accepted anytime in the previous half decade. The resulting Treaty of Utrecht almost seemed like a victory to Frenchmen. Despite losing most of the battles and generating an enormous debt, "in a very real sense, France had won the war: the nightmare of the Habsburg encirclement that had plagued it for two hundred years was no more."[223] The king's grandson would remain on the Spanish throne, albeit after renouncing his claim to the French crown. The French kingdom again had to relinquish control of key Spanish fortresses at Charleroi, Namur, and Luxembourg as well as cede Pré Carré first line fortresses at Ypres, Furnes, and Tournai. Failure to maintain the last, in particular, had been a disappointing blow to Versailles since it "greatly weakened the French defensive system on the vulnerable northeastern frontier."[224] The French quickly set to work restoring the Pré Carré fortification system, which would help the kingdom remain secure from invasion until the French Revolution prompted another coalition to attack in 1793–94 along the Spanish Netherlands frontier.[225] Even then, the Pré Carré fortresses abetted republican efforts to push back the invading armies. The fortifications of Vauban did not become completely obsolete until mid-nineteenth century advances in armaments.

Conclusion

While large parts of the old northeastern frontier have become highly developed over the last one hundred years, the small French town of Le Quesnoy survives as a monument to Louis XIV's strategic defense system. Standing atop its essentially intact walls, this one-time Pré Carré fortress helps one readily visualize the iron frontier in its full flowering. The double line of fortifications facing the Spanish Netherlands must have been an impressive site for Frenchman and foe. By the end of the 1680s with the extension of strong strategic defenses to the eastern frontier, adversaries inspecting the edge of French-controlled territory would have found the position uninviting. Vauban—the man most directly responsible for the strategic defenses—was amazed that "(except for a couple of gaps) you would be within earshot of French fortress guns all the way from the Swiss border to the Channel."[226] Their physical magnitude clearly warrants such entrancement, but how should their contribution to the security of late-seventeenth-century France be judged?

From the perspective of the 1675–76 winter, the establishment of defensible frontiers had a powerful logic. Combining strong territorial positions with stout fortifications allowed the French to develop a formidable barrier along the kingdom's most critical frontier. It addressed the military, diplomatic, and psychological security needs of French leaders, above all Louis. France's strategic culture, military capability, and resources all pointed to this approach as the optimal way to safeguard a country surrounded by adversaries. Psychologically, it bolstered Louis' confidence that the kingdom and his gloire would be safe from invasion. By contrast, the alternatives of dominance and reassurance had lost their appeal or potential for success by the mid-1670s. A decade earlier, one could have argued the merits of all three policies, but a different court and an alarmed European community essentially left France with only one viable alternative. Beyond the king's sense of gloire, a sound argument exists for pushing forward the Pré Carré in the northeast to increase its distance from Paris. Given that the nature of military affairs at the time, fortifications would have been plentiful regardless of the Pré Carré, making this case the hardest to imagine a counterfactual. The absence of robust strategic defenses would have left the instinctively insecure French king feeling more vulnerable and likely to take provocative actions that would have probably entailed deleterious consequences.

The failure of the powerful anti-French coalition in the War of Spanish Succession to succeed in overwhelming the Pré Carré strategic defense system ultimately stands as an indication of its operational effectiveness. Even late in the conflict when massed modern artillery and dwindling French resources allowed both lines along the northern frontier to be pierced, the cost and time required for these victories saved France from defeat. Many individual fortresses fell, but the defense system in toto could not be circumvented and greatly complicated attacks, encouraging the caution that allowed France to obtain peace. During the primary construction of these works in the 1670s and 1680s, the effectiveness of strategic defense systems on military balance was even more pronounced, especially given the poor siegecraft of French adversaries. Louis XIV's frontière de fer established a robust defense and provided a stout base of operations from which the French army could advance first in the spring and push aggressively with confidence that its rear would be secure. The Pré Carré best illustrates walls' or barriers' dual impact on the military balance as both solid anchors of defense and strong platforms for offense.

This offensive potential combined with the aggressive means in which the French king pursued the territory for his enhanced strategic defenses ensured that adversaries would regard the French works as highly threatening regardless of Louis' intention. As Robert and Isabelle Tombs aptly put it, France's "defensive" perspective "depended on which side of Vauban's grim new ramparts you were standing."[227] Beginning with the seizure of Condé and Bouchain in 1676, the French government pursued a long list of desirable terrain to strengthen its strategic defenses. The brusque acquisition of even needed territory through a combination of military action and faux legal maneuvering exacerbated European fears of French hegemony. Ultimately, after twelve years of expansion, the seizure of Philippsburg finally touched off the major war against all the other powers of western Europe that the French sought to avoid. It is difficult to see how France could have obtained the desired land in a more "acceptable" way, although at least part of the expansion in the 1680s—occupation of territory east of the Rhine and the Alps—appears unnecessary for a strong strategic defense and particularly inflammatory given the alienation produced in other European capitals.

Ultimately, Louis' aspiration for these forward areas, especially controlling both sides of all bridgeheads on the Upper Rhine, reflected the king's drive for absolute security, a goal significantly influenced by his extant strategic defenses. Chronically fearful of invasion, the French leader seems to have been repeatedly seduced by the notion that just one more fortress town would ensure safety, or at least markedly improve it. The result of this thought process repeatedly extended French control and placed it in a strong position for further expansion. Whether moving against the Spanish, the Dutch, the Germans, or others, the French would inevitably appear threatening. While historians focused on France generally regard Louis' orientation as defensive after the mid-1670s, historians taking a broader perspective or concentrating on his adversaries often characterize the French king as pursuing hegemony or "universal monarchy."[228] This disconnect is striking but understandable given that France's absolute security could best be achieved by maximizing the vulnerability of its adversaries—an excellent example of the modern security dilemma concept. No existing arrangement would likely have ever been completely satisfactory.

Somewhat contradictorily, his existing strategic defenses appear to have given him a false sense of security or, more accurately, promoted a miscalculation of the risk involved in further efforts to strengthen frontier security. He and other

French officials believed they could employ bullish behavior to gain desired territory without considerably greater danger. The king's lack of concern about the start of the Nine Years' War against the rest of the powers of western Europe exemplifies this attitude. Moreover, Louis and his court mistakenly believed that the fortress barrier obviated the need for talented commanders, a reality that would be exposed in the Nine Years' War and War of Spanish Succession. Louis, like many wall-builders, tended to view strategic defense systems as a virtual panacea rather than a complementary tool that required solid management, manning, and maintenance to be effective. The bottom line was that strategic defenses provided Louis XIV with a solid approach to security and ultimately saved him, but this requirement likely only resulted from his getting carried away with their potential to lead to absolute security. As a result of the exhausting wars, he severely weakened France for most of the eighteenth century. Louis was a sui generis figure, but did the basic dynamics of strategic defenses feed his imprudence in a way that suggests the existence of a more general effect on wall-builders? This question will be addressed when the concluding chapter considers the strategic defenses' influence on subsequent internal decision making.

Notes

1. Philippe Erlanger, *Louis XIV*, trans. Stephen Cox (London: Weidenfeld and Nicholson, 1970), 51.

2. Andrew Lossky, *Louis XIV and the French Monarchy* (New Brunswick, NJ: Rutgers University Press, 1994), 166.

3. John Lynn, *The Wars of Louis XIV, 1667–1714* (London: Longman, 1999), 75; and Janis Langins, *Conserving the Enlightenment: French Military Engineering from Vauban to the Revolution* (Cambridge: MIT Press, 2004), 70–71.

4. Paddy Griffith, *The Vauban Fortifications of France* (Oxford: Osprey, 2006), 12.

5. John Lynn, "A Quest for Glory: The Formation of Strategy under Louis XIV, 1661–1715," in *The Making of Strategy: Rulers, States, and War*, eds. Williamson Murray, MacGregor Knox, and Alvin Bernstein (New York: Cambridge University Press, 1994), 193.

6. Lynn, *Wars of Louis XIV*, 32.

7. Christopher Duffy, *Siege Warfare: The Fortress in the Age of Vauban and Frederick the Great, 1660–1789* (New York: Routledge, 1985), 85.

8. Griffith, *Vauban Fortifications*, 13–16; Langins, *Conserving the Enlightenment*, 71; and Duffy, *Siege Warfare: Age of Vauban*, 9.

9. Langins, *Conserving the Enlightenment*, 71; Griffith, *Vauban Fortifications*, 13–16; and Duffy, *Siege Warfare: Age of Vauban*, 9.

10. John Lynn, *Giant of the Grand Siècle: The French Army, 1610–1715* (New York: Cambridge University Press, 1997), 564, 592; Duffy, *Siege Warfare: Age of Vauban*, 81–82; and Griffith, *Vauban Fortifications*, 13–16, 21, 24, 44.

11. Langins, *Conserving the Enlightenment,* 51, 55; Duffy, *Siege Warfare: Age of Vauban,* 81–82; and Jamel Ostwald, *Vauban under Siege: Engineering Efficiency and Martial Vigor in the War of the Spanish Succession* (Leiden: Brill, 2007), 76–77.

12. Lynn, *Giant of the Grand Siècle,* 583–84.

13. Quoted in ibid., 584.

14. Lynn, *Wars of Louis XIV,* 8.

15. See ibid., 6; Christopher Duffy, *Siege Warfare: The Fortress in the Early Modern World, 1494–1660* (New York: Routledge, 1979), 45, 116, 121; and Ben Scott Trotter, "Marshal Vauban & Administration of Fortifications under Louis XIV (to 1691)" (PhD diss., Ohio State University, 1993), 21.

16. Duffy, *Siege Warfare: Early Modern World,* 121–22; and Peter Sahlins, "Natural Frontiers Revisited," *American Historical Review* 95 (December 1990): 1433.

17. Duffy, *Siege Warfare: Early Modern World,* 124.

18. Trotter, "Marshal Vauban," 28.

19. Erlanger, *Louis XIV,* 40, 48–51; and Trotter, "Marshal Vauban," 33.

20. Duffy, *Siege Warfare: Early Modern World,* 135.

21. Lynn, *Wars of Louis XIV,* 12.

22. See Lossky, *Louis XIV,* 62–63, 117–18; and Jeremy Black, *From Louis XIV to Napoleon: The Fate of a Great Power* (London: UCL Press, 1999), 34–35.

23. Lossky, *Louis XIV,* 60.

24. Ibid.

25. Erlanger, *Louis XIV,* 115.

26. Trotter, "Marshal Vauban," 57.

27. Lynn, "Quest for Glory," 203.

28. See Lossky, *Louis XIV,* 68, 74, 77, 118–19; Black, *From Louis XIV to Napoleon,* 38–39; and Lynn, *Wars of Louis XIV,* 33.

29. Duffy, *Siege Warfare: Age of Vauban,* 12; see also Lynn, *Wars of Louis XIV,* 33–34; Black, *From Louis XIV to Napoleon,* 40; and Lossky, *Louis XIV,* 132–33.

30. Lossky, *Louis XIV,* 134–35.

31. Ibid., 135.

32. See Lossky, *Louis XIV,* 103, 129, 134–36, 139; and Lynn, *Wars of Louis XIV,* 109–11.

33. See Lynn, *Wars of Louis XIV,* 157; Lossky, *Louis XIV,* 136, 144; and Erlanger, *Louis XIV,* 177, 181.

34. Lynn, *Wars of Louis XIV,* 157.

35. See Ibid., 117; Lossky, *Louis XIV,* 142, 144; and Carl Ekberg, *The Failure of Louis XIV's Dutch War* (Chapel Hill: North Carolina University Press, 1979), 14, 112.

36. Trotter, "Marshal Vauban," 11.

37. See Ibid., 11, 128, 130; Langins, *Conserving the Enlightenment,* 71; and Geoffrey Parker, *The Military Revolution: Military Innovation and the Rise of the West, 1500–1800* (New York and Cambridge: Cambridge University Press, 1988), 42–43.

38. Quoted in Lynn, "Quest for Glory," 193.

39. Ekberg, *Failure of Louis XIV's Dutch War,* 117.

40. See John Wolf, *Louis XIV* (New York: Norton, 1968), 231–32; Ekberg, *Failure of Louis XIV's Dutch War*, 22–23, 116–17, 119; and Trotter, "Marshal Vauban," 339.

41. Lossky, *Louis XIV*, 150.

42. See Lynn, *Wars of Louis XIV*, 121; Ekberg, *Failure of Louis XIV's Dutch War*, 62, 93–94, 99; Black, *From Louis XIV to Napoleon*, 43; and Lossky, *Louis XIV*, 148.

43. Lynn, *Wars of Louis XIV*, 34.

44. See Ekberg, *Failure of Louis XIV's Dutch War*, 127, 130, 137–38, 167, 182; and Lynn, *Wars of Louis XIV*, 123, 136, 144–45.

45. Lossky, *Louis XIV*, 148; and Ekberg, *Failure of Louis XIV's Dutch War*, 143–44, 151–52.

46. Lossky, *Louis XIV*, 151.

47. Ibid.

48. Trotter, "Marshal Vauban," 350.

49. Lossky, *Louis XIV*, 155.

50. See Wolf, *Louis XIV*, 147; Lossky, *Louis XIV*, 153, 159; and Lynn, *Wars of Louis XIV*, 127, 141.

51. See Lynn, *Wars of Louis XIV*, 123, 136, 184–85; Wolf, *Louis XIV*, 247; John Rule, ed. *Louis XIV and the Craft of Kingship* (Columbus: Ohio State University, 1969), 66; and Lossky, *Louis XIV*, 155–56.

52. Langins, *Conserving the Enlightenment*, 124.

53. Erlanger, *Louis XIV*, 204.

54. Wolf, *Louis XIV*, 231.

55. Lynn, *Wars of Louis XIV*, 35.

56. Quoted in Lynn, "Quest for Glory," 199.

57. Ibid., 178.

58. Lossky, *Louis XIV*, 41.

59. See Lynn, *Giant of the Grand Siècle*, 566; Lynn, *Wars of Louis XIV*, 14; Lossky, *Louis XIV*, 42, 129; and Erlanger, *Louis XIV*, 222.

60. See Lynn, *Wars of Louis XIV*, 14; and Lossky, *Louis XIV*, 42.

61. Langins, *Conserving the Enlightenment*, 73–74; and Lynn, *Wars of Louis XIV*, 14.

62. Lossky, *Louis XIV*, 108; Lynn, "Quest for Glory," 199; and Griffith, *Vauban Fortifications*, 37.

63. Lynn, *Giant of the Grand Siècle*, 7, 68; and Lossky, *Louis XIV*, 89, 94.

64. See Langins, *Conserving the Enlightenment*, 107–9; Duffy, *Siege Warfare: Age of Vauban*, 81–82; Griffith, *Vauban Fortifications*, 21, 23; and Ostwald, *Vauban under Seige*, 48–49.

65. Duffy, *Siege Warfare: Age of Vauban*, 12.

66. See Lynn, *Giant of the Grand Siècle*, 46, 51, 60, 62–63, 567; Lynn, *Wars of Louis XIV*, 50–51, 123; and Parker, *Military Revolution*, 39–40, 306. Although the Army listed 279,610 soldiers on paper at the beginning of 1678, Lynn estimates an actual force of 253,000 men (Lynn, *Giant of the Grand Siècle*, 51; and Lynn, *Wars of Louis XIV*, 144–45).

67. Lynn, *Wars of Louis XIV*, 103.

68. Black, *From Louis XIV to Napoleon*, 37, 42; Lynn, *Wars of Louis XIV*, 83–84, 98; and Ekberg, *Failure of Louis XIV's Dutch War*, 162.

69. Lynn, "Quest for Glory," 178, 185; and Ekberg, *Failure of Louis XIV's Dutch War*, 44–45.

70. Lynn, *Wars of Louis XIV*, 32.

71. Ibid., 44.

72. Ibid., 37.

73. Erlanger *Louis XIV*, 182.

74. Wolf, *Louis XIV*, 256.

75. Lynn, *Wars of Louis XIV*, 43–44, 46.

76. Ekberg, *Failure of Louis XIV's Dutch War*, 28.

77. Sahlins, "Natural Frontiers Revisited," 1425; see also ibid., 126, 1450; Lossky, *Louis XIV*, 38, 46; Wolf, *Louis XIV*, 261; and Langins, *Conserving the Enlightenment*, 65–66, 73–74.

78. Lynn, *Wars of Louis XIV*, 162.

79. Langins, *Conserving the Enlightenment*, 73.

80. Lynn, *Giant of the Grand Siècle*, 531.

81. Lynn, *Wars of Louis XIV*, 71.

82. Lynn, *Giant of the Grand Siècle*, 549.

83. Parker, *Military Revolution*, 167; see also ibid., 16, 24, 43–44; Lynn, *Giant of the Grand Siècle*, 82, 515, 530–31, 549, 576; Langins, *Conserving the Enlightenment*, 15, 122–24, 126–27; Ostwald, *Vauban under Seige*, 2–3, 7, 17–18, 216.

84. Erlanger, *Louis XIV*, 120–22, 147; Lossky, *Louis XIV*, 108; Parker, *Military Revolution*, 43, 62.

85. Robert Tombs and Isabelle Tombs, *That Sweet Enemy: The French and the British from the Sun King to the Present* (New York: Alfred A. Knopf, 2007), 4.

86. See Lynn, *Giant of the Grand Siècle*, 21–29; Langins, *Conserving the Enlightenment*, 125; Lossky, *Louis XIV*, 37; and Erlanger, *Louis XIV*, 51.

87. Lynn, *Giant of the Grand Siècle*, 141.

88. See ibid., 185, 196–97, 205, 213–14; and Parker, *Military Revolution*, 65–66.

89. See Lossky, *Louis XIV*, 165; Parker, *Military Revolution*, 62; Ekberg, *Failure of Louis XIV's Dutch War*, 177; Black, *From Louis XIV to Napoleon*, 44; Lynn, *Giant of the Grand Siècle*, 21; and Erlanger, *Louis XIV*, 280.

90. Lossky, *Louis XIV*, 68, 74; Lynn, "Quest for Glory," 184; and Erlanger, *Louis XIV*, 135.

91. Lossky, *Louis XIV*, 68.

92. Lynn, "Quest for Glory," 179, 185–86; and Erlanger, *Louis XIV*, 167.

93. Langins, *Conserving the Enlightenment*, 62–64, 80, 122, 126; Griffith, *Vauban Fortifications*, 5; and Lynn, *Giant of the Grand Siècle*, 293, 305.

94. Lossky, *Louis XIV*, 24, 168; Lynn, *Giant of the Grand Siècle*, 71–72; and Wolf, *Louis XIV*, 252–53.

95. Wolf, *Louis XIV*, 252–53.

96. Lossky, *Louis XIV*, 24, 87–88; Erlanger, *Louis XIV*, 139–40; and Lynn, *Wars of Louis XIV*, 19–21.

97. See Erlanger, *Louis XIV*, 139, 160, 162, 176; Lossky, *Louis XIV*, 28, 93–94, 96, 141; Rule, *Louis XIV and the Craft of Kingship*, 52, 212; Ekberg, *Failure of Louis XIV's Dutch War*, 9; and Trotter, "Marshal Vauban," 64, 79, 161.

98. See Lynn, *Giant of the Grand Siècle*, 282–83, 303; Wolf, *Louis XIV*, 248; Langins, *Conserving the Enlightenment*, 62–63; Lynn, *Wars of Louis XIV*, 22; Rule, *Louis XIV and the Craft of Kingship*, 52, 212; and Trotter, "Marshal Vauban," 360.

99. Reginald Bloomfield, *Sébastien le Prestre de Vauban, 1633–1707* (New York: Barnes and Noble, 1971), 127.

100. See Duffy, *Siege Warfare: Age of Vauban*, 71, 75; Lynn, *Giant of the Grand Siècle*, 559–60; Trotter, "Marshal Vauban," 9, 11, 250, 252, 321, 339; Langins, *Conserving the Enlightenment*, 62–64, 72, 80; Erlanger, *Louis XIV*, 204; Lynn, "Quest for Glory," 193; and F. J. Hebbert and G. A. Rothrock, *Soldier of France: Sébastien Le Prestre de Vauban, 1633–1707* (New York: Peter Lang, 1989), 52–53.

101. Lossky, *Louis XIV*, 165.

102. Ibid., 150.

103. Lynn, *Wars of Louis XIV*, 81.

104. Ibid., 158; see also Trotter, "Marshal Vauban," 363.

105. Lossky, *Louis XIV*, 60, 135; and Erlanger, *Louis XIV*, 115.

106. Lynn, *Wars of Louis XIV*, 45.

107. Lossky, *Louis XIV*, 150.

108. Parker, *Military Revolution*, 42–43, 171; and Lynn, *Giant of the Grand Siècle*, 61–64.

109. Quoted in Lynn, *Giant of the Grand Siècle*, 63.

110. Ibid., 61, 567.

111. See Lynn, *Wars of Louis XIV*, 35, 368–69; Langins, *Conserving the Enlightenment*, 80; Lynn, "Quest for Glory," 196; and Ostwald, *Vauban under Seige*, 3–4, 317.

112. Lynn, *Wars of Louis XIV*, 37.

113. Ibid.

114. Duffy, *Siege Warfare: Age of Vauban*, 12.

115. Trotter, "Marshal Vauban," 363; Wolf, *Louis XIV*, 248; and Lynn, *Wars of Louis XIV*, 80, 156, 371.

116. Lynn, *Wars of Louis XIV*, 159.

117. Ibid., 145; and Wolf, *Louis XIV*, 248.

118. Wolf, *Louis XIV*, 254.

119. See Wolf, *Louis XIV*, 240, 254–56; Lynn, *Wars of Louis XIV*, 146–47; and Griffith, *Vauban Fortifications*, 32.

120. Lynn, *Wars of Louis XIV*, 149; Wolf, *Louis XIV*, 248, 257, 260; and Duffy, *Siege Warfare: Age of Vauban*, 12.

121. Duffy, *Siege Warfare: Age of Vauban*, 12.

122. Lynn, *Wars of Louis XIV*, 34.

123. See Wolf, *Louis XIV,* 161–62, 260–61; Lossky, *Louis XIV,* 160; Black, *From Louis XIV to Napoleon,* 45; and Lynn, *Wars of Louis XIV,* 152,156.

124. See Lynn, *Wars of Louis XIV,* 151, 156, 164; Lossky, *Louis XIV,* 161, 165; Rule, *Louis XIV and the Craft of Kingship,* 202; and Griffith, *Vauban Fortifications,* 32.

125. Wolf, *Louis XIV,* 264; Rule, *Louis XIV and the Craft of Kingship,* 66; Lossky, *Louis XIV,* 161–62; and Black, *From Louis XIV to Napoleon,* 44.

126. Duffy, *Siege Warfare: Age of Vauban,* 12.

127. Lossky, *Louis XIV,* 162.

128. Rule, *Louis XIV and the Craft of Kingship,* 67; Lynn, *Wars of Louis XIV,* 35, 158; and Trotter, "Marshal Vauban," 363.

129. Rule, *Louis XIV and the Craft of Kingship,* 67.

130. Ibid.; Lynn, *Wars of Louis XIV,* 35; and Wolf, *Louis XIV,* 260.

131. Rule, *Louis XIV and the Craft of Kingship,* 67–68.

132. Ibid., 202.

133. See Lynn, *Wars of Louis XIV,* 159, 160; Lossky, *Louis XIV,* 169; and Rule, *Louis XIV and the Craft of Kingship,* 67–68, 330.

134. Lynn, *Wars of Louis XIV,* 170; Rule, *Louis XIV and the Craft of Kingship,* 53; and Lynn, *Giant of the Grand Siècle,* 550.

135. Griffith, *Vauban Fortifications,* 12.

136. Parker, *Military Revolution,* 166.

137. Trotter, "Marshal Vauban," 363; Griffith, *Vauban Fortifications,* 29–30; Lynn, *Wars of Louis XIV,* 75; Langins, *Conserving the Enlightenment,* 54, 125; and Rule, *Louis XIV and the Craft of Kingship,* 53.

138. Lynn, *Wars of Louis XIV,* 162.

139. Lynn, *Giant of the Grand Siècle,* 549–50; Duffy, *Siege Warfare: Age of Vauban,* 11; and Ostwald, *Vauban under Seige,* 216.

140. Wolf, *Louis XIV,* 231.

141. See Erlanger, *Louis XIV,* 236; Lynn, *Wars of Louis XIV,* 161–62, 170; Wolf, *Louis XIV,* 231; Sahlins, "Natural Frontiers Revisited," 1430, 1433; and Langins, *Conserving the Enlightenment,* 72–74.

142. Rule, *Louis XIV and the Craft of Kingship,* 53.

143. See ibid., 68, 330–31; Duffy, *Siege Warfare: Age of Vauban,* 19, 27, 87; and Lynn, *Wars of Louis XIV,* 37, 161, 164.

144. Lynn, *Wars of Louis XIV,* 161.

145. Lynn, "Quest for Glory," 200.

146. Lynn, *Wars of Louis XIV,* 164.

147. Langins, *Conserving the Enlightenment,* 74.

148. Lynn, "Quest for Glory," 200.

149. Black, *From Louis XIV to Napoleon,* 45.

150. Lossky, *Louis XIV,* 170; Lynn, *Wars of Louis XIV,* 160–61; and Black, *From Louis XIV to Napoleon,* 45.

151. Black, *From Louis XIV to Napoleon*, 46; Lossky, *Louis XIV*, 173; and Lynn, *Wars of Louis XIV*, 38, 165, 167.

152. Erlanger, *Louis XIV*, 249.

153. Lossky, *Louis XIV*, 174; Lynn, *Wars of Louis XIV*, 167; and Erlanger, *Louis XIV*, 250.

154. Lynn, *Wars of Louis XIV*, 169.

155. Black, *From Louis XIV to Napoleon*, 47.

156. Lynn, *Giant of the Grand Siècle*, 565; and Lossky, *Louis XIV*, 175.

157. Rule, *Louis XIV and the Craft of Kingship*, 172.

158. Lossky *Louis XIV*, 171–75; and Lynn, *Wars of Louis XIV*, 169–70.

159. See Duffy, *Siege Warfare: Age of Vauban*, 20, 90; Lynn, *Wars of Louis XIV*, 171; Griffith, *Vauban Fortifications*, 33; and Langins, *Conserving the Enlightenment*, 50.

160. Lynn, *Wars of Louis XIV*, 160, 169; Tombs, *Sweet Enemy*, 9; and Sahlins, "Natural Frontiers Revisited," 1434.

161. Black, *From Louis XIV to Napoleon*, 49.

162. Lynn, *Wars of Louis XIV*, 38.

163. See Lossky, *Louis XIV*, 72, 172, 228–29; Lynn, *Wars of Louis XIV*, 177–78; Black, *From Louis XIV to Napoleon*, 50; and Tombs, *Sweet Enemy*, 9.

164. Lossky, *Louis XIV*, 229–30; Black, *From Louis XIV to Napoleon*, 51–52; and Lynn, "Quest for Glory," 199, 201.

165. Hebbert and Rothrock, *Soldier of France*, 113; Lossky, *Louis XIV*, 230; and Lynn, *Wars of Louis XIV*, 38–39.

166. Lossky, *Louis XIV*, 230.

167. Rule, *Louis XIV and the Craft of Kingship*, 332; Lossky, *Louis XIV*, 230; and Lynn, *Wars of Louis XIV*, 39, 191, 193.

168. Black, *From Louis XIV to Napoleon*, 67.

169. Parker, *Military Revolution*, 171; Griffith, *Vauban Fortifications*, 30–31; and Lynn, *Giant of the Grand Siècle*, 592.

170. Lynn, "Quest for Glory," 183; see also Lynn, *Giant of the Grand Siècle*, 304.

171. Hebbert and Rothrock, *Soldier of France*, 187.

172. See ibid., 186–88; Griffith, *Vauban Fortifications*, 13.

173. Tombs, *Sweet Enemy*, 10–14; Lynn, *Wars of Louis XIV*, 39; and Black, *From Louis XIV to Napoleon*, 52.

174. Erlanger, *Louis XIV*, 279.

175. Lossky, *Louis XIV*, 231; and Lynn, *Wars of Louis XIV*, 191,195.

176. Lynn, *Wars of Louis XIV*, 195.

177. Ibid., 196–99; and Duffy, *Siege Warfare: Age of Vauban*, 32.

178. Erlanger, *Louis XIV*, 276.

179. Rule, *Louis XIV and the Craft of Kingship*, 332; Lossky, *Louis XIV*, 243; and Lynn, *Wars of Louis XIV*, 50–51.

180. Hebbert and Rothrock, *Soldier of France*, 140.

181. Duffy, *Siege Warfare: Age of Vauban*, 87; Langins, *Conserving the Enlightenment*, 74; and Lossky, *Louis XIV*, 251–52.

182. Lynn, *Wars of Louis XIV*, 99, 241; and Tombs, *Sweet Enemy*, 22.

183. Ostwald, *Vauban under Seige*, 80, 228, 285; Duffy, *Siege Warfare: Age of Vauban*, 27; and Griffith, *Vauban Fortifications*, 32–33, 36.

184. Lynn, *Giant of the Grand Siècle*, 207; see also ibid., 85, 208; Duffy, *Siege Warfare: Age of Vauban*, 84–85; Griffith, *Vauban Fortifications*, 30; and Lynn, *Wars of Louis XIV*, 209.

185. Duffy, *Siege Warfare: Age of Vauban*, 84.

186. Lynn, *Wars of Louis XIV*, 247.

187. Duffy, *Siege Warfare: Age of Vauban*, 31; Ostwald, *Vauban under Seige*, 92; Black, *From Louis XIV to Napoleon*, 55; and Lynn, *Wars of Louis XIV*, 262.

188. Lynn, *Wars of Louis XIV*, 39.

189. Griffith, *Vauban Fortifications*, 33; and Ostwald, *Vauban under Seige*, 92.

190. Lossky, *Louis XIV*, 256; see also Hebbert and Rothrock, *Soldier of France*, 193, 195; and Langins, *Conserving the Enlightenment*, 50, 55.

191. Parker, *Military Revolution*, 166.

192. Lossky, *Louis XIV*, 257; and Lynn, *Wars of Louis XIV*, 268.

193. Lynn, *Wars of Louis XIV*, 269; and Lossky, *Louis XIV*, 263.

194. Hebbert and Rothrock, *Soldier of France*, 198; and Duffy, *Siege Warfare: Age of Vauban*, 34.

195. Duffy, *Siege Warfare: Age of Vauban*, 35.

196. See Ostwald, *Vauban under Seige*, 105–8; Griffith, *Vauban Fortifications*, 33; and Duffy, *Siege Warfare: Age of Vauban*, 35.

197. Lynn, *Wars of Louis XIV*, 79, 275–76, 299; and Duffy, *Siege Warfare: Age of Vauban*, 35–36.

198. Duffy, *Siege Warfare: Age of Vauban*, 35.

199. Black, *From Louis XIV to Napoleon*, 61; and Lynn, *Wars of Louis XIV*, 41, 294.

200. Black, *From Louis XIV to Napoleon*, 62.

201. Ostwald, *Vauban under Seige*, 100–101; and Lynn, *Wars of Louis XIV*, 306–7.

202. Ostwald, *Vauban under Seige*, 110.

203. Duffy, *Siege Warfare: Age of Vauban*, 38.

204. Ostwald, *Vauban under Seige*, 101.

205. Ibid., 257–64.

206. Ibid., 264.

207. Lynn, *Wars of Louis XIV*, 321; Ostwald, *Vauban under Seige*, 101, 310; and Duffy, *Siege Warfare: Age of Vauban*, 38.

208. Lynn, *Wars of Louis XIV*, 321.

209. Ostwald, *Vauban under Seige*, 103.

210. See ibid., 102, 142–43, 253, 259–60, 300; Duffy, *Siege Warfare: Age of Vauban*, 38–39, 41; Griffith, *Vauban Fortifications*, 33, 36; and Langins, *Conserving the Enlightenment*, 115.

211. Griffith, *Vauban Fortifications*, 33.
212. Ostwald, *Vauban under Seige*, 318.
213. Parker, *Military Revolution*, 55.
214. Duffy, *Siege Warfare: Age of Vauban*, 41–44; and Lynn, *Wars of Louis XIV*, 79, 338, 343–44.
215. Duffy, *Siege Warfare: Age of Vauban*, 36.
216. Lynn, *Wars of Louis XIV*, 343.
217. Duffy, *Siege Warfare: Age of Vauban*, 41.
218. Ostwald, *Vauban under Seige*, 103.
219. Lynn, *Wars of Louis XIV*, 341, 345; and Tombs, *Sweet Enemy*, 26–27.
220. Lossky, *Louis XIV*, 276; Lynn, *Wars of Louis XIV*, 351; and Duffy, *Siege Warfare: Age of Vauban*, 43–44.
221. Duffy, *Siege Warfare: Age of Vauban*, 44; Ostwald, *Vauban under Seige*, 104, 300, 307; and Lynn, *Wars of Louis XIV*, 352.
222. Duffy, *Siege Warfare: Age of Vauban*, 87.
223. Lossky, *Louis XIV*, 278.
224. Black, *From Louis XIV to Napoleon*, 65.
225. Duffy, *Siege Warfare: Age of Vauban*, 44; Langins, *Conserving the Enlightenment*, 130; and Griffith, *Vauban Fortifications*, 12, 36.
226. Duffy, *Siege Warfare: Age of Vauban*, 87.
227. Tombs, *Sweet Enemy*, 9.
228. See ibid., 4; Lossky, *Louis XIV*, 135; Lynn, *Wars of Louis XIV*, 32, 35, 38, 61; Black, *From Louis XIV to Napoleon*, 47, 49; and Rule, *Louis XIV and the Craft of Kingship*, 67.

6

The Maginot Line

France's Great Folly or Reasoned Response to the German Threat

Introduction

By the twentieth century, advances in technology had produced a quantum leap in the mobility and destructiveness of military power; nevertheless, strategic defenses continued to be constructed, most notably the maligned Maginot Line. This largely subterranean French fortification system, while lacking the grandeur of Hadrian's Wall or the Great Wall of China, ranks among the strongest defense barriers in history. It is also often cited as a badly misguided policy that critically contributed to France's rapid defeat in 1940. Facing a stronger adversary, could the strategic defense system productively shape German behavior? Given the perception of Berlin's revisionist commitment, the ability of the Maginot Line to influence the Germans depended greatly on its operational effectiveness. Often presented as an obsolete legacy of World War I, its impact on the military balance requires closer examination. While its effects on the adversary and military balance have been criticized, particularly strong condemnation has been attached to the Maginot Line's impact on French decision making. This barrier does provide an excellent example of the pronounced psychological as well as material impact that defensive obstacles may produce, but did it create the debilitating "Maginot mentality" often declaimed?

Blanket condemnations or strident apologies do not promote proper understanding of the effects of the Maginot Line. Appreciating this barrier requires an awareness of the contextual factors that motivated the initial choice and an understanding of how the defense system subsequently shaped the strategic environment. The first half of this chapter explains why France decided to build the Maginot Line. More specifically, why did France choose to fortify part of its frontier while leaving the remaining area with minimal fixed defenses? The barrier had a long incubation period as the Army High Command debated the merit, location, and form of defense for most of the 1920s. While construction of the Maginot Line progressed in the 1930s, calls for major changes to frontier defense policy emerged in light of growing German threat perception, shifting alliance dynamics, evolving military technology, and fluctuating French politics. The chapter considers the two peaks in such questioning, 1932 and 1936, and the effect of the Maginot Line's existence on the debate. Ultimately, France did not extend fixed defenses to cover the entire eastern frontier although the government actually encouraged the impression of broad coverage, which became widespread at home and overseas. The final section considers its wartime performance. After the Wehrmacht sliced through the Ardennes forest and defeated France in six weeks in 1940, the Maginot Line obtained global renown as a symbol of flawed military policy.

A pivotal moment in the fortification's history occurred when War Minister André Maginot addressed the French Chamber of Deputies on December 10, 1929. After a decade of internal military and government debate on the subject of frontier defense, Maginot had come to obtain money for the barrier that would ultimately bear his name. While having limited involvement in the conception of this strategic defense, he spoke with passion and authority on its behalf. Beyond being a long-standing military expert among the French political leadership, the minister's stature resulted from a debilitating leg wound suffered at Verdun in World War I. Maginot's moving oration and political acumen ensured appropriation of the funds necessary for this massive construction project. Widespread recognition among French political and military elites of a need to bolster frontier security ameliorated Maginot's task. By the late 1920s, the attempted accommodation between Foreign Minister Aristide Briand and his German counterpart, Gustav Stresemann, had begun losing momentum. This approach was always regarded as naïve by senior French officers. Nor did they believe nascent efforts at collective security could be relied upon to protect the homeland. Alternatively, international and especially domestic constraints had prompted the French military to view a purely offensive-based strategy as impractical.

The national security debate in the 1920s increasingly focused on developing a strong defensive-based approach, but which variant to pursue against the Germans was a subject of considerable debate. In theory, the French had four options: (a) forward defense, (b) linear defense along the entire eastern border, (c) strongpoint defense at key sections of the border combined with mobile field forces, and (d) defense-in-depth. The key decision makers preferred some combination of these approaches, albeit with varying points of emphasis. Ultimately, the plan Maginot presented to the French assembly entailed a compromise of strongpoint and linear defense along the borders with Germany and Luxembourg while relying on a forward defense in Belgium to the north.

At the core of this defense approach was the Maginot Line with its underground fortresses. Rather than individual forts, the *ouvrages* (works) linked multiple firing positions and support elements through tunnels lying more than fifty feet below ground. Although local terrain dictated their size and shape, the French built two basic types. The *gros ouvrages* (large works) garrisoned up to one thousand troops with artillery while the *petit ouvrages* (small works) filled in gaps with one hundred to two hundred soldiers primarily employing infantry weapons. Given the Maginot Line's frontline role directly engaging the enemy, the French decided to emphasize rapid-fire, lower caliber weapons, especially improved 75-mm guns. The French designed the system to enable most gros ouvrages to cover not only the nearby petit ouvrages but also the closest gros ouvrage on the right and left. By the end of the 1930s, the French had completed a total of forty-four gros ouvrages and fifty-eight petit ouvrages.[1]

An array of lesser defense obstacles including some pre–World War I German forts supported the ouvrages and guarded the other frontier sectors.[2] The most common structure was the casemate, reinforced concrete bunkers in a variety of forms along the fortified sectors as well as the unfortified parts of the eastern borders. The army added a host of other barriers including blockhouses, *abris* (troop shelters), antitank traps, barbed-wire fences, and land mines. Some of these obstacles were placed in front of fortifications to provide early warning and hamper attacking forces, but they did not constitute a discrete barrier. Behind the main line, the French in the late 1930s began erecting small blockhouses as a stop line, but this modest effort was not completed before the war. Due to resource constraints, Chief of Staff Maurice Gamelin and the high command had rejected plans in Lorraine for building a second line of robust defenses. The French strategic defense system would not have depth.[3]

This description of fortification types facilitates a brief characterization of the fronts guarding the eastern frontier. The French army classified frontier segments into three types in order of decreasing relative strength: fortified regions (RFs, *région fortifiée*), fortified sectors (SFs, *secteur fortifié*), and defense sectors (SDs, *secteur défensif*). The 125-mile Maginot Line proper encompassed the two fortified regions, Lauter and Metz, with the weak Sarre Gap defense sector between them to help protect Alsace and Lorraine. The Lauter RF initially guarded the fifty miles from the Rhine River to the Sarre River with six gros ouvrages and two petit ouvrages, but the French extended its western end with three petit ouvrages after the Saarland voted in 1935 to reintegrate with Germany. These additions narrowed the low-lying Sarre Gap, which contained only blockhouses, casemates, and reservoirs for contingency flooding. West of the gap, the Metz RF extended over sixty miles near Longuyon (southwest of Luxembourg) guarding the critical Lorraine industrial basin. With fourteen gros ouvrages and twenty-four petit ouvrages, this stretch held the most formidable defenses along the entire French frontier.[4]

The remainder of France's eastern frontier contained weaker fortifications. The strong natural obstacles of the Rhine River front (the water barrier and the

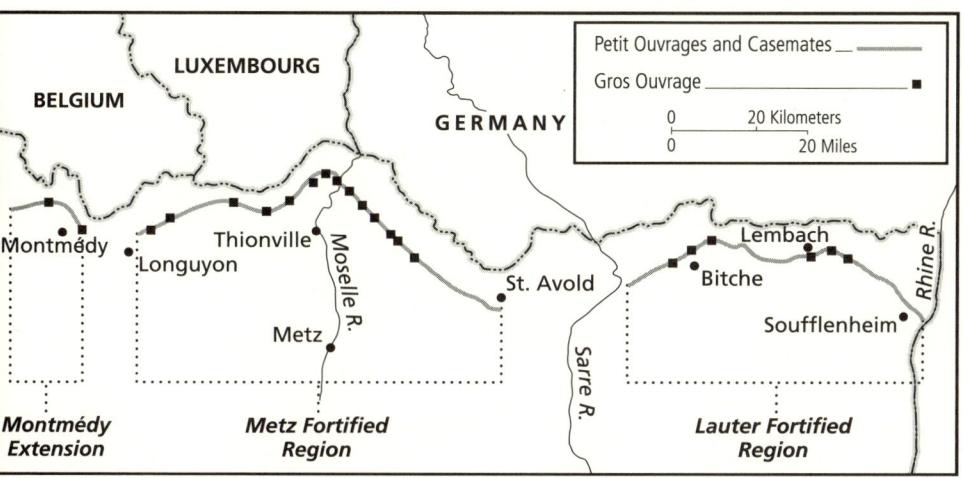

Figure 6.1 Metz and Lauter Fortified Regions, 1940

parallel Vosges Mountains) convinced the army to forgo building any ouvrages, adding only two or three lines of casemates and abris on the three fortified sectors. Natural terrain also greatly abetted defending the Italian frontier, where the French built the so-called Maginot Line of the Alps or Little Maginot Line. In the Savoy and Dauphiné fortified sectors, the Alps prevented any penetration except for passes that could be guarded exclusively with smaller fortification variants (nine gros ouvrages and ten petit ouvrages). The Italians' best invasion route was through the less rugged Maritime Alps, where the French constructed thirteen gros ouvrages and twelve petit ouvrages to shield the last thirty-five miles to the coast. Despite containing almost as many ouvrages as along the northeastern front, the army expended far fewer francs on this less worrisome region with some works still incomplete at the start of World War II.[5]

North of the Maginot Line proper, the French divided the frontier into relatively weak fortified sectors and even weaker defenses sectors. In the mid-1930s the French had built up the so-called Montmédy bridgehead, often characterized as an extension of the Maginot Line with two petit ouvrages and two small gros ouvrages. These works possessed a limited ability to offer mutual fire support, and they were separated from the Metz RF guns by the Marville defense sector. Above the Montmédy SF lay the minimally protected Ardennes defense sector, where the French counted heavily on natural terrain. The French divided the northern front above the Ardennes into four segments with only the Maubeuge SF possessing any significant fortifications (four petit ouvrages) along Germany's 1914 invasion route.[6]

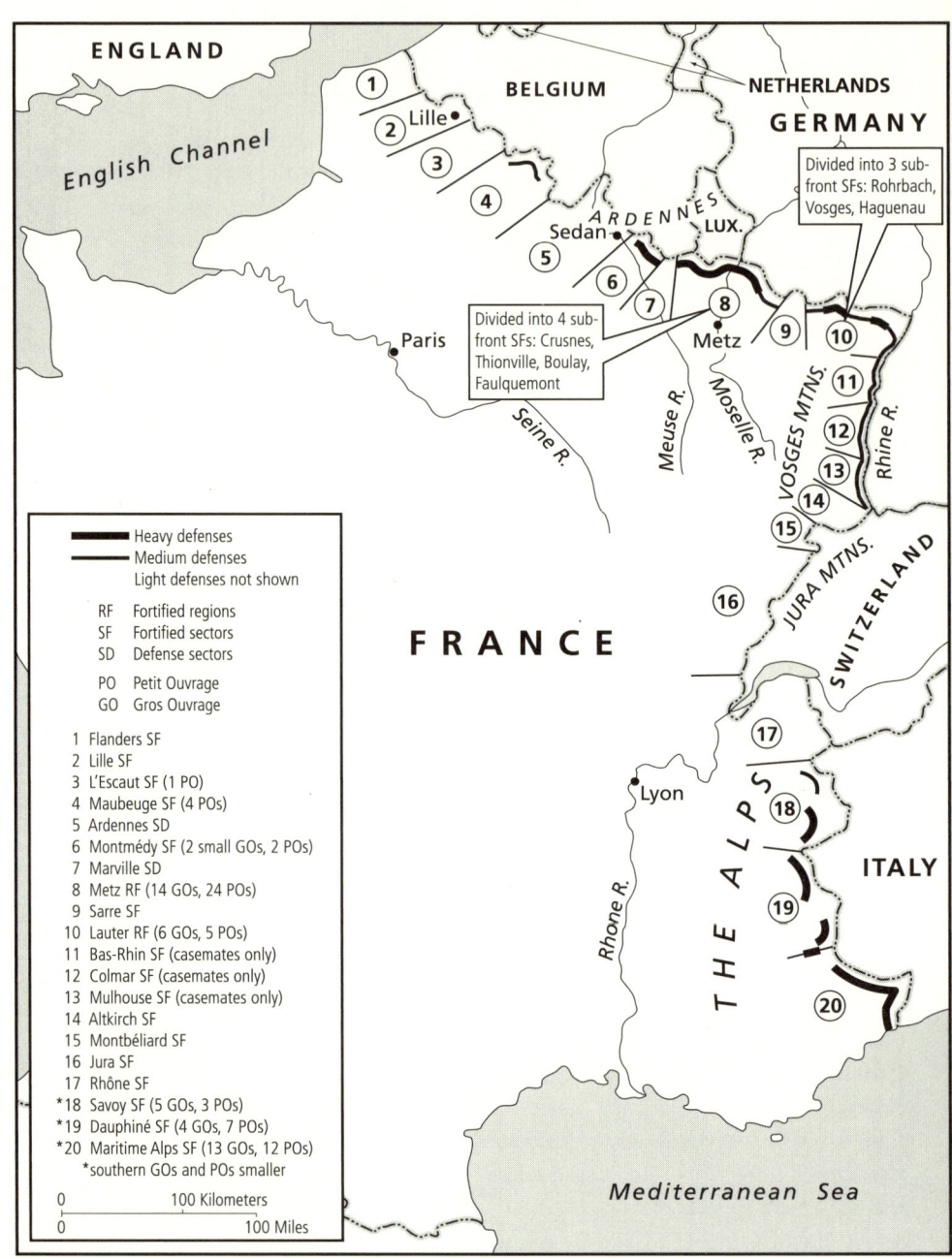

Figure 6.2 French Frontier Sectors with Key Fortified Areas, 1940

Limited defense work would continue up to the eve of war with Germany, but France's basic system with the Maginot Line as the anchor was in place by the mid-1930s. The total expenditure on all fixed defenses is extremely difficult to calculate, but about 7 billion francs were spent on the Maginot Line proper along the northeast frontier between 1930 and 1937.[7] This immense project involved fifteen thousand workers erecting more than 9 million cubic yards of earthworks, pouring more than 1 million cubic yards of concrete, and emplacing 150,000 tons of steel.[8] It has been labeled "a technological marvel, far and away the most sophisticated and complex set of fortifications built up to that time."[9] Troops, raised as elite outfits, wore distinctive khaki uniforms and berets with the motto "*On ne passe pas*" (None Shall Pass).[10] The sobriquet "Maginot Line" became the preferred way to characterize the frontier defenses soon after its September 1935 appearance in the press.[11] Some French and foreign newspapers erroneously described the Maginot Line as being a strong continuous barrier from the English Channel to the Mediterranean, and the government did not try to discourage this misperception and often fostered excessive faith in fixed defenses.[12]

Facing Off against a Stronger Germany

French decision makers in the 1920s appreciated the nation's long history with strategic defenses. Vauban's legacy and institution building resulted in fortification knowledge being a staple of French military thinking, even through the offensive-minded Napoleonic era. The rise of a unified German state in the nineteenth century intensified French fortification interest, especially after the loss of Alsace and most of Lorraine in the Franco-Prussian War in 1870–71 left them far more vulnerable. Gen. Raymond Séré de Rivières led fortification advocates pressing for "a barrier stretching from Calais to Nice, and behind it a general defensive scheme in depth as far as Paris," but political and fiscal constraints forced concentration on the Alsace-Lorraine frontier.[13] Often characterized as the Maginot Line's foundation, the Séré de Rivières fortifications consisted of a forty-mile line of strongpoints along the Meuse River from Verdun to Toul and a second line from Epinal to Belfort.[14] The French army had left a forty-three-mile gap between these two zones and another north of Verdun, hoping to channel future German attacks as well as use them for counterattacks. After the 1880s, however, an increasingly confident French High Command, yearning to regain Alsace-Lorraine, embraced a more offensive mindset.[15]

World War I and Lessons Learned

Although some of the Séré de Rivières' fortifications decayed and others were dismantled, enough remained in combination with terrain obstacles to persuade the Germans that violating Belgium's neutrality provided a more efficacious invasion route at the outset of World War I. The Germans, armed with new 420-mm guns, shocked Europe by rapidly overcoming the renowned fortifications around the key Belgian town of Liège. News of the collapsed Belgian works followed by the loss of French fortresses at Maubeuge and Montvilliers left the high command pessimistic about fortifications and even prompted a partial disarmament of the Verdun works.[16] Despite a growing appreciation of defense's dominance, the area's fortifications had remained undermanned and underequipped when the Germans launched a major 1916 offensive against the psychologically important town. France's fierce, costly, and ultimately successful resistance at Verdun led the battle to have an influential legacy on subsequent war and postwar policy. In contrast to the Liège fortifications, which suffered from design flaws and substandard materials, the Verdun works proved incredibly resilient even against the 420-mm "Big Bertha" guns. The battle certainly stood as a testament to the difficulty caused by strong fortifications, if not a "vindication of General Séré de Rivières."[17] Although the French launched another disastrous offensive in the spring 1917, they subsequently stayed on the defensive until the infusion of resources from the United States' entry into the war ensured success.

Victory after four long years in which France suffered proportionally more than any belligerent would inevitably produce significant lessons for its military and civilian leaders. Above all, officials appreciated that conflict could no longer be considered simply in military terms given the vast requirements of modern war.[18] Efficient use of natural and industrial resources had become paramount, especially when facing a larger, richer adversary such as Germany. Thus, French security officials almost uniformly agreed on the need for effective economic mobilization planning. Such uniformity did not exist over the war's military lessons, with senior officers split between offensive and defensive advocates symbolized by France's two premier soldiers.[19] Marshal Ferdinand Foch, overall commander during the victorious 1918 offensive, concluded that this success highlighted the potential for forward movement. Marshal Philippe Pétain, the hero of Verdun, saw defense as dominant. Although sometimes presented as a pure dichotomy, their perspectives actually reflected different emphases. Foch appreciated the difficulty of overrunning well-prepared positions while Pétain understood that carefully planned offensives with superior numbers could succeed and were essential for victory. In time, Pétain's defensive-minded orientation would gain more influence given its better fit with France's political context as well his position as de facto commander of the army. Senior officers did agree upon two central points related to defenses.[20] Effectiveness depended on fortified zones integrating strongpoints because isolated fortresses were unable to resist for extended periods. Second layers (defense-in-depth) proved valuable in rebuffing attacks by grinding down the aggressor.

Versailles and Postwar Developments

The French government attempted to minimize the need to implement military lessons learned by pursuing "a Carthaginian peace" that would permanently weaken Germany, but it had to settle for far less.[21] Beyond regaining Alsace-Lorraine, France sought huge financial reparations for war damage, a small conscript German army without heavy weapons, and, most significantly, the permanent division of the German state.[22] French Premier Georges Clemenceau, placing priority on securing American and British assurances of assistance against future German aggression, had to accept the return of Alsace-Lorraine, the assignment of significant parts of eastern Germany to Poland, and a fifteen-year allied occupation of the Rhineland with the right of indefinite expansion should treaty terms be violated.[23] The Rhineland was to be demilitarized once the allies pulled out while the Germany army would be limited to a one-hundred-thousand-man force without tanks, aircraft, poison gas, or a general staff. Although history has come to regard the Treaty of Versailles as excessively harsh, most French reacted with disappointment. A prescient Foch characterized it as a "twenty-year truce" rather than a peace treaty.[24] As such, it was troubling because, "while assuring a breathing space, [it] could not compensate for French demographic and industrial weaknesses."[25] During the subsequent ratification debate in the Chamber of Deputies, Maginot typified conservative sentiment by declaring that "fifteen invasions in less than six centuries give us the right to insist upon a victor's treaty that will offer something more realistic than temporary solutions and uncertain hopes."[26] Such an attitude existed even before the U.S. Senate rejected the treaty, undermining the United States' commitment to French security.

Although to foreigners the French "seemed prematurely gloomy," French leaders, especially in the officer corps, entered the 1920s with a strong sense of the need to prepare for the German threat.[27] Beyond securing the eastern frontier, the military had to assist allies in eastern Europe, protect the colonies, and secure the lines of communication between them and France. Thus, the government attempted to institute organizational changes to facilitate defense preparations. Conflicting political interests prevented passage of a new mobilization law, and the resurrected civilian coordination body suffered from irregular meetings and a failure to monitor decision implementation.[28] Reconstitution of the general staff and the higher war council (*Conseil Supérieur de la Guerre,* CSG) did enhance the ability to direct army affairs, although political leaders' longstanding suspicion of soldiers prompted authority to be split between a chief of staff with day-to-day responsibility and a designated wartime commander. The CSG would be the de facto senior military body during the interwar period despite only including army officers. It essentially functioned as a forum for deliberation on key issues including frontier defenses. The president of the Third Republic technically served as the nonvoting chair, but the minister of war usually took his place. Marshal Pétain was the body's vice president, signifying his position as France's highest ranking soldier and designated wartime commander in chief. Other members of the CSG included the minister of war, Chief of Staff Edmond Buat, all marshals, and senior generals expected to be army or army group commanders in a future war.[29]

At Minister of War André Lefèvre's direction in early 1920, the CSG began exploring how best to secure the eastern frontier. The group's first serious discussion of the issue that May, however, only revealed sharp philosophical differences exacerbated by the personal animus between Pétain and Marshal Joseph Joffre. The next meeting on the subject did not occur for two years, by which time members had further coalesced into two camps. One group, led by Pétain and Buat, argued for creating a continuous line of defense works along the border. In a 1921 document Pétain stressed that "modern defense systems can no longer be anything else than battlefields for armies, pre-arranged in times of peace."[30] This faction wanted essentially to replicate the French lines that, in their view, had proved so effective during World War I. Relatively inexpensive, such defenses could be erected over long stretches of the frontier and layered to create defense-in-depth.[31]

The competing group urged the creation of strategically placed fortified regions with large fixed defenses between which the French army could attack Germany under favorable circumstances. Proponents of this approach noted that even if ultimately successful, the World War I–type "prepared battlefields" resulted in grievous casualties that no Frenchman wanted to repeat. Underlying this group's perspective was skepticism that the absolute inviolability of frontiers could or should be the basis of French defense policy. Joffre and Foch led the advocates of this combined offense–defense approach, with the former warning that France would be "doomed to defeat for seeking to establish a new wall of China."[32] Other key members of this group were Gen. Adolphe Guillaumat, commander of French forces on the Rhine, and future chief of staff Gen. Marie-Eugène Debeney, who lacked his cohorts' zeal for the offense but favored discrete fortified areas over a continuous line.[33]

The divided senior officers could only agree to study the issue further by establishing the Commission for the Territorial Defense in June 1922. The group favoring fortified regions achieved a bureaucratic victory with Joffre's presidency of this body. Even though sparring with Pétain soon prompted Joffre to quit, the like-minded General Guillaumat replaced him as chair. Not surprisingly, the commission recommended permanent fortified zones, but Buat and Gen. François Hergault provided a vigorous dissent. In an attempt to assuage them, the report also endorsed the principle of defense-in-depth. Despite the commission's recommendations, sufficient division between the two camps prevented any decisions throughout the first half of the decade except for an understanding that the northeast frontier (Alsace-Lorraine) would be the focus of any strategic defense system.[34]

The escalation of the Ruhr crisis in late 1922 and other issues would distract senior officers from the frontier defense question until 1925. With Germany resisting compliance of the Treaty of Versailles, frustrated allies occupied key Ruhr cities in March 1921 to compel disarmament and obtain a war reparations deal. Berlin agreed to terms but then resumed its obstreperous behavior after the removal of allied soldiers. French premier Raymond Poincaré, facing considerable pressure from hardliners and provoked by German behavior, approved an early 1923 occupation of the Ruhr Valley with Belgian troops despite American and British opposition.[35] The Germans responded with passive resistance strikes that required increasing the occupation force to more than one hundred thousand soldiers and precipitated an unexpectedly long and costly operation. Berlin, suffering an economic collapse, blinked first and ended resistance in September 1923. Poincaré, however, failed to leverage the occupation into a broad settlement, and an upset French public replaced him with Édouard Herriot.[36] Diplomats over the next few years embarked on a vigorous effort to obtain a rapprochement with Germany while trouble in the colonies distracted the military.[37] Native revolts in Syria and Morocco proved difficult to quell. In particular, defeating the Moroccan insurgency eventually required more than 150,000 troops and transfer of some units from the Rhineland occupation force. Beyond weakening defenses in central Europe, this action highlighted the need for the high command to address decisively the issue of frontier fortifications.

Decision Context

Context strongly shaped the French decision to build the Maginot Line given that "from national security policy to squad level tactics, French possibilities were severely limited."[38] As true in the previous cases, decision makers generally feared trying to break free of these constraints. With the policy choice emerging slowly from 1925 until the late 1929 effort to secure funding for fixed defenses, the subsequent discussion characterizes the evolution of these factors over this five-year period.

Threat Perception

Although improved relations with Berlin after the Ruhr crisis generated hope among some French diplomats and citizens, senior officers and many others never wavered from seeing Germany as the nation's primary threat.[39] They regarded it as a revisionist actor desirous of Alsace-Lorraine, whose restraint would only last until Berlin calculated favorable prospects for war. Germany's escape from the Paris Peace Conference largely intact left it with a significantly greater resource base than France. By the mid-1920s senior army officers increasingly worried about a shifting balance of power, especially with the diminishing allied presence in the Rhineland.[40] Ultimately, as a part of the Young Plan (1929) on German war reparations, the French would agree to remove all remaining units in 1930.

Exacerbating French threat perceptions was the precarious location of the nation's vital industrial and demographic centers. The restoration of Alsace-Lorraine provided valuable commodities, including almost all of the nation's iron, but these critical resources lay extremely close to German territory. In general, the triangular region from Lorraine to Paris to Dunkirk possessed most of France's natural resources, a majority of its heavy industry, and a significant percentage of the population, despite being only a small part of the nation. Fretting about conflict with a bigger and richer Germany, French leaders regarded "every ounce of coal and iron and every factory" as essential.[41] Preventing a German victory made protection of these frontier regions vital.

France could not focus exclusively on the German threat. On the European continent, concern about Italy grew after 1924.[42] By 1928 the mercurial and ambitious Italian leader Benito Mussolini was demanding significant concessions for cooperation. While mountainous terrain along most of the 219-mile border and Italy's less capable military limited worry about the homeland, Rome represented a threat in the Mediterranean with its potential to endanger shipping routes between France and its colonies. The resilient rebellions in Syria and Morocco highlighted an ever-present danger in the colonies. Given French officials' expectation that the colonies would help offset resource inferiority to Germany, they remained committed to securing the empire despite its high protection costs. Even with these other concerns, officials largely remained fixated on the so-called German problem.[43]

Senior officers' view that the Germans would launch a lightning strike to seize the resource-rich border areas greatly influenced policy deliberations. Since an *attaque brusquée* (sudden attack) imperiled France in both a limited and total war fashion, it loomed threateningly, as evidenced by frequent discussion in military journals and at meetings at the time.[44] Concern about it grew sharply in the late 1920s with the shrinking French army, its impending withdrawal from the Rhineland, and the improving Reichsheer (German army). Guarding against such a strike left France "deeply committed to the preservation of the political and territorial status quo."[45] But securing the frontier was complicated, with the Germans possessing five potential routes into France: (a) through neutral Switzerland, (b) across the Rhine into Alsace, (c) directly into Lorraine, (d) across the Ardennes forest, and (e) through central Belgium.[46]

French strategists assessed these options as presenting sharply contrasting vulnerabilities. The Germans could swing south of the Rhine River, advance through neutral Switzerland, and cross the line of the Jura Mountains. Even if willing to violate Swiss neutrality, the Reichsheer would then have to penetrate the easily defensible 12-mile Belfort gap between the Jura and Vosges mountains. The 110-mile stretch of the Rhine River, which provided the French–German border from Switzerland to Lauterbourg, also offered a strong natural obstacle to attack, especially given that the Vosges Mountains ran roughly parallel 15 to 25 miles to the west of the river. The French did not regard the Ardennes massif, running with few roads, continuous hills, and thick forests through northwest Luxembourg and southeast Belgium, as being conducive for offensives. Plus, behind the Ardennes, the Germans would face the Meuse River, which offered a naturally strong position from which reinforcements could erect a stout defense. In 1927 an army commission did not assess this front as "impenetrable," but it estimated the Germans would require nine days to navigate the demanding terrain and thus was unfavorable for an attaque brusquée, especially against modest defense preparations.[47]

Alternatively, the two other potential avenues greatly alarmed French civilian and military leaders. On the northeast frontier, the 115-mile section running west from Lauterbourg until reaching Longwy near the southwest corner of the Luxembourg–Belgium border had negligible terrain obstacles.[48] Robert Young aptly labels this front "a natural autobahn" facilitating the movement of men and mechanized formations.[49] The other inviting route for the Germans lay across central Belgium, the approach employed in World War I. No severe water, mountain, or forest barrier stood in the way, either in Belgium or along the French–Belgian border. Moreover, heavily industrialized French areas, such as Lille, were almost in Belgium, making any defense along the French–Belgian border problematic. An attaque brusquée on this route did seem less likely given that the Germans would have to sacrifice the surprise element. Nevertheless, widespread agreement among senior French officers existed on this being the likely attack path if France took appropriate precautions to safeguard Lorraine.[50]

Military Capability

The French army's quantitative and qualitative deterioration enhanced the threat perception, especially given the implications of the 1927–28 laws on military service and organization. Leftist politicians had finally realized a longstanding goal of reducing active duty conscription to twelve months, beginning in 1930. Shortened conscription length meant a contracted force structure. Despite declaring forty-one divisions as the minimum necessary in 1920, six years later the CSG had been compelled to accept a planned twenty-division force.[51] While the French government counted on its independent colonial force to bolster the metropolitan army in a crisis, its recent performance against the Moroccan rebels revealed its own inadequacy and conscript reduction also negatively impacted this force.[52] Moreover, colonial units would be of no assistance in protecting against an attaque brusquée.

Senior officers expressed even more concern that shortened conscription would diminish the quality of individual soldiers and units. With one-year service, troops would only receive six months of training, despite the World War I experience that had demonstrated to the French that adequate instruction required at least nine to ten months.[53] This judgment would greatly influence doctrine and strategy as it encouraged a belief that soldiers were only capable of defense and tightly controlled battle. Also, fear that short-term conscripts lacked the ability to operate advanced weapons undermined advocates of relying on technology to compensate for the army's decreasing size, such as mid-1920s minister of war Gen. Charles Nollet. As a part of their grudging acceptance of one-year conscription, the high command won legislative language that it could have a larger number of professional soldiers. Poor pay and benefits, however, left the army struggling to fill the authorized level. Inadequate numbers of professional soldiers combined with short-term conscripts to produce poor performance on training exercises, according to reports by both French officers and foreign observers.[54]

Given the limitations on the regular army, the French knew that reserve mobilization would be critical even against a sudden German attack. The high command determined that a covering force to protect the frontiers required at a minimum 1 million soldiers. Reaching this size necessitated rapidly mobilizing the *disponsibles*—ready reservists from the three youngest classes—to augment the regular army. However, it would take up to two weeks to activate them, prompting the CSG in December 1927 to raise serious questions on the adequacy of this approach.[55] Even if this covering force bought time for full mobilization of the twenty-four older classes, senior officers had grave concerns about the capability of reservists to form the core fighting force, especially at the early stages of a war.[56] Gen. Antoine Targe typified sentiment by observing "only a professional army could go beyond our frontiers ... a militia army is apt for the defensive at prepared positions, but is not apt for maneuver."[57] Nevertheless, the notion of creating a professional army did not appeal to most senior officers, even if it had been politically feasible.[58] While such a force might best address an attaque brusquée, it could not defend against a mass German invasion. This recognition prompted the high command to include every active division in its mobilization plan. The army "could not fight a limited war without placing in risk its entire mobilization system and its capacity to fight a total war."[59]

Recognizing the limits of their own capability, the French aggressively pursued allies to help counter Germany. France's hope to sustain the victorious

World War I coalition evaporated when the U.S. Senate rejected the Treaty of Versailles. As Washington retreated into isolationism in the security realm, Paris concentrated on wooing London. The British had made their commitment to France conditional on U.S. assistance, allowing them to nullify the defense treaty. Regarding French concern over the Germans as excessive, London during the 1920s would act more as an arbiter between France and Germany than as a firm ally to the former. Even though the French expected British support during a true crisis, the absence of prior cooperation and general staff planning would limit Britain's contribution to protecting French frontiers in the critical early stages of a future war.[60]

Only two alternatives existed in Europe to even partially offset the lack of British cooperation: Italy and the Soviet Union. Although the French worried about Italian aims in the Mediterranean and North Africa, its resources and strategic location made Rome an attractive partner. Italy offered a land bridge to eastern Europe, helping encircle Germany and ensuring a multifront war as well as protection of shipping between France and North Africa. An alliance seemed possible at times, but insufficient common interests and mutual suspicion prevented meaningful progress. The Soviet Union potentially offered a more valuable partner, resurrecting the two-front concept to prevent German concentration. But sharp ideological differences, French demands for satisfactory compensation for huge Tsarist-era debts, Soviet nationalization of private property, and sensitivity to its Polish ally complicated cooperation. Paris recognized the communist government in 1924, but it did not seriously explore a security relationship despite the abstract appeal.[61]

Instead, France futilely attempted to replace Russia through a series of bilateral agreements with eastern European states. Most notably, it entered into a mutual defense pact with Poland in 1921. As a country with a significant border with Germany and a large army that had just beaten the Soviet Union in a war, Poland initially appeared a strong ally. Later in the decade, France added bilateral agreements with Czechoslovakia, Rumania, and Yugoslavia. The Czechoslovakian relationship was clearly the most important, given its German border, prosperity, capable military, and outstanding Skoda armament works. With maximum cooperation, these states were a poor substitute for Russia, but the situation was far from optimal as the East Europeans constantly bickered over territorial disputes. Plus, Poland, which exhibited greater concern about the Soviet Union than Germany, experienced a 1926 coup that essentially ended cooperation between the two general staffs. The inability to align with Italy and obtain a land bridge to eastern Europe further dampened the French military's enthusiasm for these allies.[62]

Ultimately, the unsatisfactory search for allies left policymakers at the end of the 1920s cognizant that France would have to rely heavily on its own efforts, especially at the early stages of a future war.⁶³ Still, the high command viewed one nation as critical for the initial war phase—neighboring Belgium. Given its desire to fight on the northern frontier in central Belgium, cooperation was necessary to prevent a German victory before French forces arrived. Belgium's pre–World War I neutrality policy had clearly been a failure, seemingly leaving collaboration with France as the only alternative. However, great suspicion of France existed within the country, exacerbated by its split between the generally pro-French Walloons and the skeptical if not hostile Flemish. With a formal alliance politically impossible, the French army had to accept a 1920 vague and semisecret accord with its Belgian counterpart. The French, seeing their interests as inextricably linked and underestimating Belgian angst, regarded the defense relationship as strong throughout the decade.⁶⁴

Strategic Culture

After World War I, France's strategic culture encompassed contradictory elements. Since the late nineteenth century, the political left and the right had been battling over competing military visions: a citizen-soldier army versus a more professional model. The leftist vision became increasingly popular with centrists culminating in the aforementioned 1927–28 defense laws. Supporters believed that a nonprofessional force would best defend France against both external and internal threats, with leftists focused more on preventing a right-wing coup than stopping a German attack. An army composed of short-term conscripts (or militia) would supposedly not be willing to support a coup since the high command lacked time to indoctrinate soldiers. Senior officers accepted the move "from an active force to a potential force," given that it at least ensured the nation's full-scale participation in future wars.⁶⁵ Ultimately, by the late 1920s the nation-in-arms concept ("the sense of total commitment and universal military service") had been definitively adopted.⁶⁶

This concept fit poorly with the belief that France's existing frontiers should be inviolable.⁶⁷ Such an objective required preparedness at the outset of any future war, a weakness of the nation-in-arms model. While Beth Kier suggests that the army and the right manufactured the "inviolability of the frontier" to ensure larger defense budgets and active duty forces in the face of the public's increasingly powerful attachment to the citizen-soldier approach, its appeal appears strong.⁶⁸ Beyond the aforementioned need to protect vital resources along the eastern frontier, four years of enormously destructive battles on French soil during World War I created a widespread political impetus to avoid a recurrence. Being a status quo–oriented actor fueled a heightened regard for the sanctity of frontiers in contrast to the pre-1914 drive to recover Alsace-Lorraine. These material and psychological needs repeatedly emerged in policy discussions so that "the future integrity of France's frontiers was the unalterable, inescapable, demand made of French strategists after 1918."[69]

The influence of the "nation-in-arms" and "inviolability of frontier" concepts combined to encourage an army culture that increasingly emphasized defense by the late 1920s. The core tenets of the defensive approach had been articulated in a 1921 document known as the "Bible" by French officers. Reflecting Marshal Pétain's outlook above all, it conveyed three main lessons about modern combat: inherent strength of defense, superior value of firepower, and advantage of methodical battle.[70] In particular, the document stressed the strength of well-prepared defensive positions. Even if breakthroughs occurred, they would attrite the enemy, allowing penetrations to be mitigated with defense-in-depth. Although offensives would have to occur for victory, they should only be attempted after stopping enemy progress and obtaining numerical superiority to allow a battering-ram type advance. In essence, the French army had shifted to a "more balanced emphasis on the defense."[71]

Whether on defense or offense, the French army embraced two other key military principles—firepower and methodical battle. Senior officers had an abiding faith in firepower's advantage on the battlefield, influenced by Pétain's famous utterance, "*le feu tue*" (fire kills). The desire to minimize casualties, avoiding World War I–level losses and husbanding a smaller manpower base, fueled this attraction to firepower, especially artillery. The high command also believed its emphasis ameliorated the danger of relying on less-skilled conscripts and reserves who lacked the ability to maneuver proficiently. But obtaining superior firepower with an inferior resource base required efficiency and prompted adoption of the methodical battle (*bataille conduite*) concept. This approach entailed careful planning and central command to allow concentration of units and weapons. French commanders contended that junior officers, soldiers, and, above all, reservists needed strict guidance. Senior commanders essentially believed that only they had the experience and information to make sound decisions about the battlefield. Modern commentators unfailingly stress the severe rigidity produced by this approach, but the French either minimized this consequence or saw little alternative. While knowing that the Germans embraced somewhat different principles for the current military environment, the high command found the tenets of defense superiority, firepower, and methodical battle best fit with its understanding of war and the existing context.[72]

Resources

French decision makers obsessed about their inherent resource disadvantage vis-à-vis Germany. With a deficit of more than 20 million in population, France's ominously lower birth rate prompted projections that German recruits would more than double their French counterparts by the late 1930s.[73] This growing gap incorporated the dreaded "hollow years" when the full effect of World War I losses would limit conscript class size. Although France's colonial population was almost 60 million, significant concerns existed over the ability and wisdom of employing nonnative manpower as soldiers.[74] Similarly, even with the recovery of the rich Alsace-Lorraine territory, French natural resources and industrial capabilities could not match German assets; the latter's "industrial production was reckoned to be at least twice that of the French."[75] Some officials had grandiose notions of the empire offsetting Germany's economic edge, but the colonies could provide little beyond agricultural products.

Resource inferiority may have been an immutable problem, but the government's ability to underwrite security efforts fluctuated considerably. In the early postwar years, a tremendous strain existed from the debt accumulated during World War I, the enormous expense of reconstruction, and the considerable financial losses from the collapsed Russian and Ottoman empires.[76] The government's preference to fund expenses through borrowing rather than taxation meant dependence on American and British financiers and thus greater susceptibility to external pressure. German resistance to paying reparations added to the challenging environment. Thus, the 1919–26 period was marked by increasing budget deficits, currency depreciation, and inflation, especially after 1923 franc collapse.[77] This fiscal difficulty coincided with sizeable military operations in the Ruhr (1923–24) and Morocco (1925–26). France was spending a higher percentage of its gross national product on defense than any other great power, but it still had to sacrifice long-term programs such as armaments and fortifications.[78]

The rapid improvement of France's fiscal position from 1927 offered an opportunity to end this neglect and prepare for a "normal" Germany. In part, the issues of interallied debt and German reparations were resolved, albeit artificially, through the circular flow of American capital. A devaluation of the franc to one-fifth of its former value in 1926 stabilized the currency and refilled government coffers with a positive balance of payments. Beyond specific financial measures, the formation of a government by the respected Poincaré in July 1926 critically reestablished national confidence and stability. France would be the most prosperous nation in Europe during the late 1920s, leaving the government with a budget surplus to fund security policy. The question for senior French military and civilian officials was how best to use this improved financial condition.[79]

Domestic Politics

The ever-shifting governing coalitions during the 1920s complicated such policy discussions. Maintenance of the centrist alignment that ruled during

World War I was not possible with moderate parties drifting to the left or right, depending on their proclivity. Rather than produce an alternating and relatively stable left-right dynamic, severe schisms within both the left and right resulted in chaotic politics with brief regimes and difficult policymaking. The right generally ruled when the moderately conservative secular and catholic blocs partnered, but these groups found it difficult to cooperate and govern effectively.[80] Conservatives tended to highlight the German threat and focus attention on the need to secure the nation's frontiers, especially after the Ruhr occupation.[81] The right favored high defense spending and an army composed of more professional soldiers and long-term conscripts, both to counter Germany and revolutionary leftist forces at home. Although usually outnumbered in parliament, leftist parties represented a powerful if usually fragmented force in French politics.[82] Outside of the communists and hard-line socialists, French leftists were not antimilitary in contrast to their counterparts in many European nations.[83] While wanting to limit defense spending, they recognized a need for security and avoidance of an encore to the 1870–1914 era. Leftists, however, possessed a distinct perspective on how France should pursue security, what today would be called "nonprovocative" defense.

Seven different leftist governments ruled in the mid-1920s until economic calamity brought to power a moderate-conservative coalition under Poincaré that managed to retain power for nearly the remainder of the decade. Operating under the Union Nationale label, the stability-minded regime included figures from moderate parties such as the left-leaning Paul Painlevé, who remained minister of war. The reduction of conscription length during this period illustrates the continuing influence of the left as well as the idea's public popularity. The April 1928 election, however, shifted relative power further rightward; thus, governing dynamics moved in a more conservative direction. The formation of the André Tardieu government late in 1929 marked the emergence of a truly rightist regime.[84]

Decision-making Process

Amid the political chaos, national security decision making operated through a clear division of labor between senior officers, diplomats, and politicians.[85] David Chuter notes the pervasive "feeling that the military should concern themselves with technical military matters, the diplomats with foreign policy questions alone, and politicians with only general political questions."[86] Whatever the theoretical wisdom of deferring to expertise, the resulting French security policy suffered from a lack of integration. Even at the apex of Foreign Minister Briand's push for an accommodation with Germany (1925–27), the military conducted its affairs almost as if the diplomats did not exist. Senior officers were "without challenge in their own domain," although French political leaders established a broad framework through their control of resources.[87] Given the recent World War I experience, it is not surprising that many members of parliament were veterans who tended to sympathize with the military. In particular, moderate and conservative political elites interpreted the military challenge similarly to army commanders, adding to the deferment of the former.[88]

The armed forces' lack of centralization and the army's somewhat convoluted command structure complicated its own decision-making process.[89] Fear of military intervention in domestic politics had prompted the left to block a unified command structure. The separation of the designated wartime commander from the chief of staff position diffused authority, with decisions tending to be worked out among a handful of senior commanders. The CSG—"glittering and prestigious summit of the French High Command"—became the forum for these critical strategic discussions, despite its being technically only an advisory body.[90] On the frontier security issue, the CSG "played a decisive role in the entire process—from the initial concept to the final strategy."[91] Its pivotal meetings in the second half of the 1920s will be addressed later in the chapter.

The key participants in these sessions offered a variety of contrasting and conflicting positions on frontier security. Marshal Pétain, the generalissimo, was clearly the most influential man in uniform, possessing wide appeal within the army, across the political spectrum, and among the public. Nevertheless, Pétain's views did not win out when opposed by a majority of the other senior army commanders. Wanting to conserve manpower and maximize firepower, the marshal possessed a more defensive orientation than most other CSG members. With Foch's direct involvement declining and his disciple, Gen. Maxime Weygand, not yet playing a central role in the frontier debate, General Guillaumat would lead the opposition to Pétain. General Debeney, by virtue of his position as chief of staff and holding views somewhat between Guillaumat's and Pétain's, was a pivotal figure. Despite sometimes being characterized as a disciple of Pétain after serving under him during the war, Debeney's outlook leaned more toward Guillaumat, as will be clear in the subsequent discussion. Ultimately, compromise would be necessary among these figures on key frontier policy questions, "for no one was able to establish clear priorities."[92]

Two politicians, Paul Painlevé and André Maginot, exercised significantly more influence over defense policy than did other civilians throughout the decade, including during the crucial choices of the late 1920s. Possessing considerable experience on defense issues, one or the other would be minister of war for most of the decade, despite the rule of numerous governments. Painlevé, having replaced Gen. Charles Nollet as minister of war in April 1925, would almost continuously hold the office until late 1929. On frontier defense, the minister preferred stronger fortified regions rather than a Pétain-type continuous line.

The conservative Maginot, who had been minister of war in the early 1920s, was head of the Chamber of Deputies' Army Commission until joining the government in late 1928 as minister for the colonies. While possessing contrasting political ideologies, Painlevé and Maginot developed an effective working relationship in the second half of the decade. The influential Maginot would succeed Painlevé as minister of war in 1929 and would attempt to win funds for the army's strategic defense concept. Ultimately, even these important figures largely deferred to the expertise of the high command.[93]

Frontier Strategic Options

The French parliament, press, and public possessed a "craving for security — *sécurité d'abord*," but disagreement existed over the best path to achieve it.[94] Consistent with the preceding discussion on the decision-making process, the French government pursued distinct diplomatic and military tracts. The army's favored political option of partitioning Germany had long passed from consideration; instead diplomats and some politicians regarded establishing a French–German rapprochement or building collective security institutions as offering ways to avoid conflict. The high command focused on military answers, considering offensive, combined offense-defense, and purely defensive approaches. All of the political and military options suffered from weaknesses, but the following discussion will show why some negatives were regarded as more manageable.

Diplomatic Options

Facing a threatening, stronger adversary encouraged consideration of a conciliatory policy with Germany. Foreign Minister Briand reputedly uttered, "I make the foreign policy of our birth rate."[95] The failure of aggressive efforts in the early 1920s culminating with the Ruhr occupation created enthusiasm for a kinder, gentler approach. After the Germans in early 1925 expressed an interest in rapprochement, negotiations quickly led to the breakthrough Locarno Pact in which Germany, France, and Belgium accepted their existing borders. Building on the "spirit of Locarno," Briand worked with Germany to achieve détente through his counterpart, Foreign Minister Stresemann. Recognizing the need for establishing linkages to advance the relationship and supported by financiers and industrialists, Briand pursued economic agreements including a pan–European Union.[96]

While many Frenchmen supported Briand's initiatives in the hope of removing the German threat and allowing the nation to reduce military spending, grave doubt existed about the potential of a conciliatory approach. British ambassador Lord Crewe had already detected after Locarno "an increasingly strong undercurrent of distrust of Germany in official circles here [France]."[97] As German diplomats hardened their positions, it became clear by mid-1928 that progress would only occur with significant French concessions. Many previously open Frenchmen now soured on accommodation, seeing no reason for "abject surrender" especially given hostile German behavior.[98] Stresemann's death in 1929 eroded diplomatic potential, but even the foreign ministers "held different and opposing conceptions of European security; Briand wanted a French Europe, Stresemann a German one."[99]

Concern that Germany could later abandon cooperation prompted many French diplomats and citizens to emphasize collective security—an alternative to the traditional alliance system.[100] For example, key foreign ministry officials had stressed that rapprochement with Germany "must be pursued only within a broad European framework and a system of collective security."[101] Integral to the completion of the Locarno treaties had been the willingness of Great Britain, Belgium, and Italy to serve as essentially guarantors of French security. At least the French interpreted the language as providing such a guarantee.[102] Central to this collective security effort was the nascent League of Nations, where France had significant influence. By the late 1920s, its diplomats were seeking more expansive accords, most notably the 1928 Kellogg-Briand pact outlawing war. With war "outlawed" and collective security established, disarmament seemed the logical next stop. Many discussions were held on the subject, but negotiators struggled to even agree on the elements to be covered.

Whatever the theoretical appeal of collective security, this untested approach left most French policymakers unsettled. Given their familiarity with national interest motivations, they worried that German threats or even attacks would not generate sufficient support for France.[103] As a result, France also pursued more traditional alliances. Although "the French did not purposely undermine the League's system of collective security," their insurance efforts "against its possible incompetence" did diminish the potential.[104] Also damaging was diplomats' tendency to conclude agreements without adequate enforcement mechanisms. The grandiose Kellogg-Briand pact represented the extreme example, outlawing war without an enforcement mechanism. In general, policymakers' interest in collective security waned with a rise of German contentiousness and other states' lack of commitment.

Military Options

While Briand and his colleagues pursued an amicable Europe, the French High Command attempted to design a military policy to guard against German aggression. The dilemma was that "France had to gamble on a quick victory or bow to the necessity of a long war."[105] Theoretically, an offensive-based approach of invading Germany in response to attack offered considerable benefits: fighting on foreign soil, aiding eastern European allies, and obtaining a rapid victory.[106] French commanders recognized that speed offered the best way to nullify Germany's superior resources. Longstanding advocates of the offensive, however, had to adjust to a less favorable environment in the late 1920s with the reduced conscription length and increased reliance on reserves. Plans to break up the active units upon mobilization made taking the offensive early in a war problematic. While the German force remained small, the French ominously had detected signs of improvement fueling fear that a major advance would leave the frontier vulnerable. Finally, after the 1930 withdrawal from the Rhineland, the French would lose their strong forward position from which to attack. As a result of these factors, even formerly strong adherents of the offensive started abandoning this approach. At first its advocates gravitated to an offense–defense approach in which frontier fortifications would serve as a force multiplier to free up the bulk of the army to advance into Germany. Even this combined strategy became increasingly hard to endorse by the end of the decade.[107]

Growing sentiment existed for a defense-based approach in which strong fortifications undermined German prospects in a lightning attack and provided time for mobilization. Only defenses functioning as a force multiplier could offset the disadvantage of facing a larger and richer opponent in an attritional war. For senior commanders who saw a long war of attrition as unavoidable, defenses would be essential for victory. Still, the consensus among senior French officers on the need for some fortifications left significant debate and disagreement over two fundamental questions: where to defend and how to defend. In terms of where to defend, the issue had both a vertical and horizontal component. First, the French could pursue a forward defense (beyond the border), a frontier defense (along the border), or a defense-in-depth (multiple lines within France). Second, the French had to consider the five avenues (Switzerland, Rhine, Lorraine, Ardennes, and Belgium) available to an invading German army. Interrelated to this evaluation was the second key question: how to defend. Two basic options existed for employing man-made obstacles to bolster security. The army could erect strong, fortified regions to cover the most vulnerable areas or establish a continuous line of prepared battlefields with trenches, barbed wire, and other smaller defense works. The next section addresses how the high command ultimately answered these questions, but it is worthwhile to consider the strengths and weaknesses of these options from the French perspective.[108]

Forward Defense

Although forward defense largely meant sacrificing employment of major fortifications, French commanders understandably found the idea tremendously appealing. It would spare France from again serving as a battlefield, safeguard the vital natural resources and industry along the frontier, and keep the Germans out of range of shelling Paris. The occupation of the Rhineland had facilitated a forward defense, but the impending withdrawal diminished the already declining feasibility of this approach. Although the Rhineland was to be demilitarized facilitating an advance to a forward defense position, the shift toward shorter-term conscripts and a corresponding de-emphasis on maneuver hampered the army's ability to move forward. The similarity of forward defense in the Rhineland to aggression also would complicate obtaining funds from the legislature to equip the forces necessary for such an advance.[109] In the international arena, such a movement at the outset of a crisis risked alienating neutrals and would-be allies, whose cooperation was viewed as necessary to sustain a long war effort.

By contrast, on the northern front, Belgium's location between France and Germany enabled a more appealing forward defense variant mounted on allied, rather than enemy, territory. Geography on this frontier also favored a forward defense because central Belgium offered significantly greater terrain obstacles, especially the Meuse River, than the flat, open countryside of the French–Belgian border. In addition, the front would be significantly narrowed. Such an approach would also add the small but capable Belgian army to the defense effort and allow use of prepared defenses in central Belgium. Diplomatically, the French knew fighting the Germans inside Belgium increased the probability of Britain joining the war effort.[110]

While French commanders found these advantages alluring, a forward defense approach even in Belgium entailed some risks. Most notably, it required Belgian cooperation. Although such a partnership seemed likely at the time, it was not guaranteed. The aforementioned tension between the pro-French Walloons and the suspicious Flemish made Belgian politics unpredictable and somewhat unstable. Beyond cooperation, France needed the Belgians to prepare sufficiently to mount a credible defense against an initial German assault. If the Germans quickly overwhelmed the Belgians before French troops arrived, the advancing French and Germans would meet on open ground in western Belgium—precisely the type of "improvised and unprepared encounter battles" the French army wanted to avoid.[111]

Defense-in-Depth
The opposite approach employed a defense-in-depth strategy in which the army established multiple prepared lines within France. In a theoretical sense, this approach fit well with a nation needing time to mobilize its military strength and gain support from its erstwhile allies, Britain and the United States. Being a relatively large nation, France seemingly could afford to exchange ground for time. In 1895 the French army briefly had adopted a war plan based on this strategy.[112] But the lessons of World War I had convinced French civilian and military

policymakers of its inapplicability against Germany. Although trading ground for time might allow the army to mobilize and obtain allied support, the latter was not guaranteed and the former would be of limited effectiveness after the Germans captured the critically needed resources of the frontier regions. Even if senior officers had favored such a strategy, it would have been vigorously opposed by politicians with constituencies in the vulnerable and heavily populated border districts.[113]

Frontier Defense
Attention naturally focused on the intermediate option of erecting a strong defense along the frontier. Such an approach could protect critical French resources and industry as well as the local population. In particular, it would best enable the army to guard against an attaque brusquée and provide time for mobilization, a critical objective stressed by Foch, Pétain, and others in the late 1920s.[114] Many senior officers focused on the value of fortification as part of this covering effort, not "a Gallic version of the Chinese Wall."[115] Although sometimes referred to derisively as passive defense, this less aggressive approach would also be more effective in gaining the support of the British and Americans.[116]

The two basic variants of frontier defense—fortified regions (also characterized as centers of resistance) or continuously prepared battlefields—entailed sharply different strengths and weaknesses. Given that not all sections of the frontier were of equal import or vulnerability, many French believed they could concentrate their efforts. The cost of erecting strong fortifications against all possible avenues of attack was simply too high, especially along the flat, open northern frontier. Instead, a focus would be on erecting large, expensive, concrete-based fortifications in key areas to rebuff even the strongest advances. The French commanders knew from the writings of senior German commanders that Berlin had generally tried to avoid strongly fortified regions during World War I.[117] Moreover, the army could emphasize firepower and technology instead of maneuver and manpower. Beyond safeguarding certain areas, the French theoretically could channel German attacks along preferred routes. With the strong works serving as a force multiplier, the army could safely concentrate troops along these open channels and other frontiers. Fitting well with the French military capability and army culture, this approach would be likely to find a generally receptive political environment, critical for funding the necessary structures.[118]

Building fortified regions, however, did entail some negatives. First, the concentration of resources on key areas would potentially leave other regions exposed. If the enemy saw a vulnerability that the French had missed, the implications would be severe. The French High Command's analysis that the Ardennes sector was easily defensible with light obstacles illustrates the danger.[119] Beyond strategic rationale, the concentration of defenses in particular areas would inevitably raise the ire and opposition of politicians from other frontier areas.[120] The high cost of fortified regions would likely prevent a fallback position should the initial defenses be penetrated or outflanked. As a combination offense–defense approach, this would require not only these expensive works but also funding an army of adequate mobility. Even the survivability of large, concrete fortresses was open to question given the ever-increasing destructiveness of modern artillery and airpower.[121]

Alternatively, the French could erect prepared battlefields along the entire eastern frontier. Essentially analogous to the trench-based defenses that emerged on the western front in World War I, these barriers would be built in peacetime to ensure their readiness for a German attack. Although such works were greatly inferior to concrete fortresses, their much lower cost meant that France could afford to cover the entire eastern frontier and complicate dangerous German outflanking maneuvers. In addition, the French could build multiple lines to wear down any German attack. While World War I had shown the severe strategic costs for losing ground, it also clearly highlighted that defense-in-depth could be extremely effective from an operational perspective.[122] The absence of obvious targets for German artillery and airpower, in contrast to concrete fortresses, also made this approach less vulnerable to barrage tactics.

The significant benefits of this approach had to be weighed against considerable weaknesses. Such defenses would be effective if properly manned, but the availability of sufficient soldiers from the shrinking French army, especially at the outset of a conflict, made them questionable.[123] Moreover, the necessary precaution of back-up lines added to manpower requirements. Even if successful, the fighting along such lines would likely produce high casualties, as occurred in World War I.[124] Many senior officers worried about suffering such losses given the smaller manpower base and morale considerations. The approach risked overextending the French army, turning the theoretical advantage of denying outflanking maneuvers into an actual disadvantage of likely penetrations. For advocates of offensive action, such a system, in contrast to the fortified region model, would not function as a force multiplier to facilitate early advances. Finally, the approach jeopardized assistance from allies. If the French obviously intended to stay behind their own borders, the Germans could concentrate on the east before turning to the west. Thus, it undercut the decades-old belief of the need for a two-front war.

Decisions for a Strategic Decision System

Faced with changing contextual pressures and a set of flawed options, it is not surprising that French policymakers' choice would slowly emerge from late 1925 through the end of the decade. Equally to be expected, the French High

Command ultimately adopted a compromise approach with elements of forward and frontier defense as well as somewhat integrating fortified region and prepared battlefield concepts. A review of the CSG's key debates on the subject provides insights into senior officers' rationale for what became the Maginot Line. The December 1925 CSG meeting marked the beginning of concrete steps toward major frontier fortifications. At first, Pétain and Foch resumed their longstanding disagreement between preparing a continuous front and fortifying select zones. The reading of deceased Chief of Staff Buat's 1923 views in support of a continuous front must have exacerbated the sense of déjà vu. New Minister of War Painlevé and others brought a strong urgency for progress. President Gaston Doumergue tried to facilitate momentum by asking two basic questions: (a) should there be a defensive system on the frontier; and (b) should forts be erected to create a continuous border battlefield? An alliance including Foch, Debeney, and Guillaumat decisively answered both questions—yes to a defense system, no to continuous fortifications along the entire border. The group was "not only authoritative, it was highly articulate," in overriding Pétain.[125] The CSG formally "advised the creation in peacetime of a discontinuous system of fortified regions" as well as recommending establishment of the Frontier Defense Commission, chaired by General Guillaumat, to explore the details.[126]

After investigating and deliberating for most of 1926, the Guillaumat Commission reported to Painlevé on November 6 that three fortified regions should be erected on the northeast frontier. An RF in the Metz-Thionville area was necessary to protect the vulnerable and valuable Lorraine plateau and Moselle River valley. They recommended a second region, to be known as the Lauter RF, from where the Rhine ceases to be the border with Germany westward through the Haguenau Forest to the Lower Vosges range. At this early date, offensive advocates could envision the Metz RF functioning as a hinge to support advances on the northeastern and northern frontiers while the Lauter RF would cover Alsace and protect the flank of an army advancing into the Saarland.[127] As a lower priority, members wanted a third smaller RF to ensure adequate protection of the Belfort gap south of Alsace between the Jura and Vosges mountain ranges. The commission concluded that the Rhine front with its major water obstacle did not require strong fortifications, nor should such works be erected on the northern frontier. Guillaumat warned that "a wall of France is a dream, in financial terms . . . and could be a danger from a military point of view. It could lead to the subordination of all war plans . . . to existing or projected fortifications."[128]

At its December 1926 meeting, the CSG approved the recommendations on RF locations, but disagreement persisted over the form of defenses and even the potential for longer prepared battlefields. Pétain still argued for a continuous front and defense-in-depth while his critics vigorously cautioned against an over-reliance on defenses. Pétain fought with Inspector General of Engineers Étienne-Honoré Fillonneau over the type of structures to construct. The marshal had more success contending that trenches or subterranean bunkers represented a better form of defense than the massive aboveground concrete fortifications favored by the commission. Despite acknowledging the merit of such bunkers, Fillonneau and others worried about their cost.[129]

Political movement toward reducing conscription to one year and other unwelcome changes was shifting sentiment among CSG members in favor of a more defensive approach. The minutes from the December 1926 meeting reveal that "support for their [fortifications] offensive employment was slowly dissolving."[130] Coalition members favoring construction of fortified regions had never been in clear agreement on the offensive component, with Foch and Guillaumat seeing the fortresses as abetting an advance into Germany while Painlevé and Debeney focused on their defensive potential.[131]

During the CSG discussions of frontier defenses in January, July, and October of 1927, even hardliners began to acknowledge difficulties of any offensive with a corresponding increase in the importance of erecting adequate barriers.[132] The CSG now viewed fortifications as the only option to "enable France to overcome its disadvantage against Germany," especially in facilitating sufficient protection against the dreaded attaque brusquée to enable mobilization.[133] The army's growing defensive orientation increased Pétain's influence, allowing him to re-energize the campaign, especially at the July 1927 meeting, for creating wider and deeper positions to guard against breakthroughs.[134] The marshal's conception of a "frontier line" and a back-up "barrage line" initially overcame the strong opposition of some CSG members such as General Fillonneau. But shortened conscription also presented a severe difficulty for Pétain given that longer barriers raised manning requirements. Unable to resolve this problem, which critics such as General Nollet seized upon, Pétain abandoned his effort for "prepared battlefields" and took off on a frontier inspection trip to reassess the matter.[135]

Although Gen. Louis Maurin and a few others remained promoters of two lines of machine gun casemates, Pétain's presentation at the October 12, 1927, CSG meeting appeared reminiscent of the Guillaumat Commission's recommendations for fortified regions. The marshal had essentially capitulated, embracing the other side's view with the primary difference being the types of works to employ in the fortified regions. He persuasively argued that underground structures linked by tunnels would greatly reduce vulnerability. CSG members concurred on this approach, albeit with modifications to minimize the number of operating personnel. Given the need to resolve technical design questions and create an entity to oversee the construction process, the army had already in August established a new commission (*Commission d'Organisation des Régions Fortifiées*, CORF) under General Fillonneau. After seven years of debate, the French High Command was now united on a basic defense approach for the northeastern region that combined terrain obstacles and manmade works. The approach most closely reflects the view held by Chief of Staff Debeney throughout the process.[136]

CSG members appreciated that protecting Lorraine with robust defenses would likely direct a German attack northward. To the immediate north lay the thick Ardennes Forest. The Guillaumat Commission had concluded that the Germans would need nine days to penetrate this obstacle if it was bolstered by minimal defenses.[137] This interval would provide sufficient time for the French to organize reinforcements along the formidable Meuse River behind the Ardennes. Thus they expected the Germans to strike further north through central Belgium, where a forward defense would have to be employed. Inherent risks existed for this approach "if the Belgian defenses had not been prepared, if agreement had not been reached on exact troop dispositions and locations, if the call for help were to come too late," but no other option appeared feasible.[138] The CSG did recommend building minor defenses at key points along the Franco-Belgian border, but the half-hearted contingency was not a serious factor. In essence, the high command had devised a strategy in which each of the three interrelated frontiers most threatened by Germany would be defended in a different manner—strong fortifications along the northeast frontier, defense-in-depth building on rugged terrain and a river obstacle in the Ardennes sector, and forward defense in central Belgium protecting northern France.[139]

Despite carrying great authority, the CSG's recommendations would only become a reality if approved and funded by the government. While squabbles continued over fortification details, Pétain briefed the civilian ministers' defense body in June 1928. They supported the defense concept, albeit with some concern that the areas around and between the RFs needed better protection. Painlevé had already obtained limited funds to initiate work on high priority sites, but significant opposition existed in the legislature to the large budget outlays necessary for the entire system. Many liberals, citing détente efforts, opposed high defense spending while the Banque de France, fearful of jeopardizing hard won financial stability, objected to major government programs. Painlevé proved unable to overcome this resistance, leaving the task of obtaining the money to the more politically adroit Maginot in November 1929. Seeking greater support, the government reduced the projected cost by cutting the lower priority Belfort RF.[140]

Maginot orchestrated an effective campaign that culminated with the parliament's approval of 2.9 billion francs for fortifications on January 14, 1930.[141] Fear of a lightning strike by a revitalized German army combined with the impending withdrawal from the Rhineland allowed him to win strong support from the right and many centrists on national security grounds. While some left-leaning politicians also worried about national security, Maginot gained the approval of organized labor and many liberal deputies by astutely playing up the project as a massive employment initiative. Moreover, he argued that erecting a defensive line would signal France's peaceful intentions to the rest of Europe and bolster, not undermine relations with, Germany. Most criticism of the government plan resulted from its neglect of certain regions, particularly the northern frontier.[142] Prominent legislator Edouard Daladier typified this sentiment by observing that "it would be ... dangerous ... to become hypnotized ...by ... Lorraine" and leave "open the route from the north to Paris."[143]

Maginot, in his key December 10, 1929, speech, had expressed the government's view that "we could hardly dream of building a kind of Great Wall of France, which would in any case be far too costly. Instead we have foreseen powerful but flexible means of organizing defense ... taking full advantage of terrain."[144] Beyond cost, Maginot stressed that diplomatic and topographical factors meant France could not erect similar fortifications in the north. It would have to fight a conventional battle on this frontier, if war ever came. In between the fortified regions, the government stressed its intention to erect rudimentary defense works and willingness to consider lengthening them if necessary. In November 1930 the credits were increased to a total of 3.4 billion francs for expanded defenses in the Metz RF and the addition of works on the frontier facing Italy. Ultimately, despite concentrating on the fortified regions, the army and supporting politicians would tend to play up publicly these interval defenses as a part of a continuous front and their commitment to "inviolability" of the frontier. While effective politically, this behavior abetted the misperception of the Maginot Line extending along the entire eastern frontier and shaped the security policy debate in the 1930s.[145]

Security Developments along a Partially Fortified Frontier

The basic decisions about defending the frontier had been made by 1930. Given that "whatever new problems might arise ... necessarily [were] considered within the framework of that system," this well-documented case allows consideration of how strategic defense systems shape decisonmakers' perceptions, deliberations, and choices.[146] Immediately upon passage of the funding bill, full-scale construction of the fortifications began under the new CORF director, Gen. Charles Louis-Joseph Belhague. The French army was anxious to complete the works by 1935 when the "hollow years" of small conscript classes would begin.[147] While laborers toiled away, external developments exacerbated perceptions of the German threat and prompted questions about the adopted defense approach. In particular, two key periods stand out. In 1932 chaos in the French political system coincided with rising alarm about Germany. Then, in 1936, German remilitarization of the Rhineland and other events removed any doubt about the threat to France. Concern focused in both periods on the northern frontier, especially with Belgium's decreasing cooperation. Ultimately, the French did not significantly deviate from their security conception at the beginning of the decade, but they could have chosen otherwise, especially in 1932.

Staying the Course, 1932

Threat perceptions mounted from the beginning of the 1930s with the accelerating deterioration of Franco–German relations and the disappointment with the League of Nations. By the time of Briand's departure as foreign minister in January 1932, any sense of détente had evaporated as Paris and Berlin increasingly adopted hard-line positions.[148] Collective security had already suffered a severe blow in 1931 when the League of Nations reacted meekly to Japan's invasion of Manchuria. This climate prompted French politicians to force a reconsideration of defense policy. Not surprisingly, representatives from uncovered regions along the frontier, particularly the Nord departments, protested their taxes being spent in Lorraine and boisterously agitated for better protection.[149] The French case illustrates how the dynamics of operating strategic defenses across only part of the frontier differ somewhat for democracies than the previous authoritarian cases. Not only can regional officials exert more pressure on national decision makers but the latter—who had solid reasons to neglect this area—are also strongly tempted to respond by artificially playing up modest efforts to prompt subjective security. While potentially effective in the short run, such successes create artificial expectations that if punctured may have severe political and psychological consequences.

With the Senate Army Commission pressing for fixed defenses on the Franco-Belgian border, a divided CSG reviewed the matter on May 28 and June 4, 1932.[150] Although the genesis of these sessions was the best use of a $250 million financial credit offered by the Senate for fortifications in the north, "in practice it was the means of defending the whole Franco-Belgian theatre that was at issue."[151] Minister of War François Pietri, Prime Minister André Tardieu, and President Albert Lebrun all favored additional fixed defenses, but politicians remained deferential to senior officers. Pétain's replacement, Maxime Weygand, and new chief of staff Maurice Gamelin supported spending the offered funds on northern front defenses, essentially as a fallback position. Gamelin in particular regarded it as wise "to harness the prevailing political tide—not swim against it," especially since the money was only available for fortifications.[152] The retired Pétain and his allies on the CSG vigorously opposed the idea of building strong points on this front. They contended such works would undermine the essential forward defense by damaging Franco-Belgian cooperation and taking funds from armament and motorization efforts. Although the amount being discussed was relatively small, the precedent fueled opponents' vehemence. Pétain's nearly sacrilegious, although perhaps not serious, suggestion that the money be given to the air force shows the extent of his hostility to fortifying the northern border.[153] Despite the contentiousness, attempts to unify the high command prompted a second meeting on June 4. After the antifortification bloc prevailed by a 7–6 majority in the closest CSG vote of the intrawar period, General Weygand would declare that "the military frontier of the northern provinces is on the German-Belgian frontier."[154] The council would return to the subject later in the decade, but as Martin Alexander stresses, "fortifications were such a long-term engineering undertaking, never was so consequential a choice made."[155]

The debate within the French High Command occurred at a time when the Belgians had begun questioning the value of an integrated defense. This sentiment suggests the growing need for a French safety net but also why Pétain and others were so sensitive about alienating the Belgians. The withdrawal of occupation forces from the Rhineland had reduced the benefits of the Franco–Belgian partnership. Like the French, the Belgians wanted to avoid turning their nation into a battlefield if possible. Thus they were increasingly drawn to an all-out defense near their German border rather than a defense-in-depth strategy, especially as construction of the Albert Canal potentially provided protection of their northern flank. At a distance of 125 miles from France, however, the Belgian–German border was beyond the French army's ability to provide timely assistance. This combined with the nation's increasingly contentious domestic politics to encourage Brussels to adopt greater independence.[156]

With both a barrier along the Franco–Belgian border and forward defense seeming problematic, some Frenchmen advocated a third option—underwriting robust Belgian fortifications. In essence, they contended the best way to secure the northern frontier was to erect a "Belgian Maginot Line" that ran from the west end of the Metz RF to the Netherlands. Although the Belgians were constructing some frontier defenses, most notably the strong Eben Emael fortress, they could not afford a fortified region analogous to the French effort. Advocates in Brussels and Paris, including French prime minister Tardieu, believed such a strategic defense system was doable with significant French funding. In early 1932, Tardieu suggested providing Belgium with 1 billion francs. Some senior officers supported the idea as a way to buy time for the French army to carry out a forward defense in central Belgium. Tardieu and other politicians, however, generally viewed such a fortification effort as removing the need to equip the army to conduct a forward defense to the concern of informed soldiers. Tardieu's defeat in mid-1932 ended current discussion of this option while staunch opponents worked to squash the notion completely.[157]

While the military generally disliked Tardieu's scheme, members of the high command were dismayed by the leftists' politically transformative victory that ousted him. Voters blamed the center-right parties for France finally suffering the calamitous effects of the Great Depression. With the popularity of extremists on both the right and left growing, a series of unstable leftist coalitions governed during a period of high political turbulence. Regardless of the particular regime, these governments focused on the economy and imposed significant budget cuts on the military.[158] The ominous German behavior that followed Hitler's rise in January 1933 did not reverse the government's position on defense spending. Ultimately, the military's budget would fall by a third between 1931 and 1935.[159] Not surprisingly, severe tension existed between officers and these leftist governments, complicating effective military policymaking. Whereas coup worries had been largely theoretical in the 1920s, they now represented a legitimate concern. A sense of isolation from society and hostility toward leftist politicians grew in the officer corps, exacerbated by the death of respected politicians such as Maginot and Poincaré.[160] Weygand frequently associated with right-wing politicians and journalists, sparking fear of his installing a reactionary regime.[161]

A practical manifestation of the civil-military tension was the French High Command's lack of enthusiasm for adding more fixed defenses despite their popularity among the public and politicians. Leftists had disproportionately safeguarded fortification programs from the draconian budget cuts.[162] With already planned works behind schedule and experiencing sharp cost overruns, most senior officers favored directing additional resources to build up motorized and mechanized forces rather than construct more fortifications.[163] Weygand stressed that "even on the defensive, especially on the defensive, an army having neither the will nor the ability to maneuver is doomed to defeat."[164] The popularity of defenses with leftists and the public almost prompted an instinctive hostility within the military. At a minimum, in contrast to the late 1920s, the high command increasingly saw a trade-off between armaments and fixed defenses.[165] This attitude grew despite a reality that money not spent on works would have been redirected to nonmilitary sectors. Present and former senior officers feared a drift toward a completely static defense approach. Pétain continued to stress that the Ardennes presented a negligible danger and the north frontier had to be defended in central Belgium. Most famously, as minister of war, he testified before the Senate Army Commission in 1934 that the Ardennes was "not dangerous" as the area would be "impenetrable" with modest defenses.[166] The rare uniformed advocate for expanding frontier fortifications, such as strategist Adm. Raoul Castex, received a frosty reaction from his colleagues.[167]

While senior officers prevented a fundamental expansion of fortifications, they did agree to build additional strong points along the Alpine, Rhine, and Belgic frontiers. In the north, modest fortifications would be constructed in the Maubeuge and Valenciennes areas, covering the Sambre and Escaut River valleys, respectively. More significantly, the army reduced the span of low-lying

Sarre Gap between the fortified regions and extended protection north from the Metz RF to cover the Montmédy region. The army designed these new works in austere times to be less expensive than the initial ouvrages, but they were commensurately less robust. In July 1934 the French parliament voted another 1.275 billion francs for frontier fortifications to continue work on the existing project and fund these additions, but the ever-increasing costs of the main Lorraine works absorbed most of this money. Regarding defenses in the north largely as a sop to the civilians rather than critical to national security, the army commenced limited construction without intensity or interest.[168]

Second Reconsideration, 1936

A series of developments in 1935 and especially 1936 clarified the German threat, prompting increased French alarm about the existing defense strategy.[169] More than 90 percent of Saar residents voted for reunification with Germany in the January 1935 plebiscite. Later that year, Hitler publicly declared rearmament and reintroduction of conscription, portending a much more aggressive effort. Highlighting the German military's adaptation of a more offensive doctrine, French intelligence repeatedly exaggerated the size and capability of the Wehrmacht.[170] Most ominously, Germany remilitarized the Rhineland in March 1936, violating the last remaining core element of the Treaty of Versailles. Despite its perceived importance, the French government did not try to push back the modest three-battalion German force. The high command declared that it could not advance into Germany until a million-man covering force was in place along the frontier, a requirement necessitating at least a two-week mobilization.[171] Instead French troops for the first time manned the Maginot Line, the basic fortresses of which were largely complete after worrisome construction delays into late 1935.[172] France's anemic reaction, reflecting in part the army's organization exclusively for total war, suggested a lack of will. The relocation of Wehrmacht troops near the border sharply elevated long-standing French fears about an attaque brusquée while rapid German work on their own frontier fortifications signaled greater difficulty advancing in a future conflict.[173]

In the months after the Rhineland's remilitarization, the French sense of isolation grew with the changing landscape of western Europe. Spain soon erupted into civil war, and Germany and Italy cooperated to support the local nationalists. Beyond enhancing Franco's prospects, this partnership reflected and advanced Mussolini's decision to ally with Hitler. Now France faced the strong possibility of being surrounded by enemies as well as having to face enhanced threats in North Africa. Moreover, Germany's growing desire for *lebensraum* had become a clear threat to France's eastern European allies. Although Italy's alignment with Germany reduced the value of these partners, the ties remained and any German aggression would cause problems for France.[174]

The silver lining from these ominous developments was their unifying effect on a French polity that could no longer downplay the danger. The governing leftist alliance, known as the Popular Front, moved to upgrade the nation's military strength led by the powerful combination of Minister of War Daladier and General Gamelin. The latter had remained chief of staff after succeeding Weygand as designated wartime leader in early 1935, consolidating army leadership. The Popular Front's defense policy had three core elements: rearm the military, improve mobilization plans, and upgrade frontier defenses. Ultimately, in August 1936, parliament allocated 14 billion francs for full-scale rearmament, demonstrating the willingness of a leftist government to appropriate significant military funds.[175]

Rather than pushing the Belgians toward the French, the mounting threat perception prompted Brussels to declare neutrality on October 14, 1936. With a weak and unprepared army and the Albert Canal years from completion, the small nation's politics had become gridlocked on defense matters. Most Flemish favored disconnecting their nation from French security policy. Even pro-French Belgians urged Paris to accept neutrality as a prerequisite for passage of the critically needed army reform bill. However, any subsequent military improvement would not offset the damage from an inability to conduct joint advanced planning. Belgium's policy change threatened to undermine France's security on the northern frontier and thus the overall concept of defense given long-standing views that only a forward defense was viable in this area.[176]

Responding to Belgium's declaration of neutrality was a pivotal issue for French policymakers. The government essentially had three basic options: extend the Maginot Line, organize a mobile force, or reinforce its basic approach. With both alternatives suffering from long appreciated weaknesses, the French generals remained committed to the status quo, albeit with a greater push for weapons acquisition. By contrast, Minister of War Daladier renewed his push from the early 1930s to create a continuous barrier from the English Channel to Switzerland—"Fortress France." He toured the northern frontier with senior officers to explore potential fortification sites. Ultimately, the army identified four areas along the border, where over the next few years it would spend tens of millions of francs on fixed defenses. As senior officers knew, such levels were inadequate to establish even meaningful insurance against a breakthrough.[177]

Gamelin and the more politically savvy generals had largely taken these measures to assuage Daladier, regarding his full-scale project as impractical and dangerous given the resource implications. The chief of staff estimated that fortifying the Franco-Belgian border would cost 10–15 billion francs given the area's flat terrain and high water table. France could not invest this amount and rearm adequately. No barrier could protect key industrial areas, such as Lille, essentially on the border. These geographic and economic considerations as well as Belgium's twenty-two divisions prompted Gamelin and other senior officers to remain decisively in favor of a forward defense despite Belgium's neutrality declaration. Belgium's reorientation only reinforced the need for acquiring adequate mobile systems and bolstering the Maginot Line to permit greater concentration of troops in the north. The generals believed the key was "more 'punch' for the French army—not more concrete."[178]

This punch would be applied through the long-standing defense strategy in contrast to what senior officers regarded as Col. Charles de Gaulle's strategically unwise and politically impossible concept of offensive-oriented, independent armor units.[179] In essence, de Gaulle's approach stressed three interrelated and disputed elements: (a) importance of the tank, (b) advantage of independent armor formations, and (c) necessity of a professional army to operate the armored force.[180] De Gaulle's proposal for a one-hundred-thousand-man professional force of seven independent armored divisions would gain him great renown for prescience after France's 1940 defeat. Nevertheless, his requirement of a professional army to operate the armor force was politically impractical with a left-wing government in power and provided the basis for the CSG's July 1936 rejection of the approach.[181] Additionally, for most senior officers, this requirement was incompatible with the iconic concept of methodical battle. Despite some senior officers expressing interest and even support for armored formations, the CSG considered general motorization a higher priority given the need to advance large numbers of infantry and artillery rapidly into Belgium.[182] Brussels' declaration of neutrality had exacerbated sensitivity to this requirement, diminishing rather than enhancing the appeal of de Gaulle's argument. As the environment placed greater strain on the prospect for French defense strategy, army leaders essentially sought to avoid the risk involved with adopting an alternative strategy.[183]

Maintenance of the army's long-standing confidence in the security of the Ardennes facilitated focusing on central Belgium. Despite being the linchpin between the two main fronts, the Ardennes region has been aptly labeled the "Cinderella sector" given its inability to compete for resources and attention.[184] Similarly, the Belgians had concentrated their defense works almost entirely on the open areas north of the Ardennes. Even the minimal defense preparations often indicated as necessary to make the Ardennes "impenetrable" had been largely neglected.[185] While the generals appear to have truly regarded the region's terrain as formidable, such a characterization in the 1930s also had political value. As Ernest May observes, it "helped to fend off proposals that underground rail lines, turrets, and the rest be built north and west of Longwy, where the Maginot Line now terminated."[186] Senior officers expected mechanized reserves to be mobilized and deployed in time to block any threat that materialized through the forest, but France's delay in developing sufficient force levels left a severe vulnerability, especially if the Germans penetrated the Ardennes faster than the estimated nine days.

The Maginot Line at War

Faith in the Maginot Line helped calm nerves as conflict seemed to move inexorably closer, but it would not be viewed as sufficient to deter Germany or obviate the need to declare war on September 3, 1939, after Hitler invaded Poland. By this time the French had fully manned the fortifications to guard the front while the rest of the force mobilized. Although France wanted to aid its beleaguered Polish ally, the army's "help" amounted to a limited, tentative, and ultimately meaningless attack. A force of seven divisions quickly marched into Germany under supporting fire from the Hochwald gros ouvrage, the Maginot Line's first combat. The French troops, however, stopped upon reaching the minefields of the German West Wall system and ceased all offensive activity in less than a week. By the end of September, most of the force had been ordered back to France before the Wehrmacht could even transition troops from the east.[187]

After the completion of this German repositioning later in the year, all of France including the troops in the ouvrages waited for Hitler to give the invasion order. In the north, Belgium had dashed hopes for establishing strong forward positions by stubbornly—at least in the minds of the French—maintaining its neutrality. Although occasionally firing on German positions during the ensuing months, the Maginot forts were instructed to avoid attacking high-value targets that might prompt German escalation.[188] Historians disagree over the extent to which, by late 1939 and early 1940, the French possessed increasing confidence and even "had become convinced that Hitler would never dare an offensive against France."[189] Talbot Imlay argues more recently that the traditional optimistic view was greatly exaggerated, perhaps representing leaders' psychological attempts to bolster the nation and themselves.[190] This revised interpretation contends that some key senior French officials searched for a path to quick victory, doubtful of France's ability to win an attrition war. Regardless, the army attempted to use the interval to better equip and train forces as well as strengthen defenses, but such efforts could not remedy years of inadequate preparations. As a precaution, the French High Command retained excessive troops (forty divisions of the 2nd and 3rd Army groups) between and behind Maginot Line fortifications to ensure the security of vital Lorraine.[191] A far more damaging deployment decision came directly from General Gamelin when he unwisely in March 1940 added Breda (Netherlands) as an objective.[192] As a result, critical mobile reserves previously intended for counterattacking dangerous German penetrations were reassigned to the extreme northern flank.

Although it has been argued that "the strong but thin Maginot line invited the Germans to attempt a penetrating thrust," Berlin was deterred from attacking Alsace-Lorraine.[193] German Army Group C occupied the ground opposite the fortified regions with a limited force. As the invasion date approached, Luftwaffe commander Hermann Göring tried to mislead the French by declaring that Germany would attack the Maginot Line in two places between May 5 and 15.[194] Such blatant declarations and deployments did not alter French expectations that the enemy would attack, especially the panzers, in central Belgium. The Wehrmacht would ignore the northeast and its fortified regions while only launching a secondary attack on the northern front to distract the allies. Instead, the Germans, for numerous reasons, decided in February 1940 to shift focus to the Ardennes sector, a change that the French missed despite the existence of clear signs.

Thus, when Germany finally put Case (Plan) Yellow into action on May 10, 1940, it worked nearly perfectly. While the best French units advanced on the northern end of the battlefield increasingly far from the decisive ground, German panzers rapidly sliced through the Ardennes Forest and the feeble second-rate divisions guarding it. Instead of taking the estimated nine days to reach the Meuse, the Germans crossed the river near Sedan early on day four. Although the initial surprise put the French and their allies at a severe disadvantage, historians note it did not have to seal their fate.[195] With almost a third more troops, more tanks, a 3:1 edge in artillery, and an even number of modern vehicles, the allies might have been able to recover if possessing greater flexibility and skill. The tightly controlled, poorly led French army, however, was organized, trained, and commanded in a way that precluded such a response.

Troops in the fortified regions absorbed German bombardment and replied with their own fire, but the so-called Maginot Line extension in the Montmédy area was in the thick of the fight once the Wehrmacht attacked the petit ouvrage at La Ferté on May 17. Undermanned and soon denied assistance from flanking casemates, the small La Ferté fortification held out for two days despite German use of heavy artillery. The capture of the ouvrage only occurred after the asphyxiation of the one hundred remaining soldiers. While engaged with La Ferté, advancing German units also attacked the four petit ouvrages of the Maubeuge area to the north. Despite possessing far better troops and artillery, the Germans took five days to overcome fortress units' stout resistance. While Berlin launched a full-scale propaganda blitz on its penetration of the vaunted Maginot Line, German army commanders had gained an appreciation for the challenge of even the weakest ouvrages.[196]

Having cut off the 1st Army Group and most of the British Expeditionary Force with their dash to the English Channel, the Germans planned to finish off France with a new offensive beginning on June 5. With the French army in disarray, more than half of the reserve infantry and artillery units on the northeast frontier had been redeployed to bolster a desperately arranged front to protect Paris. On June 2, Gen. Gaston Prételat, commander of the 2nd Army Group, actually sought permission to withdraw from the entire northeast frontier, including the RFs, but he was refused. As a part of its new offensive, the Germans planned to advance into this area but avoid directly challenging the main fortifications. Instead they approached around the western end of the Maginot Line, through the Sarre Gap in the middle, and across the Rhine River to the southeast. With 88-mm guns obliterating the vulnerable casemates along the Rhine, the Germans advanced rapidly along these avenues. Moreover, Erwin Rommel's panzers raced behind the Maginot Line, threatening to cut off the 2nd Army Group. German capture of Metz on June 17 prompted a withdrawal of all remaining field units, isolating the fortifications. That evening, new prime minister Pétain, viewing continued fighting as pointless, sought an armistice, which prompted many French soldiers to simply quit fighting.[197]

By contrast, the fortress garrisons remained committed and would get their desired opportunity for battle when the rapidity of the enemy's advance prevented evacuation. The Germans began attacking some of the main fortresses in mid-June, with fighting at its peak between June 20 and 22. Despite being able to attack these works from front and rear with plentiful air, armor, and heavy artillery support, the Germans did not capture a single gros ouvrage. Although they thought the repeated assaults had caused extensive damage, the subterranean works had proved nearly impervious. For example, the Germans attacked the Schoenenbourg gros ouvrage with 160 aerial bombs and repeated 420-mm artillery salvos without significant effect. Instead French fortresses, such as Michelsberg, Fermont, and Schoenenbourg, inflicted heavy casualties and produced a stalemate, although the lack of German need to capture the positions left them unwilling to make an all-out effort. The ability of ouvrages to provide fire support for neighboring works proved extremely valuable. Even after the French government's surrender became official on June 25, some fortress units continued to resist. The frustrated Germans threatened to bomb Lyon unless the fortress troops ended their holdout, which, combined with the surrender of Paris, finally allowed the French High Command representatives to obtain the capitulation of all fortress garrisons by early July.[198]

France's defeat did not mark the end for the vast Maginot Line defense complex. Close inspection of the ouvrages impressed the Germans, who would use some works as underground factories to protect against allied bombing. When the U.S. Third Army advanced into Alsace-Lorraine in late 1944, the Germans employed particular Maginot Line combat blocs (e.g., Simershof, Schiesseck, and Hackenberg) in conjunction with some of their old pre–World War I forts around Metz to mount a defense. Even though most of the ouvrage guns had previously been transferred to the Atlantic Wall, the potential for these works to inflict significant casualties contributed to the allied command's decision to halt in Lorraine for about a month. Given the ouvrages' sturdiness, the French army set about restoring them as a central part of the nation's defense after the war. The fortifications would continue to perform this role into the 1960s when obsolescence and changing threat perceptions largely ended their military value. The French subsequently used some of the deep ammunition bunkers as a repository for tactical nuclear weapons. In the post–Cold War era, an ever-increasing number of ouvrages are being rescued as tourist destinations, but most remain closed, slowly decaying with the passage of time.[199]

Conclusion

Visitors to any of the open ouvrages see a fortification system of impressive scope and sophistication, but what should be the legacy of the Maginot Line? The Great Wall of China stands for its amazing beauty and scale, and Hadrian's Wall represents a romantic period of ancient history, but the twentieth century French strategic defense system is usually evoked as a symbol of military disaster. Since World War II, critics of particular military policies have often labeled them another "Maginot Line" to discredit the initiatives. For example, opponents of missile defense frequently characterize it as a "Maginot Line in the Sky."

Although this standing will never be completely erased, scholars have labored to modify it by stressing the barrier's success at deterrence and defense.[200] The Germans astutely avoided the Maginot Line when invading France, a noteworthy result since, as Edward Luttwak points out, "no defensive line can possibly achieve more than to dissuade the enemy from even trying to attack it."[201] Even after a month of combat when the Wehrmacht finally advanced into Alsace-Lorraine, they attacked through weak spots denuded of field troops rather than the fortified regions of the Maginot Line. The Germans ultimately did assail the main fortifications, but without capturing a single gros ouvrage despite air and ground dominance. At this point the Germans did not need to capture these works, prompting them to avoid large-scale assaults that may have been successful, albeit with a high probability of extensive casualties. The record illustrates the tremendous tactical effectiveness of these subterranean fortresses. Rather than blame the Maginot Line for defeat, historians have attributed the disaster to two military factors.[202] First, the high command did not appreciate the openness of the Ardennes sector, situated in the middle of the entire frontier. Second, the French possessed an inflexible, poorly led, and poorly trained army unable to react to the unanticipated German avenue of attack. These shortcomings together allowed the Wehrmacht to essentially avoid the Maginot Line and conquer France in six weeks.

It is appropriate to ask whether the construction and existence of the Maginot Line contributed to military defeat by prompting or contributing significantly to these two key deficiencies. Did the strategic defense system indirectly undermine protection of the Ardennes and northern frontiers while increasing security on the northeast frontier? As Col. Narcisse Chauvineau pointed out in early 1930, "to defeat the enemy in Alsace is not a success unless at the same time one is not defeated at Charleroi" (central Belgium).[203] As this chapter has shown, the decision to build the Maginot Line was the result of strong contextual pressures. No doubt exists that the construction efforts sharply influenced subsequent intrawar defense and security policy, reinforcing many influences already operative.[204] For a fortification system that arose among a majority of senior officers seeking to limit the risks of an offense-based strategy, the barrier facilitated and encouraged a defensive outlook consistent with a shrinking French army, prevailing political preferences, and critical resources near the border. Senior officers and civilians did not appreciate the extent to which building the fortifications without an army capable of offensive operations "signaled their unwillingness to enforce the Locarno agreements and to secure the neutrality of the Rhineland . . . the prospect of an invasion alone would goad them into action."[205] Minister of War Maurin reflected this new reality in the 1930s by declaring, "How could anyone believe that we contemplate the offensive when we have spent billions to establish a fortified barrier? Would we be mad enough to go beyond this barrier to I don't know what kind of adventure?"[206] Nevertheless, given the strong contextual factors, one has difficulty believing that the absence of a Maginot Line would have resulted in the French army developing a strong offensive capability.

A less environmentally determined question is whether blame for the defensive inadequacies of the French army and vulnerability of the Ardennes should be attributed to the so-called Maginot mentality—that is, the argument that these momentous fixed works psychologically blinded the French to the shortcomings of their defense policy. In answering this question, it is important to distinguish between civilians and the military. From the beginning of construction in 1930, Maginot and other government leaders had heavily publicized these defenses to comfort the French populous, validate their cost, and deter the Germans. Establishing perceptions of subjective security ("feeling safe") were critical in a French society devastated by World War I, especially after the rise of Hitler. The army and government fostered an exaggerated sense of the barrier's strength directly and in the media.[207] For example, an officer grandiosely and falsely wrote in "Maginot Line: Facts Revealed" that the "Shield and Buckler" system would safeguard the nation's frontiers, even from the Luftwaffe with its "aerial Maginot Line" component.[208] With such efforts, the Maginot Line "captured the imagination of the public and press," but left much of the civilian population mistakenly believing that the barrier protected the entire eastern frontier.[209] Thus it appears correct to characterize the "Maginot mentality" as "a civilian phenomenon, not a military one."[210] Such civilian mindsets can create a real danger, especially in a democracy employing a nation-in-arms defense approach. British general Alan Brooke articulated this risk after inspecting the

Maginot Line in early 1940: "a false sense of security is engendered, a feeling of sitting behind an impregnable iron fence; and should the fence perchance be broken, the French fighting spirit might well be brought crumbling with it."[211] The risk was magnified given that this "fence" only extended partway across its perceived expanse. The French press and public's inaccurate perception ultimately abetted German propaganda efforts after the breakthrough in the Ardennes since it suggested the Maginot Line's abject failure.

While most French senior officers and defense officials did not appreciate the downside of these propaganda efforts, they did not suffer from a similar mindset.[212] The barrier's construction had not produced a "troglodyte existence in the Maginot Line" that undermined French alertness and left the frontier vulnerable as some British officers worried in the 1930s.[213] While embracing a defensive doctrine as the only viable solution to short-term conscripts, and fortifications as essential to the protection of Lorraine, most senior commanders tried to minimize fixed defenses elsewhere along the frontier. The high command battled with politicians for most of the 1930s to prevent a significant expansion of the defense barrier. Despite being more open (or accepting of political reality) than most senior officers to some "insurance" defenses on the northern frontier, Gamelin typified military sentiment with his "rejection of linear organization in favor of defensive maneuver."[214] Similarly, General Guillaumat, a key figure in the frontier defense debate, remained consistent in the 1920s and 1930s, warning against believing, as Hughes notes, that "concrete alone could assure the integrity of French soil."[215] The high command regarded the fortified regions on the northeast frontier as facilitating a forward defense in the north, which the French expected to be the main theater of combat. If anything, one can detect the presence of a reverse Maginot mentality—that is, the desire to fend off efforts to expand fixed defenses toward the English Channel may well have contributed to the vulnerability of the Ardennes sector. Directly north of the Maginot Line, senior officers possibly stressed the area's "impenetrability" in part and perhaps subconsciously to discourage politicians' initiatives to expand the Maginot Line northward.[216]

Even if army commanders did not possess a Maginot mentality, it is often argued that the enormous cost of the fortifications left the French army inadequately funded. While the French High Command can be described "as victim rather than as practioner of Maginot-mindedness," the barrier was not destructively expensive.[217] As Alexander notes in his detailed investigation of the fortification expenditures, the fixed defenses "cost no more than half of the sum originally budgeted for the army's rearmament programme of September 1936."[218] In the late 1920s, with war not imminent, the military wanted to lay the groundwork for a defensive approach rather than weapons acquisition in a fast evolving technological environment. The high command's conception that fortifications along the northeast frontier would free up troops and weapons to concentrate on the northern frontier appears the most efficacious way to allocate human and financial resources available at the time. These appropriations occurred when the money would not have been spent on weapons systems or active duty forces in lieu of fortifications. It simply would have been redirected to other governmental programs and thus lost to the military. After the army began seeing a real trade-off between fortifications and weapons in the mid-1930s, the French actually spent relatively little on fixed defenses, especially in contrast to arms purchases. Ultimately, the failings of leadership, doctrine, and training of the French army cannot be blamed on the cost of the Maginot Line. While more money and longer conscription service would have been valuable, before the mid-1930s French politics likely would have precluded them regardless of the Maginot Line's existence.

Discounting fundamentally different contextual pressures, the most likely counterfactual of a decision to forgo the Maginot Line in the late 1920s would have meant embracing Pétain's defense philosophy and establishing prepared battlefields along the length of the frontier. These relatively inexpensive obstacles—at least in terms of francs, not lives—could have covered the northeastern and northern frontiers, but seem unlikely to have greatly influenced the military balance in an era of offense-favoring technology. Whatever greater concern in the French High Command about such a strategic defense in the early 1930s with Hitler's rise, the latter coincided with leftist ascendancy in the French government and sharp reductions in military spending. It is extremely difficult to imagine that the ruling coalition would have significantly funded armaments or allowed the type of institutional changes in the French armed forces to facilitate a more prepared French military before Germany's remilitarization of the Rhineland in 1936. Conversely, a decision to forgo the Maginot Line would not have significantly enhanced the potential for the Briand-Stresemann effort to reach political reconciliation in the late 1920s. Perceptions of national interest precluded a stable, harmonious relationship at the time. Ultimately, the sharply increased defense francs available after the rise of the German threat in the mid-1930s should have been sufficient for delivering a much better performance in 1940.

Given the failings of the French army, did the high command actually err by not pursuing a protective barrier along the entire frontier? In other words, would France have been better off had the Maginot Line extended north to the English Channel? This question is rarely asked by historians given the fiscal, engineering, and diplomatic obstacles to this approach. Above all, as Gamelin and others argued, it would have been enormously expensive—double or triple the costs of the extant Maginot Line costs—due primarily to the high water table of the northern frontier.[219] France could have afforded it, but only at the sacrifice of other defense and government programs. Although Germany's invasion and rapid victory focuses history on that threat, French strategists in the intrawar period faced an array of challenges that encouraged heavy expenditures in other areas, especially the navy.[220] Given the immense time required for constructing such a barrier, a decision would have been necessary before the Hitler threat crystallized in the mid-1930s. Ultimately, it is unknowable if a continuous Maginot Line would have succeeded better at holding off the Germans. A barrier, even one that would have been the most impressive in history, probably alone could not be expected to hold off an imaginative and determined foe such as the Germans. The successful local deterrence and defense of the Maginot Line in Lorraine has to be weighed against the existence of appealing alternative approaches into France. One should not necessarily expect the same level of effectiveness for a strategic defense across the entire eastern frontier, especially since the existence of such an obstacle would have served to foster an even more defensive mindset among the French public and politicians. Thus the high command appears correct to have derided the creation of a "Great Wall of France."[221]

Ultimately, the verdict on the Maginot Line must be nuanced. The decision to wall off part, not all, of the frontier seems the best among a set of flawed options given the political and international constraints at work.[222] The strategic defense system should be counted as a deterrence and defense success on its own front, but "it could not live up to the myth that its political creators had allowed to grow up around it."[223] The Maginot Line cannot be blamed for the military catastrophe that ensued. If the French had established adequate protection of the Ardennes sector, even erecting the modest defenses (and allocating the doctrine-stipulated force ratios) that had been cited as necessary, the battle of France might have turned out differently, although the army's operational and tactical inferiority to the Wehrmacht made its ultimate defeat likely. Instead France had a defense strategy with a severe vulnerability that the Germans exploited fully, and a flawed army that could not recover from the mistake. In this regard, the Maginot Line and French defense policy in the intrawar period illustrates two of the most salient limits of defense barriers. First, decisionmakers choosing to build such a major and costly obstacle must appreciate that its influence will affect defense policy far into the future, especially as attempts to promote a sense of security may create false outlooks and expectations. Second, such walls or lines can eliminate known weaknesses, but they cannot shield states from the unknown or unappreciated threats. This realization should encourage continuous reevaluation for potential vulnerabilities, but the existence of major strategic defenses actually discourages attempts to detect and respond to such challenges. Such a conclusion is a valuable lesson given the difficulty of diagnosing all dangers against a determined and adaptable opponent.

Notes

1. See J. E. Kaufmann and H. W. Kaufmann, *Fortress France: The Maginot Line and French Defenses in World War II* (Westport, CT: Praeger, 2006), 20–21, 24, 26–27, 34, 47, 57, 79, 81, 85; and William Allcorn, *The Maginot Line, 1928–1945* (Oxford: Osprey, 2003), 10–11, 16, 19, 35.

2. See Kaufmann and Kaufmann, *Fortress France*, 26, 70–79; and Robert J. Young, *In Command of France: French Foreign Policy and Military Planning, 1933–1940* (Cambridge, MA: Harvard University Press, 1978), 61.

3. See Kaufmann and Kaufmann, *Fortress France*, 26; and Allcorn, *Maginot Line*, 33–34, 40.

4. See Martin Alexander, "In Defense of the Maginot Line," in *French Foreign and Defense Policy, 1918–1940: The Decline and Fall of a Great Power*, ed. Robert Boyce (New York: Routledge, 1998), 181; Allcorn, *Maginot Line*, 32–33, 43; and Kaufmann and Kaufmann, *Fortress France*, 24, 47, 77.

5. See Allcorn, *Maginot Line*, 33–34, 38–39; and Kaufmann and Kaufmann, *Fortress France*, 24–26, 60, 76–77, 92.

6. See Kaufmann and Kaufmann, *Fortress France*, 81, 85, 88, 150; and Allcorn, *Maginot Line*, 33.

7. Alexander, "Defense of the Maginot Line," 181–82; Young, *Command of France*, 60; and Elizabeth Kier, *Imagining War: French and British Military Doctrine between the Wars* (Princeton, NJ: Princeton University Press, 1997), 48.

8. Young, *Command of France*, 60; Kaufmann and Kaufmann, *Fortress France*, 91; and Allcorn, *Maginot Line*, 32.

9. Allcorn, *Maginot Line*, 4.

10. Kaufmann and Kaufmann, *Fortress France*, 92–93, 128; Allcorn, *Maginot Line*, 43; and Kier, *Imaging War*, 45.

11. Vivian Rowe, *The Great Wall of France: The Triumph of the Maginot Line* (London: Putnam, 1959), 90.

12. J. E. Kaufmann and H. W. Kaufmann, *The Maginot Line: None Shall Pass* (Westport, CT: Praeger, 1997), 93–100; and Young, *Command of France*, 31.

13. Rowe, *Great Wall of France*, 21.

14. Robert A. Doughty, *The Seeds of Disaster: The Development of French Army Doctrine, 1919–1939* (Hamden, CT: Archon Books, 1985), 44–45; and Kaufmann and Kaufmann, *Maginot Line*, 1–2.

15. Robert A. Doughty, *Pyrrhic Victory: French Strategy and Operations in the Great War* (Cambridge, MA: Belknap, 2005), 12, 25.

16. Kaufmann and Kaufmann, *Maginot Line*, 4; and Doughty, *Pyrrhic Victory*, 265.

17. Rowe, *Great Wall of France*, 22–23.

18. Eugenia C. Kiesling, *Arming against Hitler: France and the Limits of Military Planning* (Lawrence: University Press of Kansas, 1996), 13; Robert A. Doughty, "The Illusion of Security: France, 1919–1940," in *The Making of Strategy: Rulers, States, and War*, eds. Williamson Murray, MacGregor Knox, and Alvin Bernstein (New York:

Cambridge University Press, 1994), 469; and Alexander, "Defense of the Maginot Line," 166, 169.

19. Judith M. Hughes, *To the Maginot Line: The Politics of French Military Preparation in the 1920s* (Cambridge, MA: Harvard University Press, 1971), 49, 72; Doughty, *Pyrrhic Victory,* 407–9, 462, 469, 476–78, 503–4; and Kier, *Imaging War,* 44–46.

20. Stephen Ryan, *Pétain the Soldier* (South Brunswick, NJ: A. S. Barnes, 1969), 258; Rowe, *Great Wall of France,* 23; and Doughty, *Pyrrhic Victory,* 265, 274, 424–26.

21. Alexander, "Defense of the Maginot Line," 167.

22. Robert J. Young, *France and the Origins of the Second World War* (London: MacMillan, 1996), 9–10; and David Stevenson, "France at the Paris Peace Conference," in *French Foreign and Defense Policy, 1918–1940: The Decline and Fall of a Great Power,* ed. Robert Boyce (New York: Routledge, 1998), 12–13.

23. Stevenson, "France at the Paris Peace Conference," 17–18, 20; Young, *France and the Origins,* 9.

24. Young, *France and the Origins,* 11.

25. Hughes, *Maginot Line,* 101.

26. Rowe, *Great Wall of France,* 17.

27. Hughes, *Maginot Line,* 81.

28. Kiesling, *Arming against Hitler,* 14–15: Doughty, *Pyrrhic Victory,* 7; and Young, *Command of France,* 24.

29. See Doughty, *Seeds of Disaster,* 17–18; Ryan, *Pétain the Soldier,* 195–96; and Hughes, *Maginot Line,* 121–22.

30. Quoted in Rowe, *Great Wall of France,* 24.

31. See Doughty, *Seeds of Disaster,* 47–49; Hughes, *Maginot Line,* 199–200; and Kaufmann and Kaufmann, *Fortress France,* 9–10.

32. Quoted in Doughty, *Seeds of Disaster,* 48.

33. See ibid., 48–49; Rowe, *Great Wall of France,* 24, 42–43; Kaufmann and Kaufmann, *Fortress France,* 9–10; and Hughes, *Maginot Line,* 200.

34. See Alexander, "Defense of the Maginot Line," 170–71; Rowe, *Great Wall of France,* 25–26, 42; Hughes, *Maginot Line,* 199–200; Kaufmann and Kaufmann, *Fortress France,* 10–11; and Doughty, *Seeds of Disaster,* 48–49.

35. John Keiger, "Raymond Poincaré and the Ruhr Crisis," in *French Foreign and Defense Policy, 1918–1940: The Decline and Fall of a Great Power,* ed. Robert Boyce (New York: Routledge, 1998), 49, 54–55, 59–60, 63; and Robert Tombs and Isabelle Tombs, *That Sweet Enemy: The French and the British from the Sun King to the Present* (New York: Alfred A. Knopf, 2007), 518–19.

36. Keiger, "Poincaré and the Ruhr Crisis," 65–66; and Hughes, *Maginot Line,* 155.

37. See Hughes, *Maginot Line,* 144, 160, 165, 170; and Douglas Porch, "Arms and Alliances: French Grand Strategy and Policy in 1914 and 1940," in *Grand Strategies in War and Peace,* ed. Paul Kennedy (New Haven, CT: Yale University Press, 1991), 136–37.

38. Kiesling, *Arming against Hitler,* 2.

39. Young, *France and the Origins*, 10–15; Doughty, "Illusion of Security," 466; Hughes, *Maginot Line*, 193–94; and Alexander, "Defense of the Maginot Line," 168.

40. Hughes, *Maginot Line*, 156, 159, 178, 188–89, 191; Alexander, "Defense of the Maginot Line," 167; and Robert A. Doughty, "The French Armed Forces, 1918–1940," in *Military Effectiveness*, Vol. 2, *The Intrawar Period*, eds. Allen Millett and Williamson Murray (Boston: Allen and Unwin, 1988), 47.

41. Doughty, *Seeds of Disaster*, 67. See also ibid., 41–43, 47; Young, *Command of France*, 15; and Alexander, "Defense of the Maginot Line," 168.

42. Pierre Guillen, "Franco-Italian Relations in Flux, 1918–1940" in *French Foreign and Defense Policy, 1918–1940: The Decline and Fall of a Great Power*, ed. Robert Boyce (New York: Routledge, 1998), 152–54; Ryan, *Pétain the Soldier*, 262; and Kier, *Imagining War*, 47.

43. Young, *France and the Origins*, 11.

44. Doughty, *Seeds of Disaster*, 25, 45, 51; Kier, *Imagining War*, 47; and Hughes, *Maginot Line*, 193–94, 198, 208.

45. Young, *Command of France*, 16.

46. Eliot A. Cohen and John Gooch, *Military Misfortunes: The Anatomy of Failure in War* (New York: Vintage Books, 1990), 218; and Young, *Command of France*, 13.

47. Doughty, *Seeds of Disaster*, 58; see also Young, *Command of France*, 13–14; Kaufmann and Kaufmann, *Fortress France*, 122; and Rowe, *Great Wall of France*, 18–19.

48. Rowe, *Great Wall of France*, 18, 119; Young, *Command of France*, 14; and Ernest R. May, *Strange Victory: Hitler's Conquest of France* (New York: Hill and Wang, 2000), 118.

49. Young, *Command of France*, 14.

50. Doughty, *Seeds of Disaster*, 60; and Hughes, *Maginot Line*, 197.

51. See Doughty, *Seeds of Disaster*, 18–21; Kiesling, *Arming against Hitler*, 63–64, 86; and Kier, *Imagining War*, 56, 65.

52. Hughes, *Maginot Line*, 164, 175–76.

53. Kiesling, *Arming against Hitler*, 64; Doughty, "French Armed Forces," 63, 65; and Kier, *Imagining War*, 73, 76–80.

54. See Hughes, *Maginot Line*, 170–71, 204; Kiesling, *Arming against Hitler*, 68; and Doughty, *Seeds of Disaster*, 19–20, 23.

55. Doughty, *Seeds of Disaster*, 20, 24, 27; Young, *Command of France*, 30; and Hughes, *Maginot Line*, 176–77, 192.

56. Kiesling, *Arming against Hitler*, 64, 85–86, 109, 115; Doughty, *Seeds of Disaster*, 32, 36, 39; and Kier, *Imagining War*, 75.

57. Kier, *Imagining War*, 75.

58. Hughes, *Maginot Line*, 209–10; Doughty, *Seeds of Disaster*, 20, 24, 36, 39; and Kier, *Imagining War*, 65.

59. Doughty, *Seeds of Disaster*, 24.

60. See Doughty, "Illusion of Security," 466, 473–74, 483; Hughes, *Maginot Line*, 158–59, 253; Tombs, *Sweet Enemy*, 507, 515, 517, 519, 524; and Martin Alexander, *The*

Republic in Danger: General Maurice Gamelin and the Politics of French Defense (Cambridge: Cambridge University Press, 1992), 248–49.

61. See Anthony Adamthwaite, *Grandeur and Misery: France's Bid for Power in Europe 1914–1940* (New York: St. Martin's Press, 1995), 136; Doughty, "Illusion of Security," 476–78; Young, *France and the Origins,* 64; and Kier, *Imagining War,* 51.

62. See Doughty, "Illusion of Security," 477, 480–81; Alexander, *Republic in Danger,* 210–11; and Young, *France and the Origins,* 17–18.

63. Kier, *Imagining War,* 50; Doughty, "Illusion of Security," 466; and Adamthwaite, *Grandeur and Misery,* 137.

64. Alexander, *Republic in Danger,* 172, 187–88; Young, *France and the Origins,* 17; and Doughty, "Illusion of Security," 476, 482.

65. Kier, *Imagining War,* 65.

66. Doughty, *Seeds of Disaster,* 16; see also Kier, *Imagining War,* 55–59, 65; Kiesling, *Arming against Hitler,* 115, 124; Doughty, *Seeds of Disaster,* 14, 57; and Alexander, *Republic in Danger,* 179–80.

67. Young, *Command of France,* 29; Doughty, *Seeds of Disaster,* 67–68; and Alexander, "Defense of the Maginot Line," 166, 168–69.

68. Kier, *Imagining War,* 50, 67–68.

69. Alexander, "Defense of the Maginot Line," 166.

70. See Kier, *Imagining War,* 42–46, 56; Hughes, *Maginot Line,* 80; and Doughty, *Seeds of Disaster,* 4, 8–10, 33; Hughes *Maginot Line,* 70–71; and Kiesling, *Arming against Hitler,* 21, 135, 137, 140.

71. Doughty, *Seeds of Disaster,* 9.

72. See Hughes, *Maginot Line,* 71; Kiesling, *Arming against Hitler,* 121, 135, 139, 140, 143; Doughty, "French Armed Forces," 53–54, 57, 60; and Kier, *Imagining War,* 73, 75.

73. Alexander, "Defense of the Maginot Line," 167; Doughty, *Seeds of Disaster,* 43; and Young, *Command of France,* 16–17.

74. Adamthwaite, *Grandeur and Misery,* 146–47; and Porch, "Arms and Alliances," 134–35.

75. Young, *Command of France,* 17.

76. Kevin Passmore, "The Republic in Crisis," in *Modern France, 1880–2002,* ed. James McMillan (New York: Oxford University Press, 2003), 108–10; Tombs, *Sweet Enemy,* 509–10, 517; and Denise Artaud, "Reparations and War Debts: The Restoration of French Financial Power, 1919–1929," in *French Foreign and Defense Policy, 1918–1940: The Decline and Fall of a Great Power,* ed. Robert Boyce (New York: Routledge, 1998), 89–90.

77. Artaud, "Reparations and War Debts," 90; Alexander, "Defense of the Maginot Line," 190; and Adamthwaite, *Grandeur and Misery,* 116.

78. Doughty, "French Armed Forces," 43; and Hughes, *Maginot Line,* 110.

79. See Artaud, "Reparations and War Debts," 102–4, 107–8, 116; Hughes, *Maginot Line,* 209; Tombs, *Sweet Enemy,* 527–28; and Passmore, "Republic in Crisis," 111–12.

80. See Passmore, "Republic in Crisis," 42, 47–50, 72; May, *Strange Victory*, 156; and Kiesling, *Arming against Hitler*, 23.

81. Doughty, *Seeds of Disaster*, 44, 57; Alexander, *Republic in Danger*, 179–80; and Kier, *Imagining War*, 55, 57, 62, 65–67.

82. Passmore, "Republic in Crisis," 42, 52, 54–56.

83. Kier, *Imagining War*, 56–57, 59–60, 64; Doughty, *Seeds of Disaster*, 57; and Alexander, *Republic in Danger*, 179–80.

84. See Adamthwaite, *Grandeur and Misery*, 115–16; Passmore, "Republic in Crisis," 51–52; and Kier, *Imaging War*, 64, 66, 84.

85. Hughes, *Maginot Line*, 101; Doughty, "French Armed Forces," 41; and David Chuter, *Humanity's Soldier: France and International Security, 1919–2001* (Providence: Berghahn Books, 1996), 128.

86. Chuter, *Humanity's Soldier*, 128.

87. Alexander, *Republic in Danger*, 185.

88. Hughes, *Maginot Line*, 101, 107; Doughty, "French Armed Forces," 41; and Young, *Command of France*, 24–25.

89. Porch, "Arms and Alliances," 141–42; Young, *Command of France*, 24–25; and Kier, *Imagining War*, 59–60.

90. Hughes, *Maginot Line*, 103.

91. Doughty, *Seeds of Disaster*, 47.

92. Porch, "Arms and Alliances," 142; see also Alexander, "Defense of the Maginot Line," 172; Doughty, *Seeds of Disaster*, 5–6, 50, 65; Hughes, *Maginot Line*, 45, 54–55, 104, 200; and Ryan, *Pétain the Soldier*, 197–98.

93. See Hughes, *Maginot Line*, 101, 120, 200; Doughty, *Pyrrhic Victory*, 337–38; and Rowe, *Great Wall of France*, 43–45.

94. Alexander, "Defense of the Maginot Line," 167.

95. Tombs, *Sweet Enemy*, 519.

96. See Adamthwaite, *Grandeur and Misery*, 115–19; Young, *France and the Origins*, 15–16; and Raphäelle Ulrich, "Rene Massigli and Germany, 1919–1938," in *French Foreign and Defense Policy, 1918–1940: The Decline and Fall of a Great Power*, ed. Robert Boyce (New York: Routledge, 1998), 133, 137–38.

97. Adamthwaite, *Grandeur and Misery*, 125.

98. Young, *France and the Origins*, 12; see also Ulrich, "Rene Massigli and Germany," 140–41; and Adamthwaite, *Grandeur and Misery*, 128, 139.

99. Adamthwaite, *Grandeur and Misery*, 138.

100. Ibid., 119, 126–29; Doughty, "French Armed Forces," 40; and Ulrich, "Rene Massigli and Germany," 137.

101. Ulrich, "Rene Massigli and Germany," 137.

102. Hughes, *Maginot Line*, 184; and Doughty, "Illusion of Security," 474–75.

103. Young, *Command of France*, 162; and Doughty, "Illusion of Security," 474–75.

104. Doughty, "Illusion of Security," 475.

105. Young, *Command of France*, 17.

106. Doughty, "Illusion of Security," 495; and Alexander, "Defense of the Maginot Line," 185.

107. See Doughty, *Seeds of Disaster*, 32, 39, 52–53, 60; Hughes, *Maginot Line*, 205, 210–11; Young, *Command of France*, 26–27; and Kier, *Imagining War*, 41–42, 54, 73, 76.

108. See Hughes, *Maginot Line*, 69, 173; Doughty, *Seeds of Disaster*, 57–58; Alexander, "Defense of the Maginot Line," 169–70; and Young, *Command of France*, 26.

109. Alexander, "Defense of the Maginot Line," 178–79, 185.

110. See Alexander, *Republic in Danger*, 172; Hughes, *Maginot Line*, 212; and Doughty, *Seeds of Disaster*, 65.

111. Alexander, "Defense of the Maginot Line," 185; see also Doughty, *Seeds of Disaster*, 62; Young, *France and the Origins*, 62–63; and Rowe, *Great Wall of France*, 61–62.

112. Kier, *Imagining War*, 66–67.

113. See Doughty, *Seeds of Disaster*, 53, 67; Alexander, "Defense of the Maginot Line," 184–85; and Kier, *Imaging War*, 66–67.

114. Doughty, *Seeds of Disaster*, 29, 32, 47, 52, 67; Kaufmann and Kaufmann, *Maginot Line*, 85–86; and Hughes, *Maginot Line*, 173.

115. Ryan, *Pétain the Soldier*, 250.

116. Alexander, "Defense of the Maginot Line," 179; and Hughes, *Maginot Line*, 58.

117. Kaufmann and Kaufmann, *Maginot Line*, 11.

118. See Doughty, *Seeds of Disaster*, 44, 55, 59; Young, *Command of France*, 31; Alexander, "Defense of the Maginot Line," 168–70, 178–79, 184–85; Ryan, *Pétain the Soldier*, 247, 251–53, 262, 278; May, *Strange Victory*, 9; and Kier, *Imagining War*, 68.

119. Alexander, *Republic in Danger*, 200; and Doughty, "French Armed Forces," 53.

120. Doughty, *Seeds of Disaster*, 44; Kier, *Imagining War*, 68; and Alexander, "Defense of the Maginot Line," 178–79.

121. Hughes, *Maginot Line*, 206; Rowe, *Great Wall of France*, 23; and Kaufmann and Kaufmann, *Maginot Line*, 11–12.

122. Kaufmann and Kaufmann, *Maginot Line*, 12; and Doughty, *Seeds of Disaster*, 53.

123. Doughty, *Seeds of Disaster*, 55, 57, 65; and Ryan, *Pétain the Soldier*, 247.

124. Kier, *Imagining War*, 42; and Hughes, *Maginot Line*, 201.

125. Alexander, "Defense of the Maginot Line," 172.

126. Doughty, *Seeds of Disaster*, 50; see also ibid., 49; Kaufmann and Kaufmann, *Fortress France*, 12–13; and Alexander, "Defense of the Maginot Line," 172.

127. Alexander, "Defense of the Maginot Line," 172.

128. Ibid., 186; see also Doughty, *Seeds of Disaster*, 50–51; Kaufmann and Kaufmann, *Fortress France*, 13; Ryan, *Pétain the Soldier*, 249; and Kier, *Imagining War*, 42.

129. Doughty, *Seeds of Disaster*, 52; and Kier, *Imagining War*, 42.

130. Doughty, *Seeds of Disaster*, 52.

131. Ibid., 56; and Kaufmann and Kaufmann, *Maginot Line*, 10–11.

132. Doughty, *Seeds of Disaster,* 52–53; and Kier, *Imagining War,* 42.

133. Doughty, "Illusion of Security," 490.

134. Doughty, *Seeds of Disaster,* 54–55, 506; and Kaufmann and Kaufmann, *Maginot Line,* 12.

135. Doughty, *Seeds of Disaster,* 55, 65; and Ryan, *Pétain the Soldier,* 254.

136. See Kaufmann and Kaufmann, *Fortress France,* 14; Doughty, *Seeds of Disaster,* 55–58, 67; Alexander, "Defense of the Maginot Line," 171; and Ryan, *Pétain the Soldier,* 254–55.

137. Doughty, *Seeds of Disaster,* 58–59.

138. Young, *France and the Origins,* 62.

139. See Doughty, *Seeds of Disaster,* 58–60, 62, 67; Hughes, *Maginot Line,* 197, 207, 213; Young, *Command of France,* 14; and Alexander, *Republic in Danger,* 172, 174–75, 200.

140. See Doughty, *Seeds of Disaster,* 57; Alexander, "Defense of the Maginot Line," 170, 172–73; Hughes, *Maginot Line,* 120; Rowe, *Great Wall of France,* 44–45; and Kaufmann and Kaufmann, *Fortress France,* 21–22.

141. Alexander, "Defense of the Maginot Line," 178, 182–83; Kaufmann and Kaufmann, *Fortress France,* 15; and Rowe, *Great Wall of France,* 50.

142. Hughes, *Maginot Line,* 205, 214–15; and Doughty, *Seeds of Disaster,* 57.

143. Hughes, *Maginot Line,* 214.

144. Alexander, "Defense of the Maginot Line," 186.

145. See Doughty, *Seeds of Disaster,* 57–58; Hughes, *Maginot Line,* 206; Kaufmann and Kaufmann, *Fortress France,* 15, 22; and Rowe, *Great Wall of France,* 17, 43–52.

146. Hughes, *Maginot Line,* 249.

147. Rowe, *Great Wall of France,* 50; Alexander, "Defense of the Maginot Line," 179; and Kaufmann and Kaufmann, *Fortress France,* 22–23.

148. Young, *France and the Origins,* 20–21; and Adamthwaite, *Grandeur and Misery,* 131–32.

149. Ryan, *Pétain the Soldier,* 265, 267; Alexander, *Republic in Danger,* 173–74, 183–85; and Kaufmann and Kaufmann, *Fortress France,* 85.

150. See Alexander, *Republic in Danger,* 174–75, 181, 184–86; and Doughty, *Seeds of Disaster,* 63, 65.

151. Alexander, *Republic in Danger,* 184.

152. Ibid., 186.

153. Ibid., 184.

154. Doughty, *Seeds of Disaster,* 63.

155. Alexander, *Republic in Danger,* 186.

156. See ibid., 173, 185–86.

157. See ibid., 175–79.

158. Young, *Command of France,* 38–39; Alexander, "Defense of the Maginot Line," 175; and May, *Strange Victory,* 121.

159. Adamthwaite, *Grandeur and Misery,* 149.

160. Alexander, "Defense of the Maginot Line," 174, 190.

161. May, *Strange Victory*, 130; Alexander, "Defense of the Maginot Line," 173; and Kier, *Imagining War*, 84.

162. Alexander, "Defense of the Maginot Line," 179–80; Kaufmann and Kaufmann, *Fortress France*, 21; and Ryan, *Pétain the Soldier*, 256, 273.

163. Alexander, *Republic in Danger*, 197; and Young, *Command of France*, 59.

164. Kiesling, *Arming against Hitler*, 131.

165. Alexander, *Republic in Danger*, 174, 181; and Young, *Command of France*, 59.

166. Doughty, *Seeds of Disaster*, 59.

167. Adamthwaite, *Grandeur and Misery*, 151.

168. See Doughty, *Seeds of Disaster*, 62, 64–65; Hughes, *Maginot Line*, 216; Kaufmann and Kaufmann, *Maginot Line*, 71; Allcorn, *Maginot Line*, 33; Alexander, *Republic in Danger*, 197; and Ryan, *Pétain the Soldier*, 268.

169. Adamthwaite, *Grandeur and Misery*, 151, 154; Alexander, "Defense of the Maginot Line," 180–81; and Young, *France and the Origins*, 25.

170. Alexander, *Republic in Danger*, 50; and Adamthwaite, *Grandeur and Misery*, 154.

171. Doughty, *Seeds of Disaster*, 39; and Tombs, *Sweet Enemy*, 529–30.

172. Allcorn, *Maginot Line*, 44.

173. Young, *France and the Origins*, 25; Doughty, *Seeds of Disaster*, 37–39; and Hughes, *Maginot Line*, 56, 245.

174. See Young, *France and the Origins*, 26, 60; May, *Strange Victory*, 148; and Doughty, "Illusion of Security," 478–79, 484, 495–96.

175. See Doughty, "French Armed Forces," 41; Alexander, *Republic in Danger*, 28; Young, *France and the Origins*, 72; Young, *Command of France*, 166, 179; Kier, *Imagining War*, 48, 61; and May, *Strange Victory*, 123, 130–31.

176. See Alexander, *Republic in Danger*, 188–91; Young, *Command of France*, 152–53, 179, 249; and Doughty, *Seeds of Disaster*, 65.

177. See Alexander, *Republic in Danger*, 196–98; Kier, *Imagining War*, 54; Ryan, *Pétain the Soldier*, 268; Young, *Command of France*, 167; and Kaufmann and Kaufmann, *Maginot Line*, 73.

178. Alexander, "Defense of the Maginot Line," 184; see also Alexander, *Republic in Danger*, 196–98, 204; May, *Strange Victory*, 288; Ryan, *Pétain the Soldier*, 269; and Young, *France and the Origins*, 63.

179. Kaufmann and Kaufmann, *Fortress France*, 6–8.

180. Chuter, *Humanity's Soldier*, 118–20; Kier, *Imagining War*, 80–82; and Adamthwaite, *Grandeur and Misery*, 151.

181. Kier, *Imagining War*, 77, 82; and Chuter, *Humanity's Soldier*, 122.

182. Doughty, *Seeds of Disaster*, 68.

183. Adamthwaite, *Grandeur and Misery*, 151.

184. Young, *Command of France*, 169.

185. Ibid.; and Alexander, *Republic in Danger*, 200–201.

186. May, *Strange Victory*, 288.

187. See Kaufmann and Kaufmann, *Fortress France*, 131, 134, 139, 150; Allcorn, *Maginot Line*, 47; and Young, *France and the Origins*, 34.

188. Kaufmann and Kaufmann, *Fortress France*, 151.

189. May, *Strange Victory*, 8; for contrasting views, see ibid., 204–7; Kiesling, *Arming against Hitler*, 170; Tombs, *Sweet Enemy*, 542–43; and Talbot C. Imlay, *Facing the Second World War: Strategy, Politics, and Economics in Britain and France, 1938–1940* (New York: Oxford University Press, 1995), 42, 50–51.

190. Imlay, *Facing the Second World War*, 42, 46–47, 51–56, 63–64, 70–73.

191. Kaufmann and Kaufmann, *Fortress France*, 122, 143, 146; and Ryan, *Pétain the Soldier*, 281.

192. Doughty, "Illusion of Security," 493–95.

193. Kiesling, *Arming against Hitler*, 169; see also Alexander, "Defense of the Maginot Line," 187; Kaufmann and Kaufmann, *Maginot Line*, 141–42; and Edward N. Luttwak, *Strategy: The Logic of War and Peace* (Cambridge, MA: Harvard University Press, 1987), 120.

194. Cohen and Gooch, *Military Misfortunes*, 220.

195. See Young, *France and the Origins*, 35; Kiesling, *Arming against Hitler*, 10, 62, 83–84, 115, 173; Doughty, *Seeds of Disaster*, 3–5, 71, 184; Alexander, "Defense of the Maginot Line," 184, 186–87; and May, *Strange Victory*, 5–7, 423–24, 448, 451–52, 460.

196. See Kaufmann, *Fortress France*, 161–62; and Doughty, *Seeds of Disaster*, 69.

197. See Doughty, *Seeds of Disaster*, 69; Kaufmann and Kaufmann, *Fortress France*, 77, 163, 165–66, 169–70; and Alexander, "Defense of the Maginot Line," 187.

198. See Kaufmann and Kaufmann, *Fortress France*, 167–74; Allcorn, *Maginot Line*, 49, 56; Doughty, *Seeds of Disaster*, 69–70; Rowe, *Great Wall of France*, 13–14; Ryan, *Pétain the Soldier*, 261; and Rowe, *Great Wall of France*, 294.

199. See Allcorn, *Maginot Line*, 58–59; Kaufmann, *Fortress France*, 181; and Alexander, "Defense of the Maginot Line," 187–88.

200. Doughty, *Seeds of Disaster*, 69–70; Alexander, "Defense of the Maginot Line," 164–65, 187; Kaufmann and Kaufmann, *Maginot Line*, 141–42; Rowe, *Great Wall of France*, 13, 294; and Ryan, *Pétain the Soldier*, 260, 262.

201. Luttwak, *Strategy*, 120.

202. See Doughty, *Seeds of Disaster*, 3–5, 71, 184; Alexander, "Defense of the Maginot Line," 184, 186–87; May, *Strange Victory*, 5–7, 448, 451–52, 460; Kiesling, *Arming against Hitler*, 10, 62, 83–84, 115; Kaufmann and Kaufmann, *Fortress France*, 157–58; and Young, *France and the Origins*, 57–59.

203. Hughes, *Maginot Line*, 213.

204. Ibid., 56, 211, 230, 245, 249; Doughty, "French Armed Forces," 52–53.

205. Hughes, *Maginot Line*, 211.

206. Alexander, "Defense of the Maginot Line," 179.

207. Rowe, *Great Wall of France*, 52; Kaufmann and Kaufmann, *Maginot Line*, 15, 93–100; Kiesling, *Arming against Hitler*, 131; and Young, *Command of France*, 31.

208. Kaufmann and Kaufmann, *Fortress France*, 134.

209. Alexander, "Defense of the Maginot Line," 179; see also Doughty, *Seeds of Disaster,* 70; Ryan, *Pétain the Soldier,* 271, 273; May, *Strange Victory,* 120; Rowe, *Great Wall of France,* 295; and Kaufmann and Kaufmann, *Fortress France,* 134.

210. Ryan, *Pétain the Soldier,* 271; see also May, *Strange Victory,* 120; and Young, *Command of France,* 31.

211. Allcorn, *Maginot Line,* 48.

212. Kiesling, *Arming against Hitler,* 130–31; Alexander, "Defense of the Maginot Line," 166; Doughty, *Seeds of Disaster,* 184; Hughes, *Maginot Line,* 203; Young, *Command of France,* 61; Rowe, *Great Wall of France,* 295; Ryan, *Pétain the Soldier,* 271; and May, *Strange Victory,* 120.

213. Alexander, *Republic in Danger,* 272.

214. Kiesling, *Arming against Hitler,* 131.

215. Hughes, *Maginot Line,* 203.

216. May, *Strange Victory,* 288–89.

217. Young, *Command of France,* 62–63.

218. Alexander, *Republic in Danger,* 180; see also Alexander, "Defense of the Maginot Line," 176–77, 182.

219. Alexander, *Republic in Danger,* 174, 182.

220. Doughty, "Illusion of Security," 495–96.

221. Alexander, *Republic in Danger,* 184; Kier, *Imagining War,* 42; and Ryan, *Pétain the Soldier,* 250.

222. Kiesling, *Arming against Hitler,* 4, 188; Doughty, *Seeds of Disaster,* 69, 184; and Alexander, "Defense of the Maginot Line," 166.

223. Chuter, *Humanity's Soldier,* 126.

7

The Bar-Lev Line

Citadels in the Sand

Introduction

Israel's Bar-Lev Line provides an excellent opportunity to examine the dynamics of strategic defenses erected on recently seized foreign soil, in contrast to the preceding cases, which generally protected established national territory or long-held possessions. Israeli leaders decided to fortify the east bank of the Suez Canal little over a year after gaining control of the Sinai Peninsula. Although not wanting to retain the area permanently, the Israelis aimed to trade it for a peace treaty with Egypt. The Israeli Defense Forces (IDF) had demonstrated a vast superiority over the Egyptian military in the Six-Day War, but holding this forward position against a determined foe presented a considerable challenge. Operating at a huge resources detriment, the IDF above all hoped to deter aggression. Failing that goal, the Bar-Lev Line attempted to minimize the cost of both low-level and intense combat. How did the obstacle influence Egyptian attitudes and behavior, especially given its placement on occupied soil? As a discontinuous, minimal barrier with an important political purpose, did it alter the military balance, and if so how? Given its limitations, a related critical question concerns how it was integrated into the broader Sinai defense effort. The barrier made a seemingly untenable situation tenable, giving Israeli decision makers the confidence to pursue a desired course of action. Although beneficial in the short term, did this contribution entail longer-term consequences that undermined Israeli security?

The chapter follows the standard format by laying out the contextual factors that bound the Israeli decision environment. The case offers an interesting angle because the nature of the challenge did not align with IDF military strengths and the nation's strategic culture. Nevertheless, the Israelis chose a barrier approach that was at odds with their preferred modus operandi. The War of Attrition (March 1969–August 1970), which commenced partially as a response to the Bar-Lev Line's construction, provides ample opportunity to evaluate its performance. The chapter then considers the disputed lessons learned amid an intense postwar debate over whether to repair the structure, alter it, or abandon it. The Bar-Lev Line would be a source of considerable tension within the Israeli High Command for the next half decade.

While the line was rebuilt and continued to play a role in defense planning for the Sinai, personnel changes and budget constraints left it in a reduced state by the Yom Kippur War (October 1973). The legacy of this conflict tarnished the barrier's reputation, despite its never being intended to play more than a modest role in the Sinai's defense. As the most recent and modest of the six strategic defenses covered in this book, the Bar-Lev Line lacks the stature and fame of its predecessors, but it provides an excellent vehicle to examine the effects of frontier works on the adversary and the wall-builder.

The decision to create this barrier began gaining critical momentum when Minister of Defense Moshe Dayan and senior IDF officers toured the devastated frontline positions on the Suez Canal's east bank on October 27, 1968.[1] Across the narrow water channel, the Egyptian force had grown to more than one hundred thousand men with large amounts of armor and artillery. Its nine-hour, one-thousand-gun shelling along the entire front the day before signaled that a similar, albeit smaller, barrage on September 8 was not an isolated, symbolic effort.[2] The latest Egyptian gunfire left 15 Israelis dead and another 34 wounded. The existing shelters, which Maj. Gen. Avraham "Bren" Adan would later lament "had been prepared very amateurishly," only exacerbated casualties by collapsing on soldiers.[3] Overall losses along the canal since the end of the Six-Day War totaled 101 dead and 300 wounded.[4] Israeli leaders had recognized since the 1967 Arab Summit Conference at Khartoum that the long struggle would continue, but now its costs threatened to rise precipitously. This state of affairs prompted anxiety among government officials, IDF commanders, and the public.[5]

For the government, the occupied Sinai Peninsula was a chit to be exchanged for peace, but until then senior commanders and officials regarded it as a valuable defense asset. The territory supplied considerable strategic depth with more than 100 miles now separating Egyptian forces from Israel proper, and 150 miles to reach Tel Aviv or Jerusalem. The narrow body of water between the large Egyptian force and Israeli troops made any large crossing a difficult and dangerous undertaking. At the time, the Suez Canal ran for approximately 100 miles, and its width, excluding the three lakes, ranged from 160 to 240 yards and its depth about 40 to 50 feet.[6] Dayan characterized it as "one of the best anti-tank ditches available."[7] Possession of the east bank, along with the Israeli Air Force's (IAF) dominance of the skies, had allowed this long front to be held with only a few thousand troops. But the recent Egyptian display of firepower and aggression prompted concern about this enormous force disparity and a decision to add reinforcements. Moreover, the canal provided no protection from shellings, whether by artillery or the thousands of lighter weapons present.

For Dayan and other key decision makers, a range of responses to the Egyptian challenge existed. The simplest reaction would have been to withdraw from the Canal Zone, but this step was regarded as a nonstarter by the Israeli government and unnecessary by the IDF General Staff. If the territorial status quo had to be maintained, Israelis could follow a traditional preference for offensive action to deter further Egyptian aggression. Although political and military factors precluded consideration of a large-scale offensive across the Suez, a reprisal, countervalue attack in the fall 1967 had produced nearly twelve months of quiet. Another such effort had to be carried out to bring home the costs and risks of aggression to Cairo (as well as satisfy the domestic audience), but decision makers did not believe it would silence the Egyptian guns for long.[8]

Thus, while planning and executing the raid, the IDF began to explore defense options for a standing long-term threat. Adan, the respected deputy commander of the Armor Corps, was tapped to lead a diverse team of experts to identify the best approach.[9] A range of defense options existed. Benefiting from the strategic depth and formidable territorial obstacles in central Sinai, the Israelis could have adopted a defense-in-depth strategy. Alternatively, holding the water line could be attempted through (a) the creation of fortifications along the front to block an assault, (b) a mobile force that advanced upon an enemy crossing and pushed the Egyptians back into the water, or (c) a combination of the two methods. Ultimately, the Adan group recommended a line of strongpoints (*maozim*) in conjunction with other obstacles along the canal to demonstrate Israel's presence and provide early warning at an acceptable cost.[10] During the approval process for this approach, senior commanders increased by 50 percent the number of maozim to enhance the barrier's defensive capability. These strongpoints and supporting elements would soon become misleadingly known as the "Bar-Lev Line" in the media after the IDF chief of staff, Lt. Gen. Chaim Bar-Lev.

By early March 1969, after three intense months of work, thousands of Israeli soldiers and civilians had nearly completed "the largest engineering operation ever undertaken in Israel."[11] While work would continue for several more months and some elements had to be abandoned in response to belated Egyptian fire, the IDF declared the barrier operational on March 15, 1969. The first component was a sand embankment along the east bank to block prying Egyptian eyes, protect against direct fire weapons, and prevent vehicles from driving over it. Behind this obstacle the IDF erected the system core of twenty-eight maozim along the Suez Canal as well as two additional strongpoints along its Mediterranean flank. At key locations (i.e., the northern and southern ends, across from

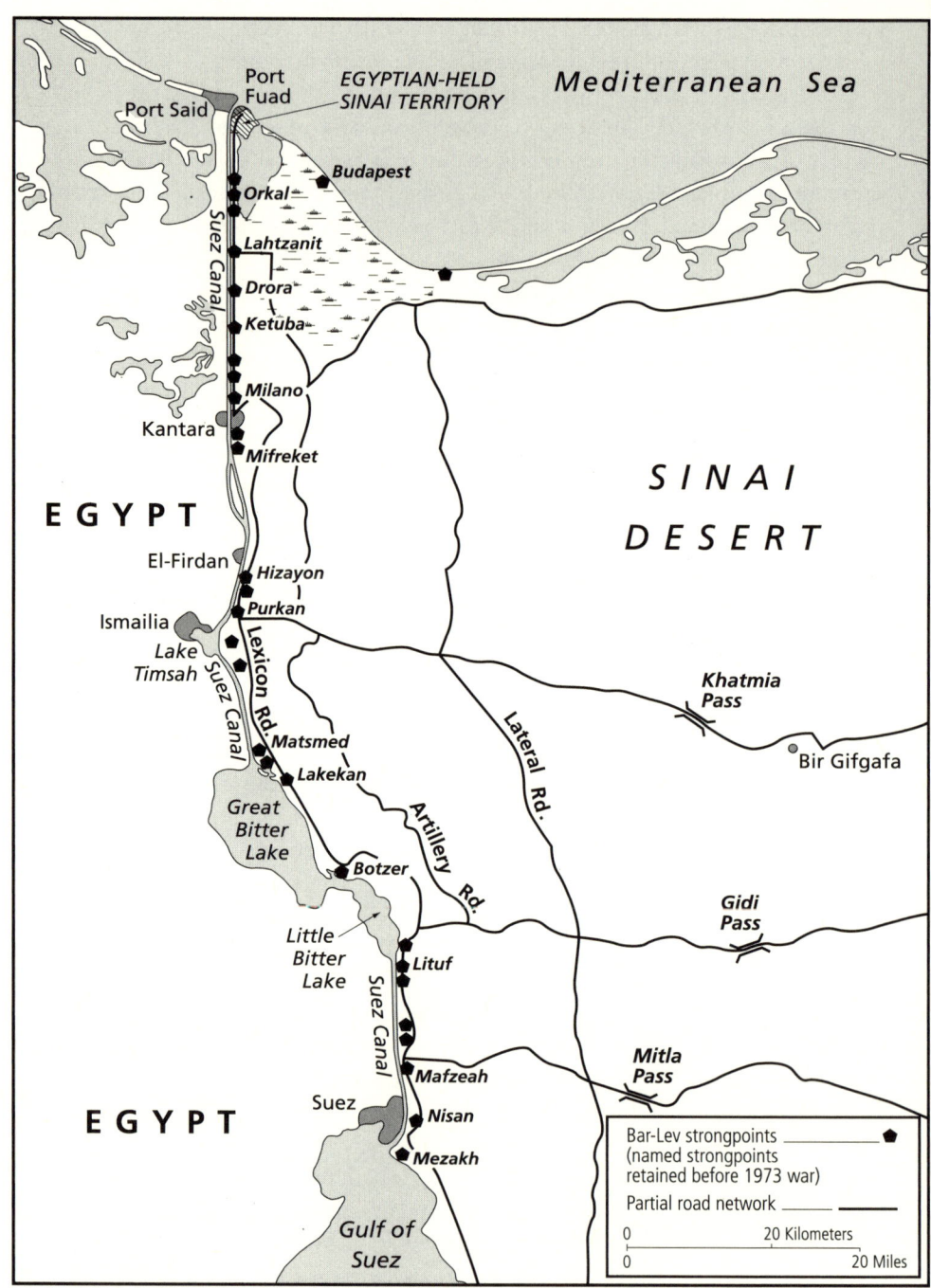

Figure 7.1 Bar-Lev Line and the Western Sinai, 1969–1970

Kantara and Ismailia) the Israelis concentrated these works, usually in groups of three, to provide mutual cover and support. Every strongpoint was actually a central command bunker with "four interconnected fighting positions, each with an attached bunker covered with steel beams as protection against artillery."[12] These bunkers had been designed to withstand intense artillery shelling and successfully tested against the heaviest caliber possessed by the Egyptian army. Equipped with small arms, machine guns, and mortars, the IDF expected the platoon-strength garrisons to hold out for twenty-four to forty-eight hours, even against an all-out attack, albeit with armor and artillery support. The Israelis used barbed wire and minefields to protect the strongpoints as well as cover the gaps between these structures. As part of the overall Sinai defense approach, behind the Bar-Lev Line the IDF added tank ramps, supply depots, artillery positions, and an improved road network. This infrastructure enabled better patrolling, support of the Bar-Lev Line garrisons, and reinforcement in a major operation. The general staff also decided to increase the Sinai-based force from two to three armored brigades, establishing Israel's first standing armored division.[13]

An Unceasing Struggle for Security

Israel's key decision makers in the late 1960s and early 1970s had been directly involved in the nation's conflict-filled first two decades, making the history particularly relevant in this case. With inexperienced soldiers and inadequate weapons, Israel in 1948 anxiously awaited invasion by the frontline Arab states after declaring independence. Lacking strategic depth, a long-standing element of security policy had been to establish border settlements to "serve as Israel's shock absorbers deterring, holding, or absorbing the first wave of incursion or attack."[14] At one of these kibbutzim (Yad Mordechai) about one kilometer north of the Gaza Strip, fewer than one hundred local men and sixteen elite Palmach soldiers held off a multibattalion, heavily armed Egyptian force for five critical days in mid-May.[15] While Arab media crowed about the eventual capture of "Israel's Maginot Line," its resistance allowed the IDF time to strengthen positions farther north and dampened the morale of the Egyptian soldiers who would never advance near Tel Aviv during the conflict.

The Israelis quickly learned that the Arabs did not regard one failed war as sufficient reason to accept coexistence. Fear remained high over defending a nation in which almost every point was within thirty miles of a hostile state. In part due to the contributions of border kibbutzim during the war, the government soon erected new frontier settlements and took over abandoned Arab villages. Organizationally, the Area Defense System consisted of a "network of fortified border settlements, backed up by military units."[16] From the beginning, Israelis regarded this effort more for fostering Jewish control and limiting small-scale infiltrations than for providing basic defense. The IDF soon concluded that offensive capability represented a better way to deter and defend the fledgling state's frontiers given its geography and the increasing firepower of enemy weapons.[17]

The 1952 overthrow of Egypt's lethargic monarchy by ardent nationalist Gamel Nasser augured greater danger, especially after it completed a huge arms purchase from Czechoslovakia in 1955. Nasser's alienation of the British and French culminating with the Suez Canal's nationalization offered the Israelis an opportunity to weaken their rival before it could fully absorb the Czech arms as well as strengthen ties with the weapons-supplying French. The vastly improved IDF rapidly carried out its component of the war plan by crushing the Egyptian army in the Sinai. The subsequent British and French phase of seizing the Canal Zone, however, unraveled under pressure from Washington. An unhappy U.S. government also coerced Israel to return the Sinai to Egypt without a peace treaty, to the lasting frustration of Israeli officials.[18] Externally the IDF had won a reputation as the premier military in the Middle East. Internally the demonstrated potential for rapid armor offensives further turned the IDF against defensive warfare. For example, a late 1950s proposal to block off with fortifications the approximately forty-mile segment of the Egyptian–Israeli border that was topographically accessible met with negligible interest.[19] As Avner Yaniv observes, given that "there are no traces of any great debate on this issue, it may plausibly be assumed that most of the participants in the debate concurred."[20] Israel's demonstrated military prowess combined with Egypt's decision to forgo basing a large number of forces in the Sinai suggested that the nation's basic security had been much improved.

The Six-Day War

Nasser, the self-proclaimed leader of the Arab world, could not avoid involvement when military skirmishes between Syria and Israel escalated in early 1967. After demanding that the United Nations (UN) remove peacekeeping troops from the Sinai, he deployed more than one hundred thousand Egyptian troops and nine hundred tanks onto the peninsula.[21] Then, despite knowing that closure of the Straits of Tiran was a casus belli, Nasser blocked this outlet on May 22, 1967. Jerusalem viewed Cairo's failure to attack as reflective of an attempt to bankrupt a mobilized Israel or wait for it to demobilize before striking. Although the status quo was unsustainable, the government of Levi Eshkol hesitated amid mounting domestic pressure.[22] In response, on June 1, Eshkol formed a National Unity government that included the main opposition parties and installed Moshe Dayan, the highly regarded former chief of staff, as defense minister.

On June 4 the Israeli government decided to strike preemptively the next day, first against Egypt and then the other Arab states. A brilliantly designed and executed air campaign almost completely destroyed the Egyptian Air Force within hours, ensuring complete air superiority. Initial plans to seize just the Gaza Strip had been dropped by Dayan in favor of a more ambitious strategy to crush Egyptian ground forces in the Sinai. The Israelis overwhelmed the opposing frontline units, prompting panic and a disorderly retreat throughout the entire Egyptian Army. Focused on eliminating Egyptian units on the peninsula, the IDF (and the government) did not have an explicit territorial objective.[23] From a purely military perspective, the canal itself marked the most natural stopping point, but Dayan had recently warned the general staff that "should the IDF reach the Suez Canal the war will never end."[24] Instead Dayan viewed control of the Gidi and Mitla passes through the mountains twenty to forty miles east of the waterway as the optimal cease-fire line. The defense minister ordered IDF troops to stay far from the Suez, but soldiers' momentum in pursuit of retreating Egyptians soon carried them to the waterline. Given this new reality, Dayan dropped his opposition and Israeli troops reached the canal in force on June 8.[25] By the time the Egyptian leader capitulated early on June 9, Israel controlled all of the Sinai except for Port Fuad at its terrain-protected extreme northeastern corner. Overall, the war ended with Israel in control of the Sinai Peninsula, the Gaza Strip, the West Bank, the Golan Heights, and East Jerusalem.

The Postwar Occupation

The rout prompted joyous celebration in Israel and astonishment throughout the world but left the government in somewhat of a quandary over the seized territory. The occupation of 26,476 square miles (23,622 square miles from the Sinai) quadrupled the area under Israeli control.[26] The annexation of East Jerusalem was a given for almost all Israelis, and other areas—especially the West Bank—had religious and historic significance. By contrast, the Sinai held no such attraction. Rather, its value was strategic, providing previously nonexistent territorial depth, satisfying a majority of Israel's oil requirement, and ensuring access through the Straits of Tiran.[27]

Leaders coalesced into two general perspectives ("the politicians" and the "security men") about the occupied territory. The politicians, including Foreign Minister Abba Eban, favored trading all the occupied territory except East Jerusalem for peace. In contrast, the security men, led by the influential labor minister Yigal Allon, believed the Arabs remained unwilling to end the struggle and wanted to retain most of the new territory to bolster Israel's security. IDF generals populated both camps, but the security men, including Chief of Staff Bar-Lev, exerted more influence. Dayan exhibited support for both perspectives by declaring "I'm waiting for the phone to ring" to exchange the occupied land for peace, but adding that he did not expect a call.[28] Similarly, Prime Minister

Eshkol tried to balance between the two groups by advocating that returned land become demilitarized zones.[29]

After several days of discussion, the cabinet on June 19 secretly approved exchanging the entire Sinai for peace under certain conditions.[30] Egypt had to (a) accept demilitarization of the Sinai; (b) guarantee freedom of navigation in the Straits of Tiran, Gulf of Aqaba, and Suez Canal; and (c) guarantee overflight rights of the Straits of Tiran and Gulf of Aqaba. Cabinet members believed peace was possible given Israel's strategic superiority and possession of valued Arab territory. Revisionist historians, however, stress that Israel's desire for even modest permanent gains including East Jerusalem undermined any grand deal while Arab politics made it problematic for Egypt to negotiate separately.[31] The broad sentiment for trading land for peace with Egypt and Syria quickly evaporated within the Israeli elite, with military leaders expressing concern particularly about relinquishing the Golan Heights.[32]

Regardless, a chagrined Nasser had no interest in a deal. After briefly resigning, he resumed office intent on rebuilding the military to recover the Sinai and restore his prestige. The Egyptians referred to the war as *Nakhsa* ("setback") rather than defeat. A frustrated and humiliated Soviet government rushed more than fifty thousand tons of military equipment to an almost defenseless Egypt and soon agreed to a long-term buildup. Bolstered by the new arms, the Egyptians soon began striking across the Suez. The first serious incident occurred on July 1 when an attack of an IDF armored patrol destroyed a few tanks, killed the unit leader, and wounded thirteen. Wanting to demonstrate control over the east bank to UN officials, the IDF front commander deployed troops to eighteen positions along the canal and laid minefields between them. Violence then broke out on the water as the parties disputed whether the cease-fire line fell in the middle of the waterway (Israel) or the east bank (Egypt). After a major skirmish with craft sunk on both sides, the Suez Canal would remain devoid of all ships. The late summer Arab conference at Khartoum accentuated Egyptian resistance. At its conclusion, the Arabs issued a communiqué avowing no negotiation with Israel, no recognition of Israel, and no peace with Israel. The "three nos" declaration confirmed what had already seemed evident to Israeli leaders: the type of "land for peace" exchange approved by the cabinet on June 19 would not occur.[33]

With its military sufficiently recovered to deny an easy Israeli advance toward Cairo, the Egyptian government escalated attacks on IDF targets. Beginning with a raid on Israeli shipping in the Gulf of Suez, the Egyptians commenced a half dozen artillery barrages in September. Israel's modest return fire caused limited damage, but it did prompt many Egyptian civilians to flee the canal cities. On October 21, a ship in Port Said harbor sank the Israeli destroyer *Eilat*, which had been patrolling nearby. The loss of the navy's flagship in conjunction with the earlier attacks prompted anger and frustration in Israel. Needing to launch a stronger response, IDF artillery and aircraft shifted from military to the countervalue targets of Suez City's petroleum installations. The resulting conflagration burned for days, destroying 80 percent of Egypt's refining capacity and greatly expediting the exodus of civilians remaining in the Canal Zone. Cairo suspended attacks and concentrated on strengthening its military.[34]

Egyptian aggression in combination with the "three nos" declaration also had hardened Israel's diplomatic position. On October 30, the cabinet replaced the June 19 terms (land for peace) with a more nebulous position that agreements with Egypt (and Syria) must ensure the nation's security.[35] Many Israelis still believed that the land-for-peace formula would work, but it would have to be at a future date. In the near term, Dayan expressed Israel's challenge as, "we must sit at the Suez Canal until we achieve our goals of peace. It is difficult but possible. We must be prepared for a long sitting and to operate so that we do not surrender to pressure."[36] A tense but quiet situation would hold for nearly a year, with occasional dust-ups, until the Egyptians initiated the large-scale shellings described earlier.

Decision Context

Environmental cues complicated Israeli decision making as particular contextual factors conflicted with each other regarding security policy on the Sinai. This dynamic exacerbated by some important misperceptions helped fuel disagreement among key actors on the best approach.

Threat Perception

Although Egyptian attacks along the canal raised concern, the Israelis retained high confidence, especially against a full-scale attack. Leaders stressed that the newly acquired strategic depth meant the Egyptian army would have to cross the canal and advance over one hundred miles of desert to reach Israel. With all Egyptian airbases pushed east of the canal, warning time for air strikes had quadrupled from four to sixteen minutes.[37] Beyond the enhanced territorial position, the Egyptian military's woeful performance in 1967 suggested little reason to worry about a threat to the homeland. Adan would later sum up the attitude of senior IDF officers at the time: "since the Arabs had not succeeded in the past under better conditions for them, we felt confident—too confident—that they could not succeed in the new situation."[38] Ariel Sharon would later observe that the popular Israeli perspective was "that the Arabs were not capable of fighting a modern war . . . they had no hope of closing the gap."[39] The high command did not expect the Egyptians to attempt a major crossing of the Suez until they perceived a fundamental shift in the military balance, especially neutralization of the IAF.[40] Whereas before, the IDF had days or even weeks to mobilize while the enemy moved into the Sinai, the Egyptian army would now be massed on the west bank able to advance with little notice. Nevertheless, Israeli commanders downplayed the loss of these obvious visual cues given their optimism and extreme faith in the intelligence services.[41]

The Israelis did closely follow the Egyptian buildup along the west bank. A combination of Saudi aid and enormous Soviet largesse ensured Cairo's rapid rearmament as well as operation of a standing large army. By September 1968 Moscow had completely offset war losses with upgrades, especially for aircraft and armor. Soviet willingness to provide replacement weapons allowed the Egyptians to engage the IDF without regard to diminishing their strength. Similarly, Egypt's large population, which had surpassed 30 million, allowed maintenance of a two-hundred-thousand-man standing army without stifling the economy. The force bordering the canal in multiple lines now included more than one hundred thousand troops with five hundred tanks and hundreds of artillery pieces. The Israelis knew that the 1967 disaster had prompted Nasser to replace his politically focused military hierarchy, but they did not appreciate the significance of these changes believing "that the 'quality gap' was not declining but actually was still growing."[42]

Israeli political and military leaders underestimated the threat because they did not appreciate Egypt's intense commitment to regaining the Sinai. Before 1967, while Egyptian officials spewed anti-Israeli invective and took provocative actions, their wish for Israel's destruction was not matched by the necessary effort. Now the Egyptian leadership and society were highly motivated to recapture a large part of their nation that had been seized in humiliating fashion by a hated enemy regardless of their pre-1967 attitude toward the lightly populated area.[43] As Yaniv observes, "The thought that the Egyptians would find the continued occupation of the Sinai by the IDF an intolerable situation, whose termination justified almost any price, seldom occurred to the Israelis."[44] The Egyptians believed their possession of disproportionate interests helped offset their military inferiority.

Although Israeli decision makers underestimated the costs and risks Egyptian leaders would be willing to run in pursuit of the Sinai's recovery, pessimism grew about a negotiated solution. Even before the heavy shellings of September and October, many Israeli leaders including Dayan and Eshkol had become bearish about ever reaching a peace agreement with Nasser. By late September 1968 even the usually optimistic Eban lamented Egypt's "hardening of the ideological intransigence, extreme adherence to the principles formulated in Khartoum, and total refusal even to dream of peace with Israel."[45] After the October 26 attack, officials realized they had to "reassess Egyptians intentions behind local belligerency and to seek new means of deterrence for both the long and short runs."[46] Israeli leaders did not regard such a "warming up" of the front as prelude to a general war but rather an attempt to pressure change by making the position of frontline IDF soldiers intolerable.[47] Plus, if Cairo created enough instability, the great powers might intervene and coerce Israel's withdrawal without requiring a full Arab–Israeli peace agreement. Increased Egyptian provocations only prompted the Israelis to see "continuation of the territorial, political, and military status quo as the condition for securing the wished-for peace and security."[48]

Given resource limitations, this section concludes with a brief sketch of Israeli thinking about the other security challenges. Vengeful Syrians wanted to regain the Golan Heights as much as, if not more than, the Egyptians wanted the Sinai. Yet Jerusalem believed that Damascus, with a far smaller resource base, would not launch a major attack unless in conjunction with Cairo.[49] Jordan had suffered the greatest losses in the war, significantly eroding its military capability and political will to continue the struggle. Still, with frequent Palestinian assaults against Israeli targets originating from Jordanian territory, "a very considerable proportion of Israel's defense effort at the time was being invested in activities along this border."[50] These attacks, along with strikes from the Gaza Strip and south Lebanon, were part of an emerging low-intensity guerrilla-warfare challenge as the Palestinians more directly assumed the fight for the "homeland." While increasingly frequent small-scale violence on the northern and central fronts occupied many IDF soldiers, it lacked the volume or gravitas to distract the Israelis from the Egyptian front. Furthermore, Nasser's inability to mobilize the other Arab states to open a second front allowed the IDF to continue confidently orienting its structure, organization, and doctrine toward battling the Egyptians.[51] But the massive September and October 1968 shellings had educated the IDF General Staff about the Egyptians' potential to extract a high cost for Israel's retention of the east bank.[52]

Military Capability

The Israelis' limited threat perception in large part resulted from an abiding faith in the capability of the IDF after its Six-Day War performance. Learning lessons from such a textbook success is problematic and, not surprisingly, the IDF moved to reinforce its strengths in the late 1960s. In particular, the Israelis focused on the trinity of air power, armor, and intelligence. The air force, combining first-rate dogfighting skills with striking prowess, was the cornerstone of Israeli defense policy. It received an increasingly large share of military appropriations to enable missions ranging from air superiority to close air support for the army. Its effectiveness at this latter task had allowed the army to neglect its own fire support assets. The key to IAF success was primarily the superior training and skill of its pilots although possession of better equipment in some key areas, especially avionics and air-to-air missiles, helped.[53]

IAF commanders were confident in maintaining superiority, but they fretted about force structure limitations and, to some extent, growing technical challenges. Surface-to-air missiles (SAMs) had not been a major hurdle to carrying out battlefield-air-interdiction or close-air-support missions during the war, but future systems seemed likely to be more dangerous. Even in the virtuoso war performance of destroying more than ten Arab aircraft for every lost Israeli plane, the IAF sacrificed about 25 percent of its first-line combat airframes.[54] The United States and France had initially embargoed advanced combat aircraft deliveries hoping the Soviet Union would mimic this restraint. After the Soviets delivered capable MiG-21s to the Arabs, the United States eventually proceeded with delivery of badly needed A-4 Skyhawks. IDF commanders felt a need to husband aircraft and avoid risking the fleet in nonessential operations, especially given that no deal had been completed for fifty supersonic F-4 fighter/bombers.[55] Protection of the Israeli skies largely fell to three aging Mirage III squadrons, only one of which had direct responsibility for the Egyptian front.

The IAF received the lion's share of accolades after the war, but the army's seizure of the Sinai and other captured territories in less than a week stood as testament to its performance. While it had traditionally been dominated by the paratroop and armor branches, the latter increasingly held sway. A first-rate capability continued to improve, but combat experience promoted a belief in armor's invincibility on open, desert battlefields. As a result, the army was becoming increasingly unbalanced with "the totality of the tank" concept. Several infantry brigades became armor units to enable a quadrupling of the tank force. The combination of armor emphasis and Suez Canal frontline made the army's lack of bridging capability a notable deficiency. Another shortcoming was the army's lack of significant artillery for counter-battery fire against the massed Egyptian guns. Ultimately, whatever approach was taken to protect the Sinai, Chief of Staff Bar-Lev stressed that the army not be distracted from "maintenance of a schedule of regular training exercises and the reshaping and strengthening of the armored forces."[56]

A critical dimension of the army was its heavy dependence on mobilized reserves, about 80 percent of the ground force. Reservists included many highly experienced, skilled, and dedicated soldiers, but the small active force, along with the air force and navy, had to provide the forty-eight to seventy-two hours necessary for mobilization. Upon activation, designated Southern Command units would be rushed across the Sinai to positions as near the east bank as possible. This reserve-based defense concept was vulnerable to surprise, explaining the emphasis Israel placed on intelligence services as the key third leg of defense policy. High confidence existed in the excellent and well-resourced intelligence agencies, but they now faced a much greater challenge with the frontline on the east bank of the Suez Canal.[57]

Even fully mobilized, the severely outnumbered IDF now had to protect approximately four times as much territory as before June 1967. Jonathan Shimshoni stresses "*effectively* the army had shrunk and would have to grow numerically to meet the same tasks as before."[58] Similarly, the air force had to patrol a quadrupled air space, while the navy had to guard a quintupled coastline.[59] Although the new territory provided strategic depth and seemed to offer enhanced security, it represented something of a dilemma, given "far longer internal lines, with a shift to—in essence—forward deployment, a method reducing Israel's early warning and underlining its abject numerical inferiority."[60] Moreover, policing the Palestinian-populated territories in the West Bank and Gaza Strip added another burden to the IDF. This day-to-day demand reinforced awareness that they army could not remain mobilized for long without severely damaging the Israeli economy. Ultimately, the army could not grow enough to approach the force-to-space ratio that existed before June 1967.[61]

Recognition of the army's limited resources prompted the Israelis to seek security assistance from a great power. The Six-Day War marked the end of Israel's traditional strategic relationship with France as Paris took the preemptive attack as an opportunity to sever security ties and stress its pro-Arab bona fides. The French arms embargo bluntly reinforced the danger of arms dependence, but despite an expanding defense industry, Israel could not produce critical weapons such as advanced combat aircraft.[62] Fortunately, amid the demoralizing Vietnam struggle, the enthusiastic reaction by American elites and the public to Israel's stunning victory created the potential for improved relations and greater weapons acquisition. The prospect even existed for a full-fledged alliance, but Israeli leaders deemed the price of a pullback from all occupied territory as too high, especially given the apparent U.S. willingness to provide the necessary weapons without it.[63] While Israeli commanders embraced the shift from French to superior U.S. weapon systems, the transition would take time, prompting heightened sensitivity to losses.

Strategic Culture

Israelis possessed a highly developed strategic or security culture (*bitkhonism*) as a result of the nation's precarious position and constrained context. Jewish history, culminating with the Holocaust, conveyed constant danger, even the threat of extermination. Upon obtaining statehood, Israelis viewed themselves as a small population without natural resources living on a tiny piece of land surrounded by not simply adversaries but enemies seeking their destruction. As a result, they possessed a profound sense of isolation, a belief in the need for self-reliance, and a tendency to attribute worst-case motivation to others. Unable to engage in "normal" diplomatic affairs with other regional actors, Israelis appreciated the central role of force in external relations.[64]

In addressing the Arab challenge, Israelis essentially subscribed to a concept known as the "iron wall." This term originated in a 1923 article ("On the Iron Wall: We and the Arabs") written by Zeev Jabotinsky, an ardent nationalist and founder of Revisionist Zionism. He argued that peaceful coexistence with the Arabs and Palestinians would only be possible after they became convinced that Israel could not be defeated militarily. Fostering that evaluation required the Jews to maintain a robust defense capability (an iron wall) to repel repeated assaults. While possessing a fundamentally different political outlook, mainstream Zionists such as David Ben-Gurion embraced the concept in spirit without using Jabotinsky's language. Revisionist historians have stressed the iron wall theme as a way to conceptualize Israeli security thinking as well as demonstrate its flaw since in their view military success prompted expanded Israeli aims, which undermined negotiation prospects. The debate over Israel's culpability in the failure to achieve a lasting peace between traditional and revisionist scholars is not germane to this chapter, but the widely shared perspective of an iron wall among Israeli decision makers is important to remember. Lacking the resources to achieve absolute victory, Israel needed the Arabs to abandon the fight.[65]

Israelis wanted to discourage challenges to the iron wall as much as possible, explaining their fascination with the concept of the deterrence.[66] Allon epitomized the Israeli view by arguing that "in the long term deterrence leads to resignation and resignation to peace."[67] Achieving such an evaluation required that the Arabs be denied any gains from military action, which placed a high burden on the IDF. Although Israel's commitment to deterrence never wavered, its approach shifted over the nation's first two decades. Yaniv stresses "the emphasis in the first package, during the 1949–1956 period, was primarily defensive—namely, on deterrence by denial. The second package, which evolved between the Sinai campaign and the Six-Day War, shifted the emphasis markedly to deterrence by punishment."[68] This change reflected a widespread view that deterrence by punishment (credibly threatening retaliatory destruction of strategic targets) fit better with Israeli strengths than deterrence by denial (convincing the adversary that aggression will not achieve its objective).[69] Israelis appreciated that deterrence would periodically require the actual use of force "to recharge the failing batteries" of a strong military reputation.[70]

When waging war, the strategic environment combined with combat experience to crystallize three basic tenets. First, Israelis wanted to fight on enemy territory given that any combat inside the small nation jeopardized significant population and infrastructure. To avoid such battles, Adan stresses, "Israeli security doctrine held that the best defense is a good offense."[71] Maj. Gen. Israel

Tal pithily adds, "the IDF is the 'Israel Defense Forces' by appellation but 'Israel Offense Forces' in substance."[72] Israelis came to believe that fighting and thus ending wars on enemy territory bolstered future deterrence. At the end of the 1950s, Allon reflected common thinking by averring that "no modern country can surround itself with a wall," particularly a small, elongated state surrounded by ardent enemies with vastly larger militaries.[73]

A second and related principle was that wars needed to end quickly with decisive victory. Tal stresses that "the art of war by the few is averse to static lines and wearying, inconclusive operations."[74] Israelis believed that any war beyond three or four weeks would cause serious economic harm.[75] They also realized that swift, overwhelming success prevented external actors from providing the Arab states meaningful assistance. Achieving such quick, decisive victories required that the IDF possess superior military skill, speed, and maneuverability, especially given the proclivity for fighting multifront wars. Israelis came to recognize that the tank and aircraft provided the best instruments for enabling this objective, reflecting their emphasis. The preference for a mobile rather than fixed defense also encouraged the IDF over time to invest "in assault forces at the expense of vital stocks of ammunition and equipment."[76]

Israelis' recognition that its military power and deterrence did not guarantee security prompted the third tenet—a belief in preempting threats. The standard definition of preemption restricts attacking to cases when adversary aggression is imminent, but the Israelis possessed a more liberal understanding, or perhaps a broader definition of aggression prompted a wider use of preemption. Beyond allowing the IDF "to project maximum power through a minimal resort to force," preemption answered enemy attempts to weaken or bankrupt Israel by forcing it to remain in a state of perpetual mobilization.[77] The strong appeal of striking first even led Israelis to embrace the more controversial notion of prevention (attacking to deny the adversary particular weapons or levels of military capability that could be used in future aggression).[78] Leaders justified these military actions morally by citing "*ein breira*" (no choice or no alternative).[79]

The applicability of these well-developed military principles was strained by the 1967 victory's significant alteration of the security context. The historic rout and captured territory raised doubt about the Arabs being an existential threat. Although still a relatively small nation surrounded by enemies, Israel now possessed some natural obstacles on each front and a degree of strategic depth. Possession of these buffer zones lessened the need and the ability to take the battle to the enemy through mobile offensive operations. Moreover, strategic depth combined with the IDF's display of military prowess appeared to vitiate the "no choice" concept that had underpinned preemption. In particular, it made U.S. acceptance of such future actions far less likely, a significant factor given the United States' growing role as weapons supplier and strategic ally. Finally, the changed boundaries complicated deterrence by leaving fewer clear red lines to cross on the way to war.[80]

Instead of appreciating this new security environment and reassessing requirements, Israeli leaders tended to emphasize what had led to their prior success.[81] Reuven Pedatzur observes that even though victory "made it possible, for the first time, to raise doubts about some of the basic assumptions upon which the 'security culture' was based ... these doubts did not affect the national consensus to the degree necessary to change the main components of the 'security culture.'"[82] Civilian and military policymakers tended to regard strategic depth exclusively as a bonus. They failed to appreciate that the possession of the occupied territory complicated employing deterrence by punishment, especially given "the sudden irrelevance of Israel's casi belli."[83] Moreover, Israeli commanders saw the war as validation of their military approach, reinforcing a "cult of the offensive."[84] Expectations of similar success in the future were widely held, including winning with low casualties, because the army "never seriously comprehended the major blunders committed by the Arabs that had allowed for such a decisive victory."[85] For a minority of Israeli officials, "the perception of security which resulted from the newly acquired strategic depth and Israel's military advantage vis-à-vis its Arab neighbors fostered a willingness to adopt a defensive approach."[86]

Resources

A central limiting factor in security policymaking was Israel's small population. In contrast to about 100 million Arabs in frontline states, with 30 million in Egypt alone, Israel had a Jewish population of approximately 2.7 million.[87] Faced with increasing demands for soldiers after the 1967 war, the government had lengthened conscription to three years, extended reserve duty obligations, recalled many older reserves to active duty, and even found a way to get religious Jews into the army.[88] As a result, the military had "stretched its manpower reserves to the very limit."[89] The fully mobilized IDF contained approximately 275,000 soldiers, but this force size required more than 10 percent of the Jewish population, a level sustainable for only a short time.[90] By contrast, this force level was less than 1 percent of the Egyptian population, allowing Cairo to maintain an army of that size indefinitely.

Israel's modest economy further constrained choices. Even discounting Israel's other enemies, Egypt had a GNP (gross national product) 50 percent higher than the Jewish state's and satisfied most of its military hardware requirements from Soviet largesse. Although the captured Abu Rudeis oilfield in the southern Sinai could satisfy more than half of Israel's oil requirement, the nation had no significant wealth-producing natural resources. Industry had achieved a ninefold increase between 1953 and 1967, but Israel remained primarily an agricultural economy with light manufacturing. Funds transferred from Jews in the United States and other countries provided a valuable resource, but U.S. government assistance was not yet meaningful. The Israelis, especially since they actually had to pay for weapons, had a limited foundation upon which to base their strong military. As a result, Israel allocated an increasing percentage of its GNP toward defense (17 percent in 1967 and 18 percent in 1968).[91]

Extracting such a high level of resources was possible because of the strong threat perception, but government officials appreciated that a limit existed. Even if "Israelis could accurately boast about being among the most heavily taxed people in the world," leaders were unable to increase the percentage of domestic resources and careful not to undermine fragile development efforts.[92] The Six-Day War had complicated the challenge by diminishing the widespread sense of existential jeopardy that provided tremendous legitimacy for government taxation and acquisition schemes. While the initial postwar euphoria at the hope for a lessened defense burden had been dashed, the victory helped unleash a demand for improved social services. With the traditionally dominant Mapai party struggling to retain power, its politicians felt more of a need to address public wants. Fortunately for decision makers, Israel in 1968 was enjoying a robust economy that improved government tax receipts in contrast to the prewar recession. This boom had the economy growing at a strong 13 percent in 1968, assisting politicians' ability to increase defense spending without affecting other popular programs.[93]

Domestic Politics

The unity, all-party government formed during the prewar crisis continued to rule, with the leftist parties obtaining stable leadership and the rightist bloc gaining credibility as a responsible governing force. This government's postwar existence reflected the declining political dominance of leftists, particularly the Mapai party from which every prime minister to date had been a member. An early 1960s schism in the party between David Ben-Gurion and other old guard figures had prompted the former to establish a breakaway party, Rafi, with other respected voices on national security, especially Dayan. Lacking defense credibility, the remaining "Old Guard" allied with the hawkish but leftist Ahdut HaAvoda party, which included distinguished military experts. The postwar political environment encouraged greater cooperation, leading to a January 1968 alignment that essentially created the Labor party. Divergent views between hawks and doves within this coalition, however, hindered taking clear positions on security issues. With their presence in the unity government, the right, only emerging as a factor in Israeli politics in the mid-1960s, had demonstrated an ability to act responsibly and shared credit for the postwar economic boom. The Arabs' rejection of the "land for peace" approach allowed Israeli politicians to avoid inevitably controversial discussions of the specific land that should be exchanged, but the Sinai's absence of religious significance removed it from this underlying divisiveness. Instead, retaining the Sinai until Cairo offered a general peace and vigorously responding to Egyptian challenges were popular positions across the political spectrum.[94]

Decision-making Process

National security decision making in Israel had traditionally been directed by a few officials despite the state being a parliamentary democracy. Even though almost everyone considered themselves a military expert by virtue of combat experience, agreement existed that the delays of representative government could not be tolerated given threats to the nation's survival.[95] Such a deferential approach required an abiding faith in leaders' skill and judgment. Initially the venerated Ben-Gurion, serving as defense minister as well as prime minister, managed to consolidate control to a considerable degree. Although successor prime ministers Moshe Sharett and Eshkol also retained the defense portfolio, they could not maintain Ben-Gurion's iron grip on security policy. Nevertheless, these leaders continued to discuss and decide matters in small groups of trusted and influential advisors.[96]

Eshkol had been prime minister for more than five years, but he now suffered from deteriorating health and popularity that would exacerbate his deferential tendency on military matters.[97] Despite considerable experience in the security arena, Eshkol was one of few Israelis who "had never handled a rifle or spent a day in uniform."[98] The prime minister had increasingly relied on former generals, especially Allon and Israel Galili of the Ahdut HaAvoda party, to moderate the influence of Minister of Defense Dayan and other Rafi members.[99] While possessing sharp divisions over West Bank policy, their agreement on retaining the Sinai until it could be traded limited civilian attention to the issue.

Moshe Dayan, the nexus between the military and the government, held enormous power but was restrained in its use. Having already been lauded as IDF chief of staff during the victorious 1956 war, assumption of the minister position right before the astonishing success in the Six-Day War earned him global renown and hero worship in Israel. Beyond being regarded as the nation's premier military expert, he was the most popular and respected Israeli. In September 1968, more than 150,000 Israelis signed a petition for him to replace Eshkol, a notion he quickly rejected.[100] While his position and stature enabled enormous influence, Dayan was quite deferential to the IDF General Staff, exhibiting reluctance to overrule the generals or even resolve disputes among senior officers.

Dayan's opinions often shifted, although at times such changes appear to reflect political or personal motivations more than strategic recalculation. This behavior encouraged other politicians and senior officers to continue to lobby him, rarely viewing a decision as final.[101]

The Six-Day War is often regarded as a transition point with the IDF subsequently exerting greater control over military policy.[102] Civilian leaders actively sought senior officers' opinions and advice to the extent that "a dependence on the military leadership was evident in the decisionmaking process."[103] The chief of the general staff was frequently invited to cabinet meetings, in contrast to the Ben-Gurion era. Politicians had to authorize actions and appropriate funds, but these functions tended to be merely formal sanctions of the military's choice. The media's worshipful attitude with the growing "cult of the generals" only exacerbated the IDF's power. Many senior officers now embraced an essentially personal journalist with the press becoming "increasingly dependent on military personnel and the information that flowed from them."[104] At the time no one questioned the merit of these changes although they would later be linked to a "decline in Israeli strategic thinking."[105]

The deferential instincts of Dayan and other civilians, however, did not leave military decision making to a unitary actor despite the efforts of the chief of the general staff. The IDF had a well-defined hierarchy that integrated the army, air force, and navy into a single command structure. Army generals had traditionally dominated this command with armor officers now exercising particular sway. The armor fraternity included the chief of staff, deputy chief of staff, half of the positions on the general staff (e.g., Tal, Adan, Shlomo Lahat, and Moshe Peled), and "beyond them, a burgeoning phalanx of brigadier-generals and colonels... all products of, or at least converts to, *Gyasot Hashiryon*—the armored corps."[106] Still, these tank commanders hardly marched in lock step on security issues, and regardless of service or specialty, the IDF leadership consisted of many strong voices. Rather than policy being commanded from the top, there had emerged "pluralism within the IDF itself, particularly among the senior staff."[107] While this philosophy promoted harmony among the military leadership, commanders also tended to massage or gloss over significant differences in search of a unified position on key strategic issues.

A number of soldiers had particularly meaningful roles on the question of how best to defend the Sinai. With the retirement of Yitzhak Rabin on June 1, 1968, Lt. Gen. Chaim Bar-Lev had become chief of the general staff. Considered "no military genius, [Bar-Lev] had a well-balanced personality who never lost his temper and spoke v-e-r-y s-l-o-w-l-y," reflecting a tendency for caution.[108] Maj. Gen. Yeshayahu Gavish, another experienced armor officer, oversaw Southern Command with the direct responsibility for defending the Sinai. Maj. Gen. Israel Tal, regarded as the IDF's premier armor expert and head of the Armor

Corps, possessed ardent views on the value of the tank and its role in defending the Sinai.[109] Maj. Gen. Ariel Sharon, the highly decorated but controversial chief of the Training Branch, was another aggressive risk-taker who firmly believed in maneuver warfare.[110] Unpopular with other generals, especially Bar-Lev, Sharon inserted himself into the debate on the Sinai. By contrast, the then-colonel Bren Adan, deputy commander of the Armor Corps, was a talented officer whose views were widely respected by others and who would be asked to play a central role in devising a defense approach.[111]

Frontier Strategic Options

While Israeli decision makers contemplated the best approach for maintaining control of the peninsula, the IDF satisfied a perceived retaliatory need for the artillery barrages by launching an October 31 heliborne commando raid. Although it caused limited damage to infrastructure targets in the Naj' Hammadi area (three hundred miles south of Cairo), the impressive range of the strike boosted Israeli morale and demonstrated Egyptian vulnerability. The "stunned" Egyptian government stopped the shellings, but it did not thin out the army massed along the canal to better protect rear areas. Regardless of being viscerally satisfying, senior Israeli commanders "fully understood that such raids were not a solution in and of themselves. They only affected the short run at best, but offered no lasting solution against a determined adversary."[112] Therefore, on the same evening of the Naj' Hammadi raid, Bar-Lev ordered Adan to lead a team of diverse experts in exploring options for the Sinai's long-term defense. The eastern part of the peninsula's topography greatly influenced the merit of potential choices. A relatively flat and passable stretch of land extended away from the east bank of the Suez Canal with the exception of swamps and lagoons on the extreme northern end. The terrain then rose to a ridge about five to eight miles from the waterline, which "afforded clear observation of most of the level strip right to the canal."[113] Behind the ridge, "virtually impenetrable" dunes extended for about twenty miles until reaching a second higher ridge, followed by another fifteen- to twenty-mile stretch of dunes that led to the mountains with the Mitla and Gidi passes.[114]

This terrain encouraged consideration of withdrawing from the east bank. The strongest natural position was the mountain passes, which a small force could defend until the arrival of reserves. Even if Egyptian troops reoccupied the abandoned eastern part of the Sinai, they would still be more than fifty miles from Israel proper. A much more limited pullback to the first ridge, which in the words of Sharon, "dominates the canal plain," would have allowed a simpler, less costly, and potentially more effective frontline defense.[115] Whatever the strategic merit for withdrawing from the east bank, Israeli decision makers gave it scant consideration. Leaders regarded the Sinai in toto as too valuable a bargaining chip to sacrifice, fearing any unilateral, partial withdrawal would signal weakness and decrease diplomatic prospects.[116] Unless the general staff informed the government it could not hold the east bank at an acceptable cost, the civilians would not consider abandoning it.

Thus the IDF set out to determine how best to maintain the territorial status quo, a goal actually involving three distinct challenges. First and most fundamentally, the IDF had to deter and, if necessary, defeat any major Egyptian invasion of the Sinai. Second, the military needed to prevent limited Egyptian attacks from seizing footholds on the east bank beyond the Port Fuad area. Critically, "there was no easy answer to the dilemma of preventing the Egyptians from capturing a bit of Sinai territory."[117] Third, the IDF had to satisfy the previous two objectives as well as absorb shellings in a way that minimized casualties. Given these demanding and somewhat conflicting goals, the Israelis would have trouble devising "an appropriate deployment formula for the supposedly ideal Suez line."[118]

Offensive-Based Approach

With defense being so challenging, one appealing option was to deter aggression through threats of unacceptable punishment. Such an offensive-based approach was consonant with Israel's military tradition and strategic culture. With Cairo fewer than one hundred miles from the canal, the Israelis could legitimately frighten Egyptian leaders by declaring their intention to cross the Suez in force. A less demanding variant would involve a sustained strategic bombing campaign against Cairo and other distant targets. Finally, the Israelis could have conducted continuous, deep raids, especially by striking targets far beyond the Canal Zone. The late October 1967 punitive attacks in response to the sinking of the *Eilat* had succeeded in bringing quiet to the front for nearly a year. The Naj' Hammadi raid had illustrated the IDF's capability to carry out such strikes along the Nile. Earlier in 1968 Dayan had conveyed confidence in such an approach, declaring, "if we want to and if we have to, we can bring them down through the civilian population. . . . The distance to Cairo today is 100 kilometers [63 miles] and that puts it within easy reach."[119]

Despite Dayan's bravura and the inherent appeal of an offensive-based approach, decision makers appreciated its severe liabilities. The limited damage from raiding made it unlikely to deter Egypt for any length of time, and the more punishing options involved excessive cost, questionable feasibility, and dubious strategic merit. In contrast to a year earlier when retaliating for the *Eilat*'s sinking and other transgressions, the Egyptians now had essentially rebuilt their military and eliminated easy countervalue targets in the Canal Zone. This depopulation and the related sacrifice of economic activity along the Canal Zone suggested Egyptian willingness to accept a high price for continued resistance. Although Dayan claimed Israel could "break the Arab will to fight," the evidence to date suggested raids were instead likely to precipitate domestic pressure on Nasser for a more aggressive policy against Israel.[120] If limited retaliatory attacks failed to cow the Egyptians, unwanted escalation would be difficult to stop.

A strategic bombing campaign or a major ground offensive entailed significant costs without offering a quick, decisive victory or even an advantageous, hard-fought success. The IAF lacked aircraft capable of effective long-range bombing. A sustained air campaign with existing planes would likely result in critical airframe losses at a time when the IAF needed to husband its precious inventory.[121] As a result, any bombing campaign probably would inflict limited damage and thus have insufficient deterrent value. A large land crossing seemed even more dubious. Even if the IDF obtained the lacking bridging equipment, any attack would inevitably be costly given the highly developed Egyptian positions, the difficulty of surreptitiously moving the necessary forces forward and across the canal, and the unlikelihood of being able to precede such an operation with a preemptive air strike. Moreover, the IDF would overcome Egyptian defenses "only to fall into a nation of thirty million people."[122] It is unclear what would represent viable war aims; any territorial gains would likely leave Israel with a far more difficult defense assignment while enhancing Egyptian motivation for continuing the struggle. The bottom line was that significant military and political shortcomings undermined the credibility of such punishment threats, whether against all-out or limited Egyptian aggression.[123]

Defense-in-Depth

Because a deterrence-by-punishment approach seemed inadvisable, the Israelis identified a range of defense-based options both to facilitate deterrence by denial as well as actually block aggression. Taking advantage of the vast Sinai desert, the Israelis could have employed a defense-in-depth given that "the canal and the Sinai did not necessarily have to be defended along the water line."[124] In contrast to the previously discussed unilateral withdrawal, in this option the IDF would retain control of the east bank and defend against raids but not hold the position against a strong Egyptian push. Instead the small frontline forces and other Sinai-based units could trade space for time until the arrival of mobilized reserves.[125] Engaging in such a fluid style of combat would play to the IDF's strengths, allowing it to attrite the Egyptians at modest cost. Upon full mobilization and Egyptian attrition, the enemy would be vulnerable to an IDF counterattack that restored control of the Sinai.

Although a defense-in-depth approach appears to best fit the strategic context and military balance of forces for defeating a major invasion, it was less effective with regard to limited attacks. In essence, although the area involved was not intrinsically valuable, government leaders had imbued it with political import.[126] They wanted to signal a commitment to retain the east bank, a more difficult challenge for a defense-in-depth strategy. Even against an all-out invasion, this approach would greatly diminish the value of the Suez Canal—"the world's greatest tank ditch"—and delay the IDF's plans to launch a punitive counteroffensive into enemy territory.[127] Moreover, if the Egyptians crossed en masse to seize a sizeable bridgehead on the east bank and then stopped, the Israelis after mobilizing would have to counterattack into fixed positions without prior attrition, lest they appear weak. The Israelis might not even be able to launch such a counterattack if the superpowers quickly intervened. As Adan would later write, in such a case "the only outcome would be the loss of territory."[128]

Mobile Armor-Based Defense

To maintain a near-continuous defense of the east bank, a static or position-based approach or a forward deployment of mobile forces could be employed. In the latter approach, tanks would be placed along the first and second ridges largely beyond Egyptian artillery range to limit enemy targets and potential casualties. Armor on the first ridge could respond to an attack within thirty to sixty minutes while larger, second-echelon forces would provide the rapid punch for a counterattack to push any limited Egyptian penetration into the water. If the scale of the attack required full mobilization, these forward forces would deny the enemy a secure bridgehead until reserves arrived. Tanks along with mechanized infantry would constantly and vigorously patrol the flatlands between the first ridge and the canal to search for interlopers and to demonstrate Israeli presence. This approach would theoretically allow control of the waterline without fixed positions, fitting with the IDF's military culture and combat strengths.[129]

Holding a fixed position represented an unorthodox way to use armor, violating a core principle of mobile defense involving the trade of time for space.[130] It would be an attempt to satisfy political conditions without deviating from the preferred form of combat. Given the size of available forces and the long front to be secured, the option was better for addressing the major attack challenge than for deterring and defending against limited aggression. The Israelis, however, worried far less about an all-out attack in the near future than minor provocations given the perceived favorable military balance. Bar-Lev, Gavish, and others stressed that "one of the main dangers that Israel would have to face would be a sudden Egyptian move to gain a foothold, however narrow, along the east bank, followed by an attempt to achieve an immediate cease-fire by international agreement."[131] Such a success would embolden the Egyptians and other Arabs while pressuring Israelis. The desire to prevent Egyptian seizure of even an inch of occupied territory undermined the appeal of the mobile approach. The potential for significant equipment losses from combat and usage if the IDF conducted frequent, large patrols in the Canal Zone also discouraged its adoption. Aggressive patrolling appeared likely to be quite costly in machines and casualties for the IDF's core armor units while restricting such activity would invite greater probing advances by the Egyptians.[132]

Position-Based Defense

Alternatively, the IDF could construct fortifications along the east bank to achieve a strong position-based defense. These structures would have political value as emblems of Israeli control over the Sinai. Beyond symbolism, fixed defenses offered the potential to defend the east bank against the full range of Egyptian options. Such works would allow continuous observation of the Egyptian forces on the other side of the Suez, providing early warning of any crossing attempts. Additionally, their presence would facilitate a rapid response to small-scale operations, whose defeat was crucial to preventing the feared Egyptian effort to slowly creep eastwards upon achieving a foothold. Although the inadequacy of extant frontline works during the October barrage demonstrated that a far sturdier set of fortifications would be required for a positional defense, these deterrence and defense gains could theoretically be achieved without massive or continuous works given the canal's size.[133]

A purely static defense model, however, also suffered from shortcomings. For a military based on maneuverability and flexibility, fortifications seemed an anathema. They represented stalemate with long, costly battles, the type of warfare best suited to Egyptian strengths of artillery, large active duty forces, and causality tolerance. Frontline defenses would also provide targets of opportunity for Egyptian guns, as well as force vulnerable resupply and troop rotation convoys to operate in harm's way. The Israelis were well aware that penetration of a strategic defense line tends to render the rest of the fortifications and their forces useless. At the time, the Israelis did not sufficiently appreciate another significant negative: such positions risked being cut off in all-out invasion, thus requiring costly efforts at relief. Finally, the value of fortifications to blunt or even slow down any sizeable Egyptian attack was questionable if resource constraints limited their scale and numbers, leaving considerable space between them. In June 1968 the Southern Command's plan to construct company-size fortifications along the front had not been acted upon in part because of their enormous financial cost and manning requirements.[134] Practical considerations meant that, for any fixed defenses, the IDF had a choice of "either putting a lot of troops up front or leaving great gaps on the Suez line."[135] Given the army's increasing armor orientation, need to limit reserve mobilization, and desire to maintain a rigorous training schedule for all-out war, any Sinai defense would have to function with great economy of manpower. But too much efficiency would leave a vulnerability that could be exploited by the Egyptians, especially because they would possess the initiative on when and where to strike.[136]

Decision for a Strategic Defense System

At the end of 1968 senior Israeli officers weighed these options. Although the general staff technically considered withdrawal, offense, and defense, only defensive-based approaches received meaningful attention. Bar-Lev subsequently summed up the restricted decision by noting that "the mission assigned us was to defend the canal waterline."[137] The question of which defense variant to pursue was difficult. After touring the frontline and exploring the issue, Adan's team realized "we faced a dilemma: on the one hand, we had ideal conditions for a mobile defense and, on the other, the sensitive political-strategic considerations of a small nation for which 'trading' territory was anathema."[138] Not surprisingly, they resolved the dilemma by recommending a combined approach. Maozim ("strongpoints") should be placed approximately every 6.5 miles along the canal. With soldiers able to observe about half that distance in daylight, this spacing allowed complete coverage of the east bank. Of course, nighttime was problematic, but IDF scientists informed Adan—erroneously—that electronic sensors could provide surveillance of the relatively flat, straight area. Beyond providing early warning, the maozim would demonstrate Israeli commitment by "showing the flag" and defeating small-scale attacks. Stoutly built but modestly sized strongpoints garrisoning fifteen to twenty soldiers in noncrisis times could satisfy these limited goals, keeping the total manning requirement to fewer than five hundred full-time troops.[139]

The maozim represented only part of the Adan group's recommendation for defending the east bank. Given the distance between strongpoints and their lack of heavy weaponry, they could not be mutually supportive when under attack. Armored units patrolling between the strongpoints would help preserve day-to-day Israeli control while the armor force would rush forward upon the Egyptian army's advance. From the first ridge, tanks could advance to the maozim in thirty to sixty minutes while artillery provided additional support. Ultimately, Adan's plan reflected the prevailing political-strategic need for a physical presence on the east bank while relying on armor to carry out most of the combat.[140]

This combination approach was inherently logical and generally embraced by the high command, but individuals maneuvered to place emphasis on either the mobile or positional elements. Generals Tal and Sharon expressed a preference for greater reliance on mobile forces as well as putting any defense line along the first ridge, not the east bank.[141] Responding to the political requirement for physical entities along the canal, Sharon recommended a token presence of "one or two locations, on the Great Bitter Lake, for example, where we would not be directly under their guns."[142] By contrast, typifying the view of many IDF senior officers, Southern Front Commander Gavish, as Chaim Herzog relates, believed "if the Canal was to be considered a physical barrier, there was no option but to establish a physical presence along it."[143] This attitude prompted General Gavish to add multiple maozim to Adan's plan at likely crossing points (e.g., across from the Egyptian canal towns of Kantara, El-Firdan, and Ismailia as well as along the roads to the Mitla and Gidi passes). Chief of Staff Bar-Lev felt similarly and added even more works on the northern and southern ends of the line, which he considered particularly exposed. As a result, the line kept gaining a more prominent defensive role throughout the approval process. Tal and Sharon would intensify their opposition in the coming months and years after gaining a clearer appreciation that the maozim would have a broader defense mission beyond early warning. Ultimately, the final approved plan increased the number of works by 50 percent over the twenty recommended by Adan.[144]

The policy requirement for holding the canal's east bank was the most determinative factor in the decision to build strongpoints, but after establishing this requirement, the Eshkol government played no role in the particulars of how the IDF accomplished it. Despite some division among the high command, civilians embraced both the barrier and the broader conception for defending the Sinai. Dayan has been cited as an ardent supporter of the barrier by some scholars, but critics of the fixed positions believed he was sympathetic to their view and continued to lobby for his assistance.[145] At a minimum, he considered the decision to fall within the realm of the IDF and did nothing to block construction of the barrier. Eshkol's death on February 26, 1969, and his replacement with Golda Meir would prompt no policy change regarding Egypt, the Sinai, or the defense approach.[146]

Enemy shelling would have greatly impeded construction of the Bar-Lev Line, even possibly preventing its completion, but the Egyptians watched without major reaction as thousands of civilians and soldiers worked twenty-four hours a day until the system was largely built. Cairo eventually became alarmed that the barrier reflected Israeli plans to remain on the east bank permanently, prompting them in February 1969 to initiate small arms fire and plan a major escalation. By the time heavy Egyptian shelling commenced in March, the Bar-Lev Line was nearly ready especially along the northern section. The IDF rushed to complete the defenses as hostile interference caused many casualties, which complicated enhancing the sand berm and finishing the remaining maozim on the southern part of the canal. Nevertheless, while limited work continued for months, the IDF declared the Bar-Lev Line operational on March 15, 1969.[147]

Security Developments along a Fortified Frontier

The Bar-Lev Line would significantly shape the struggle over the east bank, presenting the Egyptians both an obstacle and opportunity. Cairo regarded the barrier as an impediment that had to be addressed before its army could advance into the Sinai. At the same time, these strongpoints created tantalizing targets against which to demonstrate Egyptian resolve and inflict Israeli casualties.

War of Attrition

In early March, one-thousand-plus Egyptian guns opened up along the entire canal, providing the first tactical test of the maozim. Despite several artillery hits, the structures proved effective, suffering only modest damage. IDF guns could respond with just a fraction of the Egyptian salvos, but a fortuitous shot on March 9 killed Egypt's capable chief of staff during a frontline inspection. In part because of his death, Egyptian fire slackened sharply. Although satisfied with the Bar-Lev Line's performance, Brig. Gen. Shlomo Lahat, Adan's replacement, faced the one-hundred-thousand-plus Egyptians with only two thousand IDF troops along the entire front.[148]

In early April, the Egyptian army resumed aggressive attacks that would essentially continue for sixteen months. On April 19, they escalated by sending a fifteen-man commando force across the water near Ismailia to attack one of the *maoz*. The garrison repelled this raid, but it signaled the initiation of limited crossings, usually at night, to mine roads, strike small convoys, and occasionally hit the strongpoints. Efforts against the maozim did not bear success, but the eightfold rise in Egyptian-directed incidents in April tripled the number of monthly IDF deaths. While the Bar-Lev Line contributed to denying the Egyptians operational victory, it could not deter all aggression. Thus, the Israelis tried to deter attacks through retaliatory strikes beginning with another mission against Naj' Hammadi on April 29. The successful strike did not stop Egyptian fire. Despite Nasser's May 1 declaration that 60 percent of the Bar-Lev Line had been destroyed, "in reality, not one *maoz* had been seriously damaged."[149] Dayan, after experiencing a heavy shelling, raised the prospect of withdrawal at least from the most frequently targeted strongpoints at the northern and southern ends, but senior commanders convinced him not to pursue redeployment. Appreciating Israeli desire to avoid both a long war and escalation, frustrated

Egyptian officials hoped to inflict enough pain to obtain Israeli withdrawal. Alternatively, they sought to engender enough instability to create international, especially U.S., pressure on Israel to pull back.[150]

Faced with unappealing escalatory, capitulatory, and long war options, the Israelis endured months of Egyptian attacks with only limited replies until mounting pressure in mid-1969 prompted officials to employ air power. The Bar-Lev Line strongpoints continued to absorb punishment without problem, but casualties were inevitable and garrison soldiers suffered low morale.[151] Efforts to resupply the maozim and rotate personnel accounted for most IDF losses, while the sustained struggle unavoidably caused wear and tear to armor and artillery. The situation generated some public discontent, but it remained modest as the barrier not only helped keep physical costs limited but minimized the sense of insecurity felt by Israelis.[152] Leaders had been reluctant to introduce airpower, believing it would only increase the costs, especially to critical frontline airframes and pilots, without ending the conflict. In July, however, casualties doubled from the previous monthly high, making the status quo intolerable. Critically, Dayan shifted from an opponent to supporter of escalation, in part because of a particularly bold commando attack on a tank depot in early July that reinforced intelligence assessments of an impending major canal crossing.[153] A consensus emerged that restoration of the cease-fire required using airpower as well as enhanced commando operations. As Chief of Staff Bar-Lev memorably put it, Israeli policy was "escalation for the sake of deescalation."[154]

In late July 1969 the IAF commenced this new phase of the war by sweeping the skies of the revamped Egyptian Air Force and pounding frontline ground targets.[155] This intense eight-day air assault reflected a tactical escalation in an attempt to deter a significant canal crossing. Believing that Egypt had abandoned such plans and wanting to gauge reaction, Israel suspended air strikes on July 28. When Egypt intensified attacks on the Bar-Lev Line, the IAF soon resumed its air strikes to force a cease-fire. For the rest of the year, Israeli aircraft were somewhat able to suppress artillery fire, but the Egyptians countered by sharply increasing use of smaller, less vulnerable weapons such as mortars and light arms. The monthly average of fire incidents along the Bar-Lev Line now exceeded five hundred, pressuring the IDF to undertake deep strike missions.[156] On January 7, 1970, a frustrated Israeli government began bombing military targets around Cairo and Upper Egypt with its recently acquired long-range F-4 fighter/bombers. Despite somewhat appreciating the risk of Soviet intervention, Israeli leaders wanted to drive home Egyptian vulnerability, obtain a cease-fire, and bolster long-term deterrence.

While putting up a brave front and continuing attacks on the Bar-Lev Line, an alarmed Nasser reacted to the strategic bombing campaign by seeking far greater Soviet assistance. Without it, he claimed defeat would result. The Soviets, unwilling to see Egypt again beaten or, far worse, defect to the west, reluctantly decided to supply greater quality and quantity of key weapons as well as essentially take over the air defense of central Egypt. Thus, strategic bombing triggered the major escalation that Israel had tried to avoid throughout the struggle. Wanting to prevent direct conflict with the Soviets and further accidental hits on civilian facilities, the Israeli government sharply limited air raids in March and ended them completely in mid-April. Instead the IAF concentrated on the area within twenty to twenty-five miles of the canal while seeking U.S. diplomatic assistance to counter Soviet involvement. The Egyptians, with their rear secure, intensified punishing artillery and mortar attacks along the Canal Zone to the dismay of the IDF.[157]

Some officers now urged consideration of a withdrawal, but the political imperative to avoid looking weak scuttled any serious discussion.[158] The normally dovish Eban illustrated the extent to which the Bar-Lev Line and control of the Canal Zone had seized Israeli political and military leaders. In a July 13 speech to the Knesset, he breathlessly declared that "the battle on the canal line is the battle to preserve the very existence of the state of Israel."[159] Israeli officials believed that the territorial and political status quo was unsustainable if the IAF lost air superiority over the Canal Zone.[160] Thus, as David Korn stresses, "The Israeli air force's battle to stop the movement of the Egyptian-Soviet missile network toward the canal was, in fact, a battle for the Bar-Lev line. . . . If the Israelis could not bomb, they could not hold the Bar-Lev line itself, at least not as it was conceived."[161] The Soviets created a much more formidable challenge for the IAF by expanding high-level SA-2 batteries, introducing low-level SA-3 sites, and integrating them with radar-controlled antiaircraft guns. The Israelis destroyed many forward SAM networks under construction, but the enemy kept slowing advancing replacement systems, and "the rate of exchange of planes [especially F-4s] for SAM batteries quickly became untenable."[162] With airpower unable to stop increased Egyptian attacks along the Bar-Lev Line, fears even grew of a major crossing that included Soviet forces.[163]

Israel's dire perspective, however, was shared by an Egyptian government that did not sense the prospect of victory. Attacks on the Bar-Lev Line had reached an all-time high, but Egyptian casualties finally reached levels painful enough to encourage a temporary halt to the aggression.[164] The Israeli government's acceptance of UN Resolution 242, which established the principle of land for peace for the occupied territories, provided Egypt the political cover to accept a cease-fire beginning on August 7, 1970. The Egyptians and Soviets signaled their intention to resume hostilities at a later date by immediately advancing the SAM umbrella to within thirty miles of the canal. This major cease-fire violation allowed them to cover the air space over the Bar-Lev Line, prompting many IDF senior officers to argue for a renewal of the war.[165] The government, however, regarded returning to the status quo ante as excessively costly, and no realistic escalatory options remained. After Nasser's death on September 28, the cease-fire continued indefinitely with a tense but quiet frontline.

Postwar Debate about the Bar-Lev Line

Most Israelis believed that Egypt had won the War of Attrition, or at least tied, which they regarded as a loss when compared to the prior conflicts. This judgment, in conjunction with Israel's acceptance of UN Resolution 242, ended the National Unity Government. In its place emerged a shakier leftist regime, albeit with Prime Minister Meir and most key leaders continuing in office. The war's outcome combined with the enemy's postwar advance of a SAM network to cover the Canal Zone were reasons to expect a revised policy. But many government officials and senior officers actually believed that Israel won the war by preserving the territorial status quo and denying Egypt success in a form of warfare that favored it. This conclusion inclined them against changing their political and strategic perspectives. Even with Egypt's advanced SAM network and expanded armor and mechanized units, the IDF remained confident that Israel could retain the east bank of the Suez Canal at an acceptable cost.[166]

Within this broad political-strategic position, however, an intense battle emerged among military leaders over the Bar-Lev Line's effectiveness as well as the best approach to defend the east bank. Tension over the barrier had increased even before the war's end when critic Sharon replaced the pro-line General Gavish as head of Southern Command in April 1970 and quickly maneuvered to close some of the maozim.[167]

A fundamental discussion of the way forward could only occur after the war, which had left the strongpoints badly in need of repairs.[168] For Bar-Lev Line critics, the war experience intensified their opposition. The maozim had served as inviting targets for Egyptian fire and death traps for exposed forces that had to support them. In October 1970, General Tal vigorously asserted the line's combat ineffectiveness, stressing the inability of isolated strongpoints to provide mutual support to prevent water crossings. Led by Tal and Sharon, they agitated for a more mobile approach. Tal, then at the ministry of defense, proposed replacing the Bar-Lev Line outposts with "armored infantry squads on armored personnel carriers and to rotate them every twenty-four hours."[169] Sharon added that the proper place for any line of fortifications was along the first ridge, where they could provide long-range observation and support for mobile armored patrols covering the ground between the line and the canal.[170]

By contrast, Bar-Lev and other advocates of the extant barrier asserted its substantial wartime accomplishments, including reducing casualties along the frontline, limiting Egyptian raids, and discouraging larger crossings to establish a bridgehead. The chief of staff pointed out that the 260 battlefield deaths suffered during the conflict were less than half the casualties from Israeli car crashes in 1970 alone.[171] Despite sixteen months of near constant Egyptian attacks, not one maoz had to be abandoned or even faced grave jeopardy. Bar-Lev and his cohorts worried that the proposed alternative of a mobile, armor-based defense would be vulnerable to limited Egyptian advances that would cost Israel control of the east bank in sections. For them, the war actually provided evidence of a mobile approach's impracticality. Ambushes and mines had inflicted high casualties on armored patrols operating in the frontline areas away from maozim. The Egyptians had deposited so many mines that the IDF ultimately abandoned tank patrols in these areas, given the high loss rate. They contended that the Israelis lacked enough active-duty armor forces to sustain a mobile approach, at least without inhibiting training for general war. Instead they argued to rebuild the strongpoints, incorporating tactical lessons as a part of the combination static-mobile defense approach.[172]

Barrier opponents' inability to argue convincingly for the practicality of their approach ensured Bar-Lev Line repairs and upgrades, leaving Sharon to shift focus to the addition of company-sized fortifications along the first ridge. He apparently hoped this second line of *taozim* (strongholds) would diminish the Bar-Lev Line over time, facilitating a more mobile approach. Continued Egyptian efforts to elevate their opposing artillery positions increased exposure of the Bar-Lev Line and bolstered Sharon's call for a line beyond enemy observation. He added during a major attack frontline troops would be able to withdraw from the maozim to the larger taozim while armored forces engaged the Egyptians.[173] The possibility of a negotiated withdrawal from the east bank also encouraged erecting this second line as a contingency. Given these factors and with the Bar-Lev Line improvements already approved, the taozim scheme was not vigorously studied or debated, with the IDF building eleven such structures. This fortification compromise with the existence of both maozim and taozim only further muddied Israel's Sinai defense strategy with harmful repercussions.[174]

While senior officers argued over the military approach to safeguarding the east bank, the aforementioned possibility of a negotiated withdrawal had emerged. To some Israelis, new Egyptian leader Anwar Sadat appeared more open and flexible. Dayan, always uncomfortable with occupying the east bank, indirectly conveyed to Sadat in late 1970 a possible willingness to pull back if Cairo reopened the canal to all traffic.[175] The Israeli defense minister believed that the financial benefits from transit fees and rebuilt cities along the waterway would discourage Egyptian aggression. Sadat expressed his interest in a February 4, 1971, speech, although "unlike Dayan, the Egyptian leader saw a partial Israeli pull-back as catalyzing, not indefinitely delaying, a final withdrawal" from the Sinai.[176] Moreover, he wanted to place Egyptian security forces on the east bank and demanded that Israeli troops withdraw beyond the natural defense positions provided by the Mitla and Gidi passes. Many Israeli officials harbored grave reservations about this initiative, with policymakers unable to agree on how far Israel should pull back. Dayan, Tal, and Sharon favored the Mitla and Gidi passes while Meir, Bar-Lev, and Allon opposed a move beyond the first ridge, allowing the IDF to dominate the east bank. This division prevented an Israeli counterproposal, but more basically Meir and most policymakers remained leery that any agreement without a peace treaty would create significant pressure for further withdrawals.[177] Though talks through U.S. auspices lasted for another year, the moment had passed by April. Ultimately, Dayan "failed to convince his colleagues that a reopened Suez Canal constituted a better guarantee against attack than did the Bar-Lev Line."[178]

The restored strategic defense system would be weakened over the next few years. Chief of Staff Bar-Lev's retirement at the end of the 1971 shifted power toward barrier opponents with Tal becoming IDF chief of operations and then deputy chief of staff while Sharon remained Southern Front commander. They, along with Maj. Gen. (Res.) Mattityahu Peled, sought approval for dismantling the barrier at meetings in January and May 1972.[179] The new chief of staff, Lt. Gen. David Elazar, having served primarily in the north, had not played a major role in Sinai decision making. He had expressed a strong dislike for extended, defensive war, observing that "nothing is worse than a war of attrition in which 300 Egyptians and 4 Jews will fall in battle each day."[180] But he was close to Bar-Lev and favorably disposed to retaining the existing fortification system, explaining "even if I thought that the strongholds were worthless from the military point of view, I would be in a quandary over whether to abandon them from the political standpoint. When I factor in that they do help to secure the line and provide a little intelligence, I'm no longer faced with a dilemma."[181] However, the chief of staff would approve Sharon's proposal to thin out the line to save money. Despite considerable military activity on the west bank, the absence of actual Egyptian fire brought pressure to curtail defense spending, which now accounted for about a quarter of the nation's GNP. Thus the general staff approved closing nearly half of the strongpoints, including reducing each cluster to a single maoz.[182] By the end of Sharon's stint as Southern Commander in mid-1973, only sixteen strongpoints (plus two partially manned maozim) remained active.

The continuing ambiguity over the Bar-Lev Line's role throughout the early 1970s had essentially prompted individual commanders to employ their own interpretations, which risked confusion if war broke out. The May 1972 meeting on defense of the Sinai exemplified this problem because "the function of the line in the event of a new war or an Egyptian crossing was not explicitly determined."[183] Given Sharon's weakening of the frontline defenses, they were now "more of political than military importance."[184] Many Israeli senior officers did not necessarily share this view, and no clarification existed. Sharon lobbied for their immediate abandonment in an all-out invasion. General Elazar appreciated this military logic and stressed that responsibility for the Sinai's defense rested solely with the armor corps.[185] Still, he reportedly uttered before the 1973 war that "we've got to kill them on the canal," and he expected the maozim to at least play an indirect role in defense by channeling Egyptian forays.[186] Ultimately, Elazar appeared to regard evacuation as "a tactical decision, to be made under operational conditions."[187] A reasonable view but one that would promote confusion, especially as commanders interpreted battlefield signals through their own conception about the barrier.

Before considering the Bar-Lev Line's role during the Yom Kippur War, it is necessary to briefly highlight the IDF's two basic plans for defense of the Sinai. In response to a limited attack or an all-out war with limited warning, the military would implement *Shovach Yonim* (Dovecote). This called for the active-duty armored division in the Sinai to block the enemy advance, counterattacking within forty-eight hours against any limited effort and holding for seventy-two hours against an all-out invasion. In the latter scenario, the IDF would also be implementing *Sela* (Rock) in which two reserve armored divisions and supporting forces would join the fight upon mobilization. The resulting one-hundred-thousand-plus army with more than one thousand tanks would push the Egyptians back across the canal and even cross to the west side if necessary. The full Rock deployment required five days advance notice while Dovecote needed a minimum of twenty-four hours to advance the two regular armor brigades to the frontline and replace the maozim garrison troops with elite paratroopers.[188]

Maj. Gen. Shmuel Gonen, upon taking over Southern Command from Sharon in July 1973, wanted to boost the prospects for these defense plans by strengthening the Bar-Lev Line. Notably, he sought to reopen the maozim closed by Sharon, but a lack of time and higher priority construction projects behind the front line prevented any action before the Egyptian attack.[189] Thus, at the beginning of October 1973 on the Bar-Lev Line, the IDF had sixteen maozim in operation with two additional strongpoints partially manned. The eleven taozim along with supporting guns and forward armor elements were along the first ridge, five to eight miles to the rear. Ultimately, as the Yom Kippur War approached, "neither of the two defense concepts was discernibly predominant. This lack of clarity was decidedly to Israel's disadvantage during the first few days of the war."[190]

Yom Kippur War

When the Egyptians launched their all-out offensive on October 6, 1973, only 451 soldiers (just 331 combat personnel) manned the weakened Bar-Lev Line.

With the exception of the three most southern and exposed strongpoints, inexperienced reservists from the Jerusalem Etzioni brigade occupied the maozim. These frontline troops performed their early-warning mission adequately, reporting suspicious and somewhat unprecedented Egyptian activity for days (e.g., minefield clearing). Key intelligence analysts and senior commanders, however, interpreted this information as consistent with the declared large-scale training exercise. On three prior occasions since late 1971, Israel had wrongly suspected Egyptian movement as presaging an attack, diminishing their sensitivity to warning indicators. Moreover, Israeli analysts believed a major attack would not occur until the Egyptians could neutralize the IAF and advance at least to the Mitla and Gidi passes. But Sadat's goal of establishing a foothold in the east bank to upset the status quo and precipitate superpower intervention did not require offsetting Israel's overall military superiority, only along a narrow piece of land. A core reason for the creation of the Bar-Lev Line had been to help prevent such Egyptian footholds, but it was designed to repel limited forces rather than the coming all-out attack.[191]

The strategic defense system would not have been able to block such an effort, but a lack of adequate warning prevented proper implementation of Dovecote. Only on the morning of the invasion did the Israelis realize war was imminent; even then the IDF expected it to commence at 6 p.m. as the Egyptians originally intended, rather than the actual 2 p.m. start time. As a result, fewer than five hundred soldiers and three tanks would precariously man the frontline vice an augmented garrison of paratroopers and nearly two hundred tanks in prepared firing positions. Moreover, continuing doubt at Southern Command headquarters about whether Egypt planned an all-out crossing prompted somewhat confusing signals to the strongpoints in the last few hours. A "shelling alert" for 6 p.m. reached the various maozim between 12:25 and 1:15 p.m., resulting in soldiers manning observation posts outside some of the strongpoints to be ordered to return to shelter. General Gonen also would not issue deployment orders for the two supporting armor brigades of Albert Mendler's division, leaving less than one hundred tanks (one brigade) for a rapid response.[192]

While the Bar-Lev Line did not deter Cairo, Egyptian commanders regarded it as a significant barrier; to overcome it, they studied and trained in great detail. Cairo commenced Operation Badr with the limited goals of neutralizing the Bar-Lev Line and establishing solid bridgeheads. Outnumbering Israeli guns by more than 40:1, Egyptian artillery fired more than ten thousand shells in the first minute and continued this barrage for nearly an hour. Under the cover of these guns, the select first wave of eight thousand assault infantry crossed on boats along the entire canal. The Egyptians' broad advance negated Israeli efforts to identify the primary points of advance. Within four hours, the thirty-two thousand men of the initial assault force were on the east bank having scaled the sand berm, which engineers subsequently cut through with high-pressure water pumps. Expecting penetration of this obstacle to take twenty-four to forty-eight hours, the Israelis were stunned when the Egyptians quickly opened sixty passageways. In less than seven hours, the enemy had twelve bridges across the canal and quickly established strong bridgeheads. As the Israelis had anticipated, these crossings generally occurred in areas out of range of fire from the dispersed maozim.[193]

The Egyptians concentrated on their general advance, but designated units moved to capture most strongpoints. Maoz commanders who took the massive barrage as renewal of the War of Attrition and ordered their troops into shelters left their forts relatively vulnerable while others put up stiffer resistance. Regardless, position commanders immediately radioed for assistance leading the onrushing first-echelon armor of Col. Amnen Reshef's brigade to break up into small relief groups. This division plus the surprise start time led to the unit's rapid decimation. They faced a lethal Egyptian combination of missile-armed infantry occupying the prepared IDF armor positions and tank/antitank systems firing from the west bank. The IAF could provide no relief, needing to first eliminate the SAM threat and facing a higher priority on the Golan Heights front. Assistance could only come from Mendler's other two armor brigades, which eventually reached the front to suffer the same fate as Reshef's unit.[194]

The debate about whether to abandon the maozim commenced almost immediately, but it did not yield a rapid decision. The strongpoints could have been evacuated on the first evening after Col. Dan Shomron's tank brigade battled through intense opposition to reach every maoz but the southernmost fortification. Chief of Staff Elazar had authorized abandoning any fortification not playing a direct role in the defense, but Gonen's orders stipulated support, not evacuation. For Sharon and Dayan, the isolated maozim served no purpose once the enemy was on the east bank, but the Southern Front commander was reluctant to give up these positions without clarity of the battlefield situation. By the time he had an accurate appreciation the following morning, Israeli losses and growing Egyptian strength prevented a controlled evacuation. With Mendler's division having lost more than 60 percent of its tanks, the remaining armor had been ordered to break contact, leaving the maozim isolated. Gonen concluded an evacuation would have to wait until the two reserve armor divisions could launch their counterattack and link up with the strongpoints.[195]

Dayan, however, in a noontime visit to Southern Command, was adamant that the evacuation begin immediately, ordering Elazar and Gonen to have the garrisons attempt to reach Israeli lines if necessary or even surrender. Gonen relayed this order, excepting works on each end of the line. By nightfall on October 7, two maozim had surrendered with another six abandoned. Eight more positions would fall under Egyptian control over the next two days, leaving only two strongholds operational. On the southern flank, the forty-two regular soldiers of Fort Mezakh continued to resist until October 13, when a shortage of ammunition and able-bodied men finally prompted surrender. On the northern flank, the less vulnerable Fort Budapest along the Mediterranean Sea held out throughout the war. Excluding the soldiers in the Budapest position, only about a third of the garrison troops and tankers who had taken refuge in the maozim made it back to Israeli lines. This dismal outcome would weigh heavily on the legacy of the Bar-Lev Line.[196]

Despite suffering a disastrous start to the war, the IDF General Staff remained confident in its overall superiority. At the cost of essentially two-thirds of the armored division, hard fighting combined with limited Egyptian effectiveness prevented the enemy in most places from reaching its Phase I territorial goal of the first ridge line.[197] Moreover, they had transferred less than half of the scheduled 1,100 tanks in the first two days. With Israel's reserve armor divisions deployed to the Sinai by the third day, the Egyptians would have to conduct their "operational hold" phase on less than optimal terrain. The overconfident IDF, however, failed to appreciate the new operational environment that had essentially destroyed Mendler's division. As a result, Sharon and Adan's divisions on October 8 repeated the previous Israeli armor charges against the dug-in Egyptians with heavy losses.

After this costly and ineffective counterattack, the IDF appreciated the need to pause and reassess. The general staff regarded retreat as unnecessary, in contrast to Dayan's call for a withdrawal deep into the Sinai to concentrate on the Golan Heights.[198] But headlong armor charges were no longer viable, and a way to bring airpower to the battlefield was needed.[199] While seeking a solution, the line stabilized from the fourth day (October 9) along the first ridge near Sharon's taozim strongholds. Adan would later acidly observe that, despite fighting along this ridge for six days, "the various divisions made no tactical use of them [the taozim] as they could be of no aid in a mobile defensive battle. They remained deserted in the midst of an area of fierce combat."[200] This result highlights the difficulty in attempting to combine mobile and fixed elements of defense into a strategy along a frontier.

Gloom overtook many Israelis who viewed the new status quo as problematic, but an answer lay to the north. The Egyptian army's cessation of forward movement had allowed the now fully mobilized IDF to concentrate on the northern front. With retreating Syrian units under intense pressure, Damascus persuaded Cairo to order its forces beyond SAM protection. A reluctant Egyptian High Command did so early on October 14, suffering severe armor losses against modest Israeli attrition. The improved balance of forces along with exploitation of a discovered gap between the two Egyptian armies allowed the IDF to advance and conduct a reverse crossing of the Suez on October 16. Soon it controlled large sections on the western side of the canal and had destroyed enough SAM batteries to facilitate heavy IAF support. With only negligible forces between the Israelis and Cairo, a panicked Egyptian government ordered the withdrawal of some troops from the east bank and sought superpower intervention to stop the war. The United States arranged a delicate cease-fire with each side controlling significant enemy territory.

Post–Yom Kippur War

While a shaken IDF aggressively pursued expansion and improvement in the following years, the Yom Kippur War sparked considerable scrutiny of the now politically obsolete Bar-Lev Line. The presence of Capt. Motti Ashkenazi, wartime commander of the Budapest maozim, among the leaders of protests after the war helped keep attention on the strategic defense system in which an expectant public had been disappointed. It is difficult if not impossible to disaggregate the defense elements from the intelligence failure when assessing performance, but officials most involved in development of the Bar-Lev Line countered critics with two points: the barrier had been greatly weakened over time, and the overall defense plan for the Sinai had been the fundamental failing. They added that a fully maintained and manned Bar-Lev Line along with adequate strategic warning and proper implementation of the Dovecote plan would have inflicted far greater Egyptian casualties, reduced Israeli losses, and significantly slowed the assault. The import of this difference was a source of contention. Bar-Lev and Gavish believed such measures along with a preemptive air strike would have blocked the entire crossing, a conclusion that may be wishful thinking from the two senior officers most inclined to view the line as having a key role in defense.[201] General Adan, in his campaign history of the war (*On the Banks of the Suez*), concluded that the IDF even with full implementation of Dovecote would not have prevented the broad, massive Egyptian attack from achieving footholds on the east bank given the IDF's lack of infantry and artillery.[202] Such a counterfactual debate has no resolution, but even in their diminished condition, the maozim provided "somewhat of an obstacle" at the outset because not one fell in the first twenty-four hours.[203] Scholar Yaacov Bar-Siman-Tov concludes, "given the conditions of the war's outbreak, and the lack of proper implementation of Shovach Yonim [Dovecote], there is no doubt that the ma'ozim fulfilled their function in the most optimal manner."[204]

For most officers, civilians, and historians, the Bar-Lev Line represented a signature failure. Long-time critics such as Tal and Sharon aggressively argued that the success of the initial Egyptian assault had revealed the Bar-Lev Line to be counterproductive and more generally condemned defenses.[205] Not surprisingly, many other armor commanders echoed this sentiment given the strongpoints service as "Egyptian bait that would lure General Mendler's tank division to its near destruction."[206] Writing thirty years after the war, Abraham Rabinovich exemplifies history's verdict by writing that "the fatal flaw of the Bar-Lev Line—its irrelevance in the face of a major attack—had been brutally exposed."[207] Herzog highlights the reason why the fortifications became a liability by noting that "over the years, they had become a compromise—between strong points designed to hold the Canal against Egyptian attack, and warning and observation outposts. As the former they were too weak and dispersed; as the latter they were too strongly manned."[208] Such judgments formed as a result of the Yom Kippur War neglect that the barrier's creation and value had always been more about deterring and defeating limited War of Attrition–type conflicts than major war. In a limited war, a purely mobile defense approach would have likely produced strong and unwanted escalatory pressure, whereas the severe losses of rushing armor against hand-held antitank missiles in the Yom Kippur War suggest the negatives of a purely mobile approach to hold the canal line against an all-out effort without strategic warning.[209]

The main strategic error was not the construction of the Bar-Lev Line; it was the government's commitment to hold the canal line ("a virtual 'sanctification' of territory that in itself had little if any intrinsic value").[210] Defending along the canal line "made a mockery of the strategic depth it [Israel] possessed . . . and turned the Territories from an asset into a self-made trap."[211] In place of exogenous strategic depth (i.e., Egypt's lightly garrisoned Sinai), "the IDF was now deployed on the outer rim of what it had previously considered to be security margins."[212] Beyond placing Israeli forces in a more difficult position, the revised frontline greatly shifted relative motivation in favor of the Egyptians. The lack of military strength to push the IDF out of the Sinai only prompted a turn to sustained, limited aggression, which the Israelis struggled to counter. Essentially, no adequate military solution existed for the political goal of maintaining the territorial status quo, especially given the IDF's reliance on a highly skilled but small active-duty force.[213] Of course, the political leadership would not have attempted to hold the entire Sinai if the extremely confident senior commanders had not informed them that it was feasible at acceptable cost.

By contrast, after the war, Israeli leaders were willing to abandon the east bank, obviating any discussion about rebuilding the Bar-Lev Line. Even Golda Meir now appreciated the wisdom of Israel pulling back, especially given Sadat's readiness to open the Suez Canal to all traffic and repopulate the bordering cities. At a Labor Party function a month after the war, the prime minister declared that she should have embraced Dayan's 1970 call for an Israeli withdrawal ("I didn't understand what he was talking about").[214] Through Henry Kissinger's deft diplomacy, Egypt and Israel concluded two partition agreements that transferred control of the eastern Sinai. In the January 18, 1974, agreement, Israel committed to withdraw to the western entrance of the Gidi and Mitla passes; the September 4, 1975, arrangement required pulling back to their eastern entrance and surrendering the Sinai oilfields. Jerusalem had made significant concessions but obtained Cairo's acceptance of "several elements of non-belligerency."[215]

The partition agreements allowed the IDF to effectively use the Sinai's strategic depth and employ a military approach more in line with its strengths and strategic culture. Lt. Gen. Mordechai Gur, succeeding Elazar as chief of staff in April 1974, embodied the now prevalent emphasis on flexible rather than static defense.[216] The IDF subsequently maintained a watchful presence in the peninsula until long and difficult negotiations culminated with an Egypt–Israel peace treaty in 1979. As a part of this treaty, Egypt consented to keeping the Sinai essentially demilitarized and allowing continuous third-party monitoring. The last IDF soldier departed the peninsula in April 1982, leaving the Israelis ironically with its craved buffer zone "but without Israeli presence or sovereignty—a convincing proof that it is possible to achieve strategic depth not only behind Israeli forces, but also ahead of them."[217]

The Egyptian peace treaty would shift Israel's primary security challenge from a conventional military attack by frontline Arab states to small-scale Palestinian violence, a far different problem that eventually resurrected significant interest in strategic defense systems. The IDF has frustratingly spent the last thirty years trying to achieve security against the Palestinian challenge, which ultimately requires a political rather than military solution. While offensive action to diminish Palestinian capability has been a constant, the resulting gains have proven transitory. Thus, IDF officers eventually began turning to defense barriers. Upon withdrawing from most of the Gaza Strip in 1994, the IDF fenced off the territory. Similarly, with the final pullout from southern Lebanon in 2000, it established a strategic defense system along that border. When the second Palestinian intifada erupted in the same year, the Gaza barrier proved effective in blocking would-be attackers including suicide bombers while aggressors could easily advance from the open West Bank. Not surprisingly, an alarmed public and politicians began calling for a barrier to cut off the larger Palestinian area. The governing right's resulting plan to include the main Jewish West Bank settlements within the wall's perimeter upset the left while enraging the Palestinians, but Israelis' desire to reduce vulnerability outweighed all other considerations, and the project has proceeded with a concomitant decline in terrorist attacks.[218]

Conclusion

Traveling on a boat down the Suez Canal today, the east bank appears as a desolate, quiet place far removed from the struggle of the late 1960s and early 1970s. Most of the maozim have been buried under dredging for the canal, and the

Egyptians have preserved a single strongpoint as a museum.[219] Beyond lacking a physical legacy, the strategic defense system failed to leave much of an impression on history. Despite being the most recent barrier covered in this book, it is probably the least well known. Even in Israel, a nation with critical questions about defenses today, the Bar-Lev Line receives limited attention. The nation's military history apparently includes too many glorious successes to allow attention on this less appealing chapter, largely remembered for luring tanks to their doom in the early days of the Yom Kippur War.

Israel's experience with the fortification system is instructive given its effects on adversary and domestic audiences. In late 1968, seeking to reduce the costs of holding the east bank and signal commitment to remain in place, Israel constructed the Bar-Lev Line. Given these objectives, the barrier succeeded, albeit in a way that eventually prompted severe difficulties. Casualties for soldiers manning the east bank proved tolerable even through nearly eighteen months of war. The fortifications, despite frequent attack, remained intact and complicated any Egyptian plan to move across the canal. Above all, the barrier effectively "symbolized its [Israel's] desire to perpetuate the territorial, political, and military status quo."[220] Without a viable accommodation or offensive approach, any counterfactual to the Bar-Lev Line would entail a different type of defense. Jerusalem most likely would have ordered a pullback from the east bank, probably to a line through the Mitla and Gidi passes in the eastern Sinai. In retrospect, such a withdrawal would have been a superior approach, although the extent of the benefit would have depended on Israel's ability to keep the abandoned territory demilitarized rather than filled with Egyptian forces. Instead the arrangements to ensure security of the canal line represented a shift from deterrence by punishment to "a strategy of deterrence based on a supposedly impregnable defensive deployment."[221]

The potential for that strategy was compromised by the barrier being too successful symbolically. Cairo regarded it as signaling Israeli plans to remain permanently on the east bank rather than holding it until the trade for peace became possible. This context created an extremely difficult coercive dynamic, as Shimshoni notes: "Israel treated the post-1967 lines as the status quo and was engaged in trying to deter Egyptian challenge of and at these lines. But for Egypt the only relevant status quo was the 4 June 1967 disposition, so Israel was engaged in compellence. And indeed she was, for at the *strategic* level Israel was threatening to occupy until Egypt made peace. Yet while occupying, she practiced *tactical* deterrence, to minimize ongoing violence."[222] Egyptian leaders' perspective and possession of a large, well-armed, well-supplied force prompted them to be a highly motivated, cost-acceptant adversary. Such actors are likely to repeatedly test a deterrence-by-denial approach unless complemented by a credible deterrence-by-punishment threat. Israel lacked such an intimidation tool regarding the Sinai. This case exemplifies that expectations must be limited for deterrence by denial when using fortifications on adversary or disputed territory, essentially attempting tactical deterrence.

Despite their enormous motivation, the Egyptian military did not attempt to cross the canal in force for more than six years and had been unable to impose severe costs through lesser aggression. Israeli officials and the public, to an excessive degree, credited the Bar-Lev Line with contributing to this result. In part, the government, similar to regimes in other cases examined, encouraged such a perspective by exaggerating the defense barrier's strength. The sobriquet "Bar-Lev Line" alone represented a gross embellishment for small works with gaping holes along the frontier. Such myths help during peacetime or crises, but failure at the outset of war risks badly damaging civilian morale. Ironically, but logically, the myth about the line's strength grew during the "quiet" years of the early 1970s, precisely when Sharon significantly weakened the system by closing almost half of the maozim.[223]

While exaggerated expectations contributed to the harsh judgment of the Bar-Lev Line after the Yom Kippur War, more problematic for Israeli security was its role as a divisive and distracting issue among IDF senior commanders. No one in the high command expected miracles from the modest barrier; rather, even barrier proponents "saw the line as just one component in the overall defense network, of which only the forward line would be static and the rest mobile."[224] Its presence, however, created harmful ambiguity and considerable disagreement over the proper balance and integration of fixed and mobile elements.[225] Rather than resolving this lack of clarity, the barrier served as a source of continuing tension between proponents such as Bar-Lev and Gavish and critics, especially Sharon and Tal. Both groups tended to embrace oversimplified, archetypal characterizations of the strategic defense system that appear to have inhibited coherent, open-minded evaluations of the military's entire approach to defense of the Sinai. Thus, while shifting relative power by virtue of command changes led to either weakening or strengthening the line, absorption with this matter appears to have interfered with recognizing and addressing Israel's fundamental vulnerability on the east bank.

The confusion and debate over the Bar-Lev Line contributed to the IDF's failure to provide wise counsel to the civilian government about maintaining the canal frontier. Perhaps it was beyond such a confident and successful military in the late 1960s and early 1970s to conclude that the task of holding the east bank at acceptable cost exceeded its capability. Nevertheless, the fortifications, regardless of how modest in nature, facilitated an excessive comfort for political leaders with the status quo. Such a perspective discouraged them from aggressively searching for a resolution of the dispute. While during Nasser's life a negotiating partner was lacking, it was not necessarily true after Sadat rose to power, and Israel did not try to reach an accord except on inflexible terms. Moreover, the government did not seriously consider defense alternatives to holding the east bank, undermining the concept of strategic depth. Critically, a previously secondary strategic interest (i.e., a bargaining asset) had been "inadvertently redefined as primary, *intrinsic* interests (for which one *will* fight)."[226] Ultimately, Israeli leaders exhibited a typical reaction to defenses. The longer the status quo holds, the more comfortable and confident officials tend to become with the strategy, including the defense barriers employed to achieve it. With high sunk costs and fixed physical structures, linear fortifications such as the Bar-Lev Line are not well suited to the dynamic of long-term military competition with a highly motivated adversary.

Notes

1. David Korn, *Stalemate: War of Attrition and Great Power Diplomacy in the Middle East, 1967–1970* (Boulder: Westview, 1992), 95; and Yaacov Bar-Siman-Tov, "The Bar-Lev Line Revisited," *Journal of Strategic Studies* 11 (June 1988): 153.

2. Korn, *Stalemate*, 95, 98; and Avraham Adan, *On the Banks of the Suez* (Novato, CA: Presidio, 1980), 42–43.

3. Adan, *Banks of the Suez*, 43.

4. George W. Gawrych, *The Albatross of Decisive Victory: War and Policy between Egypt and Israel in the 1967 and 1973 Arab-Israeli Wars* (Westport, CT: Greenwood, 2000), 103.

5. Adan, *Banks of the Suez*, 43; and Bar-Siman-Tov, "Bar-Lev Line Revisited," 153.

6. Chaim Herzog, *The Arab-Israeli Wars: War and Peace in the Middle East* (New York: Vintage Books, 2004), 231; Adan, *Banks of the Suez*, 17; and Simon Dunstan, *Israeli Fortifications of the October War 1973* (Oxford: Osprey, 2008), 15.

7. Herzog, *Arab-Israeli Wars*, 231.

8. See Korn, *Stalemate*, 98; Jonathan Shimshoni, *Israel and Conventional Deterrence: Border Warfare from 1953 to 1970* (Ithaca, NY: Cornell University Press, 1988), 138–39; and Yaacov Bar-Siman-Tov, *The Israeli-Egyptian War of Attrition, 1969–1970* (New York: Columbia University Press, 1980), 45.

9. Gawrych, *Albatross of Decisive Victory*, 104; and Korn, *Stalemate*, 99.

10. Adan, *Banks of the Suez*, 48, 54; and Korn, *Stalemate*, 100–101.

11. Herzog, *Arab-Israeli Wars*, 202.

12. Adan, *Banks of the Suez*, 47.

13. See Bar-Siman-Tov, "Bar-Lev Line Revisited," 156; Adan, *Banks of the Suez*, 19, 47–49; Korn, *Stalemate*, 105–6, 111; Gawrych, *Albatross of Decisive Victory*, 104–5; and Herzog, *Arab-Israeli Wars*, 202–3.

14. Shimon Peres, *David's Sling: The Arming of Israel* (London: Wiedenfeld and Nicolson, 1970), 24.

15. Gary L. Rashba, "Israel's 'Maginot Line'" *Military History* 22 (August 2005): 31–36.

16. Israel Tal, *National Security: The Israeli Experience,* trans. Martin Kett (Westport, CT: Praeger, 2000), 60.

17. Martin Van Creveld, *Defending Israel: A Strategic Plan for Peace and Security* (New York: Thomas Dunne Books, 2004), 9, 14, 29–30; and Zeev Schiff, *A History of the Israeli Army, 1870–1974* (San Francisco: Straight Arrow, 1974), 214, 216, 242–43.

18. Avi Shlaim, *The Iron Wall: Israel and the Arab World* (New York: W. W. Norton, 2001), 183.

19. Avner Yaniv, *Deterrence without the Bomb: The Politics of Israeli Strategy* (Lexington, MA: Lexington Books, 1987), 100–101.

20. Ibid., 101.

21. Gawrych, *Albatross of Decisive Victory,* 15, 151.

22. Shlaim, *Iron Wall,* 238–39; and Yaniv, *Deterrence without the Bomb,* 134–35.

23. Yaniv, *Deterrence without the Bomb,* 134–35; Michael B. Oren, *Six Days of War: June 1967 and the Making of the Modern Middle East* (New York: Ballantine Books, 2002), 259–60, 311; and Gawrych, *Albatross of Decisive Victory,* 30–31.

24. Shimshoni, *Israel and Conventional Deterrence,* 123.

25. Oren, *Six Days of War,* 248–49, 259, 275.

26. Gawrych *Albatross of Decisive Victory,* 96.

27. Herzog, *Arab-Israeli Wars,* 195.

28. Oren, *Six Days of War,* 315.

29. See Oren, *Six Days of War,* 313–16; Van Creveld, *Defending Israel,* 22–23.

30. See Shlaim, *Iron Wall,* 253–54; Herzog, *Arab-Israeli Wars,* 190, 195; and Bar-Siman-Tov, "Bar-Lev Line Revisited," 151.

31. Ian Lustick, "Israel and the Hidden Logic of the Iron Wall," *Israel Studies* 1 (Spring 1996): 207–9; and Shlaim, *Iron Wall,* 254.

32. Shlaim, *Iron Wall,* 254.

33. See Gawrych, *Albatross of Decisive Victory,* 75–76; Herzog, *Arab-Israeli Wars,* 195–97; Korn, *Stalemate,* 95–96, 99; Shlaim, *Iron Wall,* 258; and Shimshoni, *Israel and Conventional Deterrence,* 132–33.

34. See Shimshoni, *Israel and Conventional Deterrence,* 127, 129; Herzog, *Arab-Israeli Wars,* 197–99; and Gawrych, *Albatross of Decisive Victory,* 101.

35. Shlaim, *Iron Wall,* 250, 254, 259.

36. Shimshoni, *Israel and Conventional Deterrence,* 133.

37. Herzog, *Arab-Israeli Wars,* 195.

38. Adan, *Banks of the Suez,* 72.

39. Ariel Sharon, *Warrior: An Autobiography* (New York: Touchstone Books, 2001), 265.

40. See Herzog, *Arab-Israeli Wars,* 227; and Adan, *Banks of the Suez,* 72, 74, 468.

41. Uri Bar-Joseph, *The Watchman Fell Asleep: The Surprise of Yom Kippur and Its Sources* (Albany: State University of New York Press, 2005), 53–55.

42. Adan, *Banks of the Suez*, 73; see also Herzog, *Arab-Israeli Wars*, 199; Oren, *Six Days of War*, 318–19; Gawrych, *Albatross of Decisive Victory*, 75–76, 102; Shimshoni, *Israel and Conventional Deterrence*, 191; and Korn, *Stalemate*, 98.

43. Shimshoni, *Israel and Conventional Deterrence*, 171, 173, 199, 208; and Bar-Siman-Tov, *Israeli-Egyptian War of Attrition*, 55.

44. Yaniv, *Deterrence without the Bomb*, 171.

45. Shimshoni, *Israel and Conventional Deterrence*, 138.

46. Ibid.

47. Bar-Siman-Tov, *Israeli-Egyptian War of Attrition*, 79; and Shimshoni, *Israel and Conventional Deterrence*, 202.

48. Bar-Siman-Tov, *Israeli-Egyptian War of Attrition*, 188.

49. Herzog, *Arab-Israeli Wars*, 206, 222–23, 293; and Yaniv, *Deterrence without the Bomb*, 147–49.

50. Herzog, *Arab-Israeli Wars*, 203.

51. Tal, *National Security*, 70.

52. Bar-Siman-Tov, "Bar-Lev Line Revisited," 153; Herzog, *Arab-Israeli Wars*, 207–8; and Korn, *Stalemate*, 98.

53. See Adan, *Banks of the Suez*, 468; Gawrych, *Albatross of Decisive Victory*, 25, 139–40; and Tal, *National Security*, 61, 64, 68, 75.

54. Gawrych, *Albatross of Decisive Victory*, 42.

55. Shimshoni, *Israel and Conventional Deterrence*, 180, 207.

56. Korn, *Stalemate*, 100; see also Abraham Rabinovich, *The Yom Kippur War: The Epic Encounter that Transformed the Middle East* (New York: Schocken Books, 2004), 34–35; Gawrych, *Albatross of Decisive Victory*, 141–42; Yaniv, *Deterrence without the Bomb*, 136; and Shimshoni, *Israel and Conventional Deterrence*, 195.

57. See Bar-Joseph, *Watchman Fell Asleep*, 2, 53–56; Reuven Pedatzur, "Ben-Gurion's Enduring Legacy," in *Security Concerns: Insights from the Israeli Experience*, eds. Daniel Bar-Tal, Dan Jacobson, and Aharon Klieman (Stamford, CT: JAI Press, 1998), 147–48; Gabriel Ben-Dor, "Dynamics of the Arab-Israel Conflict," in *Security Concerns: Insights from the Israeli Experience*, eds. Daniel Bar-Tal, Dan Jacobson, and Aharon Klieman (Stamford, CT: JAI Press, 1998), 114–15.

58. Shimshoni, *Israel and Conventional Deterrence*, 190–91. Italics in the original.

59. Dunstan, *Israeli Fortifications*, 12–13.

60. Yaniv, *Deterrence without the Bomb*, 149.

61. Ibid.

62. Michael N. Barnett, *Confronting the Costs of War: Military Power, State, and Society in Egypt and Israel* (Princeton, NJ: Princeton University Press, 1992), 196–97, 210–12.

63. Yaniv, *Deterrence without the Bomb*, 152–56; and Gawrych, *Albatross of Decisive Victory*, 97–98.

64. See Pedatzur, "Ben-Gurion's Enduring Legacy," 139, 148–50; Gil Merom, "Israel's Security Dilemma and Comparative Perspective," in *Security Concerns: Insights*

from the Israeli Experience, eds. Daniel Bar-Tal, Dan Jacobson, and Aharon Klieman (Stamford, CT: JAI Press, 1998), 38–40, 45, 48–49; Yaniv, *Deterrence without the Bomb,* 12–13; and Ariel Levite, *Offense and Defense in Israeli Military Doctrine* (Boulder, CO: Westview, 1990), 74, 154.

65. See Lustick, "Iron Wall," 199, 201, 204, 207–9, 214; and Shlaim, *Iron Wall,* 13–16, 19, 103, 251–53.

66. Yaniv, *Deterrence without the Bomb,* 1; Van Creveld, *Defending Israel,* 14; and Shimshoni, *Israel and Conventional Deterrence,* 173–74, 201–2.

67. Yaniv, *Deterrence without the Bomb,* 19.

68. Ibid., 20.

69. Tal, *National Security,* 47, 50; Yaniv, *Deterrence without the Bomb,* 20; and Levite, *Offense and Defense,* 125.

70. Yaniv, *Deterrence without the Bomb,* 162.

71. Adan, *Banks of the Suez,* 468.

72. Tal, *National Security,* 43.

73. Yaniv, *Deterrence without the Bomb,* 17.

74. Tal, *National Security,* 75.

75. Gawrych, *Albatross of Decisive Victory,* 23.

76. Tal, *National Security,* 43.

77. Yaniv, *Deterrence without the Bomb,* 18.

78. Ben-Dor, "Dynamics of the Arab-Israeli Conflict," 122.

79. Ehud Luz, "Overcoming a Tradition of Insecurity," in *Security Concerns: Insights from the Israeli Experience,* eds. Daniel Bar-Tal, Dan Jacobson, and Aharon Klieman (Stamford, CT: JAI Press, 1998), 63–64.

80. See Tal, *National Security,* 142–43; Shimshoni, *Israel and Conventional Deterrence,* 131, 194–95; Yaniv, *Deterrence without the Bomb,* 13, 128, 150–51, 183; and Levite, *Offense and Defense,* 80.

81. Rabinovich, *Yom Kippur War,* 18–19; and Gawrych, *Albatross of Decisive Victory,* 139.

82. Pedatzur, "Ben-Gurion's Enduring Legacy," 140.

83. Yaniv, *Deterrence without the Bomb,* 150.

84. Levite, *Offense and Defense,* 157–58; and Yaniv, *Deterrence without the Bomb,* 130–31, 159.

85. Gawrych, *Albatross of Decisive Victory,* 144.

86. Bar-Siman-Tov, "Bar-Lev Line Revisited," 170.

87. Shimshoni, *Israel and Conventional Deterrence,* 191; and Gawrych, *Albatross of Decisive Victory,* 3.

88. Barnett, *Confronting the Costs,* 202–3, 209.

89. Yaniv, *Deterrence without the Bomb,* 136.

90. Shimshoni, *Israel and Conventional Deterrence,* 192.

91. See ibid., 190; Gawrych, *Albatross of Decisive Victory,* 98; and Barnett, *Confronting the Costs,* 177, 186, 229, 231–32.

92. Barnett, *Confronting the Costs*, 162

93. See ibid., 153, 158, 191–92, 199–200, 206, 228, 252–53; and Gawrych, *Albatross of Decisive Victory*, 3, 98.

94. See Jonathan Mendilow, *Ideology, Party Change and Electoral Campaigns in Israel* (Albany: State University of New York Press, 2003), 43, 49, 62–63, 66–68, 71, 89; Barnett, *Confronting the Costs*, 179, 187–88, 206; Shlaim, *Iron Wall*, 251, 262, 286–87; Yaniv, *Deterrence without the Bomb*, 160; and Shimshoni, *Israel and Conventional Deterrence*, 171.

95. Pedatzur, "Ben-Gurion's Enduring Legacy," 156–57; and Barnett, *Confronting the Costs*, 74.

96. Shlaim, *Iron Wall*, 143, 220; and Yaniv, *Deterrence without the Bomb*, 20–21.

97. Yaniv, *Deterrence without the Bomb*, 21; and Shlaim, *Iron Wall*, 218.

98. Van Creveld, *Defending Israel*, 27.

99. Yaniv, *Deterrence without the Bomb*, 181–82; and Shlaim, *Iron Wall*, 222–23.

100. Martin Van Creveld, *Moshe Dayan* (London: Weidenfeld & Nicolson, 2004), 145.

101. See ibid., 124–25, 145; and Tal, *National Security*, 105.

102. Tal, *National Security*, 99–103; Schiff, *Israeli Army*, 277; and Shlaim, *Iron Wall*, 288.

103. Schiff, *Israeli Army*, 277.

104. Yoram Peri, "Changed Security Discourse in Israeli Media," in *Security Concerns: Insights from the Israeli Experience*, eds. Daniel Bar-Tal, Dan Jacobson, and Aharon Klieman (Stamford, CT: JAI Press, 1998), 221.

105. Yaniv, *Deterrence without the Bomb*, 21.

106. Ibid., 134.

107. Moshe Lissak, "Militaristic Society or a Democracy in Uniform," in *Security Concerns: Insights from the Israeli Experience*, eds. Daniel Bar-Tal, Dan Jacobson, and Aharon Klieman (Stamford, CT: JAI Press, 1998), 421.

108. Van Creveld, *Moshe Dayan*, 174.

109. Sharon, *Warrior*, 222; and Herzog, *Arab-Israeli Wars*, 201.

110. Sharon, *Warrior*, 218–20; and Van Creveld, *Moshe Dayan*, 145, 177.

111. Bar-Siman-Tov, "Bar-Lev Line Revisited," 154; and Korn, *Stalemate*, 99.

112. Gawrych, *Albatross of Decisive Victory*, 104.

113. Adan, *Banks of the Suez*, 18.

114. See Yaniv, *Deterrence without the Bomb*, 172–73; Shimshoni, *Israel and Conventional Deterrence*, 140; Korn, *Stalemate*, 99; Adan, *Banks of the Suez*, 18, 47, 87; Herzog, *Arab-Israeli Wars*, 231–32; and Sharon, *Warrior*, 220.

115. Sharon, *Warrior*, 220.

116. Bar-Siman-Tov, "Bar-Lev Line Revisited," 149, 151, 153; Korn, *Stalemate*, 105; and Yaniv, *Deterrence without the Bomb*, 160.

117. Gawrych, *Albatross of Decisive Victory*, 105.

118. Yaniv, *Deterrence without the Bomb*, 136.

119. Bar-Siman-Tov, *Israeli-Egyptian War of Attrition*, 122.
120. Shimshoni, *Israel and Conventional Deterrence*, 184.
121. Gawrych, *Albatross of Decisive Victory*, 110.
122. Shimshoni, *Israel and Conventional Deterrence*, 195.
123. Yaniv, *Deterrence without the Bomb*, 160–62, 173; Levite, *Offense and Defense*, 91, 103; and Bar-Siman-Tov, "Bar-Lev Line Revisited," 153, 170.
124. Bar-Siman-Tov, *Israeli-Egyptian War of Attrition*, 64.
125. Adan, *Banks of the Suez*, 45–46; and Levite, *Offense and Defense*, 127–29.
126. Yaniv, *Deterrence without the Bomb*, 136, 152; and Korn, *Stalemate*, 227.
127. Van Creveld, *Moshe Dayan*, 140; Herzog, *Arab-Israeli Wars*, 202; and Levite, *Offense and Defense*, 88.
128. Adan, *Banks of the Suez*, 46.
129. See Sharon, *Warrior*, 220; Korn, *Stalemate*, 103–4; Tal, *National Security*, 152–53; and Gawrych, *Albatross of Decisive Victory*, 105–6.
130. Adan, *Banks of the Suez*, 45–46; Levite, *Offense and Defense*, 127–28; Korn, *Stalemate*, 101–4, 226; and Sharon, *Warrior*, 220.
131. Herzog, *Arab-Israeli Wars*, 202.
132. See Bar-Siman-Tov, "Bar-Lev Line Revisited," 152–55; Yaniv, *Deterrence without the Bomb*, 152; Adan, *Banks of the Suez*, 46, 50; Korn, *Stalemate*, 104; and Sharon, *Warrior*, 220.
133. See Herzog, *Arab-Israeli Wars*, 201–2; Sharon, *Warrior*, 219; Adan, *Banks of the Suez*, 45; and Gawrych, *Albatross of Decisive Victory*, 142.
134. Korn, *Stalemate*, 100; Adan, *Banks of the Suez*, 44.
135. Korn, *Stalemate*, 100.
136. See Tal, *National Security*, 151; Adan, *Banks of the Suez*, 44–46; Gawrych, *Albatross of Decisive Victory*, 105–6; Korn, *Stalemate*, 100, 103–4, 226; and Levite, *Offense and Defense*, 127–29.
137. Korn, *Stalemate*, 105.
138. Adan, *Banks of the Suez*, 46.
139. See Adan, *Banks of the Suez*, 46–50, 56; Bar-Siman-Tov, "Bar-Lev Line Revisited," 153–56; Gawrych, *Albatross of Decisive Victory*, 104–5; and Korn, *Stalemate*, 100.
140. See Adan, *Banks of the Suez*, 48; Tal, *National Security*, 150–51; and Bar-Siman-Tov, "Bar-Lev Line Revisited," 154–55.
141. Sharon, *Warrior*, 220–22; Tal, *National Security*, 150–51; and Adan, *Banks of the Suez*, 48–49.
142. Sharon, *Warrior*, 219–20.
143. Herzog *Arab-Israeli Wars*, 202.
144. See ibid., 201–2; Adan, *Banks of the Suez*, 48–49, 54; Bar-Siman-Tov, "Bar-Lev Line Revisited," 155–56; Sharon, *Warrior*, 220–22; and Gawrych, *Albatross of Decisive Victory*, 105–6. Bar-Siman-Tov notes that Tal and Sharon would later portray their firm opposition to the Bar-Lev Line from the beginning, while other participants

contend it emerged later. He adds that absent access to the classified records, neither version can be verified (Bar-Siman-Tov, "Bar-Lev Line Revisited," 155).

145. Van Creveld, *Moshe Dayan*, 181–82; Bar-Siman-Tov, "Bar-Lev Line Revisited," 155; and Sharon, *Warrior*, 230.

146. Shimshoni, *Israel and Conventional Deterrence*, 141; and Shlaim, *Iron Wall*, 285–86.

147. See Dunstan, *Israeli Fortifications*, 17; Korn, *Stalemate*, 106, 110–11; Adan, *Banks of the Suez*, 47; and Herzog, *Arab-Israeli Wars*, 208.

148. See Bar-Siman-Tov, "Bar-Lev Line Revisited," 156–57; Herzog, *Arab-Israeli Wars*, 207–8; Adan, *Banks of the Suez*, 49; and Korn, *Stalemate*, 108–9, 111, 117.

149. Shimshoni, *Israel and Conventional Deterrence*, 146.

150. See Herzog, *Arab-Israeli Wars*, 207–8; Korn, *Stalemate*, 108–9, 116–18; and Shimshoni, *Israel and Conventional Deterrence*, 143–46, 154–55.

151. Herzog, *Arab-Israeli Wars*, 208; and Korn, *Stalemate*, 109, 111, 113–14.

152. Avi Kober, "From Blitzkrieg to Attrition: Israel's Attrition Strategy and Staying Power," *Small Wars and Insurgencies* 16 (June 2005), 222.

153. Shimshoni, *Israel and Conventional Deterrence*, 145–46, 149; Bar-Siman-Tov, *Israeli-Egyptian War of Attrition*, 85–86; and Gawrych, *Albatross of Decisive Victory*, 110.

154. Bar-Siman-Tov, *Israeli-Egyptian War of Attrition*, 87.

155. Shimshoni, *Israel and Conventional Deterrence*, 150–51; and Bar-Siman-Tov, *Israeli-Egyptian War of Attrition*, 88–90, 98–99.

156. Dunstan, *Israeli Fortifications*, 33; Shimshoni, *Israel and Conventional Deterrence*, 154–59, 196–97; and Shlaim, *Iron Wall*, 291–93.

157. See Shimshoni, *Israel and Conventional Deterrence*, 163; Dunstan, *Israeli Fortifications*, 34–35; Herzog, *Arab-Israeli Wars*, 214–16; Gawrych, *Albatross of Decisive Victory*, 114–15, 117; and Bar-Siman-Tov, *Israeli-Egyptian War of Attrition*, 138–41, 152–53, 205.

158. Shlaim *Iron Wall*, 294; and Korn, *Stalemate*, 228.

159. Bar-Siman-Tov, *Israeli-Egyptian War of Attrition*, 167.

160. Ibid., 159; Korn, *Stalemate*, 226–27; and Van Creveld, *Moshe Dayan*, 148.

161. Korn, *Stalemate*, 225–26.

162. Shimshoni, *Israel and Conventional Deterrence*, 166.

163. Korn, *Stalemate*, 228.

164. Herzog, *Arab-Israeli Wars*, 219–20; Korn *Stalemate*, 228–29; and Bar-Joseph, *Watchman Fell Asleep*, 15–16.

165. Sharon, *Warrior*, 235–36; Herzog, *Arab-Israeli Wars*, 219–220; and Shimshoni, *Israel and Conventional Deterrence*, 170.

166. See Bar-Siman-Tov, *Israeli-Egyptian War of Attrition*, 192–94, 198–200; Shimshoni, *Israel and Conventional Deterrence*, 169–70; Shlaim, *Iron Wall*, 296–97; and Gawrych, *Albatross of Decisive Victory*, 122.

167. Sharon, *Warrior*, 229–30; Bar-Siman-Tov, "Bar-Lev Line Revisited," 157; and Adan, *Banks of the Suez*, 50, 52.

168. Sharon, *Warrior*, 229, 237; Bar-Siman-Tov, "Bar-Lev Line Revisited," 159–60; and Dunstan, *Israeli Fortifications*, 25.

169. Adan, *Banks of the Suez*, 52.

170. See Tal, *National Security*, 152–53; Sharon, *Warrior*, 237–38; Bar-Siman-Tov, "Bar-Lev Line Revisited," 157–61; and Adan, *Banks of the Suez*, 50–53.

171. Bar-Joseph, *Watchman Fell Asleep*, 15.

172. See Bar-Siman-Tov, "Bar-Lev Line Revisited," 159–160; and Adan, *Banks of the Suez*, 52–54.

173. The southernmost taoz (Tzeider) was actually an artillery position for six 155-mm howitzers to cover the canal's entrance (Dunstan, *Israeli Fortifications*, 46).

174. See Sharon, *Warrior*, 237–38, 265; Adan, *Banks of the Suez*, 55–56; and Bar-Siman-Tov, "Bar-Lev Line Revisited," 156, 160–61, 174. As a part of the refurbishment, the IDF hatched a plan to pump oil from buried storage tanks through pipes into the canal and ignite it. After installing systems at Fort Matsmed and Fort Hizayon, a February 1971 test yielded disappointing results. The IDF decided against further systems but installed sixteen dummy sites knowing they greatly concerned the Egyptians (Rabinovich, *Yom Kippur War*, 20–21, 95; and Herzog, *Arab-Israeli Wars*, 232–33).

175. Van Creveld, *Moshe Dayan*, 150–51; and Shlaim, *Iron Wall*, 302–4.

176. Rabinovich, *Yom Kippur War*, 11.

177. Yaniv, *Deterrence without the Bomb*, 137–38; Shlaim, *Iron Wall*, 303–8; and Bar-Siman-Tov, "Bar-Lev Line Revisited," 161–62.

178. Van Creveld, *Moshe Dayan*, 155.

179. Bar-Siman-Tov, "Bar-Lev Line Revisited," 159, 162–63; and Rabinovich, *Yom Kippur War*, 18–19.

180. Kober, "Blitzkrieg to Attrition," 220.

181. Rabinovich, *Yom Kippur War*, 18.

182. See Bar-Siman-Tov, "Bar-Lev Line Revisited," 163; Adan, *Banks of the Suez*, 55; Herzog, *Arab-Israeli Wars*, 221; Sharon, *Warrior*, 263; and Barnett, *Confronting the Costs*, 154.

183. Bar-Siman-Tov, "Bar-Lev Line Revisited," 164.

184. Ibid., 165.

185. Ibid., 162–65, 167; Herzog, *Arab-Israeli Wars*, 221; Yaniv, *Deterrence without the Bomb*, 184; and Sharon, *Warrior*, 270.

186. Rabinovich, *Yom Kippur War*, 19.

187. Bar-Siman-Tov, "Bar-Lev Line Revisited," 164.

188. See Adan, *Banks of the Suez*, 57–58; Bar-Joseph, *Watchman Fell Asleep*, 56–57; and Bar-Siman-Tov, "Bar-Lev Line Revisited," 164.

189. Bar-Siman-Tov, "Bar-Lev Line Revisited," 163; and Herzog, *Arab-Israeli Wars*, 232.

190. Bar-Siman-Tov, "Bar-Lev Line Revisited," 163.

191. See Bar-Joseph, *Watchman Fell Asleep*, 99–100, 135–36, 165–66, 205; and Herzog, *Arab-Israeli Wars*, 227–29, 234.

192. See Adan, *Banks of the Suez*, 20, 81–82; and Bar-Joseph, *Watchman Fell Asleep*, 120, 204–5, 209.

193. See Rabinovich, *Yom Kippur War*, 27–28, 55, 103, 117; Adan, *Banks of the Suez*, 67, 85–86; and Herzog, *Arab-Israeli Wars*, 39–43.

194. See Adan, *Banks of the Suez*, 20, 82; Herzog, *Arab-Israeli Wars*, 242–44; Gawrych, *Albatross of Decisive Victory*, 174–75; and Rabinovich, *Yom Kippur War*, 106, 117–18.

195. See Bar-Siman-Tov, "Bar-Lev Line Revisited," 167–68; Sharon, *Warrior*, 294–95; Adan, *Banks of the Suez*, 83; Rabinovich, *Yom Kippur War*, 119–20; and Herzog, *Arab-Israeli Wars*, 250.

196. See Bar-Siman-Tov, "Bar-Lev Line Revisited," 168; Van Creveld, *Moshe Dayan*, 164; Dunstan, *Israeli Fortifications*, 45; and Rabinovich *Yom Kippur War*, 349–51.

197. Adan, *Banks of the Suez*, 58, 68, 86–87; and Gawrych, *Albatross of Decisive Victory*, 152–53.

198. Bar-Joseph, *Watchman Fell Asleep*, 230–32; and Levite, *Offense and Defense*, 130–31.

199. Herzog, *Arab-Israeli Wars*, 254–55; and Sharon, *Warrior*, 306.

200. Adan, *Banks of the Suez*, 56.

201. See Bar-Siman-Tov, "Bar-Lev Line Revisited," 165–66; Adan, *Banks of the Suez*, 83–84; and Herzog, *Arab-Israeli Wars*, 246, 317.

202. Adan, *Banks of the Suez*, 83.

203. Bar-Siman-Tov, "Bar-Lev Line Revisited," 168.

204. Ibid., 169.

205. Herzog, *Arab-Israeli Wars*, 246, 317; and Bar-Siman-Tov, "Bar-Lev Line Revisited," 166.

206. Rabinovich, *Yom Kippur War*, 106.

207. Ibid., 125.

208. Herzog, *Arab-Israeli Wars*, 246.

209. Bar-Siman-Tov, "Bar-Lev Line Revisited," 171.

210. Levite, *Offense and Defense*, 130.

211. Van Creveld, *Defending Israel*, 32–33.

212. Yaniv, *Deterrence without the Bomb*, 185.

213. Bar-Siman-Tov, "Bar-Lev Line Revisited," 166.

214. Rabinovich, *Yom Kippur War*, 494.

215. Shlaim, *Iron Wall*, 338.

216. Ibid., 335; and Bar-Siman-Tov, "Bar-Lev Line Revisited," 172.

217. Ben-Dor, "Dynamics of the Arab-Israeli Conflict," 125.

218. See Herzog, *Arab-Israeli Wars*, 389, 430–31.

219. Dunstan, *Israeli Fortifications*, 60, 62.

220. Bar-Siman-Tov, "Bar-Lev Line Revisited," 149.

221. Yaniv, *Deterrence without the Bomb*, 152.

222. Shimshoni, *Israel and Conventional Deterrence*, 174. Italics in the original.

223. See Bar-Siman-Tov, "Bar-Lev Line Revisited," 171–72; Korn, *Stalemate*, 226–27; and Dunstan, *Israeli Fortifications*, 19–20.

224. Bar-Siman-Tov, *Israeli-Egyptian War of Attrition*, 63.

225. Gawrych, *Albatross of Decisive Victory*, 104; Yaniv, *Deterrence without the Bomb*, 184; Sharon, *Warrior*, 237–38; Bar-Siman-Tov, "Bar-Lev Line Revisited," 160–61, 163–65; and Herzog, *Arab-Israeli Wars*, 221.

226. Yaniv, *Deterrence without the Bomb*, 152.

8

Conclusion

Lessons Learned about the Use and Abuse of Strategic Defenses

WHEN HEARING ABOUT THE BOOK TOPIC, people often ask whether a particular barrier was effective. While this is an understandable query, it is not a particularly constructive one. It is striking that for each of the six cases, plausible arguments could be generated for the strategic defenses being both failures and successes. Although more difficult for some cases than others, this situation highlights the problematic nature of rendering absolute verdicts. Rather than selectively employing facts and developments to construct such an overall judgment, this concluding chapter presents some common findings from the cases concerning when and how strategic defenses contributed to as well as undermined security. Answering these basic questions provides a way to consider the potential merit of future efforts and to identify the requirements to optimize their effectiveness, especially over time.

Despite the six cases spanning almost twenty-five hundred years, occurring in varied offense–defense technological balances, facing adversaries with diverse military and political capabilities, and operating under alternative regime types, common effects are evident. The variety of the cases and limited information on decision making, especially in the early cases, advises against generating a formal "theory of walls," but they do allow some basic observations for the three dimensions of strategic defense raised in the introduction. First, how do such barriers influence adversary threat perceptions and behavior? This issue provides insights into the critical questions of dissuasion and deterrence. Second, to what extent do strategic defenses alter the military balance in the immediate and longer term? This assessment must extend beyond their direct effects to consider the broader impact on generating military power and safeguarding the nation. Finally, in what ways do strategic defenses influence subsequent leadership and popular attitudes as well as policy choices in the building state? Given that barriers alone do not resolve the underlying adversarial relationships, their effects on internal behavior greatly shape whether these structures contribute to or hamper security.

When considering barrier effects for the three dimensions, it is important to appreciate the tendency to erect strategic defenses after an adversarial relationship is well established. Decision makers usually demonstrate some reluctance to construct fortification systems, especially as the focus of frontier policy. Prowall advocates clearly are present throughout in the cases, but their lobbying efforts usually take time to achieve fruition given barriers' inability to eliminate an adversary's strength or its hostility. A willingness to adopt a major work only tends to emerge after alternative courses of action appear to be problematic on political or policy grounds. Faced with an inability to pursue a viable offensive or accommodation, the logic of strategic defense becomes more appealing to enable these other approaches or, more often, to "buy time" for a subsequent change in strategic context. Even though leaders sometimes adopt heightened confidence in barriers upon deciding to erect such fortifications, it is critical to be conscious of the challenging security environment faced by political leaders and military commanders at the time. It is under such circumstances that officials are inclined to judge the effectiveness of strategic defenses rather than abstract notions of performance. Operating with detached perspective, we can gain a better understanding of the actual context and merit of fortifications, but sensitivity to the perceived pressures affecting policy choice is necessary when drawing lessons because future decision makers will likely operate with similar stresses. To assist in the forthcoming discussion of barrier effects, table 8.1 briefly summarizes the primary attributes and basic effects of each system covered in the study.

Lessons Learned

Exploration of these cases illustrates that the effects of strategic defenses on the adversary, military balance, and internal dimensions are clearly interconnected. The impressions on adversary and internal perspectives are significantly shaped by a strategic defense system's impact on the military balance. Likewise, a barrier's influence on the military balance, especially beyond the period of initial construction, is tied to adversary and internal reactions to the fortifications. During the following discussion, some of the most explicit linkages across dimensions will be addressed, but they are generally considered apart to highlight the manner and degree to which strategic defenses influence each facet.

Barrier Effects on Adversary Perceptions

A rival's reaction to construction of a strategic defense system depends on the rival leadership's understanding of what that barrier signals about intentions and how the barrier alters relative capabilities. The two elements tend to be

(*text continues on p. 314*)

Table 8.1 Summary of Case Studies

Barrier	Built	Structure	Objectives	Operational Period	External Effects	Internal Effects
Fifth century Long Walls (Athens)	Approx. 461–457 BCE; 446–442 for third wall	Continuous stone walls linking Athens with two major ports on the Saronic Gulf	Defense (facilitate concentration on navy and sea-based empire)	457–404 BCE	Adversaries appreciated this structure as impenetrable; as such, it heightened their alarm and resistance, prompting focus on inflicting damage to vulnerable Attic countryside	Increased confidence of Athenians and encouraged their instinct to seek expansion and superiority, resulting in greater risk taking that ultimately led to defeat in the Second Peloponnesian War
Fourth century Long Walls (Athens)	Approx. 394–390 BCE	Continuous stone walls between Athens and the main port of Piraeus	Defense (possibly serve as part of defense-in-depth system protecting Attica)	390–circa 301 BCE	Despite improved siegecraft, barriers remained unassailable until Macedonian era (second half fourth century); even Macedonians exercised caution because attacking probably would involve lengthy, costly undertaking	Increased subjective security, but in contrast to fifth century, these defensive-minded Athenians possibly allowed this confidence to delay their appreciation and reaction to danger of the far more capable Macedonians
Hadrian's Wall (Rome)	Approx. 122–127	Continuous wall (stone and earthen sections) with attached forts across northern England from Tyne River	Symbolism, deterrence, control, and, to an extent, defense	Approx. 127–143 and early 160s–circa 410	Long periods of relative quiet interrupted by brief outbursts of violence suggesting its "psychological weight" declined over time and could not trump con-	Barrier was valued structure, providing increased objective and subjective security; limited in ability to function as force multiplier; although imperfectly

			near North Sea entrance to Solway Firth		textual factors to provide continuous deterrence, especially when the Romans reduced troop strength to deal with problems elsewhere	and only over time, barrier helped establish the northern extent of Roman Britain
Yansui Sector, Ming Great Wall (China)	1474		Continuous earthen barrier with attached fortifications across top of Shaanxi Province	Deterrence, defense, control	1474–1644	After avoidance for several years, Mongol test of the barrier ended in triumphant Ming victory; Mongols responded by shifting attacks to nonwalled areas to the east and west, with success	Increased perceptions of subjective security help obviate perceived need to make politically painful correctives to deteriorating army and reestablish trade relationship; opposition to walls remained sufficient to prevent sustained effort at erecting defenses on adjacent frontiers

(*continued*)

Table 8.1 continued

Barrier	Built	Structure	Objectives	Operational Period	External Effects	Internal Effects
Full system, Ming Great Wall (China)	Mainly 1540s–1580s	Essentially continuous barrier with attached fortifications (earthen, brick, and stone sections) along northern China from Bohai Sea to Jiayuguan, approaching Central Asia	Symbolism, deterrence, frontier defense, frontier control	1540s–1644	Enemy struggles against well-guarded and well-maintained sectors, but the mobility of Mongol cavalry and inadequacy of Ming army abetted probing for weak points and successful attacks against them (later an abbreviated period of a combined defense and accommodation prompted notable Mongol restraint and Ming security)	Barrier encouraged Ming to "muddle through" by enhancing subjective security except for brief periods, when they begrudgingly took more accommodating positions that were abandoned as soon as possible; facilitated denial about need for fundamental changes on addressing army weakness; Ming found barrier too large and expensive to be manned and maintained adequately
Pré Carré (France)	1678 to the end of 1680s	Discontinuous barrier of multilayered fortifications across northeastern and eastern frontiers of France (from English Channel to the Alps)	Deterrence, defense	1678 through mid-nineteenth century with major upgrades	Adversaries appreciated the formidable nature of the defenses; viewed ominously by foes as reflecting and enabling Louis XIV's desire to control western Europe; both reduced French vulnerability and facilitated its power projection into neighboring territories	Increased perceptions of subjective security, but allure of achieving absolute security prompted continuous efforts to strengthen position by adding territory and building more fortifications; such behavior served to heighten alarm of others and spark nearly twenty-five years of continuous war at end of Louis' reign

Maginot Line (France)	1930–1936	Discontinuous line of defenses, anchored by subterranean ouvrages in fortified regions, especially along northern border of Lorraine	Deterrence, defense	1936–40	Drove Germans to consider invasion routes away from the vital Lorraine region; achieving strategic deterrence was not possible given the existence of vulnerabilities elsewhere	Military appreciated limitations of only blocking part of frontier, but line contributed to defensive orientation and facilitated false optimism in security approach among civilians, many of whom believed that the entire frontier was secure (a view government propaganda helped generate)
Bar-Lev Line (Israel)	1968–1969	Discontinuous strongpoints (maozim) with supporting defense obstacles along the east bank of the Suez Canal	Symbolism, deterrence, limited defense	1969–73	Given placement of the barrier on Egyptian territory, Cairo viewed it as signal of intention to retain land rather than hold until it could be traded for peace; this assessment combined with Egypt's insensitivity to costs made deterrence unachievable; still helped prompt Egyptian caution and shape their aggression	Increased confidence in maintaining status quo with acceptable costs contributed to failure to accurately appraise the situation; intramilitary dispute over proper role of line in Sinai defense scheme appears to have distracted the high command from assessing the adequacy of the overall strategy

intertwined; that is, perceived effects on capability influence assessments of intent and vice versa. The latter helps shape the tenor of the basic relationship, while the former influences the prospects for alternative courses of action. Proponents of barriers tend to stress that such structures, being "defensive" in nature, demonstrate peaceful intentions and thus should comfort the neighboring regime sufficiently to improve ties. For example, André Maginot expressed this sentiment when lobbying to erect the French fortification system that would bear his name.[1] Yet experience repeatedly shows that defense barriers tend to exacerbate rather than calm strained relations by suggesting to adversaries the builder's hostile intent and enhanced military capability.

Signaling Intentions
Not surprisingly, structures erected on disputed or enemy territory generate particularly intense concern. The Roman decision to cut off part of the Brigante tribal area signaled an intention to sharply control movement, even potentially block it. This fear apparently prompted the Brigantes, along with southern Scottish tribes, to react violently to the initiation of Hadrian's Wall. Similarly, the late seventeenth century French construction of fortresses on territorially advantageous positions seized beyond the northeastern and eastern frontiers suggested not only their intention to retain the areas to the disfavor of locals and their allies but also to advance further. As Robert and Isabelle Tombs aptly put it, one's view of the French-claimed "'defense' perspective ... depended on which side of Vauban's grim new ramparts you were standing."[2] In both cases, Roman and French leaders appear driven by military expediency without sufficient appreciation of the political ramifications for building their barrier systems. Although the Israelis did not want to hold the east bank of Suez indefinitely, their desire to secure this valued piece of trade bait signaled such an intention to the Egyptians. In each case, the benign concept of "tactical defense" seems to have served as a "strategically offensive" weapon from the adversary perspective. In a study of contemporary fencing efforts, John Donaldson similarly finds, "endowing *de facto* lines with implied permanence, these boundary security measures complicate potential dispute resolution by reducing flexibility in negotiations and increasing the political significance of changes to such lines."[3] Most of the criticism of Israel's current West Bank barrier reflects its path on disputed ground and the perception that it signifies Jerusalem's objectives for the final territorial boundary. Even the inadvertently misplaced 1.5-mile fence section built by the United States near Columbus, New Mexico, across the border has added to Mexicans' hostility toward the general barrier.[4]

A negative reaction in these cases is to be expected, but even defenses indisputably within one's own territory tend to alienate the adversary. Sparta's concern over Athens' Long Walls connecting its upper city with the main ports represents a good example. Even though the Spartans harbored no desire for their rival's soil and the barriers lay well within Attic territory, they appeared threatening by eliminating Athens' primary vulnerability. This accomplishment suggested to the Spartans that the Athenians were aiming at regional domination regardless of their denials, or at least they appeared to be giving themselves the option of pursuing it. Even when the builders possessed a clearly defensive orientation, such as in the cases of the Ming Great Wall and French Maginot Line, the construction of strategic defense systems indicated to adversaries a reduction in their leverage through threatening or committing aggression. Consistent with these historic cases, Donaldson finds for recent fencing efforts that regardless of the existence of disputed territory, "the one constant in each scenario is the negative response from the neighboring state."[5] The norm for barriers to be built after an adversarial relationship has formed and other courses of action have proven unsuccessful or impractical tends to underlie this reaction. In such contexts, defenses are likely to be viewed as a tool to facilitate advantage rather than a benign alternative to an offensive-oriented policy. As a result, they agitate rather than soothe relations, leaving foes to dream of repeating Sparta's 404 BCE destruction of Athens' Long Walls to the music of flute girls.[6]

Deterrence Effects

Barriers' exacerbation of adversary hostility raises the importance of their deterrent potential. In contrast to the more commonly used deterrence-by-punishment approach of threatening unacceptable retaliation, states aim for strategic defenses to facilitate deterrence by denial through convincing an adversary that its objective is not obtainable, at least not at an acceptable cost or risk. While the primary difficulty with the deterrence-by-punishment approach is establishing a credible commitment to retaliate, the hardest part of deterrence by denial is erecting an obstacle of such strength that the adversary concludes—preferably without being tested—that success at acceptable cost and risk cannot be achieved. History can abet this task, as George Quester suggests by noting that World War I demonstrated "the costs of testing a prepared defensive position were now obviously great; if repeated tests were required before an offensive breakthrough occurred, many nations might lack the desire to attempt these tests in the future."[7] Yet such history is not always available. Moreover, the more committed and cost-insensitive an adversary, the less likely it is to reach this conclusion.

All six defense systems examined in this book were eventually attacked, but that does not mean they did not contribute significantly to deterrence, only that their contribution needs qualification. Well-built strategic defenses clearly raise the cost and risk of aggression, but deterrent effectiveness depends on the magnitude of these increases and adversary thresholds for action. While limited information exists on the deliberations of adversaries in the earlier cases, their behavior at least appears to suggest the obstacles engendered some reticence and a search for alternatives. In the latter cases, explicit information shows that the Europeans, Germans, and Egyptians recognized the complicating factor introduced by the respective barriers and initiated determined pursuit of countermeasures. Ultimately, any deterrent effect of barriers only serves to delay aggression ("by months, years, or decades") when facing highly motivated adversaries.[8] The extent to which such deterrence can be prolonged is largely a function of the offense–defense military competition.

Nevertheless, attempts to deter exclusively or primarily through denial are prone to tests when applied against highly motivated adversaries. Whether considering the natives in northern England, the Mongols and Manchus in Asia, or the Egyptians along the Suez Canal, these opponents undertook periodic or episodic limited assaults against the strategic defense systems, whereas the seventeenth century anti-French coalition, the Macedonians, the Egyptians all eventually initiated major attacks against the works. If the only consequence of such forays is casualties to the offensive forces and a failure to achieve a breakthrough, then the disincentives for advancing are too modest to prevent attempts, especially since the adversary controls the initiative and can break off the engagement when necessary. Robust deterrence requires the addition of a retaliatory threat that convinces an adversary that aggression risks more than the status quo ante bellum. Defense barriers can help facilitate generation of a credible threat through diminishing the state's own vulnerability and thus enhancing perceptions of commitment. Of course, this contribution goes to the core of adversary angst over strategic defenses as potentially providing the builder a decisive offensive advantage (e.g., the Soviet reaction to the U.S. Strategic Defense Initiative in the 1980s). The necessity for a combination approach will be particularly strong in cases where the adversary sees the barrier as an attempt to compel rather than deter. The Bar-Lev Line case best represents this dynamic, but it may also have been true in the cases of Hadrian's Wall and the Ming Great Wall if we knew more about adversary thinking. Gaining an appreciation of the adversary's frame of mind is itself a key lesson learned because expectations for coercive strategies should be tempered in such "compellent" contexts.

Finally, a critical distinction needs to be appreciated between the barrier's potential to deter attacks against the covered area and its ability to deter adversary aggression in general. Of the six strategic defenses considered, only Hadrian's Wall truly covered the full length of the frontier from its initial construction. The Bar-Lev Line extended the length of the Suez Canal's east bank, but the limited number and scale of *maozim* positions restricted the Israelis' ability to control the frontline. Athens' Long Walls solidly linked the city with its primary ports, but they left the Attic countryside unprotected. The other barriers initially blocked a front deemed particularly valuable or vulnerable or both. Such partial obstacles shape adversary aggression, directing them toward other avenues of attack (e.g., most famously, the Wehrmacht's invasion around the Maginot Line and, most frequently, Mongol raids around walled sections of the Ming frontier). In writing about the Maginot Line, Edward Luttwak observes that "no defensive line can possibly achieve more than to dissuade the enemy from even trying to attack it."[9] Nevertheless, fortification builders often regard these barriers as facilitating a broader deterrent capability by allowing the concentration of field forces elsewhere. Some proponents of the seventeenth and twentieth century French works held this notion, as did some Israelis with regard to the Bar-Lev Line. Whether barriers function as force multipliers to facilitate greater overall military power will be addressed in the next section, but the absence of physical structures guarding alternative avenues of attack appears to make successfully conveying a general deterrence-by-denial capability to the adversary difficult to achieve. Partially for this reason as well as to bolster defense strength, a tendency exists to expand strategic defense systems over time (e.g., the Ming Dynasty's Great Wall, Louis XIV's iron frontier, and the Maginot Line to a limited extent).

Barrier Effects on the Military Balance

To a large extent, a barrier's deterrent potential corresponds to its effect on the military balance. The correlation is not complete because a wall-builder may employ defense elements that appear to convey strength even if they do not actually possess military value. In other words, deterrence rests on establishing a perception of stopping capability while military balance depends on the actual strength of the barrier. For example, even though the Israelis abandoned a plan to pump oil from buried storage tanks through pipes into the Suez Canal and ignite the fuel if the enemy began crossing, they installed sixteen dummy sites, given their awareness that the failed test generated considerable alarm among the Egyptians.[10] Similarly, the Ming expended considerable resources to build walls up mountainous terrain northeast of Beijing to show the dynasty's greatness as opposed to actually bolstering more legitimate Mongol avenues of attack. The opposite dynamic exists in which certain capabilities or obstacles provide meaningful military capability, but without a visible presence or demonstration of effect, they cannot contribute to deterrence. New covert weapons best exemplify this dynamic given that the surprise element that sharply enhances their effectiveness undermines bolstering the deterrent. Nevertheless, barriers generally facilitate both deterrence and defense.

Properly assessing walls' influence on the military balance requires considering their effects on the area directly covered as well as the general equilibrium.

Proponents of barriers cannot neglect the latter dimension given the dynamics of military competition. Additionally, a very broad conception of "military balance" must be employed, one that encompasses frontier control as well as conventional military considerations. With the exception of the Bar-Lev Line, the barriers guarded frontiers in which people and goods crossed at times.[11] Controlling and channeling those flows represented a central element of works such as Hadrian's Wall and the Ming Great Wall. Similarly, most modern barriers, such as Israel's West Bank system and the U.S. border fence with Mexico, stress this function.[12] In all these cases, opponents have had strong incentives to identify control-defying means as a part of an ongoing competition dynamic.

Efforts on the Fortified Frontier
Whether facing a conventional military challenge, a border control problem, or both, builders have been able to create meaningful obstacles that positively affected the military balance. These defense systems have worked by a variety of means, including increasing surveillance, enhancing the mobility and firepower of one's own forces along the frontier, and decreasing the enemy's options by limiting potential avenues of attack and even possibly reducing its mobility by creating firepower requirements for barrier penetration. Sparta appreciated its inability to directly challenge Athens' Long Walls. Instead, the Peloponnesians attacked—and eventually occupied—the unprotected Attic countryside, launched a surprise raid on the vulnerable port of Piraeus in an attempt to circumvent the walls, demonstrated three times in front of the fortifications to intimidate the Athenians, and ultimately negated their import by gaining naval superiority. Subsequent adversaries were more willing to challenge barriers directly, but the presence of strategic defenses sharply reduced the likelihood of penetration. All six barriers proved able to absorb enemy firepower without significant damage at the time of their construction; even the twentieth century French ouvrages and Israeli maozim could absorb direct hits despite facing weapons of vastly increased destructiveness. An obstacle, even if successfully penetrated, still ensured the attacker suffered far greater costs. Although cost-sensitivity varied among opponents, the danger of such losses prompted a tendency in all to search for alternative avenues of attack or await the development of effective counters. Even if lacking alternatives and willing to accept the high costs from a direct attack, attempting to advance through a barrier is likely to extract a toll in terms of time, increasing the wall-builder's opportunity to react militarily and politically. For example, the anti-French coalition in the War of Spanish Succession, despite possessing enhanced artillery and the willingness to suffer large casualties, required several years to bull its way almost through the Pré Carré fortifications. By this point, the underlying political dynamics of Europe had shifted, allowing France to escape its dire predicament without severe defeat.

The Pré Carré's defense-in-depth accounted for this accomplishment, highlighting a basic issue faced by all strategic defense builders: whether to concentrate on a main line or establish redundancy. Almost every strategic defense system wisely employed some degree of tactical depth with multiple elements as a way to strengthen the barrier. For instance, the Hadrian Wall system stretched more than three hundred feet with a trench, berm, pits, wall, mound, ditch, and mound from front to back.[13] Although all the layers of this system created a strong combined obstacle, the Romans did not pursue strategic defense-in-depth, reflecting the erection of distinct barrier lines separated by a significant interval (about fifteen to thirty-five miles separated fortresses between the two lines of the Pré Carré). In the abstract, a strong frontline combined with secondary barriers provides the stoutest obstacle, but finite resources usually force officials to prioritize. Only in a few cases (e.g., late seventeenth century France, and the Ming Dynasty) did decision makers construct strategic layers along even parts of the frontier. For Louis XIV, such systems facilitated attriting an advancing enemy as well as gaining time to mobilize, to garner foreign assistance, and to await a change in geopolitics. Most wall-builders, exemplified by the French in the 1920s and 1930s, have considered such secondary barriers but decided to concentrate on a main frontier barrier. A robust defense-in-depth system might more positively affect the military balance, but it is inferior at protecting against any penetration along the frontier as well as providing the visible obstacle beneficial for deterring by denial. Given the high value placed on these latter benefits, most leaders have focused on the creation of a strong and strong-appearing barrier. These decisions made sense, but future officials should be cognizant of their prioritized objective (i.e., basic defense, frontier control, and deterrence) when designing a strategic defense system.

Regardless of system architecture, history repeatedly demonstrates that the effectiveness of strategic defenses requires a level of manning and maintenance that fortification builders often neglect or cannot sustain. A tendency exists to embrace an oversimplistic view that the barrier's basic existence provides most of its value as a deterrent and defense. Yet the Genghis Khan aphorism that "the strength of walls depends on the courage of those who guard them" has held through time.[14] While well-guarded and preserved sections of the Ming Great Wall provided a formidable obstacle, the enormous structure always contained vulnerable segments with chronically undermanned or undermotivated soldiers who could be exploited. When the Romans transferred large troop vexillations from Hadrian's Wall to elsewhere in the empire, trouble seemed to soon follow in northern Britain. Only at Athens in fifth century BCE, an era with minimal siegecraft tools, could walls truly be guarded with old men and children. Plus, barriers do not negate the need for skillful management by senior officers. The Marquis de Chamlay, Louis XIV's personal military advisor in 1688, reflected his boss's forlorn hope that well-placed and strong frontier works would empower the king "to grant command of his armies to whomever it pleases him, without having anything to fear from the mediocre capacity of those to whom he confides it."[15] Alas, Louis, like others including the Ming and twentieth century French leaders, discovered that the quality of generalship significantly affects military fortune, despite the construction of frontier fortifications. Finally, barriers' many operational components and supporting weapons must be maintained. Roman and Chinese earthen walls were obvious upkeep challenges, but elements of strategic defenses have been subject to rapid decay without sufficient attention and resources. In every case, officials struggled to preserve a high state of readiness given other priorities.

Before shifting to strategic defenses' broader military effects, these structures' utility in facilitating power projection needs to be addressed. Two basic martial reasons exist for advancing beyond one's frontier: a major offensive to seize territory or weaken an adversary, and a limited, temporary foray to influence the forward area. Fortifications' reduction of vulnerability along a key front abets power projection by lowering the risk of adversary counterattack. Yet it has often been asserted that the structures themselves directly enhance forward movement by providing a secure base of operations and marshalling area. At one time, strong fortresses clearly facilitated the conduct of offensives. France's frontier fortifications in the late seventeenth century provided this benefit, as Louis XIV's neighbors always stressed. Hadrian's Wall also appeared to enable such operations fifteen hundred years earlier. As military power became more mobile, distributed, and standoff, the contribution of frontier strategic defenses in the conduct of offensives faded. Although the emergence of generally well-defined borders also lessened the traditional mission of limited advances to influence forward areas, an appreciation has reemerged for the danger of neighboring ungoverned or unstable regions (e.g., Israel and the Palestinian territories, the tribal areas near the Afghanistan-Pakistan frontier). Construction of strategic defense systems, however, have historically tended to highlight boundaries and complicate projecting influence beyond the line. The Romans apparently discovered that the failure to include outpost forts in southeastern Scotland as a part of the Hadrian Wall system diminished their ability to exert pressure. A subsequent system upgrade included the addition of several such positions to rectify this shortcoming. Similarly, Chinese frontier officials repeatedly stressed the need for adding towers beyond the Great Wall to raise awareness of trouble and influence the area. Recent U.S. operations in Iraq and Afghanistan have highlighted the value of smaller, distributed positions over weakly or ungoverned areas instead of trying episodically to project power from a few large forward operating bases. Ultimately, strategic defenses' influence on the military balance arises from their reducing vulnerability, whether to protect against invasions or safeguard against counterattacks.

Long-Term Consequences for Military Balance

Although strategic defenses initially improve the military balance, their nature complicates maintaining that position over time. In Paul Seguin's words, "a fixed and static barrier system can be viewed as a puzzle contrived for the prospective attacker to solve."[16] Whether it be new weapons to overcome obstacles (e.g., Macedonian stone-throwing catapults or increased firepower of late-seventeenth-century artillery), new capabilities to circumvent the fortifications (e.g., Sparta's attainment of naval superiority; "barbarian" acquisition of seaworthy vessels in the Roman era; Germany's development of effective mobile warfare in the 1930s), or the decline of structures (e.g., the Ming's poorly maintained or undermanned segments of its Great Wall; Israel's closure of 50 percent of the strongpoints along the Bar-Lev Line), the military balance is likely to shift negatively over time. While certainly defenses can be modified and updated as occurred with Athens' Long Walls, Hadrian's Wall, the Great Wall of China, and the Pré Carré, two factors hamper maintaining pace in this competition. First, the defender often struggles to identify mounting vulnerability. It is more difficult to design exercises and tests that diagnose the inadequacies of fixed structures than field exercises. Quester adds that "having erected a fortress on a particular location tends to inhibit speculation about what newer-model fortresses could have been put in its place."[17] When vulnerability has been identified, usually because of adversary activity, no easy or quick remedy is likely to be available. As large, solid, costly structures, these fortification systems severely restrict change possibilities without eliminating the basic system. Even a decision to adopt a radical replacement would have significant military balance repercussions by creating a window of opportunity along the contested frontier. Thus, employers of strategic defenses over time are at an inherent disadvantage against a challenger aggressively pursuing ways to defeat or counter them. Over the progression of history, this problem has intensified with the accelerating rate of technological progress. Whereas the Athenians and Romans went decades without seeing significant changes in the offense–defense balance, the effectiveness of twentieth century French and Israeli works declined in less than ten years from the rapid advancement of weaponry and related operational concepts. Considerable diagnostic efforts must be undertaken to evaluate the evolving competition and identify salient vulnerability; nevertheless, only limited remedial activities will likely be available for the extant strategic defense system.

Broader Military Effects

Both proponents and critics often note that strategic defenses have more general effects on the military balance, which prompts additional questions. Do they entail opportunity costs that critically impinge on the internal generation of military power? What is their impact on obtaining allies as an external source of military power? Barrier critics frequently assert negative responses to these questions while proponents often counter that defenses actually facilitate advantages allowing broader gains. Ultimately, their effects tend be nuanced and determined by context, but the cases examined suggest some general observations.

The most disputed question relates to their influence on the internal generation of military power. Do they serve as invaluable force multipliers or impose deleterious opportunity costs that undermine the associated armed forces? As powers facing numerous security challenges, the wall-builders in this book have generally regarded the barriers as a way to reduce a specific vulnerability while facilitating other goals. The Romans and twentieth century French sought to secure a frontier in a way that allowed safe reallocation of soldiers to other areas. The Athenians wanted to focus on the navy while the Israelis aimed to ensure most forces could concentrate on training for a conventional mobile war. The Chinese hoped to avoid the political and financial costs necessary to reform the army. While the strategic defenses examined clearly reduced the force ratios required to hold the fronts in question, the magnitude of their value as force multipliers tended to be less than initially expected or at least hoped.

Criticism of the barriers studied here as being vast wastes of treasure that undermine military strength appears even more off base. In particular, commentators focus on the two most notorious walls—wishing that the French had not poured so much money into the Maginot Line and that the Ming had exerted some restraint in building the Great Wall. Having examined among the most monumental and expensive defense works in history, one finds that two factors limit this "wasted resources" argument. First, the money employed to erect defenses often has not been available for any other course of action due to prevailing politics. For the French government in the late 1920s and early 1930s, it was build ouvrages or nothing. Similarly, the vast sixteenth century Ming Great Wall reflected the only response possible in a xenophobic and divided Ming court. While the absence of a barrier option might have prompted sufficient change in domestic politics to allow the "better" policy choice identified by critics, it seems unlikely at least in these two seminal cases.

Second, the strategic defenses were simply not so costly as to preclude other financial expenditures if deemed necessary. Excluding the Ming Great Wall for the moment, decision makers rarely disregarded other military assets because of the need to finance barriers (other factors better explain such negligence). Arguably, the Athenian, Roman, and Israeli barriers represented relatively cost-effective measures of addressing a problematic frontier that allowed greater investment on higher priorities elsewhere. Both of the French cases required significant investment, but the nation did not fail to spend on weapons and soldiers when necessary (e.g., Louis XIV's robust army, the large 1936 rearmament bill). Even in the Ming case, which clearly entailed enormous expense relative to government revenue, the dynasty probably could have afforded the walls and other needs if it had not been so politically and bureaucratically incompetent at tapping the vast wealth concentrated in southern China.

If their cost has generally not precluded the internal generation of military power, their impact on adding strength externally through alliances has also been a source of contention. In most of the cases covered, states sought allies, whether just beyond the frontier or far away. Leaders have attempted to stress that by reducing territorial vulnerability, barriers enhanced their reliability as partners. Current U.S. proponents of missile defense often assert this position. Prospective allies, however, have usually been dubious of the argument, believing instead that strategic defenses diminish the common interests that underlay any strong relationship. The answer, at least based on these cases, is that attracting "allies" depends more on strategic orientation than on the existence or absence of a frontier barrier. In cases where status quo–oriented states focused on protecting the homeland, they will have trouble generating and sustaining meaningful relationships. As Jeremy Black observes, after the 1704 defeat at Blenheim, "French strategy became mostly a matter of frontier defense, a course of action that made it difficult to gain allies."[18] Although the French maintained defense pacts with eastern European states after the construction of the Maginot Line and even declared war after Germany invaded Poland, both the eastern Europeans and the French had diminished expectations from the relationship, which produced no significant assistance. By contrast, Athens' Long Walls appear to abet Athenian willingness to support allies, including risking general war with Sparta in 433 BCE to protect Corcyra. Diminished vulnerability facilitated a predisposition for this rising power to act. Given its political and economic global interests, effective missile defense should enhance the United States' ability to attract and especially maintain allies. Of course, sharing such a capability, essentially not feasible with previous strategic defense systems, would likely go further to garner cooperation.

Barrier Effects on the Fortifying State

The general effects of barriers on adversary perception and military balance provide strong cues how to most benefit from them, yet history reveals repeated failures to sustain and maximize gains, as illustrated by the six cases covered. These breakdowns appear related to the way strategic defenses tend to influence the party that erects the structures. Thus this dimension, which at first seems less significant, may be the most critical; it is certainly the least appreciated. The final section addresses a pattern that tends to evolve internally on subsequent strategic perspective and policy choice following construction of a strategic defense. The emergence of this basic dynamic with the Athenians, Romans, Chinese, French, and Israelis despite radically different historic eras and political systems suggests a strong influence. Although it is critical to understand this pattern, its strength serves as a cautionary note that avoiding past mistakes may be difficult.

Given that strategic defenses cannot eliminate an adversarial threat, decision makers sought a reduction of their vulnerability by constructing strategic defenses to "buy time" or operate proactively in a safer environment. Despite being eminently sensible reasons and achievable objectives, experience shows that both of these motivations can entail dangerous long-run consequences. While "buying time" reflects a desire to create subsequent opportunity to deal with the adversary, the distinct patterns that emerge within a wall-building polity for the two motivations recommends treating them separately. To an extent, "buying time" and "operating safety" reflect the differences between status quo–oriented actors and rising powers, but this bifurcation is an oversimplification that fails to capture the reality of great powers who benefit from an existing geopolitical structure but also feel compelled to improve their position if possible.

The far more common circumstance involves states attempting to "buy time" through the construction of a strategic defense system. Decision makers may seek to "buy time" for contrasting reasons. They may desire an accommodation but lack a viable negotiating partner. Israel in the late 1960s had to await Egyptian president Nasser's departure from office before a diplomatic resolution would be possible. Officials may want to undertake an offensive against the enemy but need to build up strength. Yu Zijun in the early 1470s stressed to Ming emperor Chenghua that the Yansui wall would allow the local area to recover sufficiently to facilitate the much-desired seizure of the Ordos region. Finally, status quo–oriented leaders may just aim to perpetuate defensive security, not regarding accommodation or offensive viable in the future. The French army built the Maginot Line to help protect the northeastern frontier and enable broader security until such a time that alternative defense measures could be employed.

Regardless of the reason, barriers provide this breathing space not only by favorably shifting the previously discussed military balance (i.e., enhancing objective security) but also by establishing "a sense of being safe" (i.e., enhancing subjective security). Such perceptions are critical given that they drive public and elite attitudes and thus, ultimately, policy choice. The potential for perceptions of security to deviate sharply from reality exists given the likely significant degree of uncertainty over a state's objective security unless actually involved in a military engagement. Achieving a sense of safety, a vital component of any political leader's duty, requires a favorable interpretation of the situation on the ground leading officials to stress, if not exaggerate, barrier strength. Such "public relations" campaigns have been a staple of strategic defense efforts. Peter Krentz notes that the same year Athens completed the Long Walls (458

BCE), Aeschylus wrote *Oresteia* with walls playing a pivotal role in defeating the Amazonian attack, in contrast to earlier versions of the story.[19] Later efforts up through the twentieth century French and Israeli cases may have been less artistic, but they served the same purpose. Subjective security is hardly limited to the masses. Both democratic leaders (e.g., Athens, France in the 1930s, and Israel) and authoritarian rulers (e.g., Louis XIV, Chinese emperors) took great comfort from their frontier fortifications. Whether being far removed and possessing limited understanding of the defense system or intimately familiar with them, decision makers tended to see the barriers as bastions of great strength. Military commanders have usually been more circumspect in their appraisal, but efforts to convince government officials and the public of their utility have even prompted them to display excessive faith in fortifications.

The enhanced subjective as well as objective security produced by construction of a strategic defense system, however, tends to undermine pursuit of a fundamental, longer-lasting solution to the adversarial relationship. In particular, unpopular political, economic, or military changes are unlikely to occur as the pressure to undertake them has been relieved by the barrier to a critical degree. The Ming dynasty provides the foremost example. The Great Wall, even if not providing perfect security, was sufficient to forgo a politically and culturally unwanted embrace of the concessions necessary for an accommodation with the Mongols or to adopt the major economic and military reforms necessary to obtain better fighting capability. A similar dynamic appears at work with the fourth century BCE Athenians, the twentieth century French, and the Israelis. For these states, barriers not only presented the least politically painful course of action but they also removed the incentive to pursue changes that would improve long-term security prospects.

As a result, the goal of "buying time" with strategic defenses tends to morph into a policy of "muddling through" that entails increasing danger. Whereas the barrier initially enhances both objective and subjective security, over time these aspects move in opposite directions. As discussed in the previous sections, a highly motivated foe aggressively searches for counters to the physical, static structure. While a favorable answer is not inevitable, the cases examined highlight that eventually means emerge that, along with the fortifications' deterioration, decrease a strategic defense's contribution to objective security. The longer this search takes without aggression or at least successful attacks, the stronger perceptions of subjective security become among decision makers and the broader body politic. The Israeli case highlights this dynamic where subjective security with the Bar-Lev Line was highest in the early 1970s, despite half of the strongpoints being closed and the Egyptians having obtained obtaining greater offensive capability. Plato is essentially correct in observing that "walls ... tempt men to relax their guard and to trust to the false security provided by ramparts and bars," but he should have added that the passage of time exacerbates this effect.[20] Complacency discourages not only ameliorative actions that address the basic relationship but also adequate preparations for the evolving military competition.[21] As senior Ming official Wang Shu pointed out in 1484, calm in a walled area inevitably led the government to divert resources, precipitating a dangerous atrophy of defenses and associated troop readiness.[22] Thus he observed that the Ming, facing a mobile adversary, had no reason to expect lasting security.

Even if soldiers and defense experts recognize the growing danger, they will likely struggle to persuade others of the need for adaptation. Indisputable indicators of a changed balance involving barriers are almost always lacking short of conflict. Open-minded leaders would likely still be politically constrained given mass perceptions and loathe to upset them unless it were unequivocally necessary. This phenomenon is likely to be most relevant in democracies, although hardly limited to participatory political systems. Frustrated Chinese frontier officials submitted countless memoranda during the Ming Dynasty, rarely sparking a constructive reaction. The French High Command in the 1930s was constrained by civilians' possession of a "Maginot mentality" even though senior officers appear not to have subscribed to it. While a misguided sense of subjective security is so difficult to overturn without definitive proof, the provision of such evidence risks a severe backlash for holders of a falsely high level of subjective security. For example, the enemy's successful siege of France's strong fortress at Namur in 1695 shocked the court and officials, raising questions about the security provided by the kingdom's iron frontier. The twentieth century cases of the Maginot Line and the Bar-Lev Line provide excellent examples of this demoralizing potential, even though in both cases the enemy primarily maneuvered around rather than overtook the "vaunted" fortifications.

The tendency toward "muddling through" with an increasing sense of subjective security suggests the long-term peril of efforts to "buy time," yet rising powers who act more aggressively, feeling liberated by their reduced vulnerability, have also found danger. As a result of the strategic defense systems, decision makers in these rarer cases (e.g., fifth century BCE Athenians, late seventeenth century French) were more willing to take positions and actions potentially fraught with great risk in pursuit of further shifting the balance in their direction. The Athenians' provocative behavior during the run-up to the Second Peloponnesian War is a prime example as well as their eager embrace of the ill-fated Sicilian expedition in 415. Louis XIV's aggressive and extremely alienating effort through the 1670s and 1680s to strengthen the kingdom's defensible frontiers with additional territory represents another good example, albeit one affected by the king's chronic insecurity. The French appreciated, to an extent, the negative reaction sparked in other European capitals, but the presence of the extant frontier fortifications along with the continent's best army made attempts at further gains seem without too much hazard. Ultimately, both Athens and France suffered significantly as their behavior turned out to be quite risky despite the respective strategic defenses helping to limit the consequences.

If strategic defenses encouraged rising powers to commit risky action and maintaining powers to engender long-term risk by avoiding action, then how can fortifications systems be used most productively? Rather than applying a combination offensive–defensive approach or relying exclusively on a strategic defense, decision makers would appear to be best served by a combination of defense and accommodation. Such a strategy had rarely been applied in the cases examined. Even the few examples do not reflect approaches attempted with the construction of the barrier; rather, the Romans and Ming adopted it after perceptions of a declining military balance compelled employment. The policy appears to have achieved success in each case, reiterating the question of why this strategy had not been employed more often. The aforementioned effects of strategic defenses on the three dimensions combine to discourage such an approach despite its appearing to offer the best long-term prospects. After barrier construction, the adversary likely possesses a heightened threat perception and weakened military position, disinclining them to pursue a political resolution at a time of reduced leverage. The situation might force adversaries to negotiate some expedient compact, but such a coerced agreement will not lead to a legitimate, sustained accommodation. By contrast, the fortification system has strengthened the military position of the wall-builder and correspondingly lowered its threat perception, diminishing the perceived need to seek an accommodation. Somewhat counterintuitively, given these relative effects, the building state would likely have to offer more flexible or conciliatory terms to end the hostile relationship.

With strategic defenses being a "wasting asset" whose effect on the military balance is greatest at the outset, wall-builders would be wise to appreciate the value of a diplomatic push to reach a political resolution in conjunction with construction of a barrier. Although it would likely take greater flexibility of terms, such conciliatory positioning would invoke far less risk given the reduced vulnerability along the frontier. Reaching an accommodation would change the political–strategic dynamic, which should reduce the rate that the barrier's effectiveness declines over time. Eventually, the strategic defenses would hopefully become unnecessary, but its near-term maintenance as a part of a joint approach would be essential to safeguarding against the adversary backsliding toward a more confrontational frontier policy. Historians have in some cases suggested that a pure accommodation would have been the best policy, yet such efforts risk exploitation by the adversary in the short and longer term, as suggested by the counterfactuals of no barrier discussed in the conclusion of each chapter. Of course, an accommodation may not be possible given the nature of the adversary political leadership. In such cases, wall-builders must bide their time and be hypervigilant to developments that compromise the security initially generated by the barrier. Still, given what is known about the long-term dynamics, it would behoove leaders to sincerely attempt to garner the adversary's interest in a rapprochement.

If officials in Israel and the United States want to achieve more than "muddling through" with their strategic defense systems, they likely will need to overcome the political pressures that discourage a joint defense-accommodation approach. Current evidence does not produce high expectations for such a policy in either case. While Israel's array of walls increasingly cocoons the nation, they—along with periodic limited offensives—appear to be alleviating the pressure for aggressively seeking a more fundamental resolution. One can argue about the viability of a particular Palestinian leader or group as a negotiating partner, but no one should conclude that the walls obviate the need for negotiations on realistic terms. With fences covering less than 20 percent of the Mexican border and missile defense essentially still in its developmental stage, U.S. efforts have not advanced to a level that has significantly altered the military balance with respective adversaries. Nevertheless, as with the Israelis, the impression suggested by policy debates to date is that rather than facilitating a combined approach, these strategic defenses will encourage U.S. decision makers to forgo difficult choices and operate as long as possible under the safety they provide. Obviously, an earnest joint wall-accommodation approach entails some policy and short-term political risk for leaders, but leaders need to appreciate that without this approach, the longer-term risk compounds. Decision makers, especially in democracies, tend to discount future risks. Future wall-builders who do so will repeat the mistakes of their predecessors.

Notes

1. Vivian Rowe, *The Great Wall of France: The Triumph of the Maginot Line* (London: Putnam, 1959), 50.

2. Robert Tombs and Isabelle Tombs, *That Sweet Enemy: The French and the British from the Sun King to the Present* (New York: Alfred A. Knopf, 2007), 9.

3. John W. Donaldson, "Fencing the Line: Analysis of the Recent Rise in Security Measures along Disputed and Undisputed Boundaries," in *Global Surveillance and Policy*, ed. Elia Zureik and Mark B. Salter (Portland: Willan Publishing, 2005), 183.

4. "Misplaced U.S.-Mexico Fence Could Cost Feds Millions," *Associated Press*, 30 June 2007.

5. Donaldson, "Fencing the Line," 189.

6. Xenophon, *Hellenica*, Books I–IV (Cambridge, MA: Harvard University Press, 1997), II.2.23.

7. George Quester, *Offense and Defense in the International System* (New Brunswick, NJ: Transaction Publishers, 2003), 113–14.

8. Paul Seguin, *The Strategic Performance of Defense Barriers* (Fort Belvoir, VA: U.S. Army Engineer Studies Center, 1988), 23.

9. Edward Luttwak, *Strategy: The Logic of War and Peace* (Cambridge, MA: Harvard University Press, 1987), 120.

10. Chaim Herzog, *The Arab-Israeli Wars: War and Peace in the Middle East* (New York: Vintage Books, 2004), 232–33.

11. Athens' Long Walls were another exception in the sense that they did not run along a frontier.

12. Donaldson, "Fencing the Line," 178–88.

13. James Crow, "The Northern Frontier of Britain from Trajan to Antoninus Pius," in *A Companion to Roman Britain*, ed. Malcolm Todd (Malden, MA: Blackwell, 2007), 130.

14. Julia Lovell, *The Great Wall: China against the World, 1000 BC–AD 2000* (New York: Grove, 2006), 17.

15. John Lynn, "A Quest for Glory: The Formation of Strategy under Louis XIV, 1661–1715," in *The Making of Strategy: Rulers, States, and War*, eds. Williamson Murray, MacGregor Knox, and Alvin Bernstein (New York: Cambridge University Press, 1994), 183–84.

16. Seguin, *Strategic Performance of Defense Barriers*, 27.

17. Quester, *Offense and Defense in International System*, 62.

18. Jeremy Black, *From Louis XIV to Napoleon: The Fate of a Great Power* (London: UCL Press, 1999), 62.

19. Peter Krentz, "The Strategic Culture of Periclean Athens," *Polis and Polemos*, ed. C. Hamilton and P. Krentz (Claremont, CA: Regina, 1997), 64–65.

20. Josiah Ober, *Fortress Attica: Defense of the Athenian Land Frontier, 404–322 BC* (Leiden: Brill, 1985), 54–55.

21. Quester, *Offense and Defense in International System*, 62.

22. Alastair Ian Johnston, *Cultural Realism: Strategic Culture and Grand Strategy in Chinese History* (Princeton: Princeton University Press, 1995), 187.

Selected Bibliography

This bibliography is not a complete record of all the works and sources consulted in writing this book. It indicates the substance and range of reading upon which I have formed my ideas and is intended to serve as a convenience for those who wish to pursue the study of strategic defenses, especially the case studies covered in this work.

Adamthwaite, Anthony. *Grandeur and Misery: France's Bid for Power in Europe 1914–1940.* New York: St. Martin's Press, 1995.

Adan, Avraham. *On the Banks of the Suez.* Novato, CA: Presidio, 1980.

Alexander, Martin. "In Defense of the Maginot Line." In *French Foreign and Defense Policy, 1918–1940: The Decline and Fall of a Great Power,* edited by Robert Boyce, 164–94. New York: Routledge, 1998.

———. *The Republic in Danger: General Maurice Gamelin and the Politics of French Defense.* Cambridge: Cambridge University Press, 1992.

Allcorn, William. *The Maginot Line, 1928–1945.* Oxford: Osprey, 2003.

Barfield, Thomas J. *The Perilous Frontier: Nomadic Empires and China, 221 BC to AD 1757.* Cambridge, MA: Blackwell, 1989.

Bar-Joseph, Uri. *The Watchman Fell Asleep: The Surprise of Yom Kippur and Its Sources.* Albany: State University of New York Press, 2005.

Barnett, Michael N. *Confronting the Costs of War: Military Power, State, and Society in Egypt and Israel.* Princeton, NJ: Princeton University Press, 1992.

Bar-Siman-Tov, Yaacov. "The Bar-Lev Line Revisited," *Journal of Strategic Studies* 11 (June 1988): 149–76.

———. *The Israeli-Egyptian War of Attrition, 1969–1970.* New York: Columbia University Press, 1980.

Bar-Tal, Daniel, Dan Jacobson, and Aharon Klieman, eds. *Security Concerns: Insights from the Israeli Experience.* Stamford, CT: JAI Press, 1998.

Bédoyère, Guy de la. *Hadrian's Wall: History and Guide.* Stroud, Glouestershire: Tempus, 2000.

Birley, Anthony R. *Hadrian: The Restless Emperor.* London: Routledge, 1997.

Birley, Anthony R., trans. *Lives of Later Caesars: The First Part of the Augustan History with Newly Compiled Lives of Nerva and Trajan.* London: Penguin Books, 1976.

Black, Jeremy. *From Louis XIV to Napoleon: The Fate of a Great Power.* London: UCL Press, 1999.

Breeze, David. "The Edge of the World: Imperial Frontier and Beyond." In *The Roman Era*, edited by Peter Salway, 173–202. Oxford: Oxford University Press, 2002.

Campbell, Brian. *War and Society in Imperial Rome, 31 BC–AD 284.* London: Routledge, 2002.

Campbell, Duncan. *Ancient Siege Warfare: Persians, Greeks, Carthaginians and Romans 546–146 BC.* Oxford: Osprey, 2005.

Conwell, David H. *The Athenian Long Walls: Chronology, Topography, and Remains.* PhD diss., University of Pennsylvania, 1992.

———. *Connecting a City to the Sea: The History of the Athenian Long Walls.* Boston: Brill, 2008.

Crow, James. "The Northern Frontier of Britain from Trajan to Antoninus Pius: Roman Builders and Native Britons." In *A Companion to Roman Britain*, edited by Malcolm Todd, 114–35. Malden, MA: Blackwell, 2007.

Donaldson, John W. "Fencing the Line: Analysis of the Recent Rise in Security Measures along Disputed and Undisputed Boundaries." In *Global Surveillance and Policy*, edited by Elia Zureik and Mark B. Salter, 173–93. Portland: Willan Publishing, 2005.

Doughty, Robert A. "The French Armed Forces, 1918–1940." In *Military Effectiveness*, Volume 2, *The Intrawar Period*, edited by Allen Millett and Williamson Murray, 39–69. Boston: Allen and Unwin, 1988.

———. "The Illusion of Security: France, 1919–1940." In *The Making of Strategy: Rulers, States, and War*, edited by Williamson Murray, MacGregor Knox, and Alvin Bernstein, 466–97. New York: Cambridge University Press, 1994.

———. *The Seeds of Disaster: The Development of French Army Doctrine, 1919–1939.* Hamden, CT: Archon Books, 1985.

Duffy, Christopher. *Siege Warfare: The Fortress in the Age of Vauban and Frederick the Great, 1660–1789.* New York: Routledge Press, 1985.

Dunstan, Simon. *Israeli Fortifications of the October War 1973.* Oxford: Osprey, 2008.

Ekberg, Carl. *The Failure of Louis XIV's Dutch War.* Chapel Hill: North Carolina University Press, 1979.

Erlanger, Philippe. *Louis XIV.* Translated by Stephen Cox. London: Weidenfeld and Nicholson, 1970.

Fields, Nic. *Ancient Greek Fortifications: 500–300 BC.* Oxford: Osprey, 2006.

———. *Hadrian's Wall: AD 122–140.* Oxford: Osprey, 2003.

———. *Rome's Northern Frontier AD 70–235: Beyond Hadrian's Wall.* Oxford: Osprey, 2005.

Frere, Sheppard. *Britannia: A History of Roman Britain.* London: Routledge, 1987.

Fulford, Michael. "A Second Start: From the Defeat of Boudicca to the Third Century." In *The Roman Era*, edited by Peter Salway, 39–74. Oxford: Oxford University Press, 2002.

Gawrych, George W. *The Albatross of Decisive Victory: War and Policy between Egypt and Israel in the 1967 and 1973 Arab-Israeli Wars*. Westport, CT: Greenwood, 2000.

Geiss, James. "The Jiajing Reign." In *The Cambridge History of China*, Vol. 7, *The Ming Dynasty, 1368–1644, Part I*, edited by Frederick Mote and Denis Twitchett, 440–510. New York: Cambridge University Press, 1988.

Goldsworthy, Adrian. *Roman Warfare*. London: Cassell, 2000.

Griffith, Paddy. *The Vauban Fortifications of France*. Oxford: Osprey, 2006.

Hanson, Victor Davis. *A War Like No Other: How the Athenians and Spartans Fought the Peloponnesian War*. New York: Random House, 2005.

———. *Warfare and Agriculture in Classical Greece*. Berkeley: University of California Press, 1998.

———. *The Wars of the Ancient Greeks*. London: Cassell, 1999.

Hebbert, F. J., and G. A. Rothrock. *Soldier of France: Sébastien Le Prestre de Vauban, 1633–1707*. New York: Peter Lang, 1989.

Herodotus. *The Histories*. Translated by Aubrey De Selincourt. New York: Penguin Books, 1996.

Herzog, Chaim. *The Arab-Israeli Wars: War and Peace in the Middle East*, rev. ed. New York: Vintage Books, 2004.

Hucker, Charles. "Ming Government." In *Cambridge History of China*, Vol. 8, *The Ming Dynasty, 1368–1644, Part II*, edited by Denis Twichett and Frederick Mote, 9–105. New York: Cambridge University Press, 1998.

Hughes, Judith M. *To the Maginot Line: The Politics of French Military Preparation in the 1920s*. Cambridge, MA: Harvard University Press, 1971.

Johnston, Alastair. *Cultural Realism: Strategic Culture and Grand Strategy in Chinese History*. Princeton, NJ: Princeton University Press, 1995.

Kagan, Donald. *The Peloponnesian War*. New York: Viking, 2003.

Kaufmann, J. E., and H. W. Kaufmann. *Fortress France: The Maginot Line and French Defenses in World War II*. Westport, CT: Praeger, 2006.

———. *The Maginot Line: None Shall Pass*. Westport, CT: Praeger, 1997.

Kier, Elizabeth. *Imagining War: French and British Military Doctrine between the Wars*. Princeton, NJ: Princeton University Press, 1997.

Kiesling, Eugenia C. *Arming against Hitler: France and the Limits of Military Planning*. Lawrence: University Press of Kansas, 1996.

Korn, David A. *Stalemate: The War of Attrition and Great Power Diplomacy in the Middle East, 1967–1970*. Boulder: Westview, 1992.

Krentz, Peter. "The Strategic Culture of Periclean Athens." In *Polis and Polemos: Essays on Politics, War, and History in Ancient Greece in Honor of Donald Kagan*, edited by C. Hamilton and P. Krentz, 55–72. Claremont, CA: Regina, 1997.

Langins, Janis. *Conserving the Enlightment: French Military Engineering from Vauban to the Revolution*. Cambridge, MA: MIT Press, 2004.

Levite, Ariel. *Offense and Defense in Israeli Military Doctrine*. Boulder: Westview, 1990.

Lindesay, William. *The Great Wall.* New York: Oxford University Press, 2003.
Lossky, Andrew. *Louis XIV and the French Monarchy.* New Brunswick, NJ: Rutgers University Press, 1994.
Lovell, Julia. *The Great Wall: China against the World, 1000 BC–AD 2000.* New York: Grove, 2006.
Lynn, John A. *Giant of the Grand Siècle: The French Army, 1610–1715.* New York: Cambridge University Press, 1997.
———. "A Quest for Glory: The Formation of Strategy under Louis XIV, 1661–1715." In *The Making of Strategy: Rulers, States, and War,* edited by Williamson Murray, MacGregor Knox, and Alvin Bernstein, 178–204. New York: Cambridge University Press, 1994.
———. *The Wars of Louis XIV, 1667–1714.* London: Longman, 1999.
Mattern, Susan P. *Rome and the Enemy: Imperial Strategy in the Principate.* Berkeley: University of California Press, 1999.
May, Ernest R. *Strange Victory: Hitler's Conquest of France.* New York: Hill and Wang, 2000.
McGregor, Malcolm. *The Athenians and Their Empire.* Vancouver: University of British Columbia Press, 1987.
Mote, Frederick, "The Chenghua and Hongzhi Reigns." In *The Cambridge History of China,* Vol. 7, *The Ming Dynasty, 1368–1644, Part I,* edited by Frederick Mote and Denis Twitchett, 343–402. New York: Cambridge University Press, 1988.
———. *Imperial China, 900–1800.* Cambridge, MA: Harvard University Press, 2003.
Mote, Frederick and Denis Twichett, eds. *The Cambridge History of China,* Vol. 7, *The Ming Dynasty, 1368–1644, Part I.* New York: Cambridge University Press, 1998.
Murray, Williamson, MacGregor Knox, and Alvin Burnstein, eds. *The Making of Strategy: Rulers, States, and War.* New York: Cambridge University Press, 1994.
Ober, Josiah. *Fortress Attica: Defense of the Athenian Land Frontier, 404–322 BC.* Leiden: Brill, 1985.
———. "Hoplites and Obstacles." In *Hoplites: The Classical Greek Battle Experience,* edited by Victor Davis Hanson, 173–96. New York: Routledge, 1991.
Ostwald, Jamel. *Vauban under Siege: Engineering Efficiency and Martial Vigor in the War of the Spanish Succession.* Leiden: Brill, 2007.
Parker, Geoffrey. *The Military Revolution: Military Innovation and the Rise of the West, 1500–1800.* Cambridge: Cambridge University Press, 1996.
Plutarch. *The Rise and Fall of Athens: Nine Greek Lives.* Translated by Ian Scott-Kilvert. New York: Penguin Books, 1960.
Podlecki, Anthony. *Perikles and His Circle.* New York: Routledge, 1998.
Rabinovich, Abraham. *The Yom Kippur War: The Epic Encounter that Transformed the Middle East.* New York: Schocken Books, 2004.
Rowe, Vivian. *The Great Wall of France: The Triumph of the Maginot Line.* London: Putnam, 1959.

Rule, John, ed. *Louis XIV and the Craft of Kingship.* Columbus: Ohio State University Press, 1969.

Ryan, Stephen. *Pétain the Soldier.* South Brunswick, NJ: A.S. Barnes, 1969.

Salway, Peter, ed. *The Roman Era.* Oxford: Oxford University Press, 2002.

Santosuosso, Antonio. *Storming the Heavens: Soldiers, Emperors, and Civilians in the Roman Empire.* Boulder: Westview, 2001.

Sealey, Raphael. *Demosthenes and His Time: A Study in Defeat.* New York: Oxford University Press, 1993.

Serruys, Henry. "Towers in the Northern Frontier Defenses of the Ming," *Ming Studies* 14 (Spring 1982): 9–60.

Sharon, Ariel. *Warrior: An Autobiography.* New York: Touchstone Books, 2001.

Shimshoni, Jonathan. *Israel and Conventional Deterrence: Border Warfare from 1953 to 1970.* Ithaca, NY: Cornell University Press, 1988.

Shlaim, Avi. *The Iron Wall: Israel and the Arab World.* New York: W. W. Norton, 2001.

Shotter, David. *The Roman Frontier in Britain: Hadrian's Wall, The Antonine Wall, and Roman Policy in the North.* Lancaster, England: Carnegie Publishing, 1996.

Strauss, Barry S. *Athens after the Peloponnesian War: Class, Faction and Policy 403–386 BC.* London: Croom Helm, 1986.

———. *The Battle of Salamis: The Naval Encounter That Saved Greece—and Western Civilization.* New York: Simon & Schuster, 2004.

Tal, Israel. *National Security: The Israeli Experience.* Translated by Martin Kett. Westport, CT: Praeger, 2000.

Thucydides. *History of the Peloponnesian War.* Translated by Rex Warner. London: Penguin Books, 1972.

Todd, Malcolm, ed. *A Companion to Roman Britain.* Malden, MA: Blackwell, 2007.

Tombs, Robert, and Isabelle Tombs. *That Sweet Enemy: The French and the British from the Sun King to the Present.* New York: Alfred A. Knopf, 2007.

Trotter, Ben Scott. "Marshal Vauban and the Administration of Fortifications under Louis XIV (to 1691)." PhD diss., Ohio State University, 1993.

Turnbull, Stephen. *The Great Wall of China, BC 221–AD 1644.* Oxford: Osprey, 2007.

Twichett, Dennis, and Frederick Mote. *The Cambridge History of China,* Vol. 8, *The Ming Dynasty, 1368–1644, Part II.* New York: Cambridge University Press, 1998.

Van Creveld, Martin. *Moshe Dayan.* London: Weidenfeld & Nicolson, 2004.

Waldron, Arthur. "Chinese Strategy from the Fourteenth to the Seventeenth Centuries." In *The Making of Strategy: Rulers, States, and War,* edited by Williamson Murray, MacGregor Knox, and Alvin Burnstein, 85–114. New York: Cambridge University Press, 1994.

———. *The Great Wall of China: From History to Myth.* New York: Oxford University Press, 1990.

Whittaker, C. R. *Frontiers of the Roman Empire: A Social and Economic Study.* Baltimore: The Johns Hopkins University Press, 1994.

Winter, F. E. *Greek Fortifications*. Toronto: Toronto University Press, 1971.
Wolf, John. *Louis XIV.* New York: Norton, 1968.
Xenophon. *Hellenica, Books I–IV.* Translated by Carleton Brownson. Cambridge, MA: Harvard University Press, 1997.
Yaniv, Avner. *Deterrence without the Bomb: The Politics of Israeli Strategy.* Lexington, MA: Lexington Books, 1987.
Young, Robert J. *In Command of France: French Foreign Policy and Military Planning, 1933–1940.* Cambridge, MA: Harvard University Press, 1978.
———. *France and the Origins of the Second World War.* London: MacMillan, 1996.

About the Author

Brent L. Sterling is an adjunct lecturer at the School of Foreign Service, Georgetown University. He has spent the past twenty years as a Washington, D.C.–based defense analyst, including stints at the Central Intelligence Agency and consulting firms supporting the Department of Defense. Dr. Sterling's work has focused on issues of strategy, coercion, and political-military decision making.

Index

Figures and tables are indicated by *f* and *t* following the page number.

Abahai, 142–44
accommodation (political strategy): and "buying time," 6, 324; and demotivating enemy hostility, 5; French policy of, 221, 224; and Pré Carré, 175–76; and strategic culture, 121–22; and strategic defense, 309, 327–28. *See also* accommodation policy in China
accommodation policy in China: and Abahai, 143; and "absolute flexibility," 122; as defense strategy, 127–28, 146–47; Ming options for, 107, 138, 140; prospects for, 145; Yu Zijun as proponent of, 125, 127, 130, 147
Adan, Avraham "Bren": and Bar-Lev Line creation, 258, 259; and defense-in-depth strategy, 279; and national security decision making, 276, 281–82; on security defense strategy, 270; and Sinai defense, 276; and threat perception, 265; and Yom Kippur War and subsequent debate, 292, 293
Adimantus, 29
adversary perceptions, 309–14, 323. *See also* psychological aspects of fortified defense; threat perceptions
Aegina, 15, 33, 37
Aegospotami, Battle of, 44
Aeschines, 49
Aeschylus, 23, 34, 325
Afghanistan, U.S. operations in, 320
Agis, King, 43, 44

agonal (hoplite) warfare, 22–23, 28, 45
Ahdut HaAvoda party (Israel), 273, 274
Aire (France), capture of, 178, 179, 191
Aix-la-Chapelle, Treaty of, 163
Alcibiades, 41–42, 43, 53
Alexander the Great, 49
Alexander, Martin, 234, 244
Allon, Yigal: on defense strategy, 1, 271; on deterrence, 270; and national security decision making, 274; and postwar debate about Bar-Lev Line, 288; and postwar occupation, 263
Alsace-Lorraine region, 206, 209, 211, 214, 218, 229, 239
Altan Khan, 136, 138, 140
Amazonians (legendary people), 34
Ammianus Marcellinus, 94
Andocides, 36
Anne, Queen, 191
Anthemius, 4
Antigonus, 52
Antonine Wall, 65, 90, 91, 92, 95
Antoninus Pius, 89–91, 96–97
Apollodorus, 80
Appian, 81, 97
Arab–Israeli peace agreement, 267
Arab Summit Conference of 1967, 258
Archidamian War (431–421 BCE), 38–42
Ardennes region, defense of, 207, 215, 227, 231, 235, 238, 240, 242, 244, 246
Area Defense System (Israel), 261

Argos, 20, 22, 41, 42, 46
Aristides, 19
Aristotle, 47
armor-based defense, mobile, 279–80, 287, 294
Arrian, 77
Ashkenazi, Motti, 293
Athenian navy. *See* navy, Athenian
Athens' Long Walls, 8, 13–63; and Archidamian War, 38–42; army enhancements, 27; comparison of main features, 10t, 309, 310–13t; and Decelean War, 42–45; decision context of, 21–26, 53; democratic power, rise of, 16–20; domestic politics, 25–26; fourth century restored long walls, 45–49, 54; frontier fortifications, 27–28; Hadrian's observation of, 84–85; and land defense options, 26–30; Long Walls strategy, 29–30, 45–49; Macedonia and siegecraft, 49–52, 53, 54; map of, 16f, 18f; military capability, 22; and Persians, 17–18; postwar strategy, 18–19; resources for, 24–25; and Second Peloponnesian War, 37–45, 53, 54; security developments, 34–52; setbacks and war enthusiasm, 34–36; as signal of intention, 314–15; and Sparta, 20; and strategic culture, 22–24; and strategic defenses in Athens' Golden Age, 36–37; and strategic defense system decision, 30–34, 53; threat perception, 21–22, 53–54; upper city relocation, 28–29
Atilius Bradua, 80
attaque brusquée (sudden attack), 214, 215, 216, 227, 236
Attica (Greece), 15, 17, 20, 22, 27–28, 30, 35, 36, 39–40, 47–48
attrition, wars of: and ancient Athens, 38, 39, 54, 283–86; and Bar-Lev Line, 257–58, 283–86, 288, 291; and French-German relations, 225
Augsburg, League of, 183–84
Augustan History, 66, 72, 93
Augustus, 70, 74, 76, 78
Aulus Platorius Nepos, 65, 80, 87, 88

Bag Arslan, 131–33
Bai Gui, 107–8, 121, 127, 130–31, 132
ballistic missile defense, 2, 316
Banque de France, 231
barbarians, Mongols as, 116, 117, 125, 126, 128
Barfield, Thomas, 115
Bar-Kochba revolt, 78
Bar-Lev, Chaim: and military capability, 268; on military escalation, 284; and mobile armor-base defense, 279–80; and naming of Bar-Lev Line, 259; and national security decision making, 275, 276, 281, 282; and occupied territory, 263; and postwar debate about Bar-Lev Line, 286–87, 288, 297; and post-Yom Kippur War debate, 293; and Sinai defense, 276
Bar-Lev Line, 9, 257–307; comparison of main features, 10t, 309, 310–13t; debate about, 258, 286–89, 297; decision context of, 258, 265–76; defense-in-depth, 278–79; domestic politics, 273–74; frontier strategic options, 276–81; map of, 260f; military capability, 267–69; mobile armor-based defense approach, 279–80, 287, 294; offensive-based approach, 277–78, 296; position-based defense, 280–81; postwar occupation, 263–65; resources for, 272–73; security developments, 283–95; and security struggle, 261–65; and Six-Day War, 257, 262–63, 273; and strategic culture, 269–72, 277; and strategic defense system decision, 281–83, 297–98; threat perception, 265–67, 273; War of Attrition, 257–58, 283–86, 291; and Yom Kippur War and subsequent debate, 258, 289–95, 296, 297
Bar-Siman-Tov, Yaacov, 293
bataille conduite (methodical battle), 219, 238
Battle of. *See name of battle*
Batu Mongke, 134–35, 136
Behr, J. H., 171
Beijing: Mongol raid on, 138; relocation of capital to, 114

Index 341

Belfort gap, 215, 229
Belgium: and forward defense, 226; German attack through, 215; neutrality of, 237–38, 239; relationship with France, 218, 233–34; in World War I, 209–10. *See also* Maginot Line
Belhague, Charles Louis-Joseph, 232
Ben-Gurion, David, 270, 273, 274, 275
Berlin Wall, 9
"Bible" (French military document on defense), 219
"Big Bertha" guns, 210
Birley, Anthony, 85
Black, Jeremy, 162, 323
Boeotia, 21, 33, 35, 40–41, 44, 46, 47
Boeotian War (378–375 BCE), 47
Bolai, 117, 119–20
Bolé, Jules-Louis. *See* Chamlay, Marquis de
Bouchain, capture of, 177, 178, 194
Boudicca, Queen, 70
Boufflers, Marshal, 188
Boule (Athenian council), 26
Bourbon, house of, 188
Brabant entrenchment lines, 189
Brandenburg (German state), 164, 165
Breisach fortress, 186, 187
Briand, Aristide, 205, 221, 223–24, 233, 245
Brigante tribe, 65, 70–74, 82, 86–88, 90–91
Britain. *See* Great Britain
Brooke, Alan, 243–44
Buat, Edmond, 212, 229
Budapest maozim, 292, 293
"buying time" strategy, 6, 147, 234, 309, 324–25, 326
Byzantium, 50, 51

Caledonii tribe, 74, 82, 83, 90, 92, 93
Caligula, 70
Calpurnius Agricola, 91
Cambrai, capture of, 177, 179, 192
Caracalla, 93
Cartimandua, Queen, 70–71
Casale fortress, capture of, 181–82, 186

casemates (reinforced concrete bunkers), 206, 207, 230, 241
Case (Plan) Yellow (German military plan), 240
Cassander, 51–52
Cassius Dio, 65, 70, 92
Castex, Raoul, 235
Chaeronea, Battle of, 50
Chahars (Mongol tribe), 116
Chamlay, Marquis de (Jules-Louis Bolé), 173, 184–85, 190, 319–20
Charlemat-Givet fortress, 187
Charleroi fortress, 163, 164, 178, 179, 186, 187, 192
Charles II, 163, 164, 188
Charles, Archduke, 188
Chauvineau, Narcisse, 242–43
Chenghua: and accommodation strategy, 127; decision to construct Great Wall, 106, 107; and domestic politics, 123–24, 125; and military capability, 119; and Mongol settlement of Ordos, 115; and offensive strategy in Ordos, 126; and strategic defense system decision, 130, 131, 132; and wall expansion, 133–34
Chen Jing, 137
Chen Xuen, 118
China. *See* accommodation policy in China; Great Wall of China
Chongzhen, 144
Chu Dynasty (China), 111
Chuter, David, 221
Cimon, 19, 20, 26, 32, 34, 45
Claudius, 65, 70, 89
Cleisthenes, 17
Clemenceau, Georges, 211
Cleon, 41, 53
Clerville, Chevalier de, 174
Clodius Albinus, 92–93
Clyde-Forth isthmus, 71, 72, 74, 83, 89–90
Cnidus, Battle of, 46
Coehoorn, Menno van, 186
Colbert, Jean-Baptiste, 169, 172, 173
collective security, 224, 233

Commission d'Organisation des Régions Fortifiées (CORF), 230, 232
Commission for the Territorial Defense (France), 212–13
Commodus, Emperor, 92
Condé, capture of, 177, 178, 194
Condé, Prince of, 158, 166, 171, 173, 191
"Confederacy of Delos," 19
Conon, 46–47
conscription, military: Hitler's reintroduction of, 236; in Israel, 272; long-term, 221; numbers of, 220; shorter-term, 215–16, 218, 226, 230, 244
Conseil d'en-Haut (High Council), 173
Conseil Supérieur de la Guerre (CSG, higher war council), 211–12, 215–16, 222, 229–31, 233–34, 238
Constantine, 94–95
Constantius, 94
contributions (military extortion), 172, 180–81, 187, 191
Conwell, David, 23
Corbie, French defeat at, 162, 165
CORF (Commission d'Organisation des Régions Fortifiées), 232
Corinth, 14, 15, 20, 22, 29, 32, 33, 35, 37, 41, 46
Corinthian War, 46
Coronea, Battle of, 35
Cornelius Tacitus, 68, 70, 83
Corvisier, André, 181
Crewe, Lord, 223–24
Croissy, Marquis de, 180
Crow, James, 86
CSG. *See Conseil Supérieur de la Guerre*
Czechoslovakia: Egyptian arms purchase from, 262; French bilateral agreement with, 217

Dacia (Roman province), 74, 76, 79–80, 81
Dacian Wars, 71, 73, 78–79
Daladier, Edouard, 232, 237
Darius, 17
Datong sector (Chinese frontier), 108, 109, 110, 133, 134, 137, 138
Dayan, Moshe: and creation of Bar-Lev Line, 258–59; and domestic politics, 273; and national security decision making, 274–75, 282; and offensive-based approach, 277–78; and peace agreement prospects, 266; and postwar debate about Bar-Lev Line, 287–88, 294; and postwar occupation, 265; and Sadat, 287; and Six-Day War, 262–63; and War of Attrition, 283, 284; and Yom Kippur War, 291, 292
Debeney, Marie-Eugène, 212, 222, 229, 230, 231
Decebalus, 82
Decelea (Greece), 43, 54
Decelean War (413–404 BCE), 42–45
defense and defense strategies, 5–6; ballistic missile defense, 2; forward defense, 5, 205, 225–26, 229, 234; frontier, 204–5, 227–28, 229; land defense options, 26–30; mobile armor-based, 279–80, 287, 294; "nonprovocative," 221; position-based, 280–81. *See also* defense-in-depth strategy; psychological aspects of fortified defense; strategic defense system decisions
defense-in-depth strategy: and Athens' Long Walls, 52; Belgian option for, 234; French policy of, 205, 212, 219, 225–29, 231; Israeli options for, 259, 278–79; and Pré Carré, 319
de Gaulle, Charles, 238
Delian League: Athens' control of, 19, 36; and domestic politics, 25–26; fleet of, 14; military capabilities of, 22; resources from, 24, 33; and Second Athenian League, 48; setbacks of, 34–35; revolt from, 43
Dema Wall, 48
Delos, 34
Delphic Oracle, 17
Demetrius, 51–52
democracy: Athens' return to, 45; and domestic politics, 25–26; rise of, 16–20

Demosthenes, 47, 48, 49, 50
Dere Street (Scotland), 90, 91, 93
deterrence (defense strategy): and Athens' Long Walls, 27, 32, 34, 38–39, 48; and Bar-Lev Line, 267, 283, 284, 290, 316; by denial, 5, 78, 95, 129, 146, 270, 278, 296–97, 315–17; and Great Wall of China, 129, 145, 146, 316; Israel's concept of, 270–72, 296; and Maginot Line, 183, 242, 243, 246, 317; and position-based defense, 280; by punishment, 5, 78, 95, 270–71, 277, 278, 296, 315; Roman use of, 77–78, 84, 86, 95, 97; and strategic defense systems, 315–17
Diadochi (Alexander the Great's generals), 51
Dinant fortress, 187
Dionysius I, 85
diplomacy, 82–83, 223–24
domestic politics: and Athens' Long Walls, 25–26; and Bar-Lev Line, 273–74; and Great Wall of China, 123–25; and Hadrian's Wall, 79; and Maginot Line, 220–21; and Pré Carré, 172–74
Domitian, 71, 76, 82
Donaldson, John, 314, 315
Doumergue, Gaston, 229
Dovecote defense plan (*Shovach Yonim*), 289, 290, 293
draft. *See* conscription, military
Dutch War, 158, 164–67, 178–80

Eastern Mongols, 116
East Jerusalem, occupation of, 263, 264
Eban, Abba, 263, 266, 285
Eben Emael fortress, 234
Ecclesia (Athenian assembly), 26
Egypt: Air Force, 284; ancient Egypt, 14, 15; arms purchase from Czechoslovakia, 262; and Bar-Lev Line postwar debate, 286–89; and defense-in-depth, 278–79; and Israeli security struggle, 261–62; and mobile armor-based defense, 279–80; and Naj' Hammadi raid, 276; and offensive-based approach, 277–78; and position-based defense, 280–81; and postwar occupation, 264–65; and post–Yom Kippur War, 293–95; resources in, 272; and Sinai defense, 277; in Six-Day War, 257, 262–63; Soviet arms support for, 266, 268, 284–85; and Suez Canal Zone, 258–59, 277; and threat perception, 265–67; and War of Attrition, 283–86; and Yom Kippur War, 289–93
Egypt–Israel peace treaty of 1979, 295
Eilat (Israeli destroyer), sinking of, 264–65, 277
"*ein breira*" concept ("no choice"), 271
Elazar, David, 288, 289, 291, 295
England. *See* Great Britain
Ephialtes, 26
Erechthesis, 25
Esen, 114–15, 116, 134
Eshkol, Levi, 262, 264, 266, 274, 282
Euboea, 35, 36, 40, 42
Eubulus, 49
Eugene, Prince, 190, 192
eunuchs, 123–24, 125, 126, 127, 134, 137
European Union, 223
Eurybiades, 18

Farmer, Edward, 120
Favorinus, 80
Fillonneau, Étienne-Honoré, 229–30
firepower, military principle of, 219, 222, 227
First Peloponnesian War, 38–39
Flemish people, 218, 226, 237
Florus, 81, 87
Foch, Ferdinand, 210–11, 212, 222, 227, 229, 230
fortifications, terminology of, 4–5
forts and fortresses: and France's military capabilities, 169; and Great Wall of China, 110; and Pré Carré, 160–61, 164; Roman's use of, 67–68, 76; underground fortresses at Maginot line, 205–6, 242. *See also* frontiers and frontier strategic options; *specific fortresses*
forward defense, 5, 205, 225–26, 229, 234

Fossatum Africae (Saharn fortifications), 77
Four Years' War (307–304 BCE), 51–52
France: internal uprising in, 162, 167; relations with Israel, 269. *See also* French High Command; Louis XIV; Maginot Line; Pré Carré
Franco, Francisco, 236
Franco-Prussian War, 209
Freiburg fortress, 179, 187
French High Command: and Alsace-Lorraine, 209, 239; and defense options, 204, 227, 230, 234–35, 244–45; and French capitulation, 241; and Maginot mentality, 244; and military options, 224
Frere, Sheppard, 71, 86
Fronde (internal uprising in France), 162, 167
Frontier Defense Commission (France), 229
frontière de fer (iron frontier), 8–9, 178, 180, 181–84, 192, 193–94
frontiers and frontier strategic options: and Athens' Long Walls, 27–28; and Bar-Lev Line, 276–81; frontier defense, 204–5, 227–28, 229; *frontière de fer*, 8–9, 178, 180, 181–84, 192, 193–94; and Great Wall of China, 111–14, 125–30, 133–46; and Hadrian's Wall, 81–85, 88–95, 96, 97, 319, 320; "inviolability of the frontier" concept, 218–19, 232; and Maginot Line, 204–5, 223–42; natural frontiers, 170–71, 181; and Pré Carré, 161–67, 174–76, 193, 318–19; Roman "limes," 65–66; and strategic defense systems, 318–21
Fronto, 76
Fullofaudes, 94

gabelle (salt tax), 167
Galili, Israel, 274
Gamelin, Maurice, 206, 233, 237–38, 239, 244, 245
Gao Deng, 129
Gao Lu, 128–29
Gavish, Yeshayahu, 275, 279–80, 282, 286, 293, 297

Gaza Strip, 267, 269, 295
Genghis Khan, 112, 116, 139, 319
Germany: and Dutch War, 165–66; in League of Augsburg, 184; and Louis XIV, 164; and Nine Years' War, 186; Roman Empire in, 65; and War of Spanish Succession, 189. *See also* Maginot Line
Geta, 93
gloire (French concept of reputation), 170, 174, 175, 177, 178, 193
Golan Heights, 264, 267, 291
Gonen, Shmuel, 289, 290, 291
Göring, Hermann, 239–40
Gothic Line, 7
grand secretariat, Chinese, 124, 125
Great Britain: Hadrian in, 65, 66, 68, 70; relations with France, 166, 217; Roman experience in, 68–73; and War of Spanish Succession, 191–92; William III's conquest of, 185
Great Wall of China, 4, 8, 106–56; and accommodation strategy, 127–28; China's struggle for security in north, 111–15; comparison of main features, 10t, 309, 310–13t; decision context of, 115–25; and domestic politics, 123–25; frontier strategic options, 111–13, 125–30, 145–46; and Manchu challenge, 141–45; map of, 109f; military capability, 118–20; and Ming dynasty end, 141–45; and Ming frontier policy, 113–14; and Ming military decline, 114–15; and offensive strategy, 126–27, 146; resources for, 122–23, 322–23; and second Ordos debate, 136–41; security developments, 133–45; as signal of intention, 315; and strategic culture, 120–22; and strategic defense system decision, 130–33, 146–47; threat perception, 116–18; wall as strategic option, 128–30; wall expansion and Mongol challenge, 133–36. *See also* accommodation policy in China
gros ouvrages (large works), 206, 207, 239, 241, 242
gross national product (GNP), 272–73, 288

"guerre de cabinet" approach, 173
Guillaumat, Adophe, 212, 222, 229, 230, 244
Guillaumat Commission, 229, 230, 231
Gur, Mordechai, 295
Gustav Line, 7
Guyuan sector (Chinese frontier), 109

Habsburg Empire, 161–62, 163, 165–66, 182, 186, 188, 192
Hadrian: and Athens' Long Walls, 84–85; in Britain, 65, 66, 68, 70; decision-making process of, 79–80; and domestic politics, 79; and frontier strategic options, 81–85; and idea of wall, 84–85; and resource management, 79; and Roman expansion, 64, 74–75; and strategic culture, 75–78; and strategic defense system decision, 85–88
Hadrian's Wall, 2, 4, 8, 64–105; abandonment of wall, 89–90; and alternative frontiers, 83–84; comparison of main features, 10t, 309, 310–13t; decision context of, 73–80; diplomatic initiatives, 82–83; domestic politics, 79; frontier elimination, 81–82, 96; frontier strategic options, 81–85, 96, 97, 319, 320; idea of wall, 84–85; invasion and advance, 70–71, 95; map of, 67f, 69f; military capability, 74–75; resources for, 78–79, 97; return to, 90–92, 97; Roman experience in Britain, 68–73; Roman security in third and fourth centuries, 93–95; security developments with fortified frontier, 88–95; and Severan reconstruction, 92–93; as signal of intention, 314; and strategic culture, 75–78; and strategic defense system decision, 85–88, 96, 97; threat perception, 73–74; and Tyne-Solway isthmus, 71–73
Han (Chinese ethnic group), 116, 120, 147
Han Dynasty (China), 111–12, 120, 127
Han Yang, 124
Hanson, Victor Davis, 13, 19, 23, 40, 47, 49, 57n51
Helots, 20, 21, 40

Henry IV, 161
Heracles, 34
hereditary soldiery (*weisuo* system), 118, 122
Hergault, François, 212
Herodotus, 18, 25, 28–29
Herriot, Édouard, 213
Herzog, Chaim, 282, 294
Hitler, Adolf, 235, 236, 239, 243, 245, 246
Hochwald gros ouvrage, 239
Holocaust, 269
Holy Roman Empire, 166
Hongwu, 113, 116, 117, 120, 123, 124
Hong Zhengzhou, 144
Hongzhi, 134–35
hoplite warfare. *See* agonal (hoplite) warfare
Hughes, Judith M., 244
Huiyun Feng, 121

IAF. *See* Israeli Air Force
Iceni tribe, 70
IDF. *See* Israeli Defense Forces
Imlay, Talbot, 239
Innocent XI, Pope, 183
intelligence and intelligence gathering, 90, 268–69, 290
intentions, signaling of, 314–15
"inviolability of the frontier" concept, 218–19, 232
Ipsus, Battle of (301 BCE), 52
Iraq, U.S. operations in, 320
iron frontier. *See frontière de fer*
iron wall concept, 270
Isocrates, 46, 47
Israel. *See* Bar-Lev Line
Israeli Air Force (IAF): military capability of, 267–68; and offensive-based approach, 278; and Suez Canal, 258; and War of Attrition, 284–85; and Yom Kippur War, 290, 291, 293
Israeli Defense Forces (IDF): and Bar-Lev Line creation, 259, 261; and defense-in-depth, 278–79; and military capability, 267–69; missile defense systems of, 1; and mobile armor-base defense, 279–80;

Israeli Defense Forces (IDF) (*continued*) and Naj' Hammadi raid, 276; and national security, 261–62, 274–75, 282–83; and offensive-based approach, 278; and position-based defense, 280–81; and post-Yom Kippur War, 293–95; and Sinai defense options, 277, 289; in Six-Day War, 257, 263, 275; and strategic culture, 270–71; and Suez Canal military skirmishes, 264; and threat perception, 265–67; and War of Attrition, 283–85; withdrawal from Gaza Strip, 295; and Yom Kippur War, 290–92
Italy, French relations with, 214, 217, 236

Jabotinsky, Zeev, 270
James II, 185, 188
Japan, invasion of Manchuria by, 233
Jerusalem Etzioni brigade, 290
Jiajing, 136, 138, 140
Jin Dynasty (China), 141
Jingtai, 115
jiu bian zhen (nine defense garrisons in China), 119
Jiayuguan fortress, 108
Jizhou sector (Great Wall of China), 140–41
Joffre, Joseph, 212
Johnston, Alastair, 121–22, 125, 126
Jordan, Palestinian assaults from, 267
Julius Agricola, 68, 71, 75, 89–90
Julius Caesar, 70
Julius Severus, 89
Julius Verus, 90
Jurchens (tribal group), 117, 128, 141–43

Kagan, Donald, 23, 37, 48
Kammhuber Line, 4
Keegan, John, 4, 7
Kellogg-Briand pact of 1928, 224
Khalkhas (Mongol tribe), 116
Khublilai Khan, 112
Kier, Beth, 218
Kissinger, Henry, 294
Korn, David, 285

Krentz, Peter, 23, 33–34, 324–25

Labor party (Israel), 273, 294
La Ferté petit ouvrage, 240
Lahat, Shlomo, 275, 283
Lamian War, 51
Landau fortress, 186
land-for-peace approach, 264, 265, 274, 285
Lauter RF (fortified region), 206, 207f, 229, 240
La Vallière, Louise de, 158
Laws (Plato), 46
League of Augsburg, 184
League of Nations, 224, 233
Lebrun, Albert, 233
Lefèvre, André, 212
legio VI, 65, 73, 75, 80, 86–87, 90
legio VIIII, 70, 72–73, 83–84
Le Hallé, Guy, 4
Leocrates, 14
Leopold, 164, 183, 184, 188
Le Quesnoy (France), Pré Carré fortress of, 191–93
Le Tellier, Michel, 168, 173
Liaodong, defense walls constructed in, 108, 128
Life of Agricola (Tacitus), 68
Lighdan Khan, 143
Li Hsian, 124
Lille fortress, 163, 189–91, 197
"limes" (Roman frontiers), 65–66
Limes Germanicus, 66, 77
Lines of Torres Vedras, 7
Lionne, Hugues de, 173
Little Maginot Line, 207
Liu Dingzhi, 117
Liu Jin, 135
Livy, 52
Li Zicheng, 144
Locarno Pact of 1925, 223, 224, 243
Lollius Urbicus, 89–90
Longqing, 140
Long Walls. *See* Athens' Long Walls
Lorraine region. *See* Alsace-Lorraine region

Louis XIV: and accommodation approach, 175–76; assumption of power of, 163–64; domestic politics and decision making, 172–73; and Dutch War, 158, 164, 179–80; establishment of Pré Carré, 157, 160; and *frontière de fer* expansion, 181–84, 193–94; and Habsburg threat, 161; and Mazarin, 162; and military leadership qualities, 320; and new strategy implementation, 178–79; and Nine Years' War, 184–85, 187, 195; resources of, 171–72; and strategic culture, 170–71, 193; and strategic defense system decision, 176–80, 192–93, 326; and territorial expansion, 175; and threat perceptions, 167–68; and War of Spanish Succession, 188–90, 192, 195

Louvois, Marquis de: advising Louis XIV, 173–74; and Dutch War, 164, 165; and *frontière de fer* expansion, 181; and military capabilities, 168, 169; and strategic defense system decision, 158, 160, 177; and threat perception, 183; on war as necessary evil, 174–75

Lovell, Julia, 3, 112, 132, 147

Luttwak, Edward, 77, 242, 317

Luxembourg, Marshal, 173, 191

Luxembourg fortress, 181, 182, 183, 187, 192

Lycurgus, 48, 50

Lynn, John, 170, 175, 183, 197n66

Lysander, 43, 44

Lysias, 47

Maastricht (France): capture of, 165, 169, 171, 174; siege of, 178

Macedonia, 49–52, 53, 54

MacGregor, Malcolm, 25

Maeatae (Scottish tribe confederacy), 92, 93

Maginot, André, 205, 211, 222–23, 231–32, 235, 314

Maginot Line, 4, 9, 204–56; "Belgian Maginot Line," 234; and "buying time" strategy, 324; comparison of main features, 10t, 309, 310–13t; decision context of, 213–23; defense-in-depth, 205, 226–27; deterioration of Franco-German relations, 233–36; diplomatic options, 223–24; and domestic politics, 220–21; facing off against Germany, 209–13, 245–46; forward defense, 205, 225–26, 229, 234; frontier defense, 204–5, 227–28, 229; frontier strategic options, 223–32; as "Great Wall of France," 232, 246; "Israel's Maginot Line," 261; Little Maginot Line, 207; Maginot mentality, 204, 243–44, 326; map of, 208f; military capability, 215–18; military options, 224–28; resources for, 219–20, 244–46, 322; second reconsideration of, 236–38; security developments, 232–42, 243–44; as signal of intention, 315; and strategic culture, 218–19; and strategic defense system decision, 205, 228–32, 242–43, 246; threat perception, 213–15, 233, 242; Versailles Treaty and postwar developments, 211–13; at war, 239–42; World War I, lessons learned from, 209–10, 226–27

Manchus (tribal group), 107, 141–45

Mannerheim, Carl Gustav, 4

Mannerheim Line, 7

maozim (strongpoints along Bar-Lev Line): closure of, 286, 289, 297; function of, 261; increase in number of, 259; and postwar debate about Bar-Lev Line, 286–87, 288–89; and strategic defense decision, 281–84; in Yom Kippur War, 290, 291–92

Mapai party (Israel), 273

Marcellinus, Ammianus, 94

Marco Polo, 112

Marcus Appius Bradua, 72

Marcus Aurelius, 76, 91

Marcus Maenius Agrippa, 87

Marie Thérèse, 158, 163

Marlborough, Duke of, 190, 191

Maubeuge SF (fortified sector), 207, 235

Maurin, Louis, 230, 243

Ma Wensheng, 117, 124, 131

May, Ernest, 238

Mazarin, Cardinal, 162–63, 164, 174, 175–76

Medici, Catherine de, 172
Megara (Greece), 14–15, 20, 22, 25, 30, 33, 35, 37, 40–41, 44, 47
Meir, Golda, 282, 286, 288, 294
Mendler, Albert, 290, 291, 292, 294
Meng Tian, 4, 111
methodical battle (*bataille conduite*), 219, 238
metics (resident aliens in Athens), 24–25, 39
Metz RF (fortified region), 206, 207, 207f, 229, 232, 240
Mexico and U.S. border fence, 2, 314, 318, 328
Mezakh maozim, 292
military capabilities and options: and Athens' Long Walls, 22; and Bar-Lev Line, 267–69; and Great Wall of China, 118–20; and Hadrian's Wall, 74–75; and Maginot Line, 215–18, 224–28; military balance, 6, 317–23; and Pré Carré, 168–69, 193
Miltiades, 17, 19
Ming Dynasty: and accommodation, 107, 138, 140; end of, 141–45; fiscal administration, 122, 123; frontier policy of, 113–14, 118; military decline of, 114–15. *See also* Great Wall of China
Mithridates, 52
Mongols: and accommodation strategy, 128; alliance with Jurchens, 142–43; as barbarians, 116, 117, 125, 126, 128; Eastern Mongols, 116; and effectiveness of Great Wall, 107; Ming policy toward, 113–14; and offensive strategy in Ordos, 126–27; Oirats (Western Mongols), 116; and Ordos region, 107–8, 114, 115; raiding by, 114–16, 117, 128–29, 137–38, 140; stategic options against, 125, 145; and strategic culture, 121; and strategic defense system decision, 131–33; and threat perception, 116–18; and wall expansion, 133–36
Mons Graupius, Battle of, 71, 74
Montespan, Madame de, 158
Montmédy bridgemead, 207, 216, 236, 240
Montmédy SF (fortified sector), 207
Morocco: French military operations in, 220; insurgency in, 213, 214

Mote, Frederick, 117
"muddling through" policy, 106, 143, 147, 325–27, 328
Mussolini, Benito, 214, 236
Mycale, Battle of, 23
Myronides, 14–15, 25, 26

Naj' Hammadi raids, 276, 277, 283
Nakhsa ("setback"), 264
Namur fortress, capture of, 186, 189, 192, 326
Nasser, Gamel: and Arab state cooperation, 267; on destruction of Bar-Lev Line, 283; and Egyptian military, 266; leadership of, 262; and negotiation options, 297, 324; and occupied territory, 264; and offensive-based approach, 278; and Soviet military assistance, 284; and death, 286
National Unity government (Israel), 262, 286
nation-in-arms concept (France), 218–19
navy, Athenian: and army enhancements, 27; and Delian League, 14; deterrence function of, 34; in First Peloponnesian War, 38; and Long Walls strategy, 29–31, 52; and Macedonian threat, 50; maintaining power of, 36; military capabilities, 22, 23; and Persians, 17; postwar power of, 18–19; resources for, 24; restoration of power, 46
navy, French, 169
Naxos, 19
Ne Plus Ultra (No Further) entrenchment lines, 191
Neratius Marcellus, 80
Nero, 70, 76, 81
Netherlands: accord with France, 179; and Dutch War, 158, 164–67, 179–80; and Nine Years' War, 186; Spanish Netherlands, 161, 163, 166, 167–68, 177, 181; United Provinces, 164, 183, 188
Neuf-Brisach fortress, 187
Nicias, Peace of, 41–42
Nine Years' War, 184–87, 195
Ningxia sector (Chinese frontier), 135
Nollet, Charles, 216, 222, 230

"nonprovocative" defense, 221
Northern Qi Dynasty (China), 111, 112
Novantae tribe, 74, 82, 83, 89, 90, 92
nuclear weapons, storage of, 242
Numisius Junior, 90
Nurhaci, 141–42

Ober, Josiah, 23, 27, 28, 29, 47–48, 50
occupied territory, Israeli, 263–65
offense–defense theory, 3
offensive military strategy, 5; and Bar-Lev Line, 277–78, 296; and Great Wall of China, 126–27, 146; and Maginot Line, 224–25, 243, 277–78
Oirats (Western Mongols), 116
oligarchs and oligarchy (Greece), 25–26, 31
"*on ne passe pas*" motto ("None Shall Pass"), 209
Operation Badr, 290
Oracle of Delphi, 17
Orange, Prince of, 164, 178
Ordos region (China): debate of 1470s, 125, 130; Hongzhi's desire for offensive, 135; and Mongols, 107–8, 112, 114, 115, 117; and offensive strategy, 126–27; Second Ordos Debate, 106, 136–41
Oresteia (Aeschylus), 34, 325
Ottoman Empire, 175, 182, 220

Painlevé, Paul, 221, 222–23, 229, 231
Palestinians, 267, 295, 328
palisades, 84, 86
parabellum paradigm, 121, 126, 129
Paris Peace Conference, 214
Parthian War, 66, 72, 73, 77, 79
Pausanias, 44
Peace and Friendship policy (China), 112
Peace of Nicias, 41–42
Peace of Ryswick, 187
Peace of the Pyrenees, 162, 163
Pedatzur, Reuven, 272
Peled, Mattityahu, 288
Peloponnesian League, 14, 20, 21, 22, 35, 38
Peloponnesians, 14, 20, 22, 29, 33, 35, 36

Pericles: and Archidamian War, 38; and Athens' strategic position, 14–15; and defense options, 26, 54; and domestic politics, 26; and military setbacks, 35–36; and Peloponnesian League, 20; and rebuilding Long Walls, 47; and Second Peloponnesian War, 37–42, 45; and strategic culture, 23–24
Persians (Aeschylus), 23–24
Persians, 17–19, 22, 34, 43
Persian Wars, 14, 15, 23, 26, 29, 30
Pertinax, Emperor, 92
Pétain, Philippe: armistice with Germany, 241; in CSG, 212; and Franco-Belgian border defense, 233–34, 235; and prepared battlefields, 230, 245; and strategic defense, 210, 219, 222, 227, 229–31
Petilius Cerialis, 71
petit ouvrages (small works), 206, 207, 240
Phaleron 15, 30, 37, 43
Pharnabazus, 46, 47
Philip II (Macedonia), 49, 50, 53, 54
Philip V (Spain), 188, 192
Philippsburg, capture of, 179, 184, 185, 187, 194
Picts tribe, 94
Pietri, François, 233
Piraeus (Greece), 15, 27–29, 30, 36–37, 39, 40, 43, 45
Pisistratidae tyranny, 17
plague, 41, 42, 43
Plataea, Battle of, 18
Plato, 45–46, 47, 53, 325–26
Pleistoanax, King, 39
Plutarch, 32, 45
Podlecki, Anthony, 36
Poincaré, Raymond, 213, 220, 221, 235
Poland: French mutual defense pact with, 217; Hitler's invasion of, 239
Poliocretes, 52
Pomponne, Simon Arnauld de, 164, 173, 180
Popular Front (France), 237
positional warfare, 157, 171, 175, 186, 189

position-based defense, 280–81
Pré Carré, 8, 157–203; and accommodation approach, 175–76; comparison of main features, 10t, 309, 310–13t; decision context of, 167–74; and domestic politics, 172–74; and Dutch War, 164–67, 179–80; expansion policy, 157–58, 161–67, 174–75; *frontière de fer* expansion, 181–84, 193–94; frontier strategic options, 174–76, 193, 318–19; and Louis' assumption of power, 163–64; map of, 159f, 161f; and military capability, 168–69, 193; new strategy implementation, 178–79; and Nine Years' War, 184–87, 195; resources for, 171–72, 193; security developments, 180–92, 193; as signal of intention, 314; and strategic culture, 170–71, 193; and strategic defense system decision, 158, 176–80, 192–95; threat perceptions, 167–68; and War of Spanish Succession, 188–92, 193, 195, 318
preemption strategy, 271, 278, 293
"prepared battlefields": and frontier defense, 212, 225, 227, 228, 229; Pétain's support for, 230, 245
Prételat, Gaston, 240
prospect theory, 170
psychological aspects of fortified defense: and Athens' Long Walls, 30–32, 43, 44, 53–54; and Bar-Lev Line, 296–97; and efficacy of walls as defense, 3; and Great Wall of China, 52, 132, 147; and Hadrian's Wall, 85–86, 95, 97; and Maginot Line, 204, 218–19, 243–44, 326; and Pré Carré, 176–77, 193

Qi Jiguang, 139
Qin Dynasty, 8, 111–13, 129
Qing Dynasty, 143, 144
Qin Hong, 135
Qin Shi Huangdi, 111
Qiu Jun, 116
quan bin (flexibility), 121–22, 129, 132
Quester, George, 315, 321
Quintus Pompeius Falco, 66

Rabin, Yitzhak, 275
Rabinovich, Abraham, 294
Rafi party (Israel), 273, 274
rapprochement (diplomatic strategy), 213, 223–24, 328
Ratisbon, Truce of, 182
Reichsheer (German army), 214–15
Reichskrieg (war of the Holy Roman Empire), 166
reparations, war, 211, 213, 214, 220
Reshef, Amnen, 291
Richelieu, Cardinal, 162
Rock defense plan (*Sela*), 289
Roman Empire: and Hadrian's Wall, 64–105; and security in third and fourth centuries, 93–95; use of deterrence by, 77–78, 84, 86, 95, 97
Rommel, Erwin, 241
Ruhr (Germany), military operations in, 213, 220

Saar region, plebiscite in, 236
Sabina, Empress, 80
Sadat, Anwar, 287–88, 290, 294, 297
Saint Omer, capture of, 178, 179
Salamis, Battle of, 22, 29
SAMs. *See* surface-to-air missiles
Sar Hu, Battle of, 142
Sarre Gap, 206, 236, 241
Saxons (tribe), 94
Scotland, Roman advance into, 71, 89–91, 92, 93–94, 95
Sealey, Raphael, 50–51, 53
Second Athenian League, 48, 49
Second Peloponnesian War, 14, 23, 32, 37–45, 47–48, 53, 54. *See also* navy, Athenian
Secure Fence Act of 2006 (U.S.), 2
security developments: and Athens' Long Walls, 34–52; and Bar-Lev Line, 261–65, 283–95; and Great Wall of China, 133–45; and Maginot Line, 232–42, 243–44; and Pré Carré, 180–92, 193
Seguin, Paul, 321
Sela defense plan (Rock), 289

Selgovae tribe: and Brigantes, 86, 87; hostility of, 74, 82, 83; in Maeatae, 92; and Roman advancement into Scotland, 89; separation from Brigantes and Novantae, 90
Senate Army Commission (France), 233, 235
Seneffe, Battle of, 166, 171
Septicius Clarus, 80
Septimius Severus, 64–65, 92–93, 97
Séré de Rivières, Raymond, 209, 210
"Seven Military Classics," 120–21
1706–7 line, 189–90
Shanhaiguan fortress, 108, 109, 140
Sharett, Moshe, 274
Sharon, Ariel: and maozim closure, 286, 289, 297; and national security decision making, 276, 282; and postwar debate about Bar-Lev Line, 287, 288–89, 297; and Sinai defense, 276; and threat perception, 265; and Yom Kippur War, 291, 292, 293
Shimshoni, Jonathan, 269, 296
Shomron, Dan, 291
Shotter, David, 76
Shovach Yonim defense plan. *See* Dovecote defense plan
Shun Dynasty (China), 144
siegecraft: and agonal warfare, 23; and Athens' Long Walls, 14, 16, 19, 21–22, 31, 37; and Caledonii, 74; French army's ability at, 169; and Macedonia, 49–52, 53, 54
signaling of intentions, 314–15
Sinai Peninsula: defense options for, 276–77, 281–82, 287–89, 293, 297; and domestic politics, 274; occupation of, 258, 263, 266; partition agreement for, 294–95; return to Egypt of, 262, 264; and Yom Kippur War, 292
Six-Day War, 257, 262–63, 273, 275
Social War (357–355 BCE), 49
Soleil Royal (ship), 169
Song Dynasty, 111, 128
Soviet Union: arms support for Egypt, 266, 268, 284–85; French relations with, 217
Spain: civil war in, 236; French war with, 162–64, 179; in League of Augsburg, 184; Roman subjugation of, 66; Spanish Netherlands, 161, 163, 166, 167–68, 177, 181; War of Spanish Succession, 188–92, 193, 195; and War of the Reunions, 182
Sparta: and Athenian upper city relocation, 29; and Decelea, 43; defense options against, 26–28; and deterrence, 32; and Long Wall strategy, 27, 32–33, 38, 46, 54; and Peloponnesian Wars, 39, 40–45, 53; and Persians, 17; and relations with Athens, 13–15, 19–22, 34; and restoration of Long Walls, 48–49; and Thirty Years' Peace, 35, 37
Speller, Elizabeth, 76
Stanegate (Britain), 71–72, 83–84, 85, 88
Statius Priscus, 91
Stilicho, 94–95
Strasbourg, capture of, 179, 181, 183, 186
strategic culture: and Athens' Long Walls, 22–24; and Bar-Lev Line, 269–72, 277; and Great Wall of China, 120–22; and Hadrian's Wall, 75–78; and Maginot Line, 218–19; and Pré Carré, 170–71, 193
strategic defense system decisions: and Athens' Long Walls, 30–34, 53; and Bar-Lev Line, 281–83, 297–98; and Great Wall of China, 130–33, 146–47, 246; and Hadrian's Wall, 85–88, 96, 97; lessons learned from, 308–29; and Maginot Line, 205, 228–32, 242–43; and Pré Carré, 158, 176–80, 192–95; security developments, 232–42
Stresemann, Gustav, 205, 223–24, 245
sudden attack. *See attaque brusquée*
Suetonius Paullinus, 70
Suetonius Tranquillus, 80, 81
Suez Canal: and creation of Bar-Lev Line, 258–59, 279; military skirmishes along, 264; nationalization of, 262; opening to traffic of, 294; and Six-Day War, 263
Sui Dynasty, 111, 112, 129–30
Sulla, 52
Sunzi (Sun Tzu), 121
surface-to-air missiles (SAMs), 268, 285, 286, 291, 292–93

Sweden in League of Augsburg, 184
Syracuse in Decelean War, 42
Syria: and Golan Heights, 267; insurgency in, 213, 214

Tacticus, Aeneas, 48
Taizong, 112
Tal, Israel: and ineffectiveness of maozim, 286; and postwar debate about Bar-Lev Line, 288, 297; and post–Yom Kippur War debate, 293; and strategic culture, 270–71; and strategic defense system, 275–76, 282
Tanagra, battle of, 33, 35
Tang Dynasty, 110–11, 112–13, 127
taozim (strongholds), 287, 292. *See also* maozim
Tardieu, André, 221, 233, 234
Targe, Antoine, 216
Tatars, 117
taxation: in China, 122, 124, 130, 131, 138; in France, 167, 172, 233; *gabelle* (salt tax), 167; in Israel, 273
Thasos, 20
Themistius, 78
Themistocles, 4, 17–18, 23–24, 28–29, 32, 37, 45
Themistocles' Wall, 19
"theory of walls," 11, 308
Theseus, 34
Thirty Years' Peace, 35, 37
Thirty Years' War, 162, 169, 172
threat perceptions: and Athens' Long Walls, 21–22, 53–54; and Bar-Lev Line, 265–67, 273; and barrier construction, 327; and Great Wall of China, 116–18; and Hadrian's Wall, 73–74; and Maginot Line, 213–15, 233, 242; and Pré Carré, 167–68
"three nos" declaration, 264, 265
Thucydides: and Athens' expanding power, 15; and Second Peloponnsesian War, 37, 38, 40–41, 44; and strategic culture, 23–24; and strategic defense decision, 32–33; and upper city relocation, 28
Titus Flavius Secundus, 88

Tolmides, 33, 38
Tombs, Robert and Isabelle, 194, 314
Tory party (England), 191
"totality of the tank" concept, 268
total war, 214, 216, 236
Tournai, siege, 190–92
towers, 110, 113, 141
trace italienne (fortification), 8, 180
traitors, concerns about, 31–32, 44
Trajan, 66, 71–73, 76–77, 78–79, 82
Treaty of. *See name of treaty*
Trebius Germanus, 88
Truce of Ratisbon, 182, 184
Tullius Varro, 80
Tumu (China), Chinese defeat at, 115, 116, 120, 126
Turenne, Henri, 158, 164, 165, 166, 171, 173, 191
Turks, 183, 184, 186
Tu-ta Mongols (Tatars), 117
Twelfth Dynasty, 6
Tyne-Solway isthmus, 66, 71–73, 82, 83, 85, 96–97

Ulpius Marcellus, 92
UN Resolution 242 on land for peace principle, 285–86
Union Nationale (France), 221
United Nations (UN), 262
United Provinces (Netherlands), 164, 183, 188
United States: arms support for Israel, 268, 269, 271; and border fence with Mexico, 2, 314, 318, 328; operations in Iraq and Afghanistan, 320; relations with Israel, 269; and return of Sinai to Egypt, 262; Senate's rejection of Versailles Treaty, 211, 217; strategic defenses in, 1–2
"universal monarchy," 164, 165, 194
Utrecht, Treaty of, 192

Valenciennes, 177, 178
vallums (mound-ditch obstacles), 68, 90
Van Creveld, Martin, 3

Vauban, Sébastien le Prestre de, 4, 8; advising Louis XIV, 173–74; and defense fortifications, 176; on domestic unrest in France, 167; and Dutch War, 165; fortress building efforts of, 164, 188, 192; on France's expanded frontier, 186; on France's geographic vulnerability, 167; on *frontière de fer* expansion, 181; legacy of, 209; and military capabilities, 169; and natural frontiers, 171; and Pré Carré concept, 158, 160; and strategic defense, 177, 182, 183, 185, 187, 193
Vendôme, Louis-Joseph, 189
Venutius, 71
Verdun in World War I, 205, 210
Versailles Treaty, 211–13, 217, 236
Vespasian, 71, 76
vexillations (Roman military detachments), 73, 78
Villars, Marshal, 191, 192
Vindolanda, 71, 87, 95
Virius Lupus, 92
Vitruvius, 88
Votadini tribe, 74, 82, 83, 85, 89

Waldron, Arthur: on Chinese culture, 120; on decision to build Great Wall of China, 132; on domestic politics in China, 124; on Ming historical record, 107; on Ming–Mogol policy, 114; on strategic culture, 121, 122; on strategic options in China, 125; on wall building in Chinese history, 111
Walloons, 218, 226
Wang Chonggu, 140
Wang Shu, 133, 135, 326
Wang Yue: and Bag Arslan's defeat, 131–33; and Bolai's defeat, 119–20; and erection of wall, 107, 129; military contributions of, 124, 130; and offensive strategy in Ordos, 126; and wall expansion, 134
Wang Zhen, 114–15
Wan Li Chang Cheng ("ten thousand li long wall"), 111

war, outlawing of, 224
War of Attrition (1969–1970), 257–58, 283–86, 291
War of Spanish Succession, 188–92, 193, 195, 318
War of the Reunions, 182
Warring States Period (475–221 BCE), 111
wars of attrition. *See* attrition, wars of
wartime, definition of, 7
Wehrmacht (German armed forces), 205, 236, 239, 240, 242, 246
weisuo system (hereditary soldiery), 118, 122
Wellington, Duke of, 7
Weng Wanda, 137, 138, 140, 147
West Bank, 263, 269, 295
Westphalia, Treaty of, 163
Weygand, Maxime, 222, 233–34, 235
Whig party (England), 191
Whittaker, Charles, 81
William III, 164, 183, 185, 188
Winter, F. E., 32
World Disarmament Conference (1932), 3
World War I, lessons learned from, 209–10, 226–27
Württemberg, Duke of, 187
Wu Sangui, 144

Xenophon, 43, 45, 46, 47, 48, 53
Xerxes, 17–18
Xia Yan, 137–38
Xiang Zhong, 124
Xuanfu sector (Great Wall of China), 108, 109, 137, 138

Yad Mordechai, 261
Yang Yiqing, 112, 135
Yaniv, Avner, 262, 266, 270
Yansui sector (Chinese frontier), 106, 108, 110, 119, 132, 133–35
Yan Sung, 138
Year of Corbie, 162, 165
Ye Sheng, 107, 126–27, 128–29
Yom Kippur War, 258, 289–95, 296, 297
Yongle, 113, 114, 120, 123

Young, Robert, 215
Young Plan (1929) on German war reparations, 214
Ypres, 160, 187, 189, 192
Yuan Dynasty, 112–13, 115, 116, 120, 122
Yuan Zhenghuan, 143
Yu Qian, 116
Yu Zijun: 4; accommodation policies of, 125, 127, 130, 147; and "buying time" strategy, 324; and domestic politics, 124; and erection of wall, 107, 108, 128–29, 145; and strategic defense system decision, 130–31, 132, 133, 140; and wall expansion, 133–35

Zeng Xian, 137
Zhang Juzheng, 140
Zhang Quan, 142
Zhang Xianzhang, 144
Zhao Fu, 130, 131
Zhengde, 135, 136
Zhengtong, 115
Zhu Yong, 107